Security and Post-Co
Reconstruction

CH00621961

This book provides a critical analysis of the changing discourse and practice of post-conflict security-promoting interventions since the Cold War. It focuses on disarmament, demobilization and reintegration (DDR) and security-sector reform (SSR).

Although the international aid and security sectors exhibit an expanding appetite for peace-support operations in the twenty-first century, the effectiveness of such interventions is largely untested. This book aims to fill this evidentiary gap and issues a challenge to 'conventional' approaches to security promotion as currently conceived by military and peacekeeping forces. It draws on cutting-edge statistical and qualitative findings from war-torn areas including Afghanistan, Timor-Leste, Sudan, Uganda, Colombia and Haiti. By focusing on specific cases where the United Nations and others have sought to contain the (presumed) sources of post-conflict violence and insecurity, it lays out a new research agenda for measuring success or failure.

This book will be of much interest to practitioners and students of peace-building, peacekeeping, conflict resolution, conflict and development and security studies in general.

Robert Muggah is Research Director of the Small Arms Survey at the Graduate Institute of International and Development Studies in Geneva, Switzerland.

Routledge global security studies

Series editors: Aaron Karp, Regina Karp and Terry Terriff

Security and Post-Conflict Reconstruction

Dealing with fighters in the aftermath of war

Edited by Robert Muggah

Routledge
Taylor & Francis Group

LONDON AND NEW YORK

First published 2009
by Routledge
2 Park Square, Milton Park, Abingdon, Oxon, OX14 4RN

Simultaneously published in the USA and Canada
by Routledge
270 Madison Ave, New York NY 10016

Routledge is an imprint of the Taylor & Francis Group, an informa business

Transferred to Digital Printing 2009

Typeset in Times by Wearset Ltd, Boldon, Tyne and Wear

British Library Cataloguing in Publication Data
A catalogue record for this book is available from the British Library

Library of Congress Cataloging-in-Publication Data
Security and post-conflict reconstruction : dealing with fighters in the
aftermath of war / edited by Robert Muggah.
p. cm. – (Routledge global security studies ; 8)
1. Postwar reconstruction 2. Peacekeeping forces. 3. Peace-building.
I. Muggah, Robert.
JZ6374.S43 2009
355.02'8–dc22
2008023451

ISBN10: 0-415-46054-9 (hbk)
ISBN10: 0-415-54440-8 (pbk)
ISBN10: 0-203-88691-7 (ebk)

ISBN13: 978-0-415-46054-5 (hbk)
ISBN13: 978-0-415-54440-5 (pbk)
ISBN13: 978-0-203-88691-5 (ebk)

In memory of Michael Vinay Bhatia

The importance of DDR in securing a peace has been widely acknowledged. But does it actually work? Drawing on vast experience and extensive datasets, the book makes a major contribution by providing crucial empirical evidence on the effectiveness of DDR around the world. The book also helpfully cautions against loading onto 'DDR' a set of expectations and agendas that it cannot realistically support. This is essential reading for policy-makers and students alike.

David Keen, London School of Economics

A key component of peacebuilding in countries emerging from conflict involves demobilization, disarming and reintegrating former combatants. A number of leading experts discuss the difficulties of achieving these objectives and argue for a more rigorous assessment of the success or failure of such programs in the future. This is a much needed volume and will be of interest to both students and practitioners.

Gil Loescher, University of Oxford

A superb mix of in-depth case studies and thematic chapters, this volume presents a refreshingly critical and detailed analysis of the DDR record to date, bringing much-needed rigor to the evaluation of DDR impacts. It should be required reading for students and practitioners of post-conflict reconstruction, peacebuilding and development.

Roland Paris, University of Ottawa

Robert Muggah's collection illustrates clearly that DDR programs cannot hide under the banner of 'technical interventions', as they have a profound effect on the political, social and economic dynamics of countries emerging from conflict. This makes it all the more urgent that international actors be held accountable for the effectiveness of such programs. The fascinating cases in this book, by giving us the tools to measure impact, will help to create that much-needed culture of accountability.

Jennifer Welsh, University of Oxford

For much too long unsubstantiated claims about the importance of disarmament, demobilization and reintegration have proliferated like small arms after civil war. This pathbreaking book actually sheds light on these goals by subjecting them to rigorous social science and hard data. Some of the field's best young scholars apply tough evidence-based evaluation to demolish long-lived myths. Essential reading for those policy makers who face the tough jobs of peacekeeping and peacebuilding.

Stephen John Stedman, Stanford University

Contents

Illustrations

Contributors

Annan, Jeannie is a Research Fellow in the Center for Interdisciplinary Research on AIDS at Yale University. She holds a PhD in Counseling Psychology from Indiana University at Bloomington. Dr Annan's research examines the impacts of war and violence on mental health and well-being, with a particular focus on identifying the individual, social and environmental factors that protect individuals from the worst effects of violence. She is also engaged in the assessment and evaluation of post-conflict youth programmes, including the psychological effects of programmes for economic recovery and reintegration. Dr Annan has worked in northern Uganda since 1999 on psycho-social programmes and research, and since 2005 has co-directed the Survey of War Affected Youth in northern Uganda. Her other regions of interest and expertise include Liberia and Sudan.

Baaré, Anton is an international consultant and senior partner at Nordic Consulting Group Denmark. He teaches on human security at the Department of Ethnography and Anthropology, University of Aarhus. He has worked on DDR since 1993 when he was based in Uganda. He has worked extensively on security, development and rights issues. Ongoing work includes revising Denmark's National Action Plan for Security Council Resolution 1325. Between August 2006 and March 2008 he was seconded by Denmark and Sweden to the office of the H.E. Riek Machar, Vice President of Southern Sudan and chief mediator of the peace talks with the Lord's Resistance Army. In the Juba process he provided technical advice to the Cessation of Hostilities Monitoring Team and was lead expert on ceasefire and DDR negotiations.

Bennett, Jon is a socio-economist and specialist in evaluation, post-war needs assessment, food security, internal displacement, rural development and humanitarian programming. He has 32 years' experience working in Africa and Asia as Field Director, Country Representative and Team Leader posts for the UN, DFID, EC and various NGOs. He was Regional Director in Sudan for Oxfam (1986–1988), and Executive Director of ACBAR, the largest NGO coordination body in the world from 1990–1993. He was founding Director of the Global IDP Project (now IDMC) and a member of the international advisory board for the IDP Guiding Principles. From 2004–2005, he was UN Team Leader for the post-war assessment and recovery/development appeal for Sudan; and from 2005–2006, he was Team Leader for the Tsunami Evaluation Coalition, Coordination study. His published books include, *Internally Displaced People: A Global Survey* (1998), *NGOs and Government* (1987), *NGO Funding Strategies: An Introduction for Southern and Eastern NGOs* (1996), and *NGO Coordination in Practice: A Handbook* (1994, 1998).

Berdal, Mats is Professor of Security and Development in the Department of War Studies at King's College London having joined the department in 2003. He was formerly Director of Studies at the International Institute for Strategic Studies (IISS) in London with overall responsibility for the organization, funding and management of the IISS research programme. From 1997 to 2000 he was Research Fellow at St Antony's College and Research Coordinator of a research programme on 'International Organisations and Security Issues of the Post-Cold Era' at the Centre for International Studies (University of Oxford). He is contributor to and co-editor of *United Nations Interventionism 1991–2004*, published by Cambridge University Press in 2007. He is also co-editor of *Greed and Grievance: Economic Agendas in Civil Wars* (Boulder: Lynne Rienner, May 2000). He is author of *Disarmament and Demobilization after Civil Wars* (Oxford: Oxford University Press, Adelphi Paper, 1996).

Bhatia, Michael Vinay was a doctoral candidate in the Department of Politics and International Relations at the University of Oxford, where he was awarded a George C. Marshall Scholarship. He recently served as a field social scientist as part of the Human Terrain Team with the 82nd Airborne Division in Afghanistan before being killed in the line of duty in May 2008. From 2006 to 2007 he served as a visiting fellow at the Thomas J. Watson Institute for International Studies at Brown University. He was the co-author of *Afghanistan, Arms and Conflict: Armed Groups, Disarmament and Security in a Post-War Society* (London: Routledge, 2008); author of *War and Intervention: Issues for Contemporary Peace Operations* (Bloomfield: Kumarian Press, 2003); and editor of *Terrorism and the Politics of Naming* (London, UK: Routledge, 2007). He conducted research in Afghanistan for the Overseas Development Institute (ODI), Afghanistan Research and Evaluation Unit (AREU), UK Department for International Development (DfID), Small Arms Survey, and the Organization for Security and Cooperation (OSCE) in Europe; and undertook fieldwork in East Timor, Kosovo and the western Sahara.

Blattman, Christopher is an Assistant Professor of Political Science and Economics at Yale University. He holds a PhD in Economics from the University of California at Berkeley and a Master's in Public Administration and International Development from Harvard University. Dr Blattman's research examines the causes and consequences of civil war, the determinants of post-conflict reintegration of ex-combatants, the assessment and evaluation of post-conflict youth programmes, and the development of new forms of governance and peacebuilding after war. Since 2005, Dr Blattman has co-directed the Survey of War Affected Youth in northern Uganda.

Halty, Maximo has professional experience in development including policy and programme work in microenterprise support, specifically advisory and consultancy work with the Inter-American Development Bank, the World Bank, the WfP, FUNDES and a number of national small and micro-business associations throughout Latin America. He has promoted training and strategic planning service provision in Argentina, Chile, Bolivia, Peru, Ecuador, Colombia, Guyana, Venezuela, El Salvador, Guatemala, Mexico and Uruguay, and also in the Ukraine. In the field of DDR and armed violence, Mr Halty has worked as both technical adviser and programme manager developing and implementing one of the first successful national DDR programmes in Mozambique (1993–1994), with IOM. Since then, he has provided technical advice (mostly with UNDP/BCPR) to DDR and armed violence programmes in CAR, Liberia, Solomon Islands, DRC, Ivory Coast, Colombia, Guatemala, Comoros Islands, Somalia, Papua New Guinea, Philippines, Nepal Mali, Macedonia and Argentina, and has designed, implemented and managed national DDR programmes in RoC and Sudan. He has also actively participated in the development of the BCPR Practice Note on DDR and the IDDRS. In Sudan, expanding on the work done in the development of the DDR programme in CAR, Mr Halty helped develop a programme that has a broader post-conflict security focus, linking DDR to SSR and including a community security component. He is currently Chief Technical Advisor of UNDP's Threat and Risk Mapping and Analysis project in Sudan.

Humphreys, Macartan is an Associate Professor of Political Science and a research scholar at the Center for Globalization and Sustainable Development at the Earth Institute at Columbia University. He holds an MPhil in Economics from Oxford University and a PhD in Government from Harvard University. His research focuses on civil wars, post-conflict development, ethnic politics, natural resource management, political authority and leadership and democratic development and employs a variety of methods including survey work, lab experimentation, field experimentation, econometric analysis, game theoretic analysis and classical qualitative methods. He has conducted field research in Chad, Colombia, Ghana, Haiti, Indonesia, Liberia, Mali, Sao Tome and Principe, Sierra Leone, Senegal, Uganda and elsewhere. A new series of projects underway use field experiments to examine democratic decision-making in post-conflict and developing areas. Recent research has appeared in the *American Political Science Review*, *World Politics*, the *American Journal of Political Science* and the *Journal of Conflict Resolution*.

Molloy, Desmond served for 20 years as an officer in the Irish Army, primarily in an internal security and anti-terrorism role and including UN military missions in Lebanon and Cambodia. Mr Molloy is also qualified in financial management and outdoor education. Availing of early retirement, he honed his skills in emergency, relief and security coordination on missions with UN agencies and NGOs – Congo with IFRC, Bosnia with ICRC, Rwanda with Concern, East Timor with the UN, Kosovo with ARC, Ethiopia with GOAL and Head of Finance for WHO in Kosovo. He was formerly the Chief of DDR with the UN in Sierra Leone, a particularly 'successful' instance of DDR. More recently he was the Chief of the Integrated DDR Section of MINUSTAH and UNDP in Haiti. Desmond Molloy is currently a Special Research Fellow in the Peace and Conflict Studies Programme at TUFS, the Tokyo University of Foreign Studies in Japan.

Muggah, Robert is Research Director of the Small Arms Survey at the Graduate Institute of International and Development Studies. He received a PhD in Development Studies and International Relations from Oxford University and an MPhil in Development Economics at the Institute for Development Studies (IDS), Sussex University. At the Survey Dr Muggah oversees research on post-conflict transition and recovery, arms control and armed violence, disarmament, demobilization and reintegration (DDR) and security sector reform (SSR). In addition to developing tools and monitoring mechanisms to track the spatial and temporal distribution of armed violence, Dr Muggah is preparing OECD/DAC *Guidance for Armed Violence Reduction* and served as an expert on several UN panels related to governance, fragile states and post-conflict recovery. Dr Muggah has worked with multilateral, bilateral and private development and security agencies in more than 20 war-affected and post-conflict states. His work is also widely published in peer-reviewed and policy-relevant journals, academic volumes and the international media.

Patel, Ana Cutter is the Deputy Director for the International Policymakers Program at the International Center for Transitional Justice (ICTJ). Additionally at ICTJ, Ana manages a research project on Disarmament, Demobilization and Reintegration and Transitional Justice. She has 15 years of experience in international conflict prevention and peacebuilding including fieldwork, advocacy, policy research, media and public outreach, programme design, implementation and evaluation, and teaching and training. She has been a Lecturer and Fellow at the Center for International Conflict Resolution (CICR) at Columbia University since 2001. Prior to her work with ICTJ, she was a consultant with the UNDP working on conflict prevention and peacebuilding projects. From 1999–2002, she held the positions of programme officer for conflict prevention at the Carnegie Council for Ethics and International Affairs, director of media and public outreach for the Carnegie Commission on the Prevention of Deadly Conflict (1998–1999), Latin American analyst at the Newmarket Company (1997–1998), editor of the *Journal of*

International Affairs (1997–1998) and deputy head of external relations for the Corporación Andina de Fomento in Caracas, Venezuela (1993–1996). Ana served as a Peace Corps volunteer in the Dominican Republic (1990–1993) and has a Masters in International Affairs from the School of International and Public Affairs at Columbia University.

Peake, Gordon is Senior Policy Adviser, Timor-Leste Police Department Programme. He is also Practitioner Affiliate, Institutions for Fragile States, Princeton University, and a Senior Associate with Libra Advisory Group, a London-based consulting company. He holds a M.Phil in Modern Middle Eastern Studies and D.Phil in Politics and International Relations from Oxford University. He previously directed a programme on security sector reform at the International Peace Academy, New York, and has consulted on justice and security issues for the Asia Foundation, Department for International Development and OECD/DAC. His work has appeared in numerous peer-reviewed journals including *Conflict, Security and Development*, *International Peacekeeping*, and *Police Practice and Research*. His contribution to this volume does not reflect the views of the Australian Federal Police.

Pugel, James is a political geographer and research associate with the Centre for the Study of Civil War (CSCW), Peace Research Institute, Oslo (PRIO). He has served in the role of principal investigator for two separate nationwide empirical studies (supervised by UNDP and UNMIL RRR) that focused on understanding the nature of the post-conflict environment in Liberia and on the impact of national DDRR programme. James holds a MS in Strategic Intelligence with African Studies Concentration from the National Defense Intelligence College (NDIC), a MSc in Defense Geographic Information (Cranfield University), a MS in Administration (Central Michigan University), and a BS in Civil Engineering (Virginia Military Institute).

Restrepo, Jorge A. is Associate Professor of Economics at Universidad Javeriana in Bogotá, Colombia. He specializes in political economy and applied conflict analysis. He received his degree in Economics from Universidad Javeriana and holds postgraduate degrees from the University of Cambridge and Royal Holloway College–University of London. Dr Restrepo is the founder and director of the Conflict Analysis Resources Center – CERAC also based in Bogotá. Jorge is also a member Historic Memory Working Group for the Comisión Nacional de Reconciliación y Reparación.

Torjesen, Stina is a senior research fellow at the Norwegian Institute of International Affairs. She recently completed a doctorate in International Relations at the University of Oxford. She specializes in security, political economy and international relations issues and focuses on Central Asia and Afghanistan. Stina Torjesen is the coordinator for the research project 'the political economy of DDR', which is financed by the Norwegian Research Council. Recent publications by Stina Torjesen include (with Heidi Kjærnet) 'Afghanistan and Regional Instability: a Risk Assessment', NUPI report 2008 (with S. Neil MacFarlane) 'R Before D: The Case of Post Conflict Reintegration in Tajikistan', *Journal of Conflict, Security and Development*, 7 (2) 2007 and (with Katarina Ammitzbøll) 'Maximum or Minimum? Policy Options for Democratisation Initiatives in UN Peace Operations', NUPI report 2007.

Weinstein, Jeremy is an assistant professor of political science at Stanford University and an affiliated faculty member at the Center for Democracy, Development, and the Rule of Law (CDDRL) and the Center for International Security and Cooperation (CISAC). His research focuses on civil wars and communal violence, ethnic politics and the provision of public goods, and post-conflict reconstruction. He is the author of *Inside Rebellion: The Politics of Insurgent Violence* (Cambridge University Press). He has also published articles in the *American Political Science Review, American Journal of Political Science, Journal of Conflict Resolution, Foreign Affairs, Foreign Policy, Journal of Democracy, World Policy Journal*, and the *SAIS Review*. Previously, Weinstein was a research fellow at the Center for Global Development, where he directed the bi-partisan Commission on Weak States and US National Security. He has also worked on the National Security Council staff, served as a visiting scholar at the World Bank, and held fellowships at the Woodrow Wilson International Center for Scholars and the Brookings Institution. Weinstein received a BA with high honours from Swarthmore College, and an MA and PhD in political economy and government from Harvard University.

Foreword

Jean-Marie Guéhenno[1]

Global demands for peacekeeping operations have never been higher. At the beginning of 2008, there were more than 140,000 United Nations (UN) peacekeepers deployed worldwide. These men and women carry out a wide range of mandated tasks in volatile environments. They provide advice and support for political transitions, humanitarian response, the strengthening of rule of law institutions, security sector reform, the promotion of human rights and the beginnings of economic recovery in close partnership with other actors. The military and police personnel – the blue berets so symbolic of UN peacekeeping – provide critical security support, which underpins the overall peace process. Among these many tasks of peacekeeping is disarmament, demobilization and reintegration (DDR), a key component of most peace processes and the topic of *Security and Post-Conflict Reconstruction: Dealing with Fighters in the Aftermath of War*. The UN Department of Peacekeeping Operations currently manages eight ongoing DDR programmes in seven peacekeeping operations while two additional missions are in the planning stages.

The challenges facing peacekeeping operations are tremendous. By definition, they take place in politically charged and socially complex situations. Given an increasing need for peacekeeping operations and the difficulties encountered by troop-contributing countries to supply new boots on the ground, it is imperative that we continue to improve our effectiveness. *Security and Post-Conflict Reconstruction* moves beyond offering 'lessons learned' – essential elements of planning and executing DDR and other related operations. Indeed, lessons have already been covered by the United Nations Integrated DDR Standards.[2] The volume instead takes a critical look at the evidence-base of DDR and asks tough questions about what works and what does not. At a time when peacekeeping assets are shrinking relative to the global needs, the volume answers tricky questions that are routinely put to diplomats, policymakers, donors and development actors alike. Developing a culture of evidence will be crucial for improving DDR and peace-keeping practice in the twenty-first century.

Security and Post-Conflict Reconstruction applies a much needed critical lens to DDR as the international community seeks to improve on past practice and promote more people-centred security. It is true that DDR and related programmes can and should never be conceived narrowly as technical interventions: they are multi-dimensional processes that must be built into the overall peace architecture of the country. By drawing on a diverse array of cases, *Security and Post-Conflict Reconstruction* reveals how the dynamics of war, the complex factors shaping the mobilization of fighters, and the manner in which peace is secured are all crucial determinants of DDR success. The volume calls attention to how the social, economic and cultural circumstances in which DDR is undertaken are inextricably tied to programme design and outcomes. It also highlights how multilateral and bilateral agencies, including donor governments, need to take practical and realistic steps to assist post-conflict societies navigate the political transition, including supporting DDR. DDR of course can never serve as a substitute for a political process: it is a facilitator but not a driver. Even so, effective DDR can inject dynamism into a peace process. *Security and Post-Conflict Reconstruction* also provides evidence of how DDR can adapt and change to new circumstances, particularly when confronting the complex array of interests of armed groups and ex-combatants on the ground.

The challenges facing peace and development actors are only likely to grow in the coming decades. The need to address security threats such as terrorism, organized transnational crime and (regionalized) internal conflicts require global responses. In addition, the emergence of forms of localized violence – particularly in the world's massive and growing cities – challenges the ingenuity of our policy makers and the bureaucratic conventions of our practitioners. It is crucial that we draw on critical research and evidence brought to bear by the academic community to enhance our impact. We must learn from our past to make a better future. We expect that *Security and Post-Conflict Reconstruction* will contribute to such a learning process by improving the way we conduct DDR.

Note

1 Jean-Marie Guéhenno was under-secretary-general for peacekeeping operations from 2000–2008.
2 See, for example, www.unddr.org/iddrs/framework.php

Acknowledgements

The euphemism that development requires security and that without security, development cannot be achieved is entrenched in the state- and peace-building lexicon. Some scholars contend that the securitization of development (and developmentalization of security) is facilitated by the intermediacy accompanying globalization and in the wake of the post-Cold War era's so-called 'new wars'. The securitzation process evolved gradually at first. Humanitarian and relief agencies began by speaking with the enemy – exploring ways of enlisting military actors to facilitate aid delivery while not compromising their avowed neutrality and impartiality. The symptoms grew more acute over time: private security contractors gradually began assuming development and security functions once delivered exclusively by the state. Aid delivery was also for all intents and purposes outsourced to the non-governmental sector. Meanwhile, counter-insurgency operations from Iraq to Afghanistan were consciously drawing on development expertise in a bid to win hearts and minds.

One especially clear expression of the security–development nexus includes disarmament, demobilization and reintegration (DDR) and security sector reform (SSR). At one time the exclusive preserve of militaries and police forces, these interventions are now supported in equal measure by development and security actors. As generic concepts, they belie an array of contested discourses and practices. But taken together, DDR and SSR also reflect the effort by liberal democracies to restore 'stability', 'order' and 'peace' in societies affected by war. Because Western governments are increasingly preoccupied with securing the 'border-lands' and 'ungoverned spaces' – particularly following uneven interventions in Iraq and Afghanistan – DDR and SSR are seen as a kind of short-term panacea. But there's a catch. The outcomes of DDR and SSR have not been empirically tested or interrogated. There is an ominous silence in the political science, economics, security studies and peace-building literature about whether these activities actually 'work' or not. This volume represents a first attempt to critically unpack DDR, and to a lesser extent SSR, and to determine whether they achieve what they are intended to.

While authored by a few, the volume is a testament to the tireless efforts of literally hundreds of people dedicated to making the world a safer place. These practitioners, scholars and activists reflect, in many ways, the multidimensional nature of DDR and SSR. They include development and humanitarian workers, military specialists, anthropologists, sociologists, geographers, diplomats, human rights advocates, gender and child specialists, forensic pathologists and many others. Even the relatively modest numbers of scholars and practitioners consulted in the preparation of this volume are too numerous to thank here – being scattered as they are from Colombia and Sudan to Sri Lanka and Timor-Leste. Nevertheless, in giving generously of their time, energy and experience, they serve collectively as an inspiration to each of the authors. While this volume may offer a critical perspective on the outcomes of DDR, the findings presented herein should in no way diminish the worthiness of their investment and commitment.

One colleague who gave liberally of his passion, intellect and ultimately his life was Michael Bhatia. A contributor to this volume, Michael also served as a social scientist assigned to the Afghanistan Human Terrain Team in Khost Province. Michael was killed as his manuscript was being submitted. He and several colleagues were struck by an IED during operations there. In the course of his tour, Michael's work saved the lives of both US soldiers and Afghan civilians. In addition to his many published articles, Michael will be remembered for his personal courage, a powerful intellect, his willingness to endure danger and hardship, his gentle sense of humour and devoted character.

The subject of this volume – DDR – does not lend itself immediately to any clear epistemic or disciplinary tradition. International relations and political science have comparatively little say about the process except, that is, if it contributes to global or cross-border instability. Likewise, economists and geographers were comparatively slow to come to the table, though this now appears to be changing. Few academic journals have taken up the issue, though there are of course some notable exceptions. Special thanks are due, then, to Aaron Karp who planted the seed for the volume. After a decade or so spent evaluating UN and World Bank funded DDR and small arms control programmes on several continents, he convinced me to distil some of the key trends and patterns emerging from the field. Credit is due also to the staff at Routledge, including Andrew Humphreys and Emily Kindleysides, and two anonymous reviewers, who patiently steered this volume to completion. Gratitude is also owed to Ayaka Suzuki, Lotta Hagmann and several reviewers at DPKO and UNDP for their comments on certain chapter drafts.

A large number of entities and individuals supported the production of this volume. Generous funding support was provided by the Swedish Ministry of Foreign Affairs, including Ewa Nilsson and Magnus Hellgren. Likewise, the Geneva-based Small Arms Survey must be credited for supporting the volume and backing the project. There are many individuals who provided critical feedback on individual chapters. The authors of this volume would like to thank especially Charles Achodo, Katherine Aguirre Tobón, Peter Babbington, Paddy Barron, Vikram Bhatia, Edith Bowles, Susanna Campbell, Kristopher Carlson, Paul Cruickshank, Antonio Donini, Steven Feller, Brodie Ferguson, Jamie Fuller, Anthony Goldstone, Soledad Granada, Nuno Ximines Grenediro,

Jennifer Hazen, Roger Horton, Jacques Klein, Eleonora Koeb, Daniel Ladouceur, Bengt Ljunggren, Dyan Mazurana, Freida M'Cormack, Basil Massey, Edward Miguel, Sarah Nouwen, Godgrey Okot, Preston Pentony, Julio Tomas Pinto, Robin Poulton, Alan Quee, Ed Rees, Souren Seraydarian, Robin Poulton, Cyrus Samii, Shecku Silla, Gurpawan Singh, Andrea Tamagnini, Chalmer Thompson, Steve Ursino and others. Special thanks also to colleagues at the MacArthur Foundation, UNICEF Uganda, AVSI Uganda, Geneva's Graduate Institute of International and Development Studies, the UC Berkeley Human Rights Center, Bradford University, the United States Institute of Peace and the Harry Frank Guggenheim Foundation.

Introduction

The Emperor's clothes?

Robert Muggah

The breadth and reach of twenty-first century peace-support operations is unprecedented. There are nearly twice as many blue-helmets deployed in post-conflict theatres today than at the nadir of UN missions in the 1990s. Global preoccupation with channelling overseas development assistance to broken and fragile states is on the ascendant. Alarmingly, despite the ratcheting-up of peace-support operations and more targeted aid to the world's 'hot spots', the effectiveness of these interventions is still falling short of expectations. Faced with simmering violence in the Greater Middle East and Central Asia, including Iraq and Afghanistan, there is comparatively less capability or willingness to invest in areas of lower geo-strategic importance such as Africa or smaller countries in the Caribbean and South Asia. And while policy-makers and practitioners in the security and development sectors seek to improve their coherence and make their aid more effective in war zones around the world, they must also contend with arms availability and armed groups that are frustrating efforts to secure protection.

In order to meet these pressing challenges, the peace-support and peace-building arsenal has expanded in the late twentieth and early twenty-first centuries. While multilateral and bilateral agencies continue to prioritize governance and elections as the key to long-term stability, a host of shorter term security promotion activities are assuming growing importance. Together with international arms control efforts and embargoes,[1] selective amnesties and smart sanctions, interventions such as disarmament, demobilization and reintegration (DDR) and security sector reform (SSR) are commonly fielded to keep post-war countries from slipping back into conflict and to secure the 'peace'.[2] Paradoxically, as investment in such activities is growing, there are looming doubts as to whether they achieve what is expected of them. In the case of DDR, for example, critics claim that it is often too narrowly focused, inflexible and technocratic and detached from the political transition or broader recovery and reconstruction strategies. As a result, there are concerns as to whether DDR and SSR can achieve what is expected of it.

The expanding investment in DDR and SSR over the last two decades has been accompanied by the international aid architecture's erection of new pillars to promote international peace and security. From a relatively narrow peace-keeping focus designed to separate well-defined parties according to a negotiated ceasefire in the 1960s and 1970s, diplomats are increasingly confronted with irregular and fourth generation forms of war since the 1990s (Holt and Berkman 2006). States supporting peace-support operations – including troop-contributing countries – exhibited a preparedness to engage in more robust peace enforcement mandates and, more recently, peace-building. In the past decade, a growing coalition of governments revealed a willingness to transfer responsibility for specific post-conflict activities to new entities, including the recently launched Peace-building Commission (2006).[3] To many these adaptations to more firmly address insecurity are warranted: the evidence indicated that warring parties (and those who sought to separate them) were increasingly mired in conflict traps. A failure to effectively and comprehensively address the immediate and underlying causes of armed conflict meant that the embers smouldered, waiting for the next spark to reignite open collective violence following an end to formal hostilities.[4] Even now, there are legitimate concerns that DDR and SSR on their own are unable to contend with the criminal and quasi-political violence that rapidly supersedes large-scale political violence at war's end (Muggah and Krause 2008).

In spite of a growing appetite among liberal democracies for expanding the peace support agenda, the effectiveness of the broad spectrum treatment in today's conflict landscapes is largely unknown. From Colombia to Uganda and Timor-Leste there is comparatively little evidence of what kinds of interventions work and which ones do not. This volume seeks to fill this gap. It does so by focusing on a number of conventional security-promoting mechanisms designed expressly to prevent armed conflicts from resuming and keep the (presumed) sources of post-conflict violence and insecurity at bay. DDR, in particular, is one such instrument. Comprised of a cluster of activities designed at a minimum to contain arms, dismantle armed groups and prevent the recurrence of war, DDR is frequently undertaken by a constellation of international agencies and national governments.[5] Seen from a critical political economy perspective, DDR embodies the strategic and bureaucratic priorities of the security and development sectors. As such, it perpetuates the discourse and policy priorities of international donors and power-holding local elites: like the development project itself, DDR is central to neo-liberal forms of power and governmentability (Duffield 2007: viii). Put another way, DDR does not emerge spontaneously 'from below' but is part of a broader (Weberian) project of securing the legitimate control of force from above.

In the midst of the apparent enthusiasm for expanding the international peace and security agenda, the limitations of DDR and SSR have not gone entirely unnoticed. A critical literature is emerging – one that questions and challenges core assumptions underpinning the enterprise, but also explores possibilities for improving practice.[6] An overriding concern relates to the perils of glossing over complexity and artificially 'grafting' DDR or SSR programmes onto volatile post-conflict societies. Case study research reveals the genuine risks accompanying the imposition of security promotion interventions from above, particularly if they are divorced from the political, social and economic context in which such activities are inevitably embedded. Critical scholars, but also seasoned practitioners, contend that DDR is too often resorted to in a knee-jerk fashion and launched in such a way that it is isolated from the broader clutch of processes associated with governance, state consolidation and economic recovery. While the same could be said about other development interventions advanced by multilateral and bilateral donors in complex environments, the fact that DDR deals specifically with weapons and armed groups suggests an extra layer of caution is warranted.

The development aid community is also wrestling with the conceptual dimensions of certain aspects of DDR, particularly bureaucratic 'integration' of disparate UN agencies mandated to deal with such initiatives and the 'reintegration' of former fighters. In the context of wider UN reforms, there is also an ongoing debate over how best to coordinate the DDR architecture amongst disparate security and development agencies and whether they can practicably deliver the goods.[7] By the same token, there are concerns that generic approaches to reintegration cannot adequately account for the heterogeneous and differentiated motivations of armed groups. Some development workers fear that combatant-centric approaches to reintegration miss the mark entirely and that investment should be diverted instead to more inclusive or area-based programmes focusing on employment, infrastructure development and economic growth. Though these same practitioners accept that DDR amounts in some cases to a series of narrow bargains and trade-offs, criticism is emerging of the rational choice models (and monetary incentives) dominating the field (Willibald 2006).[8] Connected to this is a mounting unease among policy-makers and aid workers that DDR lacks clear benchmarks or metrics of success. As this volume shows, there are still widespread disagreements as to whether DDR amounts to a minimalist emphasis on security promotion alone or more maximalist aims associated with enhanced development and fundamental changes in governance. Not surprisingly, most interventions tend to emphasize a combination of the two. But the comparatively limited evidence available to demonstrate whether DDR achieves any of its intended effects perpetuates confusion and frustrates practice.

This volume is animated by a concern with the weak evidence base for security promotion in countries wracked by war and collective armed violence. Generating concrete evidence of why and how fighters are mobilized, what happens when they are disarmed and demobilized, and whether reintegration is effective are essential questions for which there are presently few answers. Policy-makers, aid practitioners and the taxpayers who fund such operations are especially keen to know how development assistance and security promotion can be made more contextually-appropriate, accountable and effective. Put another way, the international development and security establishments are increasingly determined to demonstrate whether their investments meet the basic tests of aid effectiveness and 'all of government' coherence.[9] Meanwhile, peace-keepers and civilian personnel working in zones experiencing simmering violence are struggling to generate results – but the priority in the field is naturally on delivery rather than monitoring and evaluation. Even so, in an era dominated by results-based management, many are also conscious of the critical importance of moving away from prescriptive approaches toward evidence-based interventions that promote genuine safety and security but have few examples of how to move the agenda forward. Appropriate metrics of success, the indicators, impacts and outcomes of DDR – together with analysis of what and why it does or does not work – are urgently required.

The extent to which social science knowledge can adequately serve policy-making on security promotion, including DDR, is necessarily limited. As with econometric and epidemiological research on the causes of conflict onset and post-conflict violence, there are acute challenges to working in this nascent area of study and with partial datasets. There is of course nothing particularly unusual about policy prescriptions changing over time in the wake of evolving methodologies and evidence (Suhrke and Samset 2007). The onus, however, is on researchers and policy-makers to prevent the misinterpretation of their findings. Researchers should approach the measurement of DDR and SSR effectiveness cautiously, in a spirit of transparency and with a willingness to acknowledge the limitations of their data. This may mean that they may lose some support (and funding) from policy-makers who are seeking certainty and general formulas. As noted by Suhrke and Samset (2007), it is equally critical that responsible policy-makers recall that much social scientific knowledge is itself comparatively soft and dynamic, and consequently be less demanding in their search for generalizable principles on which to base interventions.

A short history of DDR

Before turning to a discussion of contemporary DDR operations and the context in which they are undertaken, it is useful to trace out their origins. Although now widely heralded as a necessary feature of twenty-first century peace support and post-conflict recovery packages, DDR is in fact a comparatively new idea. Prior to the 1980s, disarmament and demobilization activities were largely conceived and executed exclusively by and for military establishments and shaped by the geo-political imperatives of Cold War cooperation. Focused on veteran soldiers and in rare cases independence and liberation movements, such processes were ordinarily designed to 'right-size' armed forces and, more unusually, as a stop-gap or stabilization measure.[10] Early experimentation with post-conflict demilitarization and decommissioning of armed groups included interventions supported by the UK in Zimbabwe in 1979 and 1980 and were narrowly conceived as a form of technical military cooperation (Mazarire and Rupiya 2000).[11] These interventions were ordinarily confined to bilateral partners and focused on the decommissioning and reform of formal military structures in lesser developed countries, including alternative employment schemes for retired officers and veteran pension schemes (Collier 1994).

Confronted with a legacy of independence wars and simmering Cold War tensions during the late-1980s, the UN and its associated agencies were increasingly invested in more expansive activities, especially in sub-Saharan Africa.[12] Multilateral and bilateral donor engagement was frequently solicited in the context of peace-keeping operations and a growing interest in, among other things, promoting democratic oversight over military institutions (Cawthra and Luckham 2003). The first formally UN Security Council (UNSC) sanctioned DDR operation was launched in Namibia (1989–1990) with support from the UN Transitional Assistance Group (UNTAG) (Dzinesa 2006). This early DDR intervention was intended to canton and dismantle South African and South West African People's Organization (SWAPO) forces and as well as various ethnic and paramilitary units.[13] Similar initiatives followed in southern Africa[14] and Central America[15] soon after (see Table I.1).

International enthusiasm for these peace-support operations and the possibilities of securitizing development in the aftermath of the Cold War spurred on renewed commitment to UN-sponsored peace-keeping and post-conflict reconstruction efforts, particularly in the Balkans and Africa (Holt and Berkman 2006; Paris 2004).[16] Although certain countries such as Ethiopia and Eritrea pursued large-scale demobilization and reintegration programmes independently of direct external UN support during the early 1990s[17] (as has Russia in the 1990s, the Philippines in the late 1990s and Colombia since 2003), UN-mandated DDR interventions – overseen by the Department for Peacekeeping Operations (DPKO) at the bequest of the UN Security Council – were launched in Angola, El Salvador, Cambodia and elsewhere.[18] Predictably, the DDR concept rapidly spread into development and security discourse and practice and was grafted into a growing array of UNSC resolutions (Muggah and Krause 2006).

Table I.1 A typology of contexts for DDR

Context	Typical intervention	Financial support	Examples
Pre-crisis/ conflict	Military/policing downsizing or 'right sizing'	Bilateral defence cooperation, and/or multilateral/bilateral loan/credit, nationally-led	CAR, South Africa, Djibouti Uganda (1992–1995)
During conflict	Limited demobilization and reintegration combined with amnesty and prosecution	Nationally-led, multilateral funding	Colombia, Northern Uganda, Cote D'Ivoire, Mindanao (Philippines)
Post 'cross-border' conflict	Demobilization, reinsertion and reintegration	Nationally-led, multilateral/bilateral funding	Ethiopia, Eritrea, Iraq, Afghanistan
Post 'internal' conflict	Disarmament, demobilization, reinsertion, and reintegration together with reconciliation and rehabilitation	UN or World Bank-led, DPKO or regional involvement, multilateral/bilateral financing, nationally-led	Angola, DRC, Rwanda, Timor-Leste, Aceh, El Salvador, Kosovo, Sudan[19]

More fundamentally, throughout the 1990s DDR programmes were introduced in a growing array of contexts with an ever-expanding array of
objectives.[20] These ranged from activities with a strict focus on demobilizing
and providing alternative livelihoods to regular and professional soldiers following a cross-border war to others promoting collective support to irregular and
rebel ex-combatants and guerrilla groups in the aftermath of so-called internal
conflicts (see Table I.1).[21] Within a short timespan, a set of orthodoxies began to
emerge: while every DDR operation was expected to be responsive to local
context, a sequenced intervention was determined to be an essential fixture of
the war-to-peace transition.[22] Technical provisions for DDR began to emerge in
peace-agreements and associated protocols (HDC 2008). Donors and UN agencies turned busily to setting-up national mechanisms so that DDR activities
would be 'locally owned' by the host state.

On the basis of accumulated experience and growing donor enthusiasm, DDR
operations began to multiply in number and reach. Interventions began to
emphasize specialized components not just for ex-combatants but for their
dependents and the communities to which they were to be returned and settled.
Facing complex challenges associated with contagion and extreme violence in
countries such as Angola, the Democratic Republic of Congo (DRC), and
Rwanda, aid agencies began to advise for the repatriation of 'foreign' ex-
combatants and focused interventions on behalf of child- and female soldiers,
HIV-AIDS-affected combatants and so-called 'vulnerable groups' (Jensen and
Stepputat 2001).[23] Donors also began to support the linking of DDR with other
thematic priorities including law and justice reform, police re-training and re-
deployment and the strengthening of government institutions. In short, DDR was
becoming a kind of hamper into which many priorities – some of them not
necessarily complementary – were added. Owing to the rapid spread of DDR
and SSR activities around the world and the high importance attached by
Western governments to their success, a bewildering array of expressions and
concepts emerged that are now regularly used by academics, policy-makers
and practitioners.[24]

Scale and distribution of DDR

The number and scale of DDR operations steadily increased during the 1990s.
Of the more than 60 documented programmes launched since the late 1980s,
some 18 were running concurrently in 2007 and 2008 (see Figure I.1). This
represented a dramatic increase on previous decades and coincided with the concomitant increase in peace-support operations more generally (DPKO 2008).
Geographically, sub-Saharan Africa is currently home to the majority of DDR
operations. Owing in large part to the scale and ferocity of conflicts on the continent, almost two-thirds of all DDR operations since 1979 were launched in
African countries – with virtually every country in the Greater Horn now also
featuring such activities. As noted above, however, there was also considerable
investment in DDR in countries throughout Central America (1980s and early

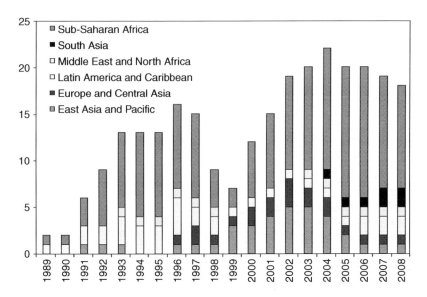

Figure I.1 Geographic distribution of DDR operations: 1989–2008.

1990s), Southeast Asia (early 1990s), the Balkans (mid and late 1990s) and even the island states of the South Pacific (late 1990s and early 2000s).

The level of global investment in contemporary DDR operations is breathtaking. A cursory review of UN and non-UN supported initiatives launched from 2000 to 2005 documented the participation of over one million ex-combatants – or 'beneficiaries'– in some aspect of DDR.[25] Although difficult to measure with precision for reasons described at length in this volume, the annual aggregate budgets of DDR programmes appeared to surpass US$630 million in 2007, although this estimation does not account for many hidden costs. While admittedly an imperfect proxy of their efficiency or effectiveness, the average expenditure on disarming, demobilizing and reintegrating a single ex-combatant in 2007 amounted to some US$1,250.

Depending on the relative geo-political importance of the country and the generosity of donors, the efficiency of the implementing agencies and the recipient state's capacity and local purchasing power, the cost of DDR varied from US$350 to over US$9,000 per capita (for absolute figures, see Figure I.2). Predictably, the ratio of spending per ex-combatant participant is comparatively lower in sub-Saharan Africa than in other regions (Hanson 2007). When compared to per capita aid contributions to others in need, say internally displaced people or those affected by malaria and other communicable diseases, DDR constitutes an especially generous form of compensation. Notwithstanding the ethical dilemmas associated with 'rewarding' bad behaviour, investment in DDR was justified by outsiders as a way of securing the peace.

Many of the countries in which these early DDR programmes were pursued

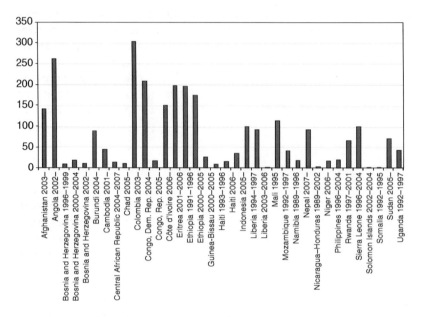

Figure 1.2 DDR budgets: 1989–2008 (in US$ millions).

constituted natural experiments in which to test and assess their potential for securing protection. And while the popularity of DDR continued to rise, the outcomes of these processes in relation to preventing a return to armed conflict were not necessarily positive. Indeed, in certain cases (e.g. Haiti, DRC, the Philippines), collective violence resumed soon after (or even before) DDR came to an end. This was not in all instances a function of 'bad' DDR, but instead reflected how limited progress on the political front and the economy could undermine more narrow security aspirations. But some critics began to detect real flaws in DDR operations: while disarmament and demobilization appeared in some cases to yield temporary improvements in relation to stability and safety, the effectiveness of reintegration was much less apparent. A report of the UN Secretary-General (UNSG 1998) emphasized this point in describing how 'disarmament and reintegration of ex-combatants and others into productive society' remained one of the priorities of 'post-conflict peace-building'.

By the end of the 1990s many in the aid community were fully committed to supporting DDR. Widely considered a central pillar of military–civilian transition operations, over 20 UN agencies were actively providing financial and technical inputs to DDR in literally dozens of countries. Dozens of non-governmental organizations (NGOs) and civil society actors were also investing in the enterprise. Prominent among them were the United Nations Development Programme (UNDP), the International Organisation for Migration (IOM), the United Nations Children's Fund (UNICEF), the United Nations High Commissioner for Refugees (UNHCR), bilateral donor governments[26] and others.[27] The

World Bank also assumed an increasingly central role in planning, financing and trust fund management for what they described as demobilization and reintegration programmes (DRPs).[28] While the World Bank expressed a certain reluctance to fund disarmament activities owing to mandate constraints,[29] it envisioned demobilization and reintegration as a pathway to unlocking core development assistance (e.g. IDA loans and credits). By the beginning of the twenty-first century, DDR was merging as a de facto feature of mainstream development.

Conventional approaches to DDR

DDR is typically described as consisting of a series of carefully designed and phased activities to create a suitable environment for stability and development to proceed. From the beginning, supporters presumed that all three components – disarmament, demobilization and reintegration – were interlocking and mutually reinforcing activities. The collection of arms and munitions – or disarmament – was from the beginning understood to comprise a necessary but insufficient means of promoting security (see Figure I.3). Many DDR supporters still insisted on disarmament as a primary step toward stabilization and highlighted the importance of generating visible and tangible evidence of success in the form of collected units of arms and munitions. On the ground, however,

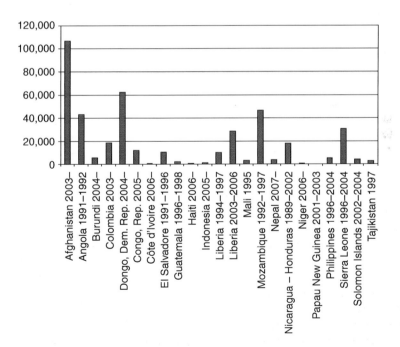

Figure I.3 DDR and disarmament: a sample of operations (number of weapons collected).

specialists were adamant that disarmament needed to be complemented with parallel activities lest they generate security dilemmas. Parallel activities such as information sharing, confidence-building and security-enhancing activities (including so-called 'reconciliation' initiatives) together with credible policing and the promotion of the rule of law were all prioritized even if unevenly implemented.[30]

A growing collection of experts were sceptical that disarmament alone could be effective in promoting genuine stability or security in societies wracked by war. Some claimed that the sheer abundance of arms left over from protracted conflicts made small-scale collection activities redundant (Spear 2005). A small minority felt that the weapons themselves did not matter – but rather they ought to be 'put beyond use'. More important than gathering up hardware was that former fighters abandoned their desire to resort to arms to solve grievances, as the experience of the Irish Republican Army (IRA) seemed to show. Optimists countered that disarmament – particularly when undertaken with verification mechanisms and when arms were destroyed[31] – could potentially build confidence between erstwhile warring parties (Spear 2006). Seasoned practitioners also emphasized the critical importance of destroying arms in order to prevent their recirculation.[32] When accompanied with destruction ceremonies as first occurred in Mali, Cambodia and Albania in the mid-1990s,[33] they appeared to offer a symbolic commitment to peace.[34]

The demobilization[35] and reintegration phases were also considered to be even more risky and complex undertakings than disarmament. It is useful to recall that demobilization can assume multiple forms.[36] Governments emerging from war frequently demobilize and reintegrate former combatants into either newly reconstituted security structures or civilian livelihoods. The challenges accompanying reintegration into either category are tremendous and well rehearsed in contemporary SSR debates. Depending on the context, security services are frequently heavily politicized and confronting major capacity gaps that can frustrate integration. Likewise, the absorptive capacities of areas for civilian reintegration are frequently exceedingly limited (Azam *et al.* 1994). Nevertheless, most conventional DDR operations have undertaken some form of demobilization (see Figure I.4).

According to Collier (1994), demobilization on its own (like disarmament) holds the potential to generate unintentional security dilemmas. Faced with an unsteady peace deal, for example, there were concerns that soldiers and rebels that remained partially organized within their existing command structure could potentially assume a spoiler function, as was the case in Sierra Leone in 2000 (World Bank 2002). Knight and Ozerdem (2004) found that, in some cases, the cantonment of ex-combatants could unintentionally reinforce latent command structures if precautions were not adopted in advance. By contrast, if former soldiers were too hastily demobilized, as was repeatedly the case in Angola, there were concerns that ex-combatants could trigger insecurity in the communities of return.[37] Such activities had the potential to contribute to the rapid dissolution of armed groups who might adopt more predatory roles including banditry in the

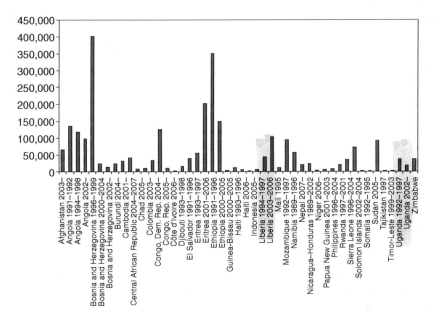

Figure I.4 DDR and demobilization: a sample of operations (number of demobilized ex-combatants).

absence of meaningful alternatives. Spear (2005), for example, documented the risks presented by hasty demobilization processes that failed to adequately dismantle command and control structures.

Another challenge relates to the sequencing of the demobilization process with other activities. Where pursued in too linear or rigid a manner and not in parallel with reintegration, it was found that demobilization could generate new challenges.[38] Likewise, in order to avoid DDR becoming orphaned or sidelined by other development priorities, donors increasingly began demanding that the entire process be aligned with and connected to sector-specific development priorities, including those supported by international financial institutions and UN agencies.[39] Development agencies involved in aspects of DDR rapidly elaborated and launched Quick Impact Projects (QIPs), ostensibly to bridge the gap between DDR and mainstream development sector priorities.[40] But the rapid injection of funds and programming options also generated new expectations on the ground. Competing priorities issued from above generated the real (and unintentional) potential to undermine more localized community-based initiatives initiated from below.

A major shortcoming of DDR since the emergence of the concept was re-insertion and reintegration (see Figure I.5). While in theory recognized as a critical component of the process, investment in livelihood alternatives, community support and the strengthening of municipal and national capacities to absorb demobilized ex-combatants regularly fell short. Part of the reason for this appeared to be connected to the integral role (and associated biases) of military and security institutions that administered DDR in the late 1980s and early 1990s. Mandated UN peace-support operations simply failed to anticipate the range of needs on the ground and lacked the necessary expertise to programme appropriately. Development agencies who relied more extensively on voluntary contributions from donors were comparatively new to the scene, and themselves struggled to identify how best to proceed (Baaré 2006). As will be described at length below, with the emergence of the World Bank and multilateral agencies such as the UNDP – some of these trends soon reversed – but the immensity of the task and the complexity of what amounted to social engineering proved a formidable challenge all the same.

Emerging independently of DDR, small arms control – or micro-disarmament – began to assume a priority for certain governments in the 1990s, particularly those emerging from bouts of acute collective violence. The period witnessed a tremendous burst of diplomatic energy and the elaboration of a rash of international and regional instruments (most politically-binding) to regulate the supply of arms – particularly controls on exports, smuggling, brokering and domestic stocks.[41] These initiatives were supply-side driven, motivated as they were by a growing global awareness of the *trans-national* dynamics of arms

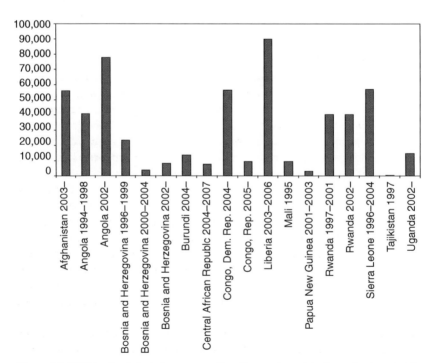

Figure I.5 DDR and reintegration: a sample of operations (number of reintegrated ex-combatants).

circulation and organized crime. Owing to the sensitivities among certain governments of what they perceived to be efforts to compromise their sovereignty with new treaties and legally-binding norms, approaches tended to privilege enhanced information-sharing and inter-agency cooperation rather than more robust and intrusive rules associated with domestic arms production or possession.

Nevertheless, alongside the UN, regional entities such as the Organisation of African States (now African Union or AU), ECOWAS and SADC elaborated regional arms control initiatives[42] together with the European Union (EU), the Organisation of American States (OAS), the Pacific Islands Forum (PIF), the League of Arab States and others.[43] At the same time, a number of innovative small arms collection and destruction programmes were quietly launched in the 1990s. These interventions sought to collect and destroy 'civilian' surplus rather than weapons from ex-combatants even if distinctions between the two were often hard to render. As such, these interventions often complemented DDR – alternately taking place before – and were supported by development agencies such as the UNDP and IOM, among others.[44]

With all of these activities taking place, efforts soon turned to standardizing and professionalizing DDR. The most recent initiative includes the *Integrated Disarmament, Demobilization and Reintegration Standards* (IDDRS) (UNWG 2006). Assembled by a UN inter-agency working group between 2004 and 2006, the IDDRS laid out a wide-ranging list of protocols and procedures covering more than two dozen separate aspects of DDR. In effect, the standards aimed to consolidate policy guidance on DDR providing a comprehensive approach to planning, management and implementation – a subject treated at length elsewhere in this volume. Constituting in some ways a new doctrine for DDR,[45] they were (self) described as 'the most complete repository and best practices drawn from the experience of all United Nations departments, agencies, funds and programmes involved in DDR'.

As is well known in military circles, doctrine is itself dynamic and also takes time to filter down from headquarters to the field.[46] Unless there is a unified chain of command, doctrine may not be effectively diffused or applied.[47] It is not surprising, then, that in spite of recent attempts to improve the predictability and coherence of DDR, there are still competing and at times contradictory visions of what it is intended to accomplish, the metrics of success, when it begins and ends, and how it ought to be undertaken. Complicating these competing visions are ideological and conceptual faultlines – commonly expressed as turf battles – that persist between implementing agencies and donors. These cleavages are due in part to their distinct mandates but also more mundane (if essential) bureaucratic and organizational issues relating to competing lines of authority and reporting.

In terms of competing vision, an unresolved question is whether DDR should be narrowly or broadly conceived.[48] Although a penchant for integrated and joined-up approaches to peace-support operations is fast becoming the norm,[49] there are real challenges to coordinating systems and institutions effectively in highly charged environments. There are also lingering concerns over how best to target beneficiaries and, indeed, who counts as a beneficiary at all.[50] These challenges throw up sharp ethical questions associated with the implications of victors' justice. If such questions are left to fester, they can potentially undermine the legitimacy of the intervention[51] in the absence of credible punitive policies, including transitional justice. While not necessarily incommensurable, these competing ideational framings of the means and ends of DDR can reproduce different assumptions and biases. Though the IDDRS and other processes explicitly encourage the adoption of shared understandings of core goals among stakeholders,[52] most implementing agencies also cannily recognize the benefits of constructive ambiguity.

Conventional DDR can be envisioned on a continuum that extends from a narrow minimalist (establishing security) to a broad maximalist (an opportunity for development) perspective.[53] More traditional security-oriented entities such as DPKO tend to adopt the former perspective. Their focus is on removing weapons, cantoning ex-soldiers and fulfilling the terms of peace agreements to the letter. Their strategic goals include a reduction of the likelihood of war recurrence while their micro imperatives are more specifically oriented toward de-linking the command and control of armed groups. By way of contrast, ostensibly 'development' agencies including the UNDP and the World Bank tend to endorse interventions that call for much broader ambition and scope. They aim to rehabilitate ex-combatants and provide for dependents, children and the infirm so that they can assume productive roles in (civil) society while also reinforcing public institutions and their legitimacy by promoting markets, infrastructure and property rights in areas of (re)integration. In many instances they may seek to redress distortions in state spending on defence, welfare and social services while seeking to enhance human capabilities and endowments.

In so-called fragile states where many actors are pushing a host of priorities, reconciling the minimalist and maximalist approaches to DDR is a formidably daunting task. While in theory their integration seems obvious, practical integration is much more difficult. On the one hand, narrowly-conceived and unambiguous targets such as collecting a specific stock of arms or demobilizing a precise group of ex-combatants is straightforward and concrete. They provide a tangible expression of results. But ensuring that such activities contribute to enhanced safety and security and the rehabilitation of former fighters and their dependents is much more challenging. Likewise, in the case of reintegration, the administration of what amounts to social engineering – from re-housing, resettling and integrating former soldiers and their families in areas that may be hostile to them – is ambitious in the extreme. Although there can be little doubt that the development sector injected creative and dynamic thinking into the process, this volume reveals how the maximalist approach to DDR often lacks focus. This is not to say that DDR is immune to adaptation. DDR is increasingly wide-ranging in its parameters and innovations. There is some evidence that DDR practitioners are already incorporating strategies focused on preventing and reducing risks associated with armed violence, enhancing the protective

factors and resiliency of affected populations, promoting community ox
security, together with community policing and provisions for tran.
justice. But unless the parameters are more clearly defined and results n
convincingly communicated, DDR may prove to be little more than anothe
passing fad.

Notwithstanding the cautions noted above, DDR programming appears to be
inexorably moving towards a more maximalist orientation. Demobilization and
reintegration initiatives funded by the World Bank in Ethiopia (2001–2007) and
Eritrea (2001–2004), for example, purposefully sought to reform national budgetary priorities. In downsizing recurrent expenditures on defence and promoting social welfare spending as part of the explicit objectives of DDR, it was
expected that more resources could be allocated to reintegrating veterans and
promoting inclusive programmes for dependents, HIV/AIDS-infected and disabled fighters.[54] Likewise, in the southern Philippines and Aceh, DDR was purposefully linked to national safety-net and food security initiatives and
urban/rural housing renewal schemes.[55] Meanwhile, DDR programmes in the
Republic of Congo, Mozambique, Sierra Leone, Sudan, Haiti and the Solomon
Islands also adopted comprehensive maximalist approaches.[56] In addition to
expanding the caseload to accommodate more beneficiaries, these initiatives
advanced culturally and socially-tailored collective incentives such as schools,
community centres, roads and water-wells rather than strict one-off cash incentives and limited training packages for demobilized ex-combatants.[57]

Structure of this volume

After the dust settles, there is actually comparatively little evidence of whether
DDR works. That is, whether it is effective in contributing to improved security
for civilians or promoting broader development objectives. Part of the reason for
this is a fundamental absence of disaggregated longitudinal baseline data with
which to render statistically valid analysis or estimations. In addition to the competing normative understandings of DDR outlined above, these basic data gaps
limit awareness and understandings of DDR outcomes and impacts. This volume
attempts to reconcile a number of these gaps through the presentation of new
and original survey data and thematic assessments of critical aspects of DDR.

Divided into two parts, the first section of the volume presents findings from
a number of country case studies. Countries featured include Colombia, Sierra
Leone, Liberia, Uganda, Ethiopia, Timor-Leste, Afghanistan, Haiti and Sudan.
The case material draws on household survey and focus groups methods to test
DDR dividends in settings involving UN missions and those where the UN was
less active.[58] The volume's second section focuses on a number of transversal
themes – namely the challenges of 'integrating' DDR interventions, the (under-)
conceptualization of reintegration during peace negotiations and the synergies
between DDR and transitional justice. Taken together, these chapters draw from
a variety of intellectual and disciplinary traditions such as economics, political
economy, public health, anthropology and sociology. The chapters are important

not only in highlighting what works and what does not, but in demonstrating how multidisciplinary research on DDR is feasible and can contribute positively to improving policy and practice.

Case studies

An overriding concern among DDR supporters is whether the process contributes to tangible improvements in real and perceived safety on the ground. Chapter 1 examines the extent to which recent disarmament and demobilization interventions focusing on Colombian paramilitaries contributed to reductions in homicidal violence. Colombia, long affected by protracted armed conflict and criminal violence, witnessed the demobilization of more than 30,000 members of the United Self-Defense Forces of Colombia (AUC) between 2003 and 2006. The AUC were widely held to be responsible for disproportionately high rates of armed violence in the preceding decade. The disarmament process yielded more than 17,000 semi- and fully-automatic military style weapons – approximately one firearm for every two demobilized combatants. Drawing on a combination of large-scale datasets, Jorge Restrepo and Robert Muggah reveal how the demobilization of actors previously expert in massacring civilians generated important but geographically differentiated reductions in homicidal violence. While the process saved the lives of between 1,400 and 2,800 people in the first two years since its inception, there is considerable national variation in relation to outcomes. Homicides actually increased in some regions, and various forms of criminality substituting for homicidal violence escalates in others. A statistical examination of the impacts of more than 35 demobilization sites on homicide rates reveals a 13 per cent reduction as compared to non-participating areas, but it remains unclear whether these gains can be sustained in the long-term.

The outcomes of DDR are potentially more ambiguous in certain countries emerging from vicious internal conflicts in West Africa, including Sierra Leone. In Chapter 2, Macartan Humphreys and Jeremy Weinstein analyse cross-sectional household survey data from a random sample of just over 1,000 ex-combatants from Sierra Leone's five warring factions. After elaborating a comprehensive definition of reintegration,[59] they seek to compare reintegration success rates between those who did and those who did not enter the DDR programme. They focus on four outcome measurements: access to employment, the extent to which fighters maintain ties with erstwhile factions, trust in the democratic process and whether combatants believe that they are accepted by family and community members. Following an examination of the programming determinants[60] and controlling for non-programmatic factors,[61] they find evidence of some level of macro success and micro failure. Specifically, they find that gender has no measurable impact on DDR outcomes, that the poor are more successful at reintegration than the wealthy and that individuals settling in wealthy areas experience more difficulty in reintegrating than those settling in poorer areas. Likewise, in examining the correlates of reintegration, they note that past participation in an abusive military faction is the strongest factor inhibiting social reintegration.[62]

Overall, the chapter reveals that there is no discernible evidence that participation in DDR programmes facilitated reintegration.

Chapter 3 considers approaches to measuring reintegration of former combatants from Liberia's brutal internal conflict. James Pugel considers the challenges of statistically analysing reintegration outcomes in data-poor contexts. The chapter considers the results of a stratified survey of over 1,200 ex-combatants and non-combatants. Separating the former fighter caseload into distinct categories, Pugel notes that while evidence of some level of impact was clearly identified in the lives of those completing the DDR programme, the failure to adequately link DDR to broad development programmes may obviate these tentative gains. Overall, the chapter considers how, without clear and cogent objectives, it is difficult to generate appropriate baseline data necessary to test outcomes. It is only by understanding how bureaucracies plan and finance DDR that the 'gap' between objectives and outcomes can be closed. More controversially, the chapter recommends re-thinking aspects of the DDR enterprise by potentially 'de-linking' disarmament and demobilization from reintegration and administering interventions in parallel. In adopting a narrower approach, Pugel contends that the quality and quantity of security provision could be improved while ensuring renewed attention from other donors and implementing agencies to development goals.

The importance of disarming, demobilizing and reintegrating child-soldiers is considered an urgent international priority. Chapter 4 questions the extent to which current DDR activities focused on children actually generate positive outcomes. Chris Blattman and Jeanie Annan note that rigorous assessments of the mobilizing habits of child soldiers – and indeed of ex-combatants in general – are few in number and largely case-based, drawing on extensive interviews with former participants and commanders.[63] In order to better understand the reintegration experiences of tens of thousands of young people forcibly recruited into the Lord's Resistance Army (LRA), the authors administered a randomized survey of approximately 740 boys and young men (half formerly abducted, half not). Theirs is the first large-scale psychological and socio-economic survey of former child soldiers, and was expected to examine the special needs of young ex-combatants during and after armed conflict. The authors reveal how interventions focusing narrowly on psychological care for traumatized and aggressive former combatants – whether child or adult – may be misplaced. They find that the main impact of war is substantially reduced education, diminished productivity and increased inequality. The impacts are greatest for children who are likely to have had school interrupted. The chapter observes that as the international community prepares an expanded DDR programme in the wake of emerging peace negotiations between the LRA and the Ugandan government, particular attention needs to be paid to its design, implementation and criteria for eligibility in light of these findings.

Chapter 5 explores a series of dilemmas confronting two DDR initiatives for former militia following the coalition-led intervention in Afghanistan. In contrast to the earlier chapters, Michael Bhatia and Robert Muggah employ

qualitative research methods, primarily testimonials and semi-structured interviews of more than 300 former combatants. Their objective is to examine
whether demobilization was effective in breaking the 'command and control' of
various armed groups and enhanced the legitimacy of the state. Overall, the
authors find that DDR should not be pursued as a technical activity by development agencies (as is currently the case). Rather, it should be conceived as a strategic 'interaction' connected to state consolidation and not a discrete technical
intervention. They find that conventional approaches to DDR tend to neglect the
many ways in which discrete activities are interpreted by local actors.
Externally-imposed interventions tend to ignore locally existing security
arrangements in areas of limited governance. They seldom adequately build on
alternative power-sharing mechanisms and inadequately account for the heterogeneous endowments of armed group members themselves. In Afghanistan,
Bhatia and Muggah find that repeated DDR activities failed to sufficiently
account for the complex motivations and interests of commanders, rank and file
and their layered relationships with communities. Instead, interventions
advanced a simple economic bias treating beneficiaries as a homogeneous caseload who would respond rationally to monetary incentives. To be effective,
planners must widen their lens to account for the ways in which former fighters
themselves are embedded in the state-building project.

Chapter 6 examines the effects of four distinct DDR initiatives designed to
assist veterans in Timor-Leste following its long war of independence. Drawing
purposefully on the lived experiences of former fighters, it considers the limited
role and programming effects of successive DDR operations in the context of
wider, dynamic societal transformation.[64] Gordon Peake adopts a qualitative
focus group approach to reviewing reintegration effectiveness, combining interviews with more than 100 veterans in several districts with small-scale semi-
structured surveys. The chapter finds that whatever credible outcomes may have
been realized immediately following DDR, these rapidly evaporated over time.
Many participating veterans had long forgotten the nature of assistance provided.
The chapter echoes the circumspection of other contributors and reaffirms the
need to deflate expectations and anecdotally-rendered claims of success. Taken
together, the chapter reveals the limited long-term impacts of DDR in Timor-
Leste, and the mounting frustration among veterans over their continued neglect.

Chapter 7 considers the reintegration experience of a World Bank and
Ethiopian government-managed DDR process. Robert Muggah and Jon Bennett
together with Aklu Girgee and Gebru Wolde consider efforts to demobilize,
reinsert and reintegrate more than 148,000 veterans recently returned from a
cross-border war with Eritrea. The chapter observes that while generally yielding positive outcomes, the intervention generated differentiated reintegration
effects. The methodology adopted a proportional size sampling strategy of more
than 800 respondents and was weighted according to geographic regions displaying the highest concentration of 'returned' veterans.[65] The chapter finds that
four years after the end of the demobilization process, income and asset holdings
deteriorated despite the fact that many veterans consider themselves to be

'empowered' and 'accepted' by their families and communities and not unduly discriminated against by political authorities. The proportion of rural and urban veterans slipping into lower income quintiles increased irrespective of the demobilization and reintegration programme, though more so in the case of the latter than the former. While there is evidence of social pathologies and dysfunctions emerging among certain clusters of veterans, they are considered more the exception than the rule. The chapter also emphasizes how certain lessons from the DDR experience in Ethiopia may be applicable to other humanitarian sectors, namely 'durable solutions' for displaced populations.

Critical themes

Chapter 8 considers the emerging orthodoxy of 'integrated missions' from a practitioner's perspective.[66] Robert Muggah, Desmond Molloy and Maximo Halty consider the integration imperative for UNDPKO and UNDP in Haiti and Sudan, two countries emerging from different types of conflict. The chapter finds that both missions contributed to far fewer demonstrable changes in real and perceived security than anticipated by their proponents. In both cases DDR itself was not wholly endorsed by the various armed groups nor were programmes themselves equipped to address the heterogeneity of these same actors. Each mission faced considerable strains and was subsequently restructured according to the needs on the ground. While the IDDRS provided a set of tentative rules to guide institutional behaviour (in the highly positivist sense), the chapter finds that integration depends as much on personalities in the field as prescriptions from headquarters. The chapter also signals a second generation of community violence reduction activities in the wake of conventional DDR. These new interventions exhibit less of a combatant-centric approach and seek in part to bolster 'agents for peace' and community leaders in areas of return. These second generation activities offer a variety of novel institutional templates for future engagement, focusing alternately on area-based, community-based and collective incentives.

DDR is frequently etched into peace agreements and UN resolutions even if negotiating parties and mediators may not be entirely sure what it is expected to do. Chapter 9 considers the way DDR – and particularly reintegration – features in the context of peace negotiations. Robert Muggah and Anton Baaré observe that while aspects of DDR may feature in formal agreements, they are often watered-down, poorly-understood and mask considerable contestation. This may be due to a lack of awareness on the part of core stakeholders and mediators. Alternately, it may reflect a strategic decision on the part of erstwhile warring parties. The chapter notes that DDR may not be effectively established in the period between an agreement and the launch of post-conflict recovery programmes – described by some as the 'the little red box'.[67] If this box is to be successfully opened, at a minimum, mediators must be well-informed about the origins, principles, approaches and outcomes of DDR. But because reintegration is largely under-conceptualized and sidelined in the rush to secure the peace, it is also often poorly understood. Competing framings of 'reintegration' and DDR can profoundly (and negatively) affect the way programmes are subsequently designed and implemented. Drawing on a wide range of experiences, particularly the case of a tentative peace agreement in northern Uganda, the chapter concludes with a series of recommendations for mediators and practitioners to better anticipate the requirements of reintegration during and after peace processes.

Chapter 10 considers the interconnections between DDR and transitional justice. Ana Patel focuses on conventional transitional justice measures such as criminal prosecutions, truth commissions, reparations for victims and vetting or other forms of institutional reform. She demonstrates that these two initiatives – one focused on justice and accountability and the other on stability – are both intent on contributing to peace but from different ontological perspectives. In signalling the lack of practical exchange and learning between the two sectors through a review of global DDR programmes, she identifies areas for more cooperation and coordination. A primary element of improved coherence is the adoption of a shared language and nomenclature.

The Conclusion ends with a review of the central themes emerging from the case study and thematic chapters. Robert Muggah, Mats Berdal and Stina Torjesen revisit a number of particular challenging aspects of DDR – the central role of context in shaping outcomes, the fundamental position of politics and state-building in shaping objectives and aspirations, its evolving bureaucratic architecture and connections to SSR, the under-conceptualization and limits of reintegration and the heterogeneous motivations of various beneficiaries. The conclusion parses out these and other themes and considers their implications for the future of DDR and security promotion more generally. Importantly, it highlights the critical importance of investing in evidence-based approaches to designing, implementing and evaluating DDR. As noted by some observers, the comparative absence of empirical research in policy making is not a dry theoretical issue:

> it has direct implications for the ability of policy makers to accurately evaluate the impact of policies and programmes, thoroughly assess what works and what does not, and effectively channel funding and resources. Empirical data can help redirect policies that did not produce expected results.
>
> (IPA 2006)

The volume does not offer a blueprint for future DDR operations. After all, a fundamental message is that templates are to be avoided: context determines all. Instead, the volume signals emerging evidence of what works and what does not. It encourages policy-makers and practitioners to infuse a dose of humility and realism in their programmes, to limit over-loading the DDR bandwagon and support flexible programming based on solid evidence. Each of the chapters also signal over-the-horizon challenges, not least the dynamic landscape of armed violence, the diminishing utility of fixed labels such as 'conflict', 'post-conflict' and 'crime' and entry-points for cost-effective monitoring and e (M&E). The volume should be read as a call for enhanced accountabilit) development and security practitioners. By shedding light on the limita\ ...s of current approaches to security promotion, it lists a number of ways to hasten course-correction. The volume offers not so much a road-map as a series of signposts for enhancing and strengthening practice in making people safer in the aftermath of war.

Notes

1 See, for example, the UN (2001), progress on the *Arms Trade Treaty* (www.arms tradetreaty.com) and OECD (2008).
2 See, for example, Collier *et al.* (2003) and Doyle and Sambanis (2000).
3 See, for example, the new set of principles and guidelines established by UNDPKO (2008); Bellamy (2004); Bellamy and Williams (2007) and Paris (2004). Interview with Carolyn McAskie, May 2008.
4 See, for example, Collier *et al.* (2003) and Harbom and Wallensteen (2007).
5 See, for example, Collier (1994); Berdal (1996) and Stedman (1997) for early discussions of DDR.
6 See, for example, Jennings (2008); Pouligny (2004) and contributing authors to this volume.
7 See, for example, de Coning (2007) and Muggah (2007).
8 The World Bank prefers cash assistance to in-kind support, and contends that it maximizes beneficiary choice and reduces administrative costs.
9 This is signalled by the *Paris Declaration* (OECD 2005d).
10 See, for example, Middlebrook (2008) who reviews issues of military restructuring and financing.
11 Interview with Martin Rupiya, 28 April 2008.
12 See, for example, Ginifer (1995) and Cilliers (1995) for a review of these early operations in Southern Africa. See also Muggah (2008b) for a review of African DDR and small arms programmes.
13 Related activities are detailed by Dzinesa (2006, 2007) and Spear (2005) in relation to the integration of former *UmKhonto we Sizwe* [Spear of the Nation] fighters into the South African military. Alternatively, former combatants may join private security companies, as was the case of Sibuyile and Thuthuka in South Africa or even Executive Outcomes which operated in Sierra Leone and Angola (Spear 2005).
14 See, for example, Dzinesa (2007) for a short review of the Namibian DDR programme and others in Southern Africa.
15 See, for example Spencer (1997) who reviews the demobilization and reintegration of some 126,000 Nicaraguan and El Salvadorian former combatants.
16 See, for example, the UN's *Agenda for Peace* (1992) which singled out these issues in detail.
17 See also Dzinesa (2007: 74) and Colletta *et al.* (1996).
18 See Clark (1996) and Colletta *et al.* (1996).
19 This does not only apply to southern Sudan. Forced disarmament is noted for Darfur in resolution 1706 but has not proven successful in practice.
20 Torunn Chaudhary and Astri Suhrke (2008) developed a typology of different categories of post-war violence ranging from 'political' and 'routine state' violence to 'economic' and 'crime-related' violence, 'community and informal justice' and 'postwar displacement' and 'land/property disputes'.
21 See, for example, UNDPKO (1999, 2000). The UN Secretary-General issued a complete definition of DDR in his note to the General Assembly on the administrative and

budgetary aspects of the financing of the United Nations peacekeeping operations (A/C.5/59/31), 24 May 2005.

22 Essential pre-conditions for DDR included buy-in to the process from parties to a conflict (e.g. peace agreement or ceasefire), agreement among donors and affected governments on a normative framework and national ownership (e.g. a national commitment) and sustained international commitment to seeing the process through (e.g. mandated funds within UN missions).

23 Also consult de Watteville (2000) and Farr (2002).

24 For example, expressions include: 'Disarmament, Demobilization and Reintegration' (DDR); 'Disarmament, Demobilization and Reinsertion' (DDR); 'Demobilization, Reinsertion and Reintegration' (DRR); 'Reinsertion et Ramassage d'Armes' (RRA); 'Demobilization, Reintegration and Rehabilitation' (DRR); 'Disarmament, Demobilization, Reintegration and Rehabilitation' (DDRR); 'Disarmament, Demobilization, Reinsertion and Reintegration' (DDRR); and 'Disarmament, Demobilization, Repatriation, Resettlement Reintegration (DDRRR). See Muggah (2004b).

25 This estimate must be treated with caution, as numbers of ex-combatants reported by the ECP (2007) are not the same as those reported by DPKO and UNDP. Countries surveyed by the ECP include Afghanistan, Angola, Burundi, Cambodia, Central African Republic, Chad, Colombia, Cote D'Ivoire, DRC, Eritrea, the Philippines, Guinea-Bissau, Haiti, Indonesia, Liberia, Nepal, Nigeria, Republic of Congo, Rwanda, Somalia, Sudan and Uganda.

26 Singled out are Japan, US, EU, the UK, Canada, Germany, Sweden, Australia, the Netherlands, France, Italy, Norway and Belgium.

27 The UNDP, as well as the IOM, European Union (EU), German Technical Cooperation (GTZ), the UK Department for International Development (DfID) and others launched various types of DDR and weapons reduction interventions in more than 50 countries – targeting a combination of civilians and ex-combatants – between 1995 and 2007.

28 See, for example, Colletta (1995) and Colletta *et al.* (1996).

29 Due to World Bank procedures (i.e. Operational Policy 2.30), World Bank funds can not be spent on disarmament.

30 Spear (2006) observes how the provision of international policing was an especially weak element of UN-supported interventions. International civilian police were often supplied too late, lacked common standards and generated uneven outcomes in enhancing local capacities.

31 Similar initiatives focused on Liberian/Sierra Leonean border to more positive effect. Weapons for development programmes in the Republic of Congo, Burundi, Mali, Niger and other countries also sought to retrieve arms for collective incentives while permanently taking them out of circulation (Muggah 2005).

32 This was the case in both Mozambique and Namibia where arms continued to be purchased on the black market and turned up in violent crime in South Africa (Dzinesa 2007).

33 Symbolic collection and destruction activities were also undertaken in Niger, Liberia, the Republic of Congo, Cote D'Ivoire, Bougainville, Solomon Islands and many other countries subsequently (see Muggah 2006). Two practitioners – Robin Poulton and David DeBeer – are often credited with being involved in the original 'flame de paix' activities in West Africa. Correspondence with Poulton, April 2008.

34 This was the case in Cote D'Ivoire in 2004 when Prime Minister Seydou Diarra handed over his arms as part of the DDR process. There was a similar process in Liberia after UNMIL launched a weapons collection programme in 2003. Both processes are now considered failures.

35 Demobilization is also referred to as 'cantonment', 'forced encampment' or – incorrectly – 'disarmament'.

36 The World Bank (2003: 56) contends, somewhat arbitrarily, that 'demobilization

would be expected to be undertaken over a period of 36 months for all countries' and that, to the extent possible, all 'procedures for regular soldiers and members of irregular forces would be similar'. Among these procedures are assembly in discharge centres, verification of status and provision of ID cards, collection of relevant data, orientation sessions, health screening, support to vulnerable groups (female troops and child ex-combatants) and transport to new sites.

37 Failed demobilization twice contributed to the resumption of armed violence between the Movement for the Liberation of Angola (MPLA) and National Union for the Total Liberation of Angola (UNITA) in the 1990s. Unless there are adequate safeguards and options for meaningful reintegration, demobilization can quickly become counter-productive, even dangerous.

38 This is doubly important since disarmament is often incomplete and it is important to capitalize on its symbolic dividends as soon as possible.

39 The case of Ethiopia shows how macro-economic changes in the transition from a command to a market economy led to widespread retrenchment in the public sector and a dampening of labour opportunities. This took place at a time when newly demobilized veterans were entering the labour market – reducing the possibility for success.

40 The World Bank and others became heavily invested in such interventions – often in financing micro-projects to rehabilitate social infrastructure.

41 The most prominent is the UN *Programme of Action to Prevent, Combat and Eradicate the Illicit Trade in Small Arms and Light Weapons in All Its Aspects* (2001).

42 See, for example, Muggah (2008b) and UNOSAA (2007) for a review of these initiatives.

43 See, for example, Small Arms Survey (2003, 2005, 2006 and 2007) for a review of international arms measures.

44 See, for example, Muggah (2006); UNDP (2006); Small Arms Survey (2005) and Muggah and Batchelor (2002) for a review of these interventions.

45 The DDR doctrine is not to be confused with DPKO's (2008) 'capstone principles'.

46 See, for example, Teamy and Sweet (2006) and Nagl (2005).

47 Militaries and security forces codify their institutional memory in doctrine. The US Army (2001: 1–45, 1–46) Field Manual 3.0 describes doctrine as 'the concise expression of how Army forces contribute to unified action in campaigns, major operations, battles and engagements … doctrine provides a common language and a common understanding of how Army forces conduct operations'.

48 See, for example, Muggah (2004b) for a treatment of broad and narrow approaches to DDR in the Republic of Congo.

49 While few observers dispute the desirability of integrated approaches to DDR in principle, many practical constraints limit its operationalization. Field personnel lament how the parameters for inter-agency collaboration are still unclear and that notwithstanding the IDDRS, few (user-friendly) guidelines are available to guide the choppy waters of agency 'turf' in resource scarce environments. See, for example, De Coning (2007) and Osland (2005) for a review of so-called integrated missions.

50 Anthropological and sociological contributions to the DDR literature emphasize the porous line distinguishing a combatant from a civilian – some may be 'part-time warriors', while others may not have played a major role in the fighting (Jensen and Stepputat 2001).

51 There are tremendous stigmas attached to certain warring parties when attempts are made to 'reintegrate' them to their original communities or another area.

52 See, for example, the Stockholm Initiative at www.sweden.gov.se/sb/d/4890.

53 Jennings (2008: 6) draws from Muggah (2006 and 2004a) in describing the minimalist and maximalist agendas with respect to 'reintegration'. A minimalist approach is 'focused on expedience, where the program aspires less to creating a lasting impact in the lives of ex-combatants and more to time-limited gains [*sic*]'. The maximalist

approach 'implies a more ambitious, transformative reintegration agenda' (Muggah 2006).

54 See Conclusion, this volume.

55 Communication with Patrick Barron (World Bank – Indonesia). See also Muggah (2004b).

56 See, for example, ECP (2007) and Muggah and Jutersonke (2007) for a short review of these programmes.

57 See, for example, Sigrid (2006) for a discussion of the merits and limitations of cash transfers versus vouchers in DDR programmes.

58 There are also other survey-based assessments underway in Burundi and Aceh that are not included in this volume. See, for example, the work of Samii, Mvukiyehe and Taylor on Burundi at http://www.columbia.edu/~cds81/burundisurvey/ and Beeke (2007) in Aceh.

59 Note that Kingma (2000) also establishes a broad definition of reintegration that accounts for social, political and economic factors.

60 These include entitlements in the form of reinsertion and reintegration packages.

61 These include endowment sets – individual group and community characteristics.

62 Specifically, high ranking combatants appear to be less trusting of democratic politics while ideologues appear more likely to remain connected to their units, as are male fighters and younger ex-combatants.

63 See Wessels (2006) for a thorough review of the literature on child soldiering.

64 Peake describes how the first international programme adopted a conventional approach to reinsertion and reintegration intended to assist cantoned veterans resume civilian life. The second internationally-supported intervention was wider in scope and took on a community-based approach. The third and fourth DDR programmes were managed by the new Timorese government.

65 More than 15 woredas were purposefully selected from four regions (i.e. Tigray, Amahara, Oromia and SNNP). Four teams of Ethiopian social scientists were trained and more than 800 urban, rural, disabled and female veterans consulted in April and May 2007. In addition, control groups were selected from non-EDRP assisted veterans and 'community' representatives. See Bennett and Muggah (2007).

66 The IDDRS are one 'formal' expression of this orthodoxy, but the spirit is widespread. Sudan and Haiti were selected to undertake integration and encountered a range of challenges – from above (e.g. coherence of the concept) and from below (e.g. operational/bureaucratic challenges). See UNWG (2006).

67 Correspondence with Kelvin Ong, formerly head of the best practices unit of DPKO.

Bibliography

Azam, J., Bevan, D. and Collier, P. (1994) *Some Economic Consequences of the Transition from Civil War to Peace Policy Research Working Paper 1392*. Washington, DC: World Bank.

Baaré, A. (2005) 'An Analysis of Transitional Economic Reintegration', *Stockholm Initiative on Disarmament, Demobilization and Reintegration (SIDDR)*. Unpublished Paper Presented at SIDDR Technical Working Group on Reintegration, April 2005, New York.

Baaré, A. (2006) 'An Analysis of Transitional Economic Reintegration', *Stockholm Initiative on Disarmament, Demobilization and Reintegration Background Studies*. Ministry of Foreign Affairs Sweden.

Ball, N. and Hendrickson, D. (2005) 'Review of International Financing Arrangements for Disarmament, Demobilization and Reintegration', Prepared for Working Group 2, SIDDR. September.

Ball, N. and van de Goor, L. (2006) *Disarmament, Demobilization and Reintegration: Mapping Issues, Dilemmas and Guiding Principles.* Clingendael Research Paper. Hague: Netherlands Institute of International Relations.

Beeke, C. (2007) 'Repaving the Road to Peace: Analysis of the Implementation of DDR in Aceh Province, Indonesia', *BICC Brief*, 35.

Bellamy, A. (2004) *Understanding Peacekeeping.* London: Polity.

Bellamy, A. and Williams, P. (eds) (2007) *Peace Operations and Global Order.* London: Routledge.

Bellamy, A., Williams, P. and Griffin, S. (2004) *Understanding Peacekeeping.* Cambridge: Polity Press.

Bennett, J. and Muggah, R. (2007) 'Making a Difference? A Beneficiary Impact Assessment of Ethiopia's Demobilization and Reintegration Program', *Executive Summary.* Addis: EDRP and World Bank.

Berdal, M. (1996) 'Disarmament and Demobilization after Civil Wars', *Adelphi Paper*, no. 303. Oxford: Oxford University Press.

Cawthra, G. and Luckham, R. (eds) (2003) *Governing Insecurity: Democratic Control of Military and Security Establishments in Transitional Democracies.* London: Zed Books.

Chaudhary, T. and Suhrke, A. (2008) 'Postwar Violence', *Background Paper for the Small Arms Survey.* Geneva: Small Arms Survey.

Cilliers, J. (ed.) (1995) *Dismissed Demobilisation and Reintegration of Former Combatants in Africa Book.* Pretoria: ISS.

Clark, K. (1996) *Fostering a Farewell to Arms: Preliminary Lessons Learned in the Demobilization and Reintegration of Ex-Combatants.* Washington, DC: US Agency for International Development, Center for Development Information and Evaluation.

Colletta, N. (1995) 'From Warriors to Workers: The World Bank's Role in Post-Conflict Reconstruction', *Leaders*, no. 204, October.

Colletta, N., Kostner, M. and Wiederhofer, I. (1996) *Case Studies in War-to-Peace Transition: The Demobilization and Reintegration of Ex-Combatants in Ethiopia, Namibia and Uganda.* Washington, DC: World Bank.

Collier, P. (1994) 'Demobilization and Insecurity: a Study in the Economics of the Transition from War to Peace', *Journal of International Development*, 6: 343–351.

Collier, P., Hoeffler, A., Elliot, L., Hegre, H., Reynal-Querol, M. and Sambanis, N. (2003) *Breaking the Conflict Trap: Civil War & Development Policy.* Oxford: Oxford University Press and World Bank.

De Coning, C. (2007) 'Coherence and Coordination in United Nations Peacebuilding and Integrated Missions', *Security in Practice*, 5, Oslo: NUPI.

De Watteville, N. (2000) *Addressing Gender Issues in Demobilization and Reintegration Programs.* Africa Region Working Paper Series.

Doyle, M. and Sambanis, N. (2000) 'International Peacebuilding: A Theoretical and Quantitative Analysis', *American Political Science Review*, 94(4).

Duffield, M. (2007) *Development, Security and Unending War.* London: Polity.

Dzinesa, G. (2006) 'Swords into Ploughshares: Disarmament, Demobilisation and Reintegration in Zimbabwe, Namibia and South Africa', *ISS Working Paper 120*. Online, available at: http://www.smallarmssurvey.org/files/portal/spotlight/country/afr_pdf/-Africa-zim-nam-sn-2006.pdf.

Dzinesa, G. (2007) Online, available at: 'Post-conflict Disarmament, Demobilization and

Reintegration of Former Combatants in Southern Africa', *International Studies Perspective*, 8(1): 73–89.

ECP (Escola de Cultura de Pau) (2007) *Analysis of the Disarmament, Demobilization and Reintegration (DDR) Programs Existing in the World During 2006*. Madrid: Escola de Cultura de Paz.

Farr, V. (2002) *The Demobilization and Reintegration of Women Combatants, Wives of Male Soldiers and War Widows: A Checklist*. Bonn: BICC.

Ghobarah, H., Huth, P. and Russett, B. (2003) 'Civil Wars Kill and Maim People – Long After the Shooting Stops', *American Political Science Review*, 97(2) (May).

Ginifer, J. (1995) *Managing Arms in Peace Processes: Rhodesia/Zimbabwe*. Disarmament and Conflict Resolution Project, United Nations Institute for Disarmament Research. New York: United Nations.

GTZ (2003) *Activity Area – Demobilization and Reintegration of Ex-combatants*, available online at: www.wedoit.net/dea/demobilisationandreintegrationofex-combatants.asp.

Hanson, S. (2007) 'Disarmament, Demobilization and Reintegration (DDR) in Africa', *Backgrounder*, Council on Foreign Relations, February.

Harbom and P. Wallensteen (2007) 'Armed Conflict, 1989–2006', *Journal of Peace Research*, 44(5): 623–634.

HDC (2008) *Negotiating Disarmament: Reflections on Guns, Fighters and Armed Violence in Peace Processes*. Geneva: Centre for Humanitarian Dialogue.

Holt, V. and Berkman, T. (eds) (2006) *The Impossible Mandate: Military Preparedness, the Responsibility to Protect and Modern Peace Operations*. Washington, DC: Stimson Center.

Humphreys, M. and Weinstein, J. (2004) *What the Fighters Say: A Survey of Ex-Combatants in Sierra Leone: June–August 2003*. New York and Stanford: Colombia University and Stanford University/PRIDE.

IPA (International Peace Academy) (2006) *Counting What Counts: Ten Steps toward Increasing the Relevance of Empirical Research in the UN System*. Meeting Note. New York. February.

Jennings, K. (2008) 'Seeing DDR From Below: Challenges and Dilemmas Raised by the Experiences of Ex-Combatants in Liberia'. *FAFO Report* (3). Oslo: FAFO.

Jensen, S. and Stepputat, F. (2001) 'Demobilising Armed Civilians', *CDR Policy Paper*. Copenhagen: CDR.

Kaldor, M. (1999) *New and Old Wars: Organised Violence in a Global Era*. Cambridge: Polity Press.

Keen, D. (1999) 'The Economic Functions of Violence in Civil Wars', *Adelphi Paper*, 320, Oxford: Oxford University Press.

Kingma, K. (ed.) (2000) *Demobilization in Sub-Saharan Africa: The Development and Security Impacts*. Basingstoke: Macmillan.

Kingma, K. (2002) 'Demobilization, Reintegration and Peace-building in Africa', *International Peacekeeping*, 9(2): 181–221.

Knight, M and Ozerdem, A. (2004) 'Guns, Camps and Cash: Disarmament, Demobilization and Reinsertion of Former Combatants in Transitions from War to Peace', *Journal of Peace Research*, 41(4).

Mazarire, G. and Rupiya, R. (2000) 'Two Wrongs Do Not Make a Right: A Critical Assessment of Zimbabwe's Demobilization and Reintegration Programmes, 1980–2000', *Journal of Peace, Conflict and Military*, March.

Meek, S. (1998) 'Buy or Barter: the History and Prospects of Voluntary Weapons Collection Programmes', *ISS Monograph Series*, 22. London: Institute for Strategic Studies.

Middlebrook, P. (2008) 'Right-Financing Security Sector Reform', *GFNSSR Bulletin*, April.

Moser, C. and McIlwaine, C. (2001) *Violence in a Post-Conflict Context*. Washington, DC: World Bank.

Muggah, R. (2004a) 'The Anatomy of Disarmament, Demobilization and Reintegration in the Republic of Congo', *Conflict, Security and Development*, 4(1): 21–37.

Muggah, R. (2004b) *Assessing the Prospects for DDR of the MILF in Mindanao. A Desk Review and Evaluation for the UNDP*. Commissioned by the UNDP in New York/Manila.

Muggah, R. (2005) *Securing Haiti's Transition: Prospects for Disarmament, Demobilization and Reintegration*, Occasional Paper 14, Geneva: Small Arms Survey.

Muggah, R. (2006) 'Emerging from the Shadow of War: A Critical Perspective on DDR and Weapons Reduction in the Post-Conflict Period', *Journal of Contemporary Security Policy*, 27(1).

Muggah, R. (2007) '(Dis)Integrated Missions: Reflections from Sudan and Haiti', *Humanitarian Practice Network*, 38. London: Overseas Development Institute.

Muggah, R. (2008a) 'A Hard Pill to Swallow: Assessing Collective Violence in Africa', *Africa Report on Violence 2008*. Harare: African Health Organisation.

Muggah, R. (2008b) 'Managing the Post-Conflict Transition: Reviewing DDR and Arms Control in Africa', *Africa Development Report 2008*. Tunis: African Development Bank.

Muggah, R. (2008c) 'No Post-Conflict Panacea: Disarmament, Demobilization and Reintegration', in V. Chetail (ed.) *Peace-building Lexicon*. Oxford: Oxford University Press.

Muggah, R. (2008d) 'Comparing DDR and Durable Solutions: Some lessons from Ethiopia', Humanitarian Practice Network 37, London: ODI.

Muggah, R. and Jutersonke, O. (2007) *Engaging DDR: A Comparative Assessment of Switzerland's Value-Added*. Berne: Department for Foreign Affairs (unpublished).

Muggah, R. and Krause, K. (2008) 'Closing the Gap between Peace Operations and Post-Conflict Insecurity: Towards a Violence Reduction Agenda', *International Peacekeeping*, 16(1).

Nagl, J. (2005) *Learning to Eat Soup with a Knife: Counterinsurgency Lessons from Malaya and Vietnam*. Chicago: University of Chicago Press.

OECD (Organisation for Economic Cooperation and Development) (2001a) *Guidelines on Helping Prevent Violent Conflict*. Paris. www.oecd.org/document/32/0,2340,en_2649_34567_33800800_1_1_1_1,00.html.

OECD (2001b) *Guidelines on Helping Prevent Violent Conflict*, Paris.

OECD (2005a) *Principles for Good International Engagement in Fragile States: Learning and Advisory Process on Difficult Partnerships (LAP)*. Paris. Online, available at: www.oecd.org/dataoecd/59/55/34700989.pdf.

OECD (2005b) *Security System Reform and Governance*. Paris. Online, available at: www.oecd.org/dataoecd/8/39/31785288.pdf.

OECD (2005c) *Preventing Conflict and building Peace: A Manual of Issues and Entry Points*. Paris. http://www.oecd.org/dataoecd/26/3/35785584.pdf.

OECD (2005d) *Paris Declaration on Aid Effectiveness: Ownership, Harmonisation, Alignment, Results and Mutual Accountability*. Paris: OECD.

OECD (2006) *Evaluating Conflict Prevention and Peace-building activities*. Norway. Online, available at: www.oecd.org/dataoecd/5/44/37500040.pdf.

OECD (2008) *Armed Violence Reduction Guidance: Draft*. Paris: Small Arms Survey/SecDev Associates.

Osland, K. (2005) 'The UN and Integrated Missions', *NUPI Conference Proceedings*. Oslo: NUPI.

Paris, R. (2004) *At War's End: Building Peace After Civil Conflict*. Cambridge and New York: Cambridge University Press.

Pouligny, B. (2004) *The Politics and Anti-Politics of Contemporary Disarmament, Demobilization and Reintegration Programs*. Paris: CERI.

Sigrid, W. (2006) 'Does Money Work? Cash Transfers to Ex-combatants in Disarmament, Demobilization and Reintegration Processes', *Disasters*, 30(3): 316–339.

Small Arms Survey (2003) *Small Arms Survey 2003: Development at Risk*. Oxford: Oxford University Press.

Small Arms Survey (2005) *Small Arms Survey 2006: Weapons at War*. Oxford: Oxford University Press.

Small Arms Survey (2006) *Small Arms Survey 2007: Unfinished Business*. Oxford: Oxford University Press.

Small Arms Survey (2007) *Small Arms Survey 2007: Guns and the City*. Cambridge: Cambridge University Press.

Spagat, M. (2006) Colombia's Paramilitary DDR: Quiet and Tentative Success, *CERAC Working Paper*. Bogota: CERAC.

Spear, J. (2005) 'Conclusions: The International Practice of DDR'. Online, available at: www.ssronline.org.

Spear, J. (2006) 'From Political Economies of War to Political Economies of Peace: The Contribution of DDR after Wars of Predation', in *Contemporary Security Policy*, 27(1): 168–189.

Spencer, D. (1997) 'Demobilization and Reintegration in Central America'. *Occasional Paper*, 8. BICC, February.

Stedman, S. (1997) 'Spoiler Problems in Peace Processes', *International Security*, 22(2): 5–53.

Suhrke, A. and Samset, I. (2007), 'What's in a Figure? Estimating Recurrance of Civil War', *International Peacekeeping*, 14(2): 195–203.

Swarbrick, P. (2007) 'Avoiding Disarmament Failure: the Critical Link in DDR: An Operational Manual for Donors, Managers and Practitioners', *Working Paper* 5. Geneva: Small Arms Survey.

Teamy, K. and Sweet, J. (2006) 'Organizing Intelligence for Counterinsurgency', *Military Review* (September/October).

UN (1992) *An Agenda for Peace Preventative Diplomacy, Peacemaking and Peacekeeping*. A/47/277–S/24111. Online, available at: www.un.org/docs/SG/agpeace.html.

UN (2000) *Report of the Panel on UN Peace Operations*. New York: DPKO. (A55/502). Online, available at: www.un.org/peace/reports/peace_operations/.

UN (2000) *Report of the Secretary-General on the Role of United Nations Peacekeeping in Disarmament, Demobilization and Reintegration*. (S/2000/101).

UN (2001) *UN Programme of Action on Combating the Illicit Trade and Trafficking of Small Arms in All Its Aspects*. http://www.iansa.org/un/programme-of-action.htm.

UN Executive Committee on Humanitarian Affairs, Working Group on Disarmament, Demobilization, and Reintegration (2000) *Harnessing Institutional Capacities in Support of the Disarmament, Demobilization and Reintegration of Former Combatants*. New York: United Nations.

UNDP (United Nations Development Programme) (2003) *UNDP Support for Disarmament, Demobilization and Reintegration of Ex-Combatants (DDR): A Brief Stock-take of Experiences and Lessons Learned*. New York: United Nations Development Programme.

UNDP (2006) *BCPR Strategic Review.* New York/Geneva: UNDP and Small Arms Survey. www.undp.org/cpr/documents/sa_control/BCPRStrategicreview.doc.

UNDPKO (United Nations Department for Peacekeeping) (1999) *Disarmament, Demobilization and Reintegration of Ex-combatants in a Peacekeeping Environment: Principles and Guidelines.* New York: Lessons Learned Unit, Department of Peacekeeping Operations, United Nations.

UNDPKO (2000) *Disarmament, Demobilization and Reintegration of Ex-Combatants in a Peacekeeping Environment.* New York: United Nations.

UNDPKO (2008) *United Nations Peacekeeping Operations: Principles and Guidelines.* New York: United Nations. Online, available at www.un.org/depts/dpko/lessons/.

UNOSAA (United Nations Office of the Special Adviser on Africa) (2007) 'Overview: DDR Processes in Africa'. *Background paper for the Second International Conference on DDR and Stability in Africa*, Kinshasa, 12–14 June.

UNSC (United Nations Security Council) (2000) *Report of the Secretary General: The Role of the United Nations Peacekeeping in Disarmament, Demobilization and Reintegration.* S/2000/101, 11 February.

UNSG (1998) *The Causes of Conflict and the Promotion of Durable Peace and Sustainable Development in Africa.* Secretary General's Report to the UN Security Council, 16 April.

UNWG (United National Working Group) (2006) *Integrated Disarmament, Demobilization and Reintegration Standards (IDDRS).* http://www.unddr.org/iddrs/.

US Army (2001) Field Manual 3–0 'Operations'. Washington, DC: GPO.

Wessels, M. (2006) *Child Soldiers from Violence to Protection.* Cambridge: Harvard University Press.

Willibald, S. (2006) 'Does Money Work? Cash Transfers to Ex-combatants in Disarmament, Demobilisation and Reintegration Processes', *Journal of Disasters*, 30(3): 316–339.

World Bank (1993) 'Demobilization and Reintegration of Military Personnel in Africa: The Evidence from Seven Country Studies', *World Bank Discussion Paper*, no. 130.

World Bank (2002) 'Sierra Leone: Disarmament, Demobilization and Reintegration', *Africa Region*, no. 81, October. Online, available at: www.worldbank.org/afr/findings/infobeng/infob81.pdf.

World Bank (2003) *Position paper: Linkages between Disarmament, Demobilization and Reintegration of Ex-combatants and Security Sector Reform*, MDRP Secretariat Paper. Washington, DC: World Bank and MDRP Secretariat.

1 Colombia's quiet demobilization

A security dividend?

Jorge A. Restrepo and Robert Muggah

Introduction

Paramilitaries are a routine feature of contemporary civil conflicts. Their involvement in persecuting violence as proxies of the state, however, is undergoing a qualitative transformation. Specifically, paramilitaries are increasingly distanced from state structures, operating in an intermediate area between public and private spheres. In many cases they are awake to the possibilities of accumulating private capital (see Duffield 2001, 2007). Moreover, in the wake of new human rights mechanisms such as the International Criminal Court (ICC), states are less inclined to invest in violence entrepreneurs than before.[1] Thus unmoored, paramilitary techniques of violence are potentially more damaging for individuals and communities. In Colombia's long-running civil war, paramilitaries are the main perpetrators of human rights violations.

Colombian paramilitaries are more likely than guerrillas or formal state military actors to be involved in violating human rights. They are increasingly less amenable to state control, much less influence from international entities. This marks a shift from the 1970s and 1980s during which time states resorted to repressive tactics to quell internal dissent and violently suppressed insurgencies by direct military action. Freed from military and legal checks and balances, paramilitaries in the early twenty-first century are more potent than ever. They increasingly exhibit cellular network structures that facilitate rapid, flexible and decentralized deployment, fewer vertical controls and lower overheads. Paramilitaries have honed the efficiency of repression, disconnected from legal or humanitarian restrictions and thus the potentially humanizing customs of war. At the coal-face of armed violence, paramilitaries may find it easier to resort to organized crime as a means of financing their operations.

Engaging with paramilitaries as part of a post-conflict recovery programme – including their disarmament, demobilization and reintegration (DDR) – is a challenging enterprise. The dividends of effective engagement, however, are also potentially much higher in terms of contributing to declines in real and perceived armed violence. This chapter considers the outcomes of a recent demobilization programme focused primarily on paramilitaries. It draws principally from large-scale datasets tracing the actions of Colombia's self-defence groups

(AUC) and their subsequent demobilization in different parts of the country. Colombia's DDR experience is exceptional in that it is one of the few processes of 'paramilitary' demobilization (as opposed to DDR of insurgent or state forces). What is more, it was pursued in the midst of an ongoing armed conflict rather than at war's end. It is also unusual in that it offered a reinsertion and reintegration process for former paramilitaries despite their wilful prosecution of extensive human rights violations.

Before turning to an analysis of the demobilization experience itself, it is important to note a number of factors that directly shaped the chapter's methodology. For the purposes of this assessment, the key metric for measuring DDR 'success' and 'failure' includes reported reductions in armed violence. Many evaluations of DDR tend to focus on broad outcomes such as a reduction of conflict or micro outputs including the number of arms collected or soldiers demobilized. This chapter constitutes an important departure in this respect. The chapter also deliberately adopts an historical perspective. A key objective is to help reconstruct an 'historical memory' and 'common truth' underlying patterns of armed violence in Colombia wherein victim and survivor narratives and testimonies are given ample visibility. While the chapter draws attention to the importance of transitional justice, including access of victims to genuine restitution and reparations, the focus is nevertheless on genuine armed violence reduction (see Chapter 10, this volume).

The chapter is divided into several sections. The first section considers the Colombian conflict and the dynamics of various paramilitary groups. The second section considers the rationale for the Colombian government's preoccupation with disarming and demobilizing the AUC and the many challenges and contradictions accompanying the process. The third section introduces the DDR programme and its conceptual and bureaucratic architecture. The fourth section briefly reviews the methods adopted to assess the effectiveness of DDR as defined above. It draws primarily from straightforward econometric methods to examine four security indicators. The final section considers the findings of the research, highlighting the heterogeneity of results, regional variations between cities and the limitations.

The dynamics of Colombia's conflict

Newly available datasets are illuminating the spatial and temporal dynamics of Colombia's armed conflict. Between 1998 and 2006 there were at least 40,000 conflict deaths, with an annual average of 2,221 killings (Small Arms Survey 2006). The vast majority of these conflict deaths (as opposed to criminal homicide) were perpetrated in isolated rural areas (Restrepo and Spagat 2005: 15).[2] In fact, 'only ten per cent of conflict fatalities have been in municipalities with population densities exceeding 200 people per square kilometre where two-thirds of the Colombian population resides' (Small Arms Survey 2006: 223). As disconcerting as these longitudinal and geographic trends are, they only tell part of the narrative.

When reviewing conflict violence and designing intervention strategies it is crucial to recognize who is killed by whom, the categories of victims and the types of events contributing to fatal outcomes. It is possible to render a distinction between 'clashes' in which two or more groups exchange fire and 'attacks', defined as one-sided events with no effective resistance. The distinction between the two is important: most victims of 'clashes' are combatants while the majority of those victimized during 'attacks' are civilians. In Colombia, most civilians that are killed in the context of war are done so during unilateral paramilitary attacks. There is evidence that the large-scale increase in Colombian conflict-related violence experienced from the late 1990s to 2002 and in early 2005 was accompanied by a 'surge' in paramilitary-related massacres and selective assassinations.

While formidable military entities in their own right, the Revolutionary Armed Forces of Colombia (FARC) and the National Liberation Army (ELN) guerrillas pursued an alternative strategy. Their methods concentrated on disrupting Colombian society, undertaking targeted bombing campaigns, storming and seizing municipal institutions and infrastructure and selective attacks against public and private interests. In the process, the guerrillas killed significantly fewer civilians than the paramilitaries. But unlike in the case of paramilitaries who kill many and tend to leave few injured, guerrilla attacks generate more injuries than deaths due to the indiscriminate nature of their explosive bombing campaigns. Unilateral attacks by state forces, though at one time sustained and regular, were comparatively more infrequent and account for a lower proportion of overall civilian deaths in the past decade. It is important to note that their role in perpetrating armed violence is nevertheless severe – in administering aerial bombardments, they have contributed to a sizeable number of civilian casualties.

Although considerable global attention is devoted to Colombia's armed conflict, organized and inter-personal criminal violence exacts an even graver human toll. In contrast to conflict casualties that are primarily rural, criminal violence is a predominantly urban phenomenon taking place in inner cities and peri-urban slums. Since 1979, between 70 and 80 per cent of all firearm-related deaths from any cause occurred in urban areas. While there are disagreements concerning the overall death toll from criminal violence in Colombia, there is consensus that it is astonishingly high: the department of national statistics records some 508,000 people killed as a result of firearms[3] between 1979 and 2007.[4]

Irrespective of the scale of conflict and criminal violence, there is widespread consensus that illegal right-wing paramilitaries are central to the issue of insecurity and armed violence in the country. When compared to either guerrillas or government forces, they are responsible for the majority of civilian conflict deaths and exhibit a high ratio of killings to injuries suggesting a significant element of intentionality.[5] More emphatically, killing constitutes an explicit strategy of 'terror' and a deterrent to ward off civilians whom the paramilitaries suspect of aiding guerrillas. In this way it contributes to the internal displacement of frequently poorer and marginalized civilians and leads to illegal land appropriation. While the majority of Colombia's paramilitaries theoretically joined the 2002 ceasefire and subsequently demobilized as part of a government-sponsored programme, there is evidence that, while substantially reduced, paramilitaries remain deeply committed to violence.

The shape and dynamics of paramilitary violence have changed over time. This has been referred to as the gradual 'commercialization of insurgency and the search for wealth' (Metz 2000). Fundamental transformations began emerging in the 1980s with the growing involvement of insurgent forces in narco-trafficking.[6] The narco-paramilitary alliance is not solely an expression of criminal profiteering or the shoring-up of capital to prosecute war against the guerrillas. Rather, a host of interests condition paramilitary involvement in the drug trade ranging from the appropriation of arable land, localized self-defence interests, counter-insurgency strategies and far-reaching aspirations related to the accumulation of power that are already transforming Colombia's political landscape.

Disaggregating the paramilitaries

Colombia's civil conflict represents a long-lasting and relatively low intensity contest for political power. Launched more than three decades ago, it features several distinguishable phases. With the exception of the wrenching communal bloodletting colloquially referred to as *La Violencia* (1946–1966) in which the country was split along political sectarian lines (i.e. liberal and conservative parties), the contemporary conflict has pitted several leftist guerrilla groups against state forces. The paramilitaries are in fact a relatively recent player.

Colombia's paramilitary movement emerged in the mid-1980s against a backdrop of escalating armed conflict between the state and guerrilla forces and the deepening of narco-trafficking in the Andean region.[7] Paramilitary groups first emerged as part of a state-sponsored counter-insurgency strategy to combat guerrillas and their perceived civilian supporters.[8] In addition to the FARC, ELN and ERP, all of which formed during the 1960s, in the 1970s new urban groups such as the *Movimiento 19 de Abril* (M-19) entered the fray. The origins of these various guerrilla groups can be traced to peasant self-defence organizations established in the mid-twentieth century. The negotiated settlement between liberals and conservatives in the 1940s and 1950s led to the dismantling of most partisan guerrilla groups, probably the first DDR process ever recorded in the country. Some guerrillas nevertheless survived and persisted with their activities until the emergence of the FARC in 1964 and the ELN in 1967. As noted above, smaller regional guerrilla groups appeared in the 1970s, including the Quintin Lame in Cauca, the only explicitly indigenous insurgency group in Latin America at the time.

By the 1980s the armed conflict was in full swing. Its intensity increased in the wake of a failed peace process initiated by Betancur's government

(1982–1986). Although the FARC's political wing (the *Unión Patriótica*) was almost exterminated in subsequent state-led attacks, this quickly led to the radicalization of the FARC and other guerrillas. The escalation of armed violence also coincided with an increase in available funding earned through kidnapping and extortion of multinational enterprises and domestic firms, cattle farmers and landowners. More ominously, the guerrillas located a profitable new income source in taxing illegal narcotic activity in isolated areas. The narcotics producers and traffickers did not take this incursion into their business lightly.

Following their gradual association with criminal drug cartels, self-defence movements were soon converted into well-armed offensive paramilitary groups. Certain political leaders, cattle ranchers and lower-income farmers [*campesinos*] began simultaneously forming themselves into disparate militia or 'self-defence' groups. Some of these latter entities conformed to traditional vigilante militia while others bore the hallmarks of war-lordism. In certain cases, these groups were linked to the narco-leadership and nurtured linkages with local political elites and state forces. These categories – self-defence, warlord and counter-insurgency – were and remain fluid and often came together in insidious ways. In what is euphemistically described as the 'dirty war', paramilitaries began federating and, together with drug cartels, focused on eliminating guerrillas, their political affiliates and sympathizers and any public authorities investigating related activities. Predictably, as the paramilitary war deepened during the 1990s, the level of conflict violence escalated. Elements within the Colombian government in certain instances allowed, regulated and authorized some of these groups to operate legally under the name *Convivir*[9] or security cooperatives.

Paramilitary activity reached its apogee in the late 1990s with the creation of the United Self-Defense Forces of Colombia (AUC). Originally established as a coordinating body to unify disparate paramilitary groups, the AUC's national conference called for a highly regimented military command structure in order to incorporate regional factions. Headed by Castaño, the AUC began expanding operations throughout the country. New mobile squads were established and, by 1997, the AUC issued statements announcing an 'offensive war according to the operational capacity of each regional [paramilitary] group' (Tate 2001: 168). The paramilitaries were soon one of the largest and best resourced armed groups in the world.[10] In some ways the AUC served as a franchise organization, providing training, arms, ammunition supplies and logistical support to its branches around the country. This arrangement not only facilitated its rapid expansion but also the seeds of its own destruction: these franchises were subject to the penetration of 'pure' narco-traffickers, prone to indiscipline, leadership rivalries and in-fighting.

One of the many challenges accompanying interventions designed to take 'spoilers' out of commission relates to diagnosing the motivations and interests of combatants (Weinstein 2006). The AUC is no exception. As noted by Sanin (2008: 7):

these are rare and elusive populations, often with poorly defined identities. Even in the midst of a demobilization process, it is difficult to differentiate combatants from other categories (friends, old time supporters, opportunist supporters, etc.). Before the paramilitary demobilization that took place in Colombia between 2005 and 2006, the size of the group was calculated by the most serious estimates, including official ones, to range between seven and 12,000 combatants. The press reported up to 50,000 participated in the process. Though several factors may have influenced competing estimates, there are clear incentives to artificially swell the ranks of the demobilized.

Reducing armed violence through DDR

Important policy and programmatic interventions to reduce armed violence – whether conflict or criminal – include DDR and small arms control (Muggah 2005). As generic concepts, these activities encompass a wide bandwidth of possible interventions ranging from discrete activities described in the Introduction of this volume to prohibitions on domestic production, imports, exports and civilian controls together with military and police enforcement measures, legislative reform and changes in incarceration procedures (Small Arms Survey 2006: 230). Notwithstanding the important contributions of these and other interventions to dramatically reducing gun violence in Colombia, this chapter focuses primarily on DDR.

During the 1970s, 1980s and 1990s, several moderately successful peace processes led a number of guerrilla groups to abandon their struggle and forge political movements instead.[11] There were in fact a variety of DDR processes introduced for various armed groups in Colombia over the past 50 years. Alluded to above, successive Colombian administrations pursued DDR since the 1950s following the relatively positive disarmament processes in the wake of *La Violencia*. In fact, there were nine separate DDR processes with distinct guerrilla groups since the 1970s. Between 1990 and 2002, more than 7,300 former guerrillas collectively disarmed and 4,715 of them entered into reintegration programmes (Small Arms Survey 2006). The character and bureaucratic shape of these DDR frameworks varied from negotiation to negotiation with no standardized approach surfacing. As noted in other chapters of this volume, DDR is a challenging political and bureaucratic enterprise in any context. In Colombia as elsewhere, a vast range of operational agencies and departments were mandated to attend to specific components of the enterprise.[12] The recurrent costs of sustaining DDR and ensuring that processes are coordinated are considerable – some US$94 million between 1998 and 2002 alone.

The most recent round of DDR targeted paramilitary groups for the first time in 2003. By December 2002, most paramilitary groups had initiated a unilateral ceasefire, albeit one that was difficult to maintain and suffered from repeated breaches. Notwithstanding several violations of the ceasefire, the suspension of hostilities paved the way for more formal negotiations to begin in 2003. As early as January 2003, the first surrendered arms began to trickle in, many of them modern and high-quality but with serial numbers erased. Since the process began, more than 31,000 paramilitaries aligned with the AUC were demobilized, handing in some 17,000 weapons of varying calibres. Paramilitaries were demobilized *collectively* in 37 mass demobilization ceremonies. Though more seldom discussed, over the same period, 9,500 mostly FARC and ELN combatants also demobilized on an *individual* basis.

The paramilitary DDR process was guided by a controversial normative framework. After several attempts to approve appropriate legislation in Congress, Law 975 – widely referred to as the Justice and Peace Law – was approved by Congress and ratified in mid-2005. The Justice and Peace Law includes provisions to apply reduced sentences to those ex-combatants who willingly disarm, demobilize, hand over minors or kidnapped victims, surrender assets obtained as a result of illegal activity, cooperate with justice and cease fighting and engaging in organized crime. At the same time, the law purports to guarantee victims' rights to justice and reparations – and installs a special unit in the Prosecutor's Office to this end. After repeated legal challenges to the law, the Constitutional Court amended it and strengthened provisions for victims' protection and reparations. The law continues to be criticized, especially on the grounds that it provides limited access to victims to justice, reparations and restitution, while the benefits to the demobilized are guaranteed by the state (see Chapter 10, this volume).

The Colombian DDR intervention was unusual for its being almost entirely administered by national public institutions and carefully monitored and evaluated. Disarmament and demobilization was initially managed by the Ministry of Defense and reintegration by the Ministry of Interior and Justice, though by late 2006 a special Presidential High Commissioner post was created to assume responsibility for the latter process. At the micro-level, most collectively disarmed and demobilized paramilitaries were processed in Reference Centres (CROs) in regional offices where beneficiaries were to receive training and other entitlements. These CROs facilitate the tracking of DDR participants, including follow-up with those not availing themselves of monthly stipends or providing 'spontaneous declarations and confessions'. Recently the conditionality of stipends on compliance with retraining and psycho-social assistance was also established. Baseline data on most paramilitaries was gathered during the collective demobilization ceremonies and compiled into a system for monitoring and evaluation (SAME) administered by the International Organisation for Migration (IOM) and overseen by the Commissioner for Peace. Socio-economic and spatial data exists for more than 80 per cent of all former combatants (HCP 2006). Regrettably, much of the data and relational information stored by the national police remains unavailable to independent researchers. Weaknesses in the criminal justice system also mean that many cases of violence are not adequately investigated and thus go unpunished: attribution of perpetration is a difficult and occasionally dangerous task.

Assessing the effects of DDR in Colombia

It is possible to analyse the impacts of paramilitary disarmament and demobilization by drawing on statistical techniques. These techniques are necessarily tailored to the dynamics of paramilitary groups and exploit the fact that different groups operated in different areas and demobilized at different times. Described at length above, the AUC consisted of a federated network of factions with localized dispersion. This made it possible to define with some precision their areas of operation. Following the 'announcement' of discrete DDR interventions, it was possible to then determine the exact time of the intervention and its geo-spatial catchments.[13] Demobilization and disarmament ceremonies took place at different points in time due to the logistical requirements of the process but also the politics of negotiation. Not surprisingly, there was also periodic pressure from the government and the public to speed-up certain interventions in 'high risk' areas.

The methodology used by the authors can be described generally as a pre-post assessment. In assessing changes to security indicators in the operational areas of each group following demobilization, the DDR process assumes the character of a quasi-controlled experiment due to the considerable variation (and semi-randomness) in the times and places of demobilization. Nevertheless, it is important to emphasize that while there appears to be a causal association between DDR and reductions in violence, there are limitations of the assessment due to the authors' inability to statistically isolate all possible effects that could also have a contemporaneous local effect on the evolution of security.[14]

There are a number of approaches to testing the impacts of DDR on security and safety. Choices range from qualitative case studies to quantitative econometric modelling. The selected approach will depend in part on the availability of data and its coverage. On the basis of the selected methodology, research tends to focus on the number of demobilized combatants and arms handed over, reintegration outcomes and, more recently, the evolution of restitution of goods, reparation of victims and the provision of justice to victims and communities. In examining the statistical relationships between DDR and armed violence, this chapter adopts a novel approach. Defining and measuring violence of course raises new conundrums. Some analysts focus on coding human rights violations while others emphasize more narrow and precise indicators such as homicide. As emphasized above, DDR is considered here as an intervention in which the principle objective – violence reduction – constitutes the key dependent variable. Indicators range from intentional homicides and assaults causing personal injury to robbery and private property-related theft. Data is drawn directly from the national police registries.[15]

In order to exploit the spatial–temporal variation arising during DDR, the chapter draws on a panel data structure, i.e. a data point corresponding to a combination of space and time observations. Spatial aggregation corresponds to municipality data and temporal aggregation of quarterly data.[16] This methodology displays an advantage over others in that it accounts for heterogeneity between spatial units (municipalities in this case)[17] and time (within a year) that might otherwise be concealed in aggregated data (Wooldridge 2003). We adopt a simple modelling strategy using this panel data structure in which the set of security indicators are a function of a set of variables that would theoretically have an impact on the former. Notice that only those time and spatial variables that actually present variations at both quarterly and municipal levels are included as their changes could theoretically have an impact on the dynamics of security.

Disaggregating demobilization and security

The analysis thus adopts a functional model to account for the relationships between four security indicators and the presence or absence of the demobilization and disarmament of one of the paramilitary groups in a given area. The presence of each paramilitary group (demobilized or not) was determined using CERAC's conflict database and data provided by the national police. The focus, then, is on measuring changes in the 'violent' presence of the paramilitary groups and not necessarily their non-violent presence.[18] Also included in the analysis are a set of controlling variables, including the relative presence of conflict violence.[19] The functional formula can be summarized as:

$$y_{it} = \beta_0 + \delta_1 d_{it} + \beta' \mathbf{x}_{it} + \alpha_i + u_{it} \tag{1}$$

According to the function, a change in the number of homicides in municipality; during period + (y_{it}) may be explained by municipal variables (x_{it}) and by the occurrence or not of a demobilization of a paramilitary group with violent presence in the area (d_{it}).[20] The parameter δ_1 will capture the size and direction of the effect of the DDR interventions on the variable of interest y_{it}. Amongst the controls $(\mathbf{x}_{it})$, we include the number of non-paramilitary-related conflict actions in order to isolate the security changes associated with conflict changes, the quarterly population level (that also involves a time dummy isolation component) to normalize and a quarterly variable for paramilitary presence in the municipality area.[21] There are also non-observable effects applicable for each individual that can be assumed to be constant in time (α_i), capturing the idiosyncratic locally determined characteristics.[22] Likewise, u_{it} is a well-behaved error term.[23]

The security indicators deployed in the application display a distribution that is far from being the common type of data observed in nature. First, they are count variables, which follow a discrete (one by one, entire-unit step) rather than a continuous distribution. Second, they do not have negative values (the distribution is bounded below zero) and exhibit a 'fat tail' to the right; i.e. there are non-negligible numbers of events in which a large number of people are affected, but the probability that small events occur remains quite large.

Theoretically, this type of data is usually assumed to follow a Poisson distribution (Cameron and Trivedi 1998). Nevertheless, one its most important characteristics relate to the equidispersion of the distribution, meaning that the two first moments (variance and mean) are the same. We test using the procedure proposed by Cameron and Trivedi (1990) in all four variables of interest and found that they did not conform to this property.[24] Taking this into consideration, we proceed to base the estimation on a negative binomial model (Cameron and Trivedi 1986; Cox 1983).

For our model we assume that the dependent variable $y_{it} \approx Poisson\ (\lambda_{it})$, in which the parameter $\lambda_{it} \approx \Gamma(\gamma_{it}, \delta)$ and $\gamma_{it} = e^{x_{it}\beta}$. Since y_{it} shows over dispersion we have $y_{it} \approx Negative\ Binomial\ (\gamma_{it}, \delta)$ with mean and variance:

$$E(y_{it}) = \frac{e^{x_{it}\beta}}{\delta} \tag{2}$$

$$V(y_{it}) = \frac{e^{x_{it}\beta} \cdot (1 + \delta)}{\delta^2} \tag{3}$$

Where β_j corresponds to the estimator of the parameters of interest and can be estimated by maximum likelihood estimators as:

$$\beta_j = \frac{\partial E(y_t \mid x_t)}{\partial x_j} \frac{1}{E(y_t \mid x_t)} \tag{4}$$

We use the Hausman test to discriminate between the fixed and the random effects model (Hausman *et al.* 1984: 928) finding that the random effects test is much more suitable for our application.

A decline in insecurity[25]

Table 1.1 shows the results of the application for the four variables under investigation – homicide, robbery, theft of property and assault. The estimation is presented for the 2003–2005 period (first column in the table) and for the 2003–2006 period (second column). For the entire period of analysis, the t-statistic and p-values are offered, as well as a 95 per cent confidence interval for the parameter variation. Results are presented in percentage terms.[26] Thus, a negative percentage figure needs to be read as the quarterly decrease in the variable of interest that an average municipality in Colombia will experience given the number of DDR processes after controlling for other influencing factors.

The analysis reveals heterogeneous but positive results as a consequence of the paramilitary DDR process. Until 2006, the (overall) fall in homicides that can be attributed to DDR varied between a –13.23 and –3.97 per cent with a central point estimate of –8.6 per cent. This indicates a sustained decline in the homicide rate that can be attributed to the DDR process. The fall in robberies to persons is of similar dimension and direction, while assaults impact is also positive and larger (a decrease of –13.16 per cent) during the demobilization period (2003–2006). These results are highly significant in statistical terms. It is worth noting, however, how thefts of property fail to be statistically significant.

Even so, when one concentrates on a shorter temporal period, the estimated outcome of DDR process on security appears to be even more substantial. The fall in homicides appears to be of –22.16 per cent and of robberies some –12.10 per cent. This indicates that the initial (larger) effects of DDR on homicide evaporate relatively rapidly. This is consistent with what can be expected: a DDR process with the paramilitary groups will cause the 'deparamilitarization' of the war, producing rather sizeable quantifiable improvements in security and safety, but not necessarily across the board. It is possible to say with confidence, then, that DDR contributed to substantial improvements in human security, but, given the continuation of the conflict, the incomplete demobilization of the paramilitary groups and the persistence of other forms of violence (like organized criminal violence), the effect is limited.[27]

Figure 1.1 displays a quarterly rolling estimation for the homicide model, with 95 per cent confidence bands for the period under analysis. It is worth emphasizing that this includes a negative axis showing the quarter-by-quarter estimation result and for each point estimate the 95 per cent confidence interval for these findings. The graph displays a rather large reduction in homicidal violence as a consequence of the demobilization, but the progressive disappearance of this effect across time.

The reason for the temporary effect of DDR on homicidal violence can be explained in a number of ways. The most likely explanation relates to the presence of newly established groups and other organized armed factions in the areas formerly occupied by paramilitaries. Because the armed conflict persists, newly established groups and criminal outfits have emerged to fill the gap left by paramilitaries. Owing to security dilemmas or disingenuous demobilization, some erstwhile paramilitary groups have also likely rearmed. The temporariness of the effect thus reflects the weaknesses of the Colombian state in effectively occupying and restoring security in areas 'cleared' of paramilitaries. Perhaps it is to be expected as a by-product of a partial DDR process: only one of the sides in the three-party conflict entered negotiations yielding some space for other groups to enter into the fray. Even so, the positive effects of DDR should not be discounted as they persist even three years after the initial paramilitary demobilization.

While the above analysis reflects national patterns, it is important to recognize the heterogeneous outcomes across regions. At the regional level it is important to stress that there are significant variations in the demobilization effect across specific areas and by types of reported armed violence. For example, the districts of Chocó and Risaralda reveal large and significant decreases in homicidal violence and similarly large and significant increases in robbery and assaults. The area of Medellín exhibits the most dramatic and sustained decrease in all four categories of violence. But in yet other regions there is no visible impact of demobilization: in the north of the Colombia, including the Sierra Nevada mountains which are known for coca production, there appears to be no significant effects of demobilization on security and safety. In five other zones, demobilization has an insignificant effect on robberies and

Table 1.1 Security promoting effects of DDR: random effects negative binomial regression

Crime indicators	Municipalities with paramilitary presence					
	Estimation (2003–2005)	Estimation (2003–2006)	t-statistic	(P-value)	Confidence interval	
Homicides	−22.16%	−8.60%	−3.739	0.000	−13.23%	−3.97%
Robberies	−12.10%	−8.65%	−3.204	0.001	−13.99%	−3.31%
Theft*	−1.42%	−4.69%	−1.340	0.184	−11.61%	2.22%
Assault	−12.99%	−13.16%	−4.538	0.000	−18.88%	−7.45%

Note
*Not significant at 5%.

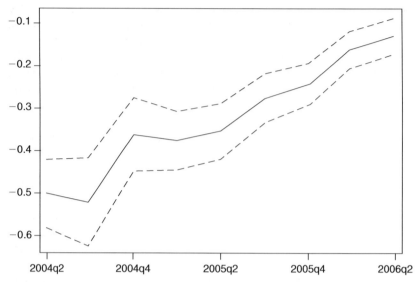

Figure 1.1 Homicides and DDR: 2004–2006.

assaults but a significant impact on homicides, negative in three cases and positive in one. Although the reasons for these variations require further investigation, they are undoubtedly connected to the persistence of conflict and similar
factors identified above.

Conclusions

The world's reception of DDR in Colombia has progressed from 'frosty to tepid'
(Spagat 2007: 4). Colombia's human rights record and the prospects of paramilitary impunity surely raised the stakes. The challenge of reconciling meaningful
justice with pragmatic peace is not unique to Colombia (see Chapters 9 and 10,
this volume). It is difficult to know how far justice can be advanced without
undermining future deals with armed groups that have yet to be militarily
defeated. Likewise, the prospect of impunity triggers strong opposition from
vocal minority groups with access to international and domestic media who
voice legitimate concerns. The Colombian government's apparent inability to
handle criticism – or at least provide satisfactory justifications for DDR – has
undermined the country's reputation and embittered domestic opposition even if
the current administration's domestic approval ratings remained undiminished.

This chapter reveals that paramilitary DDR appears to have generated a
number of positive dividends. Contrary to sharp criticism from the human rights
community and victims associations, there are sharp and correlated reductions in
armed violence in areas where demobilization was undertaken. While perhaps
unpalatable from a rights-first perspective, the average collective demobilization

appears to lower the homicide rate by (a statistically significant) 13 per cent in the area of operation of a demobilized group. A further calculation observes that between 650 and 2,300 homicides were potentially averted due to the cumulative effect of all completed demobilizations. Other forms of people-centred security also reveal large improvements. But these outcomes are spatially and temporally heterogeneous: there is clearly a need for closer monitoring and evaluation of regions. Criticisms of the DDR programme on the ground that there is a low ratio of guns handed in to demobilized paramilitaries are also misleading. The ratio is in fact higher than most surmise (see Spagat 2007), and the (high) quality of weaponry surrendered suggests a degree of genuineness of intent. Likewise, the ratio of guns to demobilized people is not necessarily a useful indicator of DDR success since it is at best weakly connected with patterns of homicide.

One of the main reasons for the lack of progress in terms of the paramilitary DDR relates to the absence of adequate state presence in those areas that were previously under paramilitary control. Despite the costly efforts of the Colombian armed forces and police to establish a presence in what were once considered isolated and marginal areas of the country, the continuation of the conflict and the emergence of new groups seem to be driving new forms of violence that undercut recent DDR gains. Like in other areas of disarmament, only the provision of strong protection centred security by the state plus DDR bring about sustained reductions in violence.

Notes

1 There is evidence, for example, that Colombia's self-defence groups (AUC), Guatemala's militia structures (PAC) and the Janjaweed in Sudan (or SSDF, PDF and others) are more clearly disconnected from state organs than before.

2 Municipalities with population densities falling below 50 people per square kilometre suffer well over 65 per cent of all conflict killing despite accounting for less than 20 per cent of the total population.

3 This includes homicides, suicides, accidents and undetermined incidents. See, for example, Small Arms Survey (2006: 227–228).

4 There has also been considerable variation over time – with firearm deaths rising from 3 per cent of all deaths in 1979 to 15 per cent by 2002. The absolute number of deaths also rose sevenfold during this period, from 3,617 to 28,989 or 16 per 100,000 to 66 per 100,000. Ibid.

5 The ratio of civilians killed to injured in operations involving paramilitaries is at least fourfold the corresponding ratio for government operations. Coupland and Meddings (1999: 2) find in their review of the literature that:

> total deaths were never more than 26% of all casualties in war, a wounded to killed ratio of 2.8. In two reports accurate casualty figures were known for soldiers wounded by rifles in a military context. The wounded to killed ratios were 1.9 and 2.2.

The Iraq Body Count project also reports an average ratio of 5.0 and a median ratio of 2.69.

6 The process began in the 1970s in the Middle East, specifically Lebanon (the Bekka valley) and the so-called Golden Triangle in Eastern Asia.

7 Marijuana cultivation supplied US markets in the 1970s. Colombia's first cartels, in

Medellín and Cali, shifted into the production and export of cocaine by the late 1970s and acquired more than 2.5 million acres of land between 1983 and 1985 alone.

8 It is worth noting that paramilitary organizations in Colombia can be traced to the 1960s, when US military advisers first recommended the formation of 'indigenous irregulars' as a fundamental component of the Colombian counter-insurgency strategy, then aimed at defeating leftist guerrilla movements. A US Special Warfare Team from Fort Bragg first proposed the strategy in 1962, and later that year a series of US Special Warfare Mobile Training Teams worked with the Colombian armed forces to implement the recommendation. The strategy was formally adopted as the basis for *Plan Lazo*, a Colombian counter-insurgency plan approved at the end of 1962 and in effect until the end of 1965. See, for example, Tate (2001: 2).

9 In 1994, President Cesar Gaviria set up Decree 356 which served as the basis of *Convivir*, or paramilitaries, which were officially launched through Resolution 368 in 1995.

10 The Small Arms Survey (2006) documented the use of AR-15 assault rifles, M60 machine guns, Galil rifles and an array of rifle and pistol silencers and night-vision equipment.

11 The most successful processes involved the M-19 (1990), and a series of smaller groups called Quintín Lame (1991), EPL (1991), CRS-ELN (1994) and the PRT (1991).

12 In Colombia, the Dirección General de Reinserción (formerly under the Ministry of Interior) oversees DDR of individuals covered under previous peace agreements. The Instituto Colombiano de Bienestar familiar ensures that the rights of youth and minors are respected during the DDR process. Meanwhile, the Ministry of Defence offers humanitarian assistance to recently demobilized people while the Fiscalía General de la Nación is charged with defining the legal situation of adult ex-combatants, an important feature of transitional justice (Patel 2007).

13 The fact that these demobilizations took place only after a day or two of being announced in most cases, due to reasons of security, is an advantage from the econometric estimation viewpoint. It is therefore possible to discern the effect of demobilization from an endogenous effect (e.g. an increase in crime, for example) that could appear due to the DDR intervention.

14 These results are preliminary since the reinsertion process and the actual negotiation has not ended. They are subject to change. The Conflict Analysis Resources Center (CERAC) in Bogotá continues to analyse these activities and was supported by the government of Canada through the Global Peace and Security Fund. The dedicated research assistance of Soledad Granada is acknowledged.

15 Although violence incidence is subject to under-reporting in most criminal systems, we do not find plausible reasons for variation in the rate of recording during the demobilization process. If in fact variation occurred it would likely have been towards a higher level of reporting given the expansion of the security apparatus taking place during the DDR period. This will nevertheless strengthen the results as it will likely contribute to increasing the positive (violence reduction) impacts of the process and may mitigate negative (violence increases) outcomes.

16 We tested results for monthly aggregations, but no substantial changes were obtained and in several cases the algorithms did not converge with this aggregation.

17 Municipalities are the smallest administrative unit in Colombia, loosely corresponding to counties.

18 In civil wars, the absence of violence might mean the temporary ascendance of one of the groups or simply the absence of contest in that particular area. This observable difficulty is difficult to resolve.

19 One of the difficulties confronting this assessment is that the DDR process occurs in the midst of the continuing guerrilla–government conflict and in the context of organized criminal activities.

20 Notice that $\mathbf{x}_{it}$ is a *vector* of several variables. By contrast, d_{it} is a step-dummy variable that takes the value of zero if no DDR process of an active group is present and will be increased in discrete cumulative intervals if, as found in several regions, a DDR process will take place in the area from the start of the exercise until t, in each municipality i. The information for this variable include reports by the Colombian Office for the High Commissioner for Peace.

21 The quarterly municipal population projections are produced by CERAC and based on census data using standard geometric population projections as described by Sadinle (2008). The basis for the projection include a time varying dummy, which, in fact, means that this variable introduces a deterministic trend component into the regression model.

22 This includes geographic characteristics, historical conditions, infrastructure, transport costs, etc. The panel data estimation approach permits a treatment of unobserved effects in two ways. First, the non-observable effects are fixed for each municipality (the so-called 'fixed effects' estimation). Second, the non-observable effects are treated like a random variable (the so-called 'random effects' estimation). The selection between the two depends primarily on the relation between the explanatory variables ($\mathbf{x}_{it} = (x_{1it}, \ldots x_{kit})$ and the non-observable factors (α_i). In the case where there exists a dependency between any kind of variable $\mathbf{x}_{it}$ y α_i, the values estimated by the static/dummy model of the parameters set out in equation (1) (β_0, δ_1, $\boldsymbol{\beta}$) do not correctly represent the 'real' values. In such cases, the best option is to use the 'fixed' effects model.

23 Robustness exercises included adding to the dependent variables (in the homicides case) disappearances and homicide data attributed to the paramilitaries. This data is drawn from the Comisión Colombiana de Juristas which are publicly available together with exercises focusing on the presence of coca and poppy crops at the municipality level. We also checked for robustness excluding several time periods and municipalities and no significant changes were discerned.

24 In this test, the unrestricted null assumes that the distribution is a negative binomial rather than a restricted (to equal mean and variance) Poisson model.

25 A compilation of results will be shortly produced in a book by CERAC. Detailed results are available upon request.

26 This is no different than the semi-elasticity interpretation of the parameter estimations.

27 We did not find a significant result with other forms of victimization such as kidnapping. Recall that paramilitaries are more expert in the most lethal forms of violence and did not engage as extensively in kidnappings as did guerrillas.

Bibliography

Cameron, A. and Trivedi, P. (1990) 'Regression-based Tests for Overdispersion in the Poisson Model', *Journal of Econometrics*, 46 (1): 347–364.

Cameron, A. and Trivedi, P. (1998) *Regression Analysis of Count Data.* London: Cambridge University Press.

Cameron, C. and Trivedi, P. (1986) 'Econometric Models Based on Count Data: Comparisons and Applications of Some Estimators and Tests', *Journal of Applied Econometrics*, 1(1): 29–53.

Coupland, R. and Meddings, D. (1999) 'Mortality Associated with Use of Weapons in Armed Conflicts, Wartime Atrocities, and Civilian Mass Shootings: Literature Review', *BMJ* 319: 407–410.

Cox, D. (1983) 'Some Remarks on Overdispersion', *Biometrika*, 70 (1): 269–274.

Duffield, M. (2001) *Global Governance and the New Wars: The Merging of Development and Security.* London: Zed Books.

Duffield, M. (2007) *Development, Security and Unending War Governing the World of Peoples.* London: Polity Press.

Hausman, J., Hall, B. and Griliches, Z. (1984) 'Econometric Models for Count Data with an Application to the Patents-R and D Relationship', *Journal of Econometrica*, 52 (4).

HCP (High Commissioner for Peace) (2006) *Desmovilizacions Colectivas de las Autodefensas: Estado de la Reintegration* (unpublished), 20 October.

IEPRI/CERAC (2006) *Hacia un Post-conflict Benigno? Demobilizaction, Reinsercion y Criminalidad en Colombia.* Bogota, February.

Metz, S. (2000) *Armed Conflict in the 21st Century: The Information Revolution and Post-Modern Warfare.* Strategic Studies Institute of the US Army War College.

Muggah, R. (2005) 'No Magic Bullet: A Critical Perspective on Disarmament, Demobilization and Reintegration and Weapons Reduction during Post-Conflict', *The Commonwealth Journal of International Affairs*, 94 (379).

Patel, A. (2007) 'Transitional Justice and Disarmament, Demobilization and Reintegration in Colombia', *Background Paper.* New York: ICTJ.

Pizarro, E. (2004) *Una Democracia Asediada: Balance y Perspectivas del Conflicto Armado en Colombia*, Bogotá, Editorial Norma.

Ramírez, W. (2005) 'Autodefensas y Poder Local', in *El Poder Paramilitar.* Bogotá: Editorial Planeta Colombiana.

Restrepo, J. and Spagat, M. (2005) 'Colombia's Tipping Point?', *Survival*, 47 (2).

Restrepo, J. and Vargas, J. (2004) 'The Dynamics of the Columbian Civil Conflict: A New Dataset', *Homo Oeconomicus*, 21.

Romero, M. (2003) *Paramilitares y Autodefensas 1982–2003.* Bogotá: IEPRI – Editorial Planeta.

Sadinle, M. (2008) 'Metodología para Interpolar Tamaños Poblacionales', *Documentos de CERAC 7*, Febrero.

Sánchez, G. and Meertens, D. (1983) *Bandoleros, Gamonales y Campesinos: el Caso de la Violencia en Colombia.* Bogotá: El Áncora Editores.

Sanin, F. (2008) 'Telling the Difference: Guerrillas and Paramilitaries in the Colombian War', *Politics and Society*, 36 (1): 3–34.

Small Arms Survey (2006) 'Colombia's Hydra', *Small Arms Survey 2006.* Oxford: Oxford University Press.

Spagat, M. (2007) 'Colombia's Paramilitary DDR: Quiet and Tentative Success', CERAC Working Paper. Bogota: CERAC.

Tate, W. (2001) 'Paramiltiaries in Colombia', *Brown Journal of International Affairs*, 8 (1).

Weinstein, J. (2006) *Inside Rebellion: The Politics of Insurgent Violence.* London: Cambridge University Press.

Wooldridge, J. (2003) *Introductory Econometrics.* Mason: Thomson South-Western.

2 Demobilization and reintegration in Sierra Leone[1]

Assessing progress

Macartan Humphreys and Jeremy Weinstein

Efforts to demobilize armed factions and reintegrate individual fighters into civilian life – the latter two elements of DDR programmes – are a central component of multidimensional peacekeeping operations (Berdal 1996). But despite the confidence of policy-makers in the impact of these efforts, there have been few systematic efforts to evaluate whether these programmes actually work. The literature is full of 'lessons-learned' assessments that attempt to parse the factors that account for the success (or failure) of a given DDR programme.[2] Surprisingly, however, this debate has typically been carried out without an appropriate source of variation in the key explanatory variables. At the macro-level, studies of DDR have typically not engaged in a comparison of outcomes in countries that did and those that did not receive interventions. At the micro-level, many studies fail to examine why some individuals and not others are able to successfully reintegrate after conflict and whether participation in DDR programmes accounts for this variation. In the absence of this kind of systematic comparison, however, it is difficult to answer the key counterfactual question: how different would things have been in the absence of these interventions?

To address the question, we focus on the Sierra Leone experience. By many criteria, the Sierra Leone case is a success story. Most importantly, Sierra Leone has seen continuous peace since the war ended in 2002. The country has experienced two democratic elections for the presidency and the most recent of these in 2007 brought a democratic change in governing party. The main rebel group, the Revolutionary United Front (RUF) has completely disbanded and there has been a dramatic decline in the number of arms in circulation. Moreover, as we report elsewhere (Humphreys and Weinstein 2004) the DDR process itself was seen as being equitable across groups, participation rates were high and, some vocal complaints notwithstanding, participants reported broad satisfaction with the programme and the training received in it.

In this study, however, we focus not on these macro-level outcomes or on individual perceptions of programme success. Instead we focus on the narrower question of understanding the *variation* in reintegration and demobilization: why are some ex-combatants more likely than others to experience problems demobilizing and reintegrating? Does participation in DDR programmes help account for this variation? Drawing on a survey of 1,043 combatants from the five warring factions in Sierra Leone's civil war, we thus seek to identify the impact of international attempts to facilitate reintegration, but also to explore how the ability of ex-combatants to reintegrate depends on their personal characteristics and on their experience of conflict.

The micro-level approach we use exploits a source of variation in individual level outcomes that can in principle establish whether a particular international program delivers the benefits attributed to it. We emphasize, however, that there are two (related) shortcomings with the approach that we employ here. The first concerns micro–macro linkages. By exploring demobilization and reintegration at the micro-level, we make an implicit assumption that the impact of a DDR programme in a given country can be discerned by comparing reintegration outcomes across individuals that did and did not participate in a programme. This assumption makes sense if the macro effects of DDR programmes work through the positive impact they have on individual combatants. To the extent that DDR is designed explicitly to break down ties within factions and facilitate economic, political, and social reintegration, these effects should, in principle, be visible at the individual level. However, there are ways in which DDR might matter without leaving any traces at the individual level. If DDR programmes work at a more aggregate level – for example, by giving a faction leader grounds on which to commit to a peace process – the impact of the intervention cannot be assessed through this micro-level approach. If these effects dominate, a cross-national approach may be more appropriate.

The second shortcoming relates to the difficulties of establishing causality in programme evaluation. Even assuming that the micro-level effects obtain, an *ex post* survey approach is only a second-best approach. A first-best approach exists, using a method of randomized intervention, in which (for example) the order in which individuals undergo DDR processes is partly randomized. This method provides enormous power for understanding the impact of external interventions. It is also an approach that is rapidly gaining ground in the evaluation of a wide range of development programmes, as evidenced for example by the extraordinary work of the Poverty Action Lab at MIT. But we know of no attempt to use the principle of randomization to evaluate DDR efforts in any post-conflict country. In the absence of randomization, we use data from *ex post* survey work to identify the correlates of successful reintegration and look for evidence of the impact of DDR programmes. The fact that our approach is second best introduces some caveats on the interpretation of our results, which we discuss in more detail below.

These caveats notwithstanding, three major findings stand out from our analysis of the Sierra Leone case. First, different processes appear to underlie distinct facets of social, economic and political integration. It is simply not the case that all good things go together – combatants who break ties to their factions are not necessarily also more likely to successfully reintegrate into the economy, their community, or the country's political life. While policy-makers conceptualize disarmament, demobilization and reintegration as steps on the path toward full reintegration for ex-fighters, it is not clear from the Sierra

Leone experience at least, that success on one front translates into progress on another.

Second, a number of individual level determinants of successful reintegration emerge from the analysis – factors that may prove important in the design of future DDR programmes. Past participation in a military faction that is highly abusive of civilians is the strongest predictor of difficulty in achieving social reintegration. For economic and political integration, we find that individuals from wealthier and more educated backgrounds face greater difficulties. Higher ranking combatants, we find, appear to be less trusting of democratic politics. On our measure of the disestablishment of military factions, the data suggest that ideologues are more likely to remain connected to their units, as are male fighters, and younger ex-combatants. Perhaps surprisingly, however, given the special attention paid to women and young people in the aftermath of conflict, we find little evidence that these groups face a more difficult time reintegrating into civilian life.

Third, and most importantly, our examination of the impact of DDR programmes produces little evidence in support of claims that they effectively break down factional structures and facilitate reintegration. Combatants not exposed to the DDR programme appear to reintegrate just as successfully as those that participated. In the absence of a randomized trial, however, there are a number of reasons why we might fail to identify effects even if they exist – chief among these are spillover, selection and sampling biases. We examine each of these in some detail. Based on the data available to us, our analysis suggests that the non-finding cannot be easily attributed to selection or sampling effects. There is, however, some evidence (for one of our four outcome measures) that spillover effects may render our ability to identify programme effects particularly difficult. Nonetheless, to discount this prima facie evidence that the DDR programme in Sierra Leone had no impact, policy-makers will need to employ more robust strategies for demonstrating the efficacy of demobilization and reintegration efforts. To the extent that policy-makers wish to build their programme designs on stronger evidentiary bases, we take this conclusion to be one of the most important outcomes of this study. We discuss what such strategies might look like, and what they can and cannot accomplish, in a concluding section.

The promise of demobilization and reintegration

One reason that policy-makers have long supported demobilization and reintegration is that such programmes are believed to reduce the risk of a return to conflict.[3] As noted above, DDR programmes are viewed as essential to decreasing the incentives for ex-combatants to take up arms in the future. Spear (2002: 141), for example, emphasizes the role of DDR in dissolving armed factions: 'peace requires breaking the command and control structures operating over rebel fighters ... thus making it more difficult for them to return to organized rebellion'. Economic dimensions of post-conflict reintegration receive priority from the International Peace Academy (2002) which argues that 'ex-combatants must be able to earn a livelihood through legitimate means'. If a higher risk of conflict results from an absence of income-earning opportunities for young men (Collier and Hoeffler 2004), then demobilization and reintegration programmes that seek to create economic opportunities for combatants should reduce these risks.

The United Nations (2000) points to the need to 'convert combatants who pursue their objectives through force to civilians who pursue their objectives through other means'. Generating confidence in a democratic alternative to militarized politics is a 'critical test of the peace process' (ibid.). Finally, civil society organizations often underscore the need for reconciliation in the aftermath of conflict. To the extent that ex-combatants gain acceptance from family members, friends and neighbours through formal or informal processes of reconciliation (which often accompany DDR programmes), communities are in a better position to reintegrate former soldiers and facilitate their reinsertion into civilian life.

Policy-makers thus recognize a range of distinct channels through which the demobilization and reintegration of ex-combatants contributes to successful peace-building. The basic hypothesis we examine in this chapter is that DDR programmes facilitate peace-building through each of these channels. Thus, we conceptualize reintegration as multifaceted, with factional, economic, political and social dimensions. We look for evidence that participation in demobilization and reintegration programmes dissolves the factional networks linking ex-combatants to one another, improves income-earning opportunities available to former fighters, generates increased confidence in the democratic process, and facilitates reconciliation with family, friends and community members.

We also explore a series of individual, group and community-level characteristics that might condition successful demobilization and reintegration. These variables are of considerable independent interest in that our study provides an opportunity to identify some of the empirical correlates of reintegration.

Table 2.1 Dimensions of reintegration

Dimension	Hypothesis	Indicators
Factional	DDR programmes break down the structure of command and control operating over fighters.	The extent of social ties among former fighters.
Economic	DDR programmes prepare ex-combatants to earn a livelihood through legitimate means.	Access to employment opportunities.
Political	DDR programmes help to generate faith in the democratic process among ex-combatants	Confidence that democratic means are the most effective means for airing concerns.
Social	DDR programmes facilitate reconciliation among fighters and victimized communities.	The extent of difficulties ex-combatants face in gaining acceptance in their communities.

Surveying DDR in Sierra Leone

In January 2002, when the government of Sierra Leone declared its more than decade-long war officially over, the international community showered it with plaudits for a successful disarmament, demobilization and reintegration programme that paved the way for a stable post-war political order. This turn of events was unexpected for a country that experienced a brutal civil war which captured international attention, a stop-and-start peace-building effort lasting more than four years, and the persistent negative spillover effects of violence in neighbouring Liberia.

The war in Sierra Leone began on 23 March 1991 with a cross-border invasion by the RUF from Liberia into the border districts of Kailahun and Pujehun.[4] The group, formed originally by student radicals opposed to the one-party regime of the All People's Congress (APC), had received training in Libya and subsequently, material support from the Liberian warlord and later president, Charles Taylor.

In 1992, the APC government was deposed by a group of junior officers of the Sierra Leone Army (SLA) and replaced by the National Provisional Ruling Council (NPRC). The NPRC sought to achieve an outright victory over the RUF by hiring a South African security firm, Executive Outcomes. Following popular rallies and a palace coup, the country returned to civilian rule in 1996. The new civilian government, led by President Ahmed Tejan Kabbah and the Sierra Leone People's Party (SLPP) coordinated its actions with local civil defence militias that had first appeared in 1993–1994, consolidating an offensive paramilitary force, the Civil Defense Forces (CDF).

In 1997, Kabbah was driven into exile following a military revolt. The coup brought a fourth group into the conflict, the Armed Forces Revolutionary Council (AFRC). The AFRC forged an unlikely alliance with the RUF, inviting the insurgents to join a power-sharing arrangement. Following a Nigerian-led intervention in 1998, the democratic government was restored and the AFRC/RUF alliance was removed from the capital. The AFRC/RUF regrouped in the bush, rebuilding its military strength with resources garnered from international businessmen and arms suppliers that were willing to provide resources up-front in exchange for mineral concessions. The combined forces launched a successful and devastating attack on the capital, Freetown, on 6 January 1999, although they were later repulsed by West African peacekeeping forces. Under tremendous pressure to consolidate control of its territory, Kabbah's government signed a peace agreement with the RUF in Lomé in July 1999.

However, this political solution to the Sierra Leone conflict was short-lived. In early 2000, a United Nations force (UNAMSIL) deployed to take the reins from the Nigerians, but it was weak and poorly organized. Distrust was high, and the RUF reacted, taking large numbers of UN troops as hostages. British intervention alongside robust action by Guinean troops substantially weakened the RUF militarily. The government arrested RUF leaders in Freetown, and with a more effective UN force in place, the warring factions were largely broken down and demobilized. President Kabbah, securely back in power, declared the war at an end in February 2002.

Surveying DDR in Sierra Leone

Given the ups and downs of the war itself, it should come as no surprise that the DDR process faced many hiccups in its implementation (Comninos *et al.* 2002). Boutros Boutros-Ghali called for a demobilization and reintegration effort in Sierra Leone as early as 1995 (Agence France Press 1995) and a DDR programme was written into the terms of the 1996 peace agreement. However, the first sustained effort to demobilize fighters began only in late 1998. Kabbah's government led this process after it was returned to power by the Nigerians. But it was interrupted by the January 1999 assault on Freetown, by which time it had registered only 3,000 ex-combatants (Molloy 2004). A second phase began in 1999, after the Lomé Accord was signed, and it continued until 2000 when the war broke out anew. During this period, slightly more than 20,000 combatants turned up to be demobilized. Although demobilization continued during negotiations, the bulk of demobilization took place after UNAMSIL was beefed up, following the British intervention, in 2001–2002. In the third and final phase close to 50,000 combatants disarmed. This brought the total caseload to over 70,000 fighters (see Table 2.2 and Molloy 2004).

The disarmament process was conducted at reception centres distributed around the country as represented in Figure 2.1. It included five phases: the assembly of combatants, collection of personal information, the verification and collection of weapons, the certification of eligibility for benefits, and transportation to a demobilization centre. Once disarmed, combatants were prepared to return to civilian life in demobilization sites where they received basic necessities, reinsertion allowances, counselling, and eventually transportation to a local community where they elected to live permanently. In the community, combatants benefited from training programmes (largely vocational skills including auto repair, furniture-making, etc.) designed to ease their re-entry into the local economy.

Table 2.2 Stages of demobilization and reintegration in Sierra Leone

		Programme phase			Total count
		1998 Count	1999 Count	2001–2002 Count	
Fighting force	SLA/AFRC	3,037	5,500	324	8,861
	RUF	140	4,871	19,284	24,295
	CDF	2	9,312	27,898	37,212
	Others	–	430	17	447
	N/A	4	2,450	268	2,722
Total		3,183	22,563	47,791	73,537

Source: National Committee for Disarmament, Demobilization, and Reintegration.

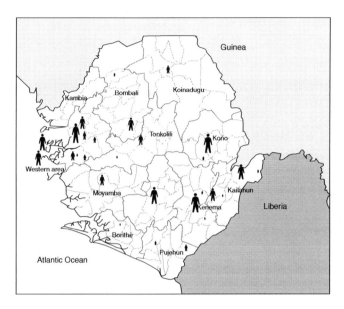

Figure 2.1 Geographic distribution of disarmament sites and caseload (source: National Committee for Disarmament, Demobilisation and Reintegration).

To assess the extent to which combatants have been able to reintegrate and identify the relative importance of participation in the DDR programme, we gathered systematic data on a sample of ex-combatants, some of whom participated in the formal DDR effort and others who remained outside of it. The survey was conducted between June and August 2003, slightly more than a year after the war came to an end. The study targeted a sample of 1,000 ex-combatants; a total of 1,043 questionnaires of ex-combatants were completed. The main method for gathering information was through the administration of a closed-ended questionnaire by an enumerator in the respondent's local language. Interviews were conducted at training programme sites and in community centres around the country and included respondents that had entered and completed DDR, those that had entered but not completed and those that never entered at all.[5]

In evaluating the impact of the DDR programme, we should note that moving more than 70,000 soldiers through this process is from an operational standpoint an accomplishment in itself. A large quantity of arms was collected during the programme, including (in phase three alone), 7,789 personal and hand weapons, 17,184 assault weapons, 487 group serviced large weapons and 810,000 rounds of unexploded ammunition (DDRP 2004). And, of course, there has been no resumption of armed conflict. Although these facts do not speak directly to the role of the DDR programme in dismantling the fighting groups, they should be kept in mind as part of any overall assessment.

Table 2.3 Success of programme implementation in Sierra Leone

	RUF	CDF	Total
Share that entered DDR	90% (375)	87% (551)	89% (926)
Share that received cash benefit	92% (339)	95% (480)	94% (819)
Share that enrolled in training	77% (336)	75% (476)	76% (812)
Share that believe training prepared them well for work	74% (141)	77% (137)	76% (278)
Share that believe the skills they learned are needed in the region	92% (149)	92% (149)	92% (298)
Share that believe they are better off socially	87% (150)	86% (150)	87% (300)
Overall rating of the training (1, Excellent to 5, Very poor)	2.45 (191)	2.45 (224)	2.45 (415)

In addition to these successes, our data suggest that programme implementation was successful in other ways: rates of participation were nearly equal across the five major factions and we found little evidence that an individual's political affiliation correlated with his or her ultimate satisfaction with the programme. As Table 2.3 demonstrates, among the two main combatant groups (the RUF and the CDF), there are no major differences in access to DDR programmes or levels of satisfaction with training. Of course, there were complaints about the programme which centred mainly on its administrative efficiency and bureaucratic design – common criticisms of UN-sponsored programmes. But there is no evidence that the process was manipulated to favour any one group to the exclusion of any other.

Moving beyond measures of access and satisfaction, we now turn to the question of whether participation in the DDR programme itself facilitated the dismantling of the factions and ex-combatant reintegration.

Four measures of demobilization and reintegration success

To reflect the multiplicity of goals associated with a DDR programme, we generated four measures intended to capture distinct dimensions of reintegration. Our first measure, DELINKED, captures the extent to which linkages with factions are maintained by the individual, recording whether or not the individual ex-combatant has successfully broken his factional ties. The measure combines an individual's responses to three questions.[6] The first asks individuals *who* they spend their time with. The second asks were they to start a business, who they would partner with. For each of these questions, one of the options available to respondents was 'Friends that I met in my faction during the war'. The final question asks individuals about the avenues they pursue when confronting ongoing, personal problems in the post-war period. The variable DELINKED takes a value of one, unless:

1   individuals spend most of their time with friends from their faction, or
2   individuals reported that friends from their faction would be their preferred business partners, or
3   individuals felt that recourse to members of their faction was among the most effective ways to deal with their problems.

The second measure, EMPLOYED, indicates whether or not an individual has reintegrated into the workforce. The measure takes a value of 0 if the individual declared his or her present occupation to be unemployed or doing 'odd jobs'. For all other responses, this measure takes a value of 1. The third measure, DEMOCRATIC, focuses on the confidence ex-combatants express in the democratic system. The measure takes a value of 1 if an individual believes that exercising voice by voting in elections or approaching government officials, either locally or centrally, is the most effective way to deal with community problems. Alternative choices included protests, complaints to NGOs, reaching out to traditional leaders or factional authorities, or taking up arms to fight. Our final measure, ACCEPTED, records whether or not individuals reported facing ongoing difficulties in gaining acceptance from their families and communities. This measure takes a value of 1 if the individual reported no problems in gaining acceptance from family members and neighbours in the post-war period; if problems are reported, the measure takes a value of 0.

Summary statistics for these four measures are provided in Table 2.4. We see from the table that there is considerable variation across these measures in the extent to which individuals can be considered successfully reintegrated. In addition, Table 2.4 shows the average scores on each of these measures for each of the two major factions in Sierra Leone's war, the RUF and the CDF.

We find that 86 per cent of combatants in our sample have broken ties with their factions, while 14 per cent still consider faction members to be among their closest friends, most likely business partners, or as a primary source of support in the event of problems. The distribution of this measure is similar across the two major factions. On employment, 84 per cent of our sample report some form of permanent occupation.[7] The problem of unemployment is found disproportionately within the RUF sub-sample; of these ex-combatants, 21 per cent report having no present full-time occupation.

Turning to democratic politics, we find that 62 per cent of combatants express confidence in electoral politics or approaches to state/local officials as among the most effective ways to respond to problems in their communities. The remainder looks either to their old factions, or more commonly, to outside actors, typically the international community, as a means to effect change. Uniquely, fighters from the CDF are less likely to be reintegrated than RUF members by this measure although the difference is not statistically significant.

Table 2.4 Measures of reintegration

Variable	N	Mean	SD	CDF (Mean)	RUF (Mean)	Difference
Delinked?	1,007	0.86	0.34	0.88	0.84	0.04
Employed?	1,037	0.84	0.36	0.90	0.79	0.11***
Democratic?	1,009	0.62	0.49	0.61	0.66	−0.05
Accepted?	1,020	0.93	0.25	0.99	0.86	0.13***

Notes
*significant at 10%.
**significant at 5%.
***significant at 1%.

Finally, on the measure of acceptance, we record the highest levels of successful reintegration, with 93 per cent reporting no problems. While this measure supports the idea that across individuals in Sierra Leone, reintegration has proceeded with great success, the difficulties faced by 7 per cent of respondents should not be under-emphasized. If our sample were entirely representative of the ex-combatant population, this figure of 7 per cent would correspond to approximately 5,000 former soldiers facing challenges in being accepted into civilian life. In fact, since our sample does not include those combatants that failed to reintegrate and elected instead to continue fighting in Liberia or Côte d'Ivoire, this number plausibly underestimates the number of non-reintegrated fighters. Note, finally, that these acceptance rates differ markedly across factions. Non-acceptance rates are much higher within the RUF than within the CDF; while CDF members almost universally report no problems of acceptance, 14 per cent of ex-RUF members report such problems.

Do these four indicators capture different facets of the same underlying phenomenon? If they were capturing a single underlying process of reintegration, we might expect to find that the measures are positively correlated with one another. Table 2.5 reports the pair-wise correlations between these measures. Uniformly, however, we find that the correlations among the measures are low.

In Sierra Leone, at least, reintegration on one dimension is typically *not* a good predictor of reintegration on another dimension. Although it would be simpler, both from the point of view of analysis and for policy reasons, to

Table 2.5 Correlation matrix of measures of reintegration

	Delinked?	Employed?	Democratic?	Accepted?
Delinked?	–	−0.02	−0.02	0.06
Employed?	−0.02	–	0.06	0.07
Democratic?	−0.02	0.06	–	0.02
Accepted?	0.06	0.07	0.02	–

generate a single measure of reintegration success, our data suggest that this is not appropriate. Distinct processes may underlie each of these measures of reintegration success.

Non-programmatic determinants of reintegration success

Recent research in social psychology and anthropology suggests some plausible factors shaping reintegration prospects including exposure to violence (Dyregrov *et al.* 2002; Husain *et al.* 1998), age (Richards *et al.* 2003), and gender (Mazurana *et al.* 2002).[8] But beyond these studies, our review of the literature on demobilization and reintegration yields little in the way of systematic theories about the conditions under which some combatants but not others will give up their arms and reintegrate into civilian life. Given the rudimentary state of our knowledge, our examination of these factors is exploratory: we seek to document the extent to which a set of demographic and social factors can account for successful reintegration across individual combatants. To do so we consider the relationship between reintegration success and 11 individual, group and community characteristics: five measures of an individual's demographic background (age, gender, ethnicity, education and wealth), four measures of an individual's experience of the conflict (whether the individual was abducted, whether he was a political supporter of the group, whether he was an officer, and a measure of the abusiveness of the unit in which an individual fought) and two measures of community characteristics (an indicator of wealth and an index of the degree to which the community suffered from abuse during the war).

Programmatic determinants of reintegration success

To assess the effectiveness of the DDR programme in facilitating reintegration, we use two measures of the 'treatment'. Our first measure emphasizes participation in the programme: 87 per cent of our sample joined the DDR programme, while 13 per cent elected to reintegrate on their own.[9] In addition, we collected a second measure that captures whether or not an individual *completed* DDR. By this measure, 46 per cent of our sample completed the DDR programme at the time of our survey and 54 per cent had not.[10] Studying both measures allows us to distinguish between the effects of initial and complete exposure to the DDR programme.

Results I: non-programmatic determinants of reintegration

We report our basic results in Table 2.6. The table reports the estimated impact of each of the 11 background indicators and the two programmatic measures on the likelihood of successful reintegration, as measured by each of the four outcome indicators. Each number in the table gives the estimated percentage change in the likelihood of reintegration success associated with variation in each of the programmatic and non-programmatic measures.

Table 2.6 Correlates of reintegration

	Delinked	Employed	Democratic	Accepted
Non-programmatic factors				
Percentage difference in the likelihood of successful reintegration…				
For each additional year of age	0.3**	0.1	0.2	0
Between men and women	−6.4***	1.5	−3.3	−0.4
Between Mende and non-Mende	−0.7	1.2	−0.4	1.4**
Between the more educated and less educated respondents	1.2	−2.2*	−0.4	−0.2
Between the pre-war poor and pre-war non-poor	0	2.5	9.1***	1.8*
Between abductees and volunteers	−0.3	−2.6	18.3***	0.1
Between those who joined for political reasons and all others	−5.9**	0.3	17.8***	−2.4**
Between officers in the factions and rank and file	−5.1	−1.1	−8.8**	0.1
Between combatants from more abusive units and those from less abusive units	−1.2	−7.6	−28.0*	−9.5***
Between ex-combatants now living in wealthy districts and all others	3.5	−9.8**	−9.4**	0.4
Between ex-combatants now living in communities that suffered abuse and all others	1.8	−16.4	49.6*	−7.7**
Programmatic factors				
Percentage difference in the likelihood of successful reintegration…				
Between ex-combatants that participated in DDR and those that did not	−4.3	12.6**	−3	−0.6
Between ex-combatants that completed DDR and all others[a]	−4.6	−1.1	−4.6	−0.6

Notes
*significant at 10%.
**significant at 5%.
***significant at 1%.
Robust z-statistics in brackets. All results in each column are based on a single probit model with errors clustered geographically at the chiefdom level. For more details on the models on which these results are based see Humphreys and Weinstein (2007) as well as the dataset made available online at http://www.columbia.edu/~mh2245/papers1/jcr2007/.

a The reported effect in this final line reflects the *joint* effects of entering and completing the programme and not the completion effect alone.

A number of key non-programmatic effects are worth highlighting. Two characteristics thought to be major factors in the reintegration process, age and gender, exhibit weak effects across dimensions. Consistent with the prevailing view that reintegration is harder for younger fighters, we find that older ex-combatants are more likely to have broken ties to their factions. But the evidence suggests that younger combatants are no less likely to be accepted by their communities, to place their faith in democratic processes, or to have found gainful employment.[11]

Perhaps surprisingly, given the extensive focus on the difficulties faced by female ex-combatants, we find significant differences between male and female ex-fighters on only one dimension. Female ex-combatants are significantly more likely to have broken ties to their factions. The difference is substantively large and significant at the 99 per cent level. While the qualitative literature has focused on the difficulties women face in the reintegration, our evidence suggests that gender has no measurable impact on most outcomes, except for the fact that men appear less willing to sever their ties to other combatants. Observers of the conflict in Sierra Leone, in particular, have noted the difficulties that women face in returning to their communities, but our results suggest that these very real challenges owe more to their membership in the RUF than to their gender.

The effects of (pre-war) poverty, and to a lesser extent, education, appear to be consistent across the indicators with less well educated and poorer individuals typically having *more* success in reintegrating. Poverty, measured at the individual level (using a dummy variable capturing whether the walls of the pre-war home were constructed of mud and sticks) is associated with a higher likelihood of adopting democratic norms, gaining acceptance by community members, and (although not significant) finding employment. Strikingly, more educated ex-combatants were less likely to find employment in post-conflict Sierra Leone. We find no relationship, however, between an individual's socio-economic status and the likelihood that they break their ties with their factions.

War experiences appear to shape the prospects of reintegration as well. If individuals joined because they supported the cause of the group, they face more difficulty gaining acceptance in the post-war period and are more likely to remain attached to their factions. Strong believers, across factions, have a harder time readjusting to civilian life. Surprisingly, however, these individuals also appear to place the greatest faith in the electoral process.

Combatants who fought in units which were highly abusive toward civilian populations also faced a more difficult path to reintegration.[12] Individuals from non-abusive units exhibit acceptance levels nearly one standard deviation higher than those from highly abusive units. This may be the result of the psycho-social impact of the conflict on individual fighters (Blattman 2006) or reflect the unwillingness of host community members to accept a returning fighter. We cannot distinguish between these explanations, although we emphasize that the result is independent of our estimate of the degree of abuse to which host communities were exposed. Individuals from abusive units are less likely to place their faith in democratic processes.

We find some evidence that community characteristics – or absorptive capacities – matter as well. Individuals who settle in wealthier locations find it more difficult to find employment and are less likely to have faith in democratic processes. Plausibly fighters relocated to wealthier districts, such as Freetown and the diamond mining areas, to improve their employment opportunities, but with little success. In addition, the degree of abuse experienced by local communities during the war is powerfully related to the level of acceptance of ex-combatants. Consistent with stories told by some of our respondents about reintegration, their membership in a faction mattered not because of their personal characteristics, but because of the reputation of the group in the area where they lived.

Results II: programmatic determinants of reintegration

The results of our analyses of programme effects are also presented in Table 2.6. The most striking result from the table is the lack of evidence that international interventions are returning the benefits attributed to them, as observed at the individual level. Evidence from Sierra Leone does not support the hypothesis that participation in a DDR programme increases the degree to which combatants are accepted by their families and communities. Nor is there a relationship between participation in these programmes and democratic attitudes, the likelihood that an individual breaks ties with his faction, or the likelihood that he returns home. The only significant result is that those that enter the programme are more likely to be employed. In fact, however, the most likely interpretation of this finding is that individuals consider themselves to have an occupation *over the period in which they are active participants in the programme*. This can be seen from the fact that there is no correlation between programme *completion* and employment. Those in programmes declare themselves having an occupation while those completing programmes declare none. Other than the short-term occupation provided during training, we find no net effect of exposure to DDR programming on the employment prospects of ex-combatants.

While the multidimensional peacekeeping operations in Sierra Leone may have been effective at the macro-level, we cannot identify an impact for the DDR component of these programmes at the micro-level. We must be cautious, however, in interpreting these findings as evidence that the DDR process had no impact. No evidence of an effect is not the same as evidence of no effect. Moreover, empirically, the strategy of comparing outcomes across 'treated' and 'untreated' ex-combatants to identify the efficacy of a national level process, is complicated by three distinct effects: *spillover effects, selection effects* and *sampling effects*. We discuss each of these possibilities in turn.

Spillover effects

Consider first the challenge posed by spillover effects. The idea here is that if fighters that did not take part in the programme nevertheless benefited indirectly from its positive impact on those that did, then our approach of comparing those that did participate and those that did not will lead to an underestimate of the programme's impact. A number of distinct mechanisms could underpin such spillover effects. For example, when a programme seeks to separate ex-combatants from their factions, success in breaking any individual's ties to the network may undermine the network as a whole. A similar dynamic might take place with respect to acceptance by families and communities. In principle, combatants that did not take part in DDR programmes may find their relationships with community members improved precisely because those combatants that did take part are successfully reintegrating with family and community members.

We tested explicitly for such positive spillover effects by generating a measure of the percentage of soldiers in a given chiefdom that participated in the demobilization programme. We then looked to see whether the reintegration trajectory of a given ex-combatant depended on how many others in his or her area were participating in the DDR programme. While such geographically structured spillovers are not the only possible type of spillover (in particular, spillovers may occur between individuals that are structurally linked but geographically separate within an organization), many plausible spillover mechanisms have a geographic component – in particular, spillover mechanisms that work through hypothesized impacts on host communities.

On three of the four measures of reintegration success, we continue to find no evidence that DDR programmes, either directly, or through spillover effects, increase the likelihood of reintegration. Notably, we find a negative relationship on our measure of delinking, which is consistent with the negative relationship we find on the direct effect, although it is not significant at conventional levels. We do, however, find some evidence of spillover effects of participation in DDR for acceptance and the impact is substantively large. Our estimates suggest that individuals that do not join the programme have a 92 per cent [95 per cent CI: 67–99.7 per cent] chance of gaining acceptance if no individuals in their chiefdom join programmes and a 99 per cent probability if all individuals enter the programmes [95 per cent CI: 95–99.9 per cent]. With 87 per cent joining (our estimated actual take-up rate), an individual not joining has an estimated 98 per cent probability of gaining acceptance [95 per cent CI: 94–99.9 per cent]. In other words, even though we find no evidence of direct effects, the estimated total effect is, in principle, large enough to overcome the problems faced by ex-combatants in gaining acceptance.

Selection effects

A second possibility is that we find no evidence of direct impacts at the individual level because there is a selection effect in operation. That is, the population of combatants who participated in DDR may be systematically different from those that elected to reintegrate without external assistance. It may be that DDR took on the very difficult cases – such as hardcore members of the RUF – while rank and file members of the CDF (which was widely seen as victorious in the conflict) decided to return home on their own. Such differences, if unobserved and not controlled for in our models, might explain the non-result. We emphasize, however, that precisely the opposite argument may be made for the bias introduced by selection effects. Plausibly, it is the difficult cases – those afraid of being identified by authorities or those unwilling to cooperate with the government – that refused to enter DDR, whereas those simply needing a means to re-enter civilian life elected to participate. If such a selection effect were in operation, we would find that participants fared better than non-participants even if the programme had no impact.

Whether or not our finding of no programme effect can be attributed to selection then depends on what form of selection was in operation. One of the advantages of a survey approach is that we could ask individuals directly why they did or did not enter, allowing for an open-ended response. The answers are revealing. In many cases, the answers do not suggest an obvious selection effect. In a number of cases, respondents reported that they had wanted to enter, but happened to be travelling or sick at the time. Other answers suggest that the selection effect is likely to work against finding evidence of an impact of the programme. Some that did not participate simply had other options; they reported having communities and jobs waiting for them. One claimed that he was 'not interested because of the delay and the waste of time'. Another explained that he did not register 'because my parents were willing to assist me'. Finally, some responses suggest a selection effect that would bias the results toward finding an effect of the programme. Some refused to enter because of distrust or suspicion: 'It was a waste of time because they were lying', one said. Another explained that 'my husband threatened that the disarmament records were going to be used after 4–5 years to punish all those who took part in the war so I gave my weapon to another member of my unit to disarm'.

Based on these open-ended responses, then, it is not clear that selection effects work either to hide or magnify a programme effect. Beyond our qualitative examination of the determinants of selection, however, there are statistical approaches we can employ to explore the issue of selection more systematically. We utilized propensity matching estimators to compare outcomes across individuals with a similar 'propensity' to take part in the programme.

Propensity matching indicators estimate, for each individual, a probability of entering DDR based on all relevant available data. Based on these probabilities, the method matches pairs of individuals that have the same estimated propensity of joining, but one of whom did and the other of whom did not join. If our estimates for the propensity of joining are accurate, then for any pair matched in this way, we can treat the difference in reintegration success for those that do join DDR and those that do not, as a result of the fact of joining. However, this method is only as good as our ability to predict joining probabilities and selection effects may still obtain if unobservable characteristics of individuals simultaneously determine their decision (or ability) to enter the programme and the likelihood of successfully reintegrating.

To employ this technique, we use all of the explanatory variables in Table 2.6 as well as an indicator of our subjects' location at the end of the war in order to predict participation. Our predictors thus capture key demographic features as well as conflict-relevant variables that we know in some cases to be related to reintegration success but that could in principle explain participation in the DDR programme as well. Together, however, they only account for 25 per cent of the variation in participation. Using the resulting propensity scores to compare similar participants and non-participants, we continue to find no evidence that participation in DDR contributed to reintegration success on any dimension.

Sampling bias

Finally, we explored the possibility that the non-result on programme effects is driven by an imperfection in our sample of respondents. In particular, it may be the case that those ex-combatants that faced the greatest difficulty reintegrating were also the least likely to be enumerated when our survey teams came to the selected chiefdoms. Indeed, if the hardcore fighters from Sierra Leone that migrated to take part in the civil wars of neighbouring countries did not demobilize and reintegrate and, in addition, were absent from our sample, it is possible that a sampling bias accounts for our non-finding.

There are three important responses to this charge of sampling bias. First, if fighters did take part in the DDR programmes and subsequently left the country to fight in other wars, then the bias works in the opposite direction. If this effect predominates, then our estimate in fact *over*estimates programme effectiveness. Relatively little is known about the fighters that left Sierra Leone to fight elsewhere in the sub-region. Perhaps the most careful study of these fighters has been undertaken by Human Rights Watch in a report on West Africa's 'regional warriors'. The report cites multiple instances of individuals that took part in the Sierra Leone DDR process and later moved to fight in Liberia, with, in some cases, recruitment to the Liberia war linked to their participation in the Sierra Leone DDR process (Human Rights Watch 2005: 22–24).

Second, it may be that for individuals that wished to take part in the DDR process but were unable to participate, their lack of access to the programme could have actively contributed both to their failure to reintegrate and their absence from the sample. Indeed, Human Rights Watch reports that, 'the majority of those [regional warriors] interviewed had negative experiences with the DDR programme in Sierra Leone … the programme's failure to engage them contributed to their decision to take up arms with another armed group'. In this case, including these individuals in the sample would lead to a more favourable measurement of the impact of DDR, but only because of the adverse effect of the programme on the untreated rather than its positive impact on the treated.

The third response relates to the fact that those populations not available to our enumerators likely reflect in part those same samples that were not available for the DDR programme. If fighters left the country to pursue more lucrative soldiering options elsewhere, and if this fact explains why they did not take part in DDR programmes, then what appears to be a sampling problem in fact masks a selection problem. It is the lack of reintegration that explains their failure to participate in the programme, not vice versa. Attributing their failure to reintegrate as evidence of the programme's success is in this case a fallacy. Instead, our goal should be to estimate the impact of the programme on the relevant population of potential programme participants (the ability of a programme to cover the full population of ex-combatants thus constitutes a second dimension for evaluation). If the same individuals that select out of the population of potential beneficiaries also select out of our sample, then in the absence of other selection effects, our estimate is not a biased estimate of programme impact on the relevant population.

In short, sampling biases could have effects in either direction; the qualitative evidence suggests, however, that the bias is likely either to result in an overestimation of the positive effects or an underestimation of the adverse effects of the programme on the untreated. These three considerations – spillover, selection, and sampling – point to the complexity of interpreting simple two-sample comparisons in the absence of a randomized intervention. We now turn to alternative designs that can surmount these challenges.

Future directions in the measurement of the impact of DDR

On many criteria, the DDR programme in Sierra Leone was a success. The most important outcomes, continued peace and the dismantling of armed groups, have been achieved. In addition the programme itself was well received and was inclusive and equitable across factions. These features are important for any overall assessment of programme success. As noted in 2006 by President Kabbah of Sierra Leone:

> From the beginning, we agreed that one of the causes of the war was exclusiveness and so a central component of the DDR process was inclusiveness. The transition was so successful that now we are regarded as model for post-conflict countries.
>
> (Summit Communications 2006)

Despite these positive features however, our direct study of programme effects yields little evidence that participation in the DDR programme increased the likelihood that combatants successfully reintegrated. These results are both surprising and disturbing. Our examination of the three major threats to the validity of our findings, however, underscores just how difficult it is to identify a programme's causal effects in the absence of an experimental design. We believe that it is not appropriate, based on the results presented here, to conclude that the DDR programme had no positive micro-level impacts in Sierra Leone.

Nevertheless we believe the non-findings should be seen as a wake-up call to advocates of these programmes. Needed now is a method that is better suited to identify causal impacts in the presence of the confounding effects we have discussed. We believe that there is such a method and that it involves the development of monitoring and evaluation systems that employ some form of randomized intervention. This method can help account for the selection and sampling problems and some (but not all) of the spillover problems.

The key issue is the following. If scholars and policy analysts are to disentangle the effects of demobilization programmes from the range of other initiatives launched as part of multidimensional peacekeeping operations, DDR programmes must be designed in such a way that the reintegration trajectories of participants can be usefully compared with those of non-participants, when both groups are identical except for the treatment itself. With an appropriate treatment and control group, data collected after the DDR programme is completed (for the treatment group) can be used to answer the relevant counterfactual: how successfully would ex-combatants have reintegrated if they had not participated in the programme? Selection effects then no longer represent the threat to valid measurement of programme effects described above.

How can practitioners identify an appropriate control group for an experimental study of DDR programmes? Evidently, it does not make sense in a post-conflict environment to simply deny 'treatment' in the demobilization process to a group of combatants for the purpose of evaluating the programme's impact. To overcome this problem, we advocate an experimental approach that randomizes the timing of participation in DDR programmes. The core idea is that, although all ex-combatants will eventually participate in the programme, the timing of their entry into the programme will be determined by lottery, allowing for comparisons of programme participants and non-participants (that is, combatants that have not yet entered the programme).

This approach to evaluating the effects of DDR is increasingly feasible as the UN and its partners have moved beyond an individual-level programme model, in which combatants register for cash payments and training, to include more community-focused forms of demobilization and reintegration, in which assistance is provided to communities with significant populations of ex-combatants. With this new model, the rollout of UN programme efforts is constrained by logistical considerations and staffing capacity, necessitating some delays in the extension of programmes to different communities. Any limits on the feasibility of providing a treatment to the full sample of recipients at a single point in time provide the opportunity for an experimental design. It is reasonable to consider making decisions about which communities should receive the programme first by lottery in order to ensure fairness, although some localities might be excluded from the process of random selection if their situation is particularly dire. With a sufficient number of communities included in the lottery, identifying programme effects by comparing participants to non-participants is feasible. Moreover, by conducting such an evaluation using a community-focused approach, both individual effects (such as those measured in this paper) and community-level outcomes, such as levels of conflict, can be assessed in the same design.

Beyond selection issues, a randomized design can also help to mitigate problems posed by spillover effects and sampling bias. With DDR programmes implemented community by community, and stratified by region within a country, one can use the (exogenous) variation in the density of treatment communities in a given geographic region as the programme is phased in, to empirically estimate the positive (or negative) externalities experienced by communities not yet included in the programme (following Miguel and Kremer 2004). Other non-geographic spillover effects may also be studied with random sources of variation in treatment at the individual or unit level. Of particular interest – because of the potential they hold to shed light on organizational cohesion and resilience – are spillovers that occur through vertical and horizontal organizational channels.

An additional advantage of a randomized intervention is that the population for which inferences can be made is well defined and identified. It is precisely that population over which the randomization in the allocation of the treatment is undertaken. Although individuals that are not available for programme assignment may fare worse systematically than programme participants, the marginal impact of the programme on the relevant population can be estimated without bias. In addition, although individuals that take part in the programme may subsequently exit a sampling frame, a randomized design with follow-up allows for this fact to be observed and accounted for.

While the discussion above underscores how randomized intervention can be useful for assessing the overall *impact* of DDR programmes on individual and community-level outcomes, the logic of experimental design can also be extended to questions of programme design. Indeed, UN officials grapple with the question of how much power to provide in community-level initiatives to ex-combatants versus community leaders; what role to reserve for women in the leadership and management of community efforts; and what forms of assistance are likely to be most beneficial for ex-combatant reintegration.

More broadly, the main advantage of this micro-level approach is that it can increase our confidence that the mechanisms attributed to work in a given case indeed function as believed. By exploiting sub-national variation, we can work out with greater confidence whether a programme is effective but also *for whom* a programme is failing. One disadvantage, however, is that this approach cannot identify programme impacts that operate at the level of factions rather than individuals. For example, if DDR programmes prevent the recurrence of conflict because they enable faction leaders to sell their soldiers on a peace deal, regardless of whether the programme itself will improve the soldier's prospects, micro-level comparisons will tell us little about programme effects. The external validity of micro-level results may also be called into question. If there is little evidence that DDR programmes were effective in Sierra Leone, this does not mean that DDR programmes are never successful. While the Sierra Leone case is an important case – regarded as a success story, elements of the Sierra Leone 'model' are being replicated in neighbouring Liberia, in Burundi, and now as far away as Haiti – it should still be seen as a single data point in a larger model that attempts to explain cross-national variation in programme effectiveness.

Ultimately, single-country experimental designs need to be complemented by attention to country-specific factors that shape the trajectory of DDR programmes. To understand how DDR contributes to successful peace-building, sub-national studies represent only the building blocks for a richer analysis of how external interventions affect post-war trajectories.

Notes

1 This research draws on a large survey led by the authors together with the Post-conflict Reintegration Initiative for Development and Empowerment (PRIDE) in Freetown, Sierra Leone. Financial support was provided by the Earth Institute at Columbia University, and logistical support came from the Demobilization and Reintegration office at the United Nations Mission in Sierra Leone (UNAMSIL). A fuller treatment of the data and analysis summarized in this chapter can be found in previous articles by Humphreys and Weinstein (2007).

2 A number of studies exist specifically for the case of Sierra Leone including Comninos *et al.* (2002); Ginifer (2003); Richards *et al.* (2003) and Stavrou *et al.* (2003).

3 Of course, investments in extensive disarmament, demobilization and reintegration programmes have also been justified in terms of their importance for reorienting government spending away from military expenditures toward investment in the social sector (Kostner *et al.* 1996).

4 This history is based on Richards (1996); Keen (2005) and Gberie (2005).

5 For more information on the sampling strategy and a discussion of the potential biases in the sample, see Humphreys and Weinstein (2007).

6 To examine the precise wording of this question and all other questions used in the analysis, please see the survey instrument, available online at www.columbia.edu/~mh2245/SL.htm.

7 It is worth emphasizing that the accurate measurement of employment in developing countries is a difficult task. A rate of 84 per cent employment may strike the reader as surprisingly high; this is because we code as unemployed those who report no occupation at all. We thus count as employed individuals who perform agricultural labour (even if they would prefer to be working in the formal sector) and those engaged in informal sector activities.

8 In this volume, Blattman and Annan also touch on the issue of resilience – identifying factors that correlate with greater or lesser difficulties in achieving post-conflict reintegration. As in Sierra Leone, they find less resilience among those youth who experienced the most severe violence and among ex-combatants who returned to unsupportive home environments.

9 In comparison, FAO estimates a total ex-combatant population (within Sierra Leone) of 84,200 (FAO 2004) and thus a participation rate in DDR, broadly construed, of 76,000/84,200 = 90 per cent. DDRP (2004) reports 72,490 disarmed which implies a higher non-participation rate; Molloy (2004) reports 'over 76,000' disarmed. In addition, Molloy reports that of the 76,000 that disarmed 11,000 either self-reintegrated, hid, or fled, for a non-participation rate in the reintegration programme *among those that entered DDR* of 14 per cent.

10 It is possible that the individual-level impact of DDR is only realized years after participation in the programme has been completed. Given the timing of our data collection, we are not in a position to explore the evidence for long-term programme impacts.

11 This finding should be interpreted with caution. Human subjects concerns prevented us from interviewing soldiers who were children at the end of the fighting. Nonetheless, our sample includes a substantial proportion of individuals who joined the factions as children and were over 18 when the war came to an end.

12 Our measure of abusiveness used answers to eight related questions given by respondents who fought in the same area, for the same faction, during the same period of the

war. The weights derived from a factor analysis were then used to create a single index of *abusiveness*, which ranges from 0 to 1.

Bibliography

Agence France Press (AFP) (1995) 'Boutros-Ghali Calls for Democracy in Sierra Leone Ahead of Trip'. 24 November.

Annan, J. and Christopher B. (2008) 'The Reintegration of Child and Youth Combatants in Northern Uganda: Myth and Reality', draft chapter, this volume.

Berdal, M. (1996) *Disarmament and Demobilization after Civil Wars: Arms, Soldiers, and the Termination of Conflict.* Adelphi Paper no. 303. Oxford: Oxford University Press.

Blattman, C. (2006) The Consequences of Child Soldiering. Manuscript. University of California, Berkeley.

Collier, P. and Hoeffler, A. (2004) 'Greed and Grievance in Civil War', *Oxford Economic Papers* 56 (4): 563–595.

Comninos, S., Stavros, A. and Stewart, B. (2002) *Assessment of the Reintegration Programmes of the National Committee for Disarmament, Demobilization, and Reintegration.* Freetown, Sierra Leone.

DDRP (2004) *Summary of Programme Achievements.* Public Presentation.

Doyle, M. and Sambaing, N. (2006) *Making War and Building Peace: United Nations Peace Operations.* Princeton: Princeton University Press.

Dyregrov, A., Jested, R. and Rundle, M. (2002) 'Children Exposed to Warfare: A Longitudinal Study', *Journal of Traumatic Stress* 15 (1): 59–68.

FAO Food and Security Atlas (2004) Sierra Leone. 2004. Online, available at: http://www.daco-sl.org/encyclopedia/2_data/2_4_fao.htm (accessed 13 April).

Gberie, L. (2005) *A Dirty War in West Africa: The RUF and the Destruction of Sierra Leone.* Bloomington and Indianapolis: Indiana University Press.

Geri, L. (2005) *A Dirty War in West Africa: The RUF and the Destruction of Sierra Leone.* Bloomington: Indiana University Press.

Ginifer, J. (2003) 'Reintegration of Ex-Combatants'. In S. Meek, T. Thokozani, J. Ginifer and P. Coke (eds), *Sierra Leone: Building the Road to Recovery.* Institute for Security Studies Monograph no. 80. Pretoria, South Africa: Institute for Security Studies.

Human Rights Watch (HRW) (2005) *Youth, Poverty and Blood: The Lethal Legacy of West Africa's Regional Warriors.* New York: Human Rights Watch.

Humphreys, M. and Weinstein, J. (2004) 'What the Fighters Say', Center for Globalization and Sustainable Development Working Paper, Columbia University, New York.

Humphreys, M. and Weinstein, J. (2007) 'Demobilization and Reintegration', *Journal of Conflict Resolution.*

Husain, S.A., Nair, N., Holcomb, W., Reid, J., Vargas, V. and Nair, S.S. (1998) 'Stress Reactions of Children and Adolescents in War and Siege Conditions', *American Journal of Psychiatry* 155 (12): 1718–1719.

International Peace Academy (IPA) (2002) *A Framework for Lasting Disarmament, Demobilization and Reintegration of Former Combatants in Crisis Situations.* New York: International Peace Academy.

Keen, D. (2005) *Conflict and Collusion in Sierra Leone.* Oxford: James Currey.

Kostner, M., Colletta, N. and Widerhofer, I. (1996) *Case Studies in War-to-Peace Transition: The Demobilization and Reintegration of Ex-Combatants in Ethiopia, Namibia, and Uganda.* Washington, DC: World Bank.

Mazurana, D., McKay, S., Carlson, K. and Kasper, J. (2002) 'Girls in Fighting Forces and Groups: Their Recruitment, Participation, Demobilization, and Reintegration', *Peace and Conflict: Journal of Peace Psychology* 8 (2): 97–123.

Miguel, E. and Kremer, M. (2004) 'Worms: Identifying Impacts on Health and Education in the Presence of Treatment Externalities', *Econometrica* 72 (1): 159–217.

Molloy, D. (2004) *The DDR Process in Sierra Leone: An Overview and Lessons Learned*. Freetown: UNAMSIL.

Richards, P. (1996) *Fighting for the Rainforest: War, Youth, and Resources in Sierra Leone*. Oxford: Heinemann.

Richards, P., Archibald, S., Bah, K. and Vincent, J. (2003) *Where Have All The Young People Gone? Transitioning Ex-Combatants Towards Community Reconstruction After The War In Sierra Leone*. Unpublished report.

Spear, J. (2002) 'Disarmament and Demobilization'. In S.J. Stedman, D. Rothchild and E.M. Cousens (eds), *Ending Civil Wars: The Implementation of Peace Agreements*. Boulder: Lynne Rienner.

Stavrou, A., Vincent, J., Peters, K., Burton, P. and Johnson, S. (2003) *Tracer Study and Follow-Up Assessment of the Reintegration Component of Sierra Leone's Disarmament, Demobilization, and Reintegration Program*. Centre for Sustainable Livelihoods, University of Ireland, Cork.

Summit Communications (2006) 'Interview with President Ahmad Tejan Kabbah' (6 March). Online, available at: www.summitreports.com/sierraleone2006/interview11.htm.

United Nations (2000) *The Role of United Nations Peacekeeping in Disarmament, Demobilization, and Reintegration: Report of the Secretary General*. New York: UN.

UNWG (2006) *Integrated Disarmament, Demobilization and Reintegration Standards (IDDRS)*. Online, available at: www.unddr.org/iddrs/.

3 Measuring reintegration in Liberia

Assessing the gap between outputs and outcomes

James Pugel

> In conflict resolution, Liberians try to find the Solomonic way forward – where everyone can be a winner. To understand the cultural context of 'forgive and forget' one must contrast and examine the 'win-win' outcome proposed by Liberians with the 'right-wrong' outcome that is often sought by Westerners. However, there will always be people who will not accept the win-win or split difference solutions and will bear grudges. Some of them can be expected to act on them.[1]

Over a decade ago Mats Berdal (1996: 66) lamented the 'general failure to plan and coordinate activities among UN agencies, donor-countries and NGOs related to both the long-term and more immediate requirements of ex-combatants'. These challenges have only grown in the intervening years. The deficiencies in DDR planning, implementation and evaluation continue to re-emerge and meaningful solutions are in short supply. Until recently, the absence of a clear DDR doctrine or widely agreed output and outcome indicators has contributed to ambiguity.[2] The paradigmatic benchmark of DDR success – whether or not a state relapses into war – takes us only so far. This chapter argues that the linkages between DDR outputs and desired outcomes remain poorly defined.

Through examination of the case of Liberia, the chapter asks why this 'gap' in expected DDR outputs and outcomes persists. The resulting confusion can frustrate field practitioners and overall intervention efforts. Generating a satisfactory answer is important in the context of peace-support operations and post-conflict recovery efforts. Owing to the emergence of Results Based Management (RBM) as a cornerstone of aid effectiveness, it is all the more important for practitioners, policy-makers and scholars to revisit approaches to DDR planning, implementation, and monitoring and evaluation in order to demonstrate legitimate returns. The chapter finds that confusion over bureaucratic roles and responsibilities with respect to DDR planning are in large part to blame.[3] Unless concepts are mutually agreed and understood, it is likely that proponents of DDR will continue to harvest only minimal returns (and confuse outputs with outcomes).[4]

Adjusting the overall scope of DDR is a critical step that can shape future policy: a parallel *vice sequential approach* to programming reintegration along side disarmament and demobilization may be in order. Put another way, it may be the case that targeted reintegration programmes are not the best mechanism for promoting combatant livelihoods. While shorter-term reinsertion benefits and assistance can play a role in incentivizing disarmament, dealing with short-run security concerns, or covering basic needs, reintegration outcomes may be better served through broader 'structural' programmes focused on improving infrastructure, getting banking systems working and attracting private sector investment. Either way, DDR supporters would do well to adopt a more robust approach to programme monitoring and evaluation. In closing the gap between ascribed outputs and outcomes, evidence-based policy can enhance understanding of the context in which DDR occurs and contribute to the generation of baseline data in order to quantify the efficacy of a given programme.

This chapter is divided into four parts. The first section provides a background on the Liberian conflict and the context within which DDR proceeded. The second section presents a range of confounding factors and intervening variables that influence the design and implementation of DDR. It also proposes a comprehensive definition of reintegration. The third section details the methodologies employed by the author in conducting field research to assess the efficacy of the Liberian DDR programme (2003–present) and considers the implications of these findings for future policy. The final section offers a number of reflections on the Liberian experience and its implications for global DDR more generally.

Liberia's long war

The war in Liberia has long roots and can be traced back to the landing of freed American slaves to the territory in 1822. It is ironic that a country first conceived as part of a 'humanitarian programme' to repatriate former slaves descended into a repressive oligarchic state (Liebenow 1969). The dream of a classless society based on equal representation quickly evaporated. While representing only a fraction of the population, the elitist class of Americo-Liberians[5] rapidly presided over indigenous Africans from its independence in 1847 until the regime was finally toppled in a military coup in 1980. According to Levitt (2005: 195), 'the coup was the manifestation of 158 years of pent-up settler-native and civil society-government (post-1950s) hostilities, spawned by a socio-political order that never evolved fully to accommodate Liberia's diverse and dynamic population'.

What is widely regarded as Liberia's contemporary civil war began in 1989 after Charles Taylor crossed into the country from neighbouring Côte d'Ivoire. The war is often divided by experts into three distinct chronological phases. The first was triggered by the Taylor insurgency (December 1989) and includes the siege of Monrovia, the first international intervention,[6] the assassination of President Samuel Doe, and an eventual 'democratic' process that installed Charles Taylor as president in 1997. The second phase entailed a brief lull (1997–1999) in the civil war during which time Taylor continued the legacy of elitist authoritarian rule in Liberia and decimated his opponents. This interlude exacerbated the disenfranchisement of many Liberians and ratcheted-up hostilities in the hinterland as well as with neighbouring countries. President Taylor's record of terror[7] set the stage for the final phase of the war (1999–2003) – an insurgency that would ultimately drive him into exile.

Crucially for this chapter, this third stage also witnessed the emergence of an insurgency that spawned a new rebel group – the Liberians United for Reconciliation and Democracy (LURD) – with backing from neighbouring Guinean President Lansana Conte in 1999. Fighting in Liberia's northern Lofa County intensified in 2001 and reached Monrovia by June 2003. By this time, a second rebel faction intent upon the removal of Taylor from power emerged from the eastern part of the country – the Movement for Democracy in Liberia (MODEL) – and was reportedly backed by the government of the Côte d'Ivoire (ICG 2003). With the capital city, Monrovia, surrounded, Charles Taylor reluctantly accepted an invitation for asylum from the Nigerian government and departed Liberia in mid-August 2003.

After more than 14 years of internal strife and external interference, the Republic of Liberia is now on the mend. With the signing of the Accra Comprehensive Peace Agreement (CPA) in August 2003, all former warring factions (including government troops) demonstrated a commitment to formal post-conflict recovery and reconstruction. A major pillar of the stabilization process included a disarmament, demobilization, rehabilitation and reintegration (DDRR) programme. By mid-September 2003 the United Nations Mission in Liberia (UNMIL) was established by Security Council resolution 1509 with a mandate to support the implementation of the ceasefire agreement. In the absence of a clear victor in the war, the CPA dictated a power-sharing agreement, and the National Transitional Government of Liberia (NTGL) was organized with a politically neutral Monrovian businessman, Charles Gyude Bryant, assuming leadership duties as chairman.

The formal completion of the disarmament and demobilization phases in December 2004 coincided with the 2005 democratic elections. Multi-party elections were relatively peaceful during October 2005, and a highly competitive, constitutionally mandated two-candidate run-off took place in November 2005. The inauguration of the first elected female African head of state occurred in January 2006, and the country has since continued the process of reconciling and rebuilding. These international and domestic developments appear to have generated some important dividends. For example, the Liberia National Police (LNP) attributed a low crime rate in 2005 to UNMIL presence and optimism that accompanied the presidential elections (LNP 2006). Much of the stability that enabled a smooth democratic transition is attributed to the focus on the disarmament process, which, paradoxically, had also been singled out as a failure in the last round of international interventions from 1994 to 1997 (UNOSAA 2005).

Defining a DDRR strategy

As noted in the Introduction, DDR is the conventional label ascribed to a cluster of post-conflict interventions focused on collecting arms, neutralizing potential spoilers, reintegrating legitimate ex-combatants into the armed forces or civilian life and preventing war recurrence. In Liberia, the CPA mandated that a DDRR[8] programme be established and launched no later than 60 days after the installation of the transitional government (CPA 2003). While the 'rehabilitation'[9] component was introduced by peace negotiators, its specific purpose and expected outcomes were never clarified. This lack of clarity persisted throughout the implementation of the DDRR process. The only tangible indication of rehabilitation appears to be the provision of a short session with a psychological counsellor during demobilization.[10]

In order to understand the extent of the gap between outputs and outcomes, this chapter first considers the historical and political context in which DDRR planners prepared the programme. Revisiting the strategic design of DDRR in Liberia can provide insights into the motivations and trade-offs facing policymakers and practitioners at the time. Indeed, crucial to any robust impact or outcome evaluation is an understanding of a given programme's objectives and assumptions.[11] From the beginning, the process was supported by a centralized committees composed of foreign experts. Relevant baseline data was extremely limited.[12] Within two months of the CPA, international donors established an interim secretariat that compiled together a *DDRR Strategic Framework*. The framework's purpose was to provide the overarching strategy and objectives for ensuring 'the consolidation of peace through comprehensive disarmament, demobilization and sustainable reintegration of all ex-combatants into civilian society' (Draft Interim Secretariat 2003: 6). In addition to the disarmament and demobilization objectives, the authors[13] of the framework laid out what they believed to be the critical indicators of social, economic and political reintegration 'success'.

While the framework usefully focused on the disarmament and demobilization objectives, the proposed outcomes for rehabilitation and reintegration were less precise. Specifically, the outcomes for social reintegration were amongst the most detailed, while indicators for economic and political reintegration were vague and difficult to operationalize or quantify. For example, economic measures of reintegration were expressed as activities and opportunities for ex-combatants rather than targeted economic outcomes.[14] Likewise, the political dimension of reintegration was curiously summarized as (a reduction in) 'socio-political instability risk' (Draft Interim Secretariat 2003: 78) arising from unmet 'peace dividends'. Combatants were also regarded as a menacing problem to be resolved: the 'government views ex-combatants as a high-risk group whose adjustment to civilian life must be assured with targeted interventions and be monitored carefully' (Draft Interim Secretariat 2003: 15).[15] Reintegration of these high-risk groups was to be achieved through 'community-based support', with 'community resources' expected to support ex-combatant reintegration to the 'greatest extent possible' (Draft Interim Secretariat 2003: 15). A later strategic reintegration framework document emphasized a more 'targeted' approach and envisaged a two-and-a-half year transition period where after former combatants would 'be treated like every other member of the community' (UNDP 2004: 8).

Implementing DDRR in Liberia

The DDRR programme was launched less than four months after the signing of the CPA and registered more than 103,000 ex-combatants and associated parties between December 2003 and December 2004. Eleven separate cantonment sites[16] were established by UNMIL in order to facilitate the disarmament and demobilization (DD) process in three separate phases from early December 2003 to late October 2004.[17] Criteria for programme inclusion were conditional and changed over the course of the intervention. For most adult males, a serviceable weapon or ammunition was required. In order to meet UNICEF standards, this condition was waived for children under the age of 18 and women recognized as being associated with the fighting forces. While the mission succeeded in processing a high volume of combatants in a short period of time, the overall numbers fell short of expectations: the highest estimate of *armed* forces predicted by the international community was only 53,000.[18] With fewer than 30,000 weapons collected for the more than 100,000 registered combatants, many observers began to doubt whether the disarmament process had been effective at all.[19]

Unlike the DD process, the reintegration component was under-funded from the beginning. Established provisions for reintegration included opportunities for vocational or agricultural training or for formal education. In early September 2006 (nearly two years after DD), only 44 per cent (45,166) of the previously disarmed ex-combatants were enrolled in a reintegration training programme.[20] By January 2007 the number climbed to near 60 per cent, but rumours of funding shortages for the remaining beneficiaries were circulating.[21] According to the head of the National Commission for DDRR (NCDDRR), by mid-April 2007 there were still an estimated 23,000 beneficiaries requiring access to reintegration assistance.[22] Confounding the monitoring of reintegration activities was the lack of external agency collaboration, particularly with the US Agency for International Development (USAID) which was reluctant to integrate its efforts into the broader UN-coordinated DDRR framework.[23] UNDP programme benefits did eventually move beyond the narrow targeting of ex-combatants and extended into communities of return. A community-based programme effort that undoubtedly generated positive spillover effects was the UNDP's Community Based Recovery (CBR) Programme.[24]

Challenges in design and evaluation

There are many challenges associated with evaluating a DDR programme. Ambiguous strategic planning throughout a programming and implementation cycle can undermine assessments and desired outcomes themselves. Although substantive empirical research is gradually emerging on DDR impacts, there is an urgent need to assist policy-makers and practitioners in staying ahead of the curve. But how does one undertake DDR in environments characterized by ongoing hostilities, with limited surveillance data, with political pressures to demonstrate success and the absence of functional monitoring and evaluation? The international community would benefit from condensing DDR into a feasible intervention instrument and agreeing on how to approach post-conflict reintegration in order to demonstrate convincing outcomes. What is more, it will need to invest in robust data collection strategies that support evidence-based policy decision-making.

The UN has made some important strides in meeting some of these objectives. As signalled in the introduction to this volume, in an effort to develop a meaningful doctrine to guide DDR, the IDDRS was launched in late 2006.[25] In the years preceding the publication of the IDDRS, DDR programmes were regularly lauded and eventually assumed an essential pillar of the war to peace transition despite systematic evaluations (Muggah 2005: 289). The absence of a robust doctrine during this period potentially hindered DDR design and evaluation. For example, each separate DDR operation administered by the UN constituted a more or less new experience that typically yielded inefficiencies, redundancies and poor planning. The absence of a coherent DDR doctrine and the inability of planners to define a realistic scope potentially facilitated the burgeoning of 'mission creep'[26] and the inflation of donor and beneficiary expectations far beyond the capacity and purpose of the enterprise.

These early security promotion activities – especially disarmament – were recognized by Western donors as prerequisites of peace-building and peace consolidation. The cognitive association of disarmament with peace appears to have cemented the importance of this intervention tool in peace-keeping missions. The early successes recorded by disarmament programmes in retrieving weapons and unearthing caches likely sustained a virtuous cycle of more investment from donors. But as these interventions rolled-on, some observers began to register concerns about the way in which disarmed ex-combatants were exposed to security dilemmas in the absence of other opportunities for meaningful reintegration. Caramés *et al.* (2006), for example, noted how while DD initiatives typically lasted 16 months,[27] the reintegration and rehabilitation processes frequently persisted much longer, extending for five years or more. While the UN struggled to ensure the stability of many post-conflict countries and performed many DD interventions, the longer-term reintegration processes have proven to be more burdensome requiring a sustained commitment long after most donors had shifted to the next hot spot.[28]

Implementation and evaluation

In the case of Liberia, not unlike other post-conflict environments, DDR was not neatly pre-packaged. While ECOWAS negotiated the ceasefire between the warring factions in Accra, the UN waited patiently until the final terms were agreed.[29] A month after the signing of the CPA, UNMIL was authorized and, within four months, disarmament operations were launched. In a country that was decimated by more than a decade of acute collective violence, the international aid and security architecture had literally four months to define a strategic plan that provided for national security, disarmament of tens of thousands of combatants, the return or resettlement of hundreds of thousands of displaced citizens, massive humanitarian aid operations, and the establishment of conditions for free and fair elections. All of this was to be done without causing unintentional harm[30] and preventing Liberia from sliding back into protracted warfare.

The sheer scale of the challenges facing the UN and its partners was breathtaking. How could the international community and the nascent government plan for long-term reintegration when the majority of the country was still inaccessible and 50 to 80 per cent of its infrastructure had been destroyed?[31] How could beneficiaries be identified and registered so as to ensure that a traumatized civilian population realized a meaningful peace dividend? How could one construct a coherent reintegration plan that accounted for a variety of displaced persons (e.g. soldiers, internally displaced persons, or IDPs, and refugees) spontaneously resettling to their communities of origin without precipitating violence? To answer these questions, it is important to gain an appreciation of the organizational dynamics that led the warring parties to conflict and develop theories of post-conflict communal reintegration that enable an accurate measurement of the progress of intervention programmes.[32]

DDR programmes should be guided by a clear strategy, coherent design, and a proper outcome monitoring and evaluation plan. For DDR interventions, evaluation (and implementation) may be confounded by a failure to appropriately develop and implement a results-based management strategy. The comparatively recent introduction of RBM approaches within the UN is expected to hasten the 'pick-up' of effective planning models in the field.[33] Central to RBM is an emphasis on a strategic framework that relates services, products and procedure to clearly articulated and transparent results. Clearly supporting evidence-based policy, the functions of outcome monitoring and evaluation are critical to RBM strategies.[34] Fundamental to both outcome monitoring and evaluation is the collection of baseline data, which for monitoring enables change tracking, and for evaluation, a tangible reference for validating programme results and why they were or were not achieved.[35] The RBM paradigm shifts the focus from programme-specific outputs (how many weapons collected) to objective outcomes (incidence of weapons-related criminal activity within a community), but the shift also requires an understanding and application of the fundamental difference between the two if the gap is to be bridged. Although outputs are an important intermediate indicator, it is outputs that genuinely measure efficacy.

In Liberia, a plethora of qualitative and quantitative studies have recently been implemented at the micro or individual level.[36] Micro-level research is intent on examining the individual-level outcomes and determinants embedded within the macro process. In the case of DDR evaluations, it is anticipated that micro-level findings will reveal important nuances within their targeted area for practitioners while simultaneously validating observed macro-level outcomes that are of concern to higher-order policy-makers. It is also abundantly clear that these empirical studies have yielded comparatively limited impact on relevant policy-makers. Externally, the International Peace Academy (IPA) critiqued UN actors for failing to back programme and policy decisions with empirical evidence (IPA 2006). A recent UNDP *Practice Note* on DDR (2006: 23) also identified shortcomings in DDR programme evaluation worldwide: 'the lack of clearly defined impact indicators for monitoring and evaluation has been a major weakness'. While the UN struggles to inject more rigour into its programmatic interventions, the impact evaluation literature must also seek to align itself more effectively to practitioner needs for relevance and ease of implementation.

Unpacking reintegration outcomes

The connection between outputs and outcomes for the process of post-conflict reintegration continue to puzzle the international community and governments. To be sure, recording the number of combatants and weapons registered and collected provide easily quantifiable measures (outputs) of disarmament. But the process of measuring reintegration outputs and outcomes is substantially more subjective and complex. Complexity alone, however, may not be a satisfactory excuse for failing to identify or design appropriate interventions to achieve the desirable outcomes. This sub-section contends that the process of establishing reintegration programmes often features ill-defined outcomes that are nevertheless vital to programming interventions and assessing their efficacy. The resulting ambiguity perpetuates the gap and impedes success.

The process of reintegration should not be envisioned in a narrow or unidimensional context if intervention outcomes are to be achieved. Anderson and Olson (2003: 11) discuss how two realities need to be acknowledged when it comes to planning peace programme interventions. First, it is import to recognize that conflicts are highly differentiated (and therefore require different strategies in designing evaluations) and second, 'process is inextricably linked to the outcome' (read: garbage in, garbage out). This raises a fundamental question: how to unpack reintegration in order to ensure a tailored process that leads to achieving desired outcomes? Arguably, part of the complexity confounding reintegration programming relates to a failure to obtain consensus on how to approach and define the overall anticipated outcome (i.e. 'successful' reintegration) and then disaggregate the phenomenon into manageable outputs.

There are considerable debates among scholars and practitioners relating to the challenges accompanying the reintegration of ex-combatants. One strand emerged in the wake of the *IDDRS* (UNWG 2006) as noted above.[37] While the recent effort to consolidate knowledge on DDF generated a greater awareness of the challenges facing practitioners, concrete and practical insights on the reintegration enigma are more elusive. But there are important precedents in the debate on reintegration. For example, Berdal (1996) acknowledged the import- ance of the 'economic' and 'social' dimensions of reintegration a decade before the IDDRS were produced. Likewise, in 2000, the UNDP noted that the agency 'should concentrate its support to *political, social and economic reintegration* of war-affected populations on restoring social and human capital while contribut- ing to political and economic stability' (UNDP 2000: 55, italics added). Kingma (2002) also adopted a threefold approach to conceptualizing reintegration while also signalling a 'psychological' facet. Baaré (Chapter 9, this volume) similarly played an important role in highlighting the multidimensional features of reinte- gration. While Berdal, Kingma, the UNDP and Baaré recognized that the process of reintegration is multifaceted, the UN (2006b) nevertheless adopted a narrow definition with that privileged social and economic determinants.[38] And while a concise definition is more user-friendly and accessible, an overly narrow definition that excludes critical components can unintentionally hinder 'effec- tiveness'.

Problematically, academics and practitioners have yet to agree on a common definition or approach to reintegration and the interconnections between separate components. Without a coherent conceptual starting point to operationalize rein- tegration it will continue to be exceedingly difficult to measure outcomes. This challenge is exemplified by the conflation of 'social' and 'societal' reintegration. The expression 'social' refers to the 'productive capacities of a human being such as health, education, age, gender, hunger and poverty' (Lichem 2006). Despite the propensity among experts to refer to 'social' indicators in the DDR literature, Lichem (2006) contends that 'societal' – which carries a very different connotation – should be the starting point.[39] Reinforcing Lichem's view after an exhaustive examination of ex-combatant reintegration, Anders Nilsson not only agrees with conceptualizing reintegration as a multidimensional process, but is astounded by the paucity of theory available to aid in informing policy decisions. His conclusion is that reintegration 'should be seen as a societal process aiming at the economic, political and social assimilation of ex- combatants and their families into civil society' (Nilsson 2005: 27).

While the debates in the qualitative literature continue to search for a way forward, two empirical studies have examined the influence of multidimensional reintegration engagements. In the case of Sierra Leone, Humphreys and Wein- stein (Chapter 2, this volume) find that, due to low correlations between various outcomes, and an insignificant reliability measure that was estimated using Cronbach's alpha, reintegration on one dimension is typically not a good predic- tor of reintegration on another dimension. Similarly, Pugel (2007a) found that an examination of reintegration as a multifaceted process offered considerable explanatory power. Exploratory cluster alignment of reintegration outcomes under the qualitative headings of 'societal' and 'economic' appeared to indicate stronger relationships within their respective clusters (multidimensional) than between them (unidimensional). While this evidence is not conclusive, it does corroborate the qualitative literature.[40]

What is needed for closing the gap between outputs and outcomes is a comprehensive definition of reintegration that adequately captures its multiple dimensions and implications. For the purpose of this chapter, reintegration is defined as *a multidimensional, post-conflict and peace-building*[41] *intervention process that enables communities to reform anew after conflict and accepts their displaced and war-affected population as fully-fledged citizens. This long-term endeavour requires a secure environment as a pre-condition to pursing the requisite societal, economic, political and psychological outcomes for sustained peace, prosperity and progress.* Thus armed with a more precise definition, it may be possible to overcome conceptual and terminological opacity that characterizes much of the programming field. Clear definitions and labels can enhance the coherence of doctrine, better align mission objectives to outcome indicators and guide effective monitoring and evaluation.

Analysis and discussion

> *They took the gun from me – they make my heart free.*
> (Male ex-combatant in Zwedru, Grand Gedeh County, February 2006)

This section reviews research undertaken on DDR in Liberia. It focuses in on the results of two impact and outcome evaluations commissioned by UNDP[42] and UNMIL[43] and compares findings from these studies with other recent assessments. The section finds that 'success' was largely obstructed by a range of confounding pre-conditions that will be reviewed below. Before turning to the findings, however, a critical first step in undertaking scientific evaluations in support of evidence-based policy is the preparation of an appropriate research design and sampling frame. Recognition of the challenges of probability sampling and sources of bias are crucial features of robust assessments. If generalizable and unbiased claims are to be rendered to guide national priority setting and resource allocation, a rigorous and transparent approach is of central importance. The section begins with a discussion of research design and methodology in order to set the context for the second half of the section which considers the findings and potential implications.

Establishing a sample frame and research design

Obtaining a sampling frame that accurately reflects the ex-combatant population in Liberia is not straightforward. At the very least, it requires a substantial knowledge about the characteristics of the population sub-group and access to denominator data drawn from registration or census exercises. Two overarching characteristics that define the population of former combatants in Liberia include:

1   those who registered for DDRR benefits, and
2   those who opted to reintegrate spontaneously and not register for entitlements.

Acknowledging this distinction is important because DDRR programme impacts were tested and analysed against both of these parameters. Latent discrimination of these characteristics in the sample frame was the first hurdle in rendering a statistical generalization. For the purposes of understanding DDRR in the context of a 'treatment' that is to be assessed (against those not treated), it is important to note that all members of the population with this characteristic self-selected themselves into the programme.

While there were over 103,000 registered, self-reported ex-combatants, the number of ex-combatants that did not register is nowhere documented. In order to establish a viable sample frame that would be reflective of the population of former combatants residing in Liberia, two independent sources were utilized. For the population of combatants who registered, a database query from the NCDDRR[44] was obtained with up-to-date beneficiary statistics. To account for the number of fighters that did not register a best-guess estimate was developed based upon the DDR non-participation rate of 13 per cent uncovered by Humphreys and Weinstein (2004: 30) in Sierra Leone.[45] Also critical to the formulation of the sampling frame was the disaggregation of the parameter of DDRR participation. Recognizing that this parameter is most likely not homogeneous, a NCDDRR database query was run so as to discriminate among those registered ex-combatants who had completed their course of reintegration training, those who were currently enrolled in reintegration training, and those who had disarmed. It is then possible to understand the utility of the respondent sample that was drawn during the studies by checking the percentages surveyed in each of the four population parameters.

As illustrated in Pugel (2007a), none of the four major population parameters in the sample deviated from the sample frame by more than 4 per cent in the February 2006 study and by no more than 8 per cent in the September 2006 study (Amara *et al.* 2006). In both studies, age appeared appropriately distributed as designed and gender-sampled proportionately in the UNDP study but slightly under-sampled in the UNMIL study. Since the DDRR programme was under way when both studies were called for and a portion of the population had already received a 'treatment' (i.e. registered and receiving benefits) and given the fact that a baseline study had not been conducted, the most appropriate research methodology was a non-equivalent control group, post-test-only, quasi-experiment design.[46]

Probability sampling methods

Both assessments employed an analogous approach to obtaining a representative, random sample with the only difference being the size of the targeted sample. The approach replicated methodologies implemented by Humphreys and Weinstein in Sierra Leone, but with modifications for the Liberian case (see Chapter 2, this volume). Many of the methods adopted in the Liberia study, including the survey instrument, may enhance future comparative assessments.[47] The UNDP study was designed to collect 1,200 interviews (600 ex-combatants and 600 non-combatants) from 30 geographic clusters of 40 respondents each, and the UNMIL study was designed to collect 1,050 interviews (all ex-combatant) from 70 geographic clusters of 15 respondents each.[48] Ultimately, 1,190 interviews were returned satisfactorily for the UNDP study and 944 for the UNMIL study. For both studies, all 66 administrative districts of Liberia were considered in a random selection process and weighted in accordance with the resettlement preferences indicated by ex-combatants on their demobilization intake forms.[49] Once the requisite geographic clusters were identified at the administrative district level, community locations were randomly selected through incorporation of unique identifiers (p-codes)[50] using a random number generation technique. Variation across Greater Monrovia was gained by randomly selecting clusters across the 12 metropolitan zones.

At the community level, data collection teams introduced themselves to the appropriate chiefs or elders and solicited their assistance in obtaining a pool of prospective candidates for the study. Consent was gained from each candidate, and a final random selection of the respondents available in the targeted location was conducted. Ideally, the pool of respondents was to be two to three times larger than the requisite numbers, and the field team would select every second or third respondent for inclusion in the study. In some of the more rural locations, however, this method was not feasible due to a lack of potential respondents. For the UNMIL study, all ages were included in the study. For the UNDP study, the sample was limited to those respondents over the age of 18. In each geographic region, the field teams were also directed to obtain a quota of 20 per cent female respondents to ensure adequate gender representation in the sample in order to ensure a sample that was reflective of the study's sample frame.

Sources of bias

Field research is challenging in any post-conflict environment and it is exceedingly difficult to completely overcome bias in a given sample. Recognizing the limitations of associated statistical generalizations that may be inferred from the collected sample becomes especially important. Many of the sources of bias detailed here are not unlike those encountered in similar country cases overseen by other researchers.[51] The longer planning and execution period as well as a favourable climate during the collection of the UNDP data mitigated a great deal of bias, while a shorter planning and execution cycle coupled with poorer weather that was characteristic of the UNMIL collection effort resulted in data that was more susceptible to bias. The ten questionnaires from the UNDP sample that were rejected for study consideration were improperly filled out by the field team and could not be used. For the UNMIL study, because of weather, time constraints, and security concerns, the field team was unable to collect 10 per cent of the targeted 1,050 surveys.[52]

Both studies also suffer from the possible introduction of bias due to four other complicating factors – respondent selection, truth telling, survey length, and spillover effects. While every effort was made to ensure a random selection, it must be recognized that the chiefs and elders of the community helped to arrange the pool of possible respondents.[53] This approach most certainly did not account for 100 per cent of the population of former combatants within the targeted town or village.[54] As with any sensitive topic, respondent deception is also another source of potential bias. While Liberian combatants were not under threat of criminal prosecution by the state at the time of the surveys,[55] truthful admission to wartime activities by some element of the sample is potentially suspect as cautioned by both Wood (2003) and Weinstein (2007: 354). The lengthy survey administered by the field team is another source of potential bias that should be considered: exhaustion by both enumerators and respondents may have led to incorrectly marked responses and a modest number of non-responses. Finally, spillover effects might have affected those respondents who did not register for benefits with the DDRR as the programme not only targeted individuals but also eventually supported the development of communities at a more meso level.

Findings and implications

With an understanding of the nature and character of the respondent samples, it is possible to discuss the findings. There are a number of theoretical and practical implications arising from the research undertaken in Liberia. Taken as a whole, they underline the persistent inability of international agencies and government planners to effectively plan and monitor DDRR interventions. Solid longitudinal assessments can push the debate on effectiveness from anecdote to fact. They also reveal contradictions to prevailing DDR orthodoxies. The remainder of the section considers a range of factors that influenced the efficacy of the Liberian DDRR reintegration intervention effort and calls into question how the intervention was designed and executed. The findings highlight the gap between outputs and outcomes and find that success for reintegration programmes are potentially inhibited by a number of confounding pre-conditions and were not corrected or accounted for.

Baseline data collection activities and missed opportunity

The way a mission is organized and its relative coherence will necessarily impact on the efficacy of subsequent reintegration programmes. In order to understand reintegration efforts, it is crucial to understand the context in which they were derived. In DDR, the registration of combatants during the disarmament phase provides practitioners with their first opportunity for large-scale primary data collection. But in the Liberian case, several factors relating to the disarmament process must be considered before synthesizing and reaching conclusions. DDRR planners responsible for developing entry criteria clearly established that they wanted to avoid the '*monetization* of weapons that comes from traditional arms buy-back programmes' and that weapons turn-in would not be a mandatory requisite for programme inclusion (Draft Interim Secretariat 2003: 13) – an important planning aspect for understanding programme outputs.

While the weapon-to-soldier ratio is one of the lowest recorded by a DDR programme (0.28),[56] it should also be recalled that 19,350 combatants were formally registered as women or children associated with fighting forces and entered without a weapon.[57] How does this output correlate with the possible objective outcome of 'reduced gun violence'? Empirical evidence collected to study the efficacy of the DDRR possibly suggests that most of the weapons were indeed either collected or pushed out of the country. Pugel (2006) indicated that in a sample of over 599 non-combatants drawn from the same geographic clusters as those in the nationwide survey of former fighters, less than 2.5 per cent of the respondents believed that small arms were a problem in their respective communities since the end of the formal disarmament period.[58] At the time of the author's study, it did not appear that a low combatant to weapon ratio could be equated with 'higher instances of gun violence' as conventional wisdom might suggest. Arguably, the mission had secured the requisite stable environment (outcome) for reintegration programmes to succeed without achieving an 'expected' output (high soldier to weapon ratio).

The manner in which prospective DDRR candidates were allowed to register in the programme, however, led to complications with ripple effects affecting the rest of the intervention.[59] The difficulties associated with registration are rooted in the ways that warring factions negotiated their force strengths (during the ceasefire talks), the way these forces were documented (by negotiators and practitioners) and how they were monitored. In the case of Liberia, mission representatives never actually knew with certainty the number of prospective combatants that would participate in DDRR.[60] The uncertainty over beneficiary numbers was compounded by the introduction of criteria that enabled a wider interpretation of the definition of combatant that allowed ammunition to be turned in lieu of weapons.[61] While this expansion of the criteria allowed unprecedented access to the DDRR programme, forecasting the number of beneficiaries was inaccurate and led to numerous complications as the programme progressed. There appears to be a general consensus that DDR interventions should be accessible to the broadest possible population.[62] Even so, accurate beneficiary predictions are required if donor confidence and support is to be sustained. The mission required that former warring factions submit accurate troop strengths, but was unable to compel faction leaders to do so during negotiations.

Compounding the inability to accurately estimate beneficiaries was a lack of attention given to the design of the disarmament intake forms – a critical baseline data collection instrument. Although a failure to properly design an intake form does not constitute a fatal threat to a DDR programme, in the case of Liberia, the mission lost a critical capability for not only understanding the circumstances of the participants to the conflict, but for planning the reintegration intervention and preparing for future monitoring and evaluation. In relation to weapons registration at the disarmament sites, the poorly formatted intake forms coupled with disastrous Military Observers' (MILOBs) handwriting resulted in significant inaccuracies entering the databases (Nichols 2005). Likewise, information critical to understanding the phenomenon of arms proliferation and acquisition was never acquired.[63] Information uniquely attributable to one of the former warring factions was also lost during the registration effort. The intake form did not originally include the option for a fighter to identify himself as government-aligned militia.[64] What is more, the intake form did provide for another category of affiliation – 'other'[65] – which only served to confuse a quantitative accounting of the combatants who engaged in the fighting. Disaggregated analysis (by faction) from the NCDDRR database is therefore biased and of limited use in analysing specific warring groups as the data are not truly generalizable with any degree of statistical certainty.[66]

Measurable outcomes: deciphering the dimensions of reintegration

As noted above, at least four dimensions of reintegration can be considered when planning a post-conflict intervention (e.g. societal, economic, political and psychological). Research efforts could usefully explore discrete indicators across these dimensions for mapping outcomes across time and space. Drawing from UNDP-supervised field collection efforts, Pugel (2007a) attempted to conceptualize and operationalize measurable outcomes of reintegration. An effort was made to evaluate reintegration against the impact of confounding factors drawn from three tiers – individual demographics, wartime experiences and community factors (see Table 3.1). Ten factors[67] were examined in light of their capacity to influence nine reintegration outcomes categorized under three of the four identified dimensions of reintegration – societal, political and economic (see Table 3.2). Unfortunately, data collected on the psychological dimension of reintegration was still under examination at the time of this writing. In examining outcomes associated with successful multidimensional reintegration (see Table 3.3), the economic dimension proved especially significant.[68] All three economic outcomes were statistically significant.[69] Across the dimension, six of the ten controlling factors (excluding the 'programmatic' variables) indicated a correlation with reintegration success, with four of the statistically significant variables impacting at least two of the three dimensional outcomes.[70]

While outcomes aligned fairly consistently with respect to magnitude across the regression models, the political dimension was especially difficult to assess. At the very least, the role of the political dimension requires attention given its notable absence from the IDDRS and related protocols. The limited attention to the political aspects of reintegration constitutes a hole in the strategic framework

Table 3.1 Quantifying dimensional outcomes of ex-combatant reintegration

Dimension	'Successful' outcome
Societal	Gains acceptance of the community
	Actively participates in social and community events
	Extended social networks beyond (ex)military circles
Economic	Engaged in livelihood-producing activities
	Earning a wage above the poverty line
	Exhibits spending patterns indicative of excess earning capacity
Political	Confidence in local community mechanism for dispute resolution
	Sever all social/economic ties with former faction members
	Confidence in democratic, non-violent political expression to effect change

of the Liberian DDRR programme. The failure to identify and operationalize this essential component area resulted in an absence of decidedly relevant information associated with ex-combatant reintegration and, subsequently, was not gathered by the integrated monitoring function of the mission's Joint Implementation Unit (JIU).[71] In a mission that is inherently political with numerous implications for human security, this gap represents a major oversight.

Of the three groupings of influencing/confounding factors – individual demographics, wartime experiences and community factors – the individual demographics were found to yield the most explanatory power in relation to interpreting reintegration success. While all five factors that were examined revealed a correlation with reintegration success, the variables marital status (married) and education level (higher) proved the most influential.

Table 3.2 Examining the factors that potentially influence reintegration outcomes

Areas of influence	Understanding factors that 'influence' reintegration	
	Estimating the impact of:	*Compare against:*
Programmatic	DDRR programme participation*	Non-participants
Individual demographics	Age: older participants	Younger participants
	Gender: female	Male
	Marital status: married	Not married
	Education: higher levels	Little to no education
	Home owners	Non-owners
Wartime experiences	Abduction (self-reported)	Recruits/volunteers
	Volunteer officers	All other officers/combatants
Community	Resettling in home community	Community 'strangers' (newcomers)
	Settling in the national capital	Settling outside of the capital
	Higher reported rates of crime	Lower reported rates of crime

Note
* Impact estimation requires assessments of three sub-samples of DDRR registered participants: those who have completed a course of reintegration training, those currently enrolled in training and those who have disarmed and demobilized but have yet to enter a training programme.

Table 3.3 What influences outcomes? (visualizing multidimensional reintegration)

Areas of influence	Factor	Reintegration dimensional effects*		
		Societal	*Economic*	*Political*
Programmatic**	DDRR programme (completed)	0 0 +	0 0 +	0 0 0
	DDRR programme (enrolled)	0 + +	0 0 0	0 0 0
	DDRR programme (no training)	0 0 +	− 0 0	− 0 +
Individual demographics	Age: older participants	0 0 0	0 0 +	0 0 0
	Gender: female	0 0 +	0 0 0	− 0 +
	Marital status: married	0 0 +	+ + +	− − 0
	Education: higher levels	0 0 +	0 + +	− 0 +
	Home owners	0 0 0	0 0 0	0 0 +
Wartime experiences	Abduction (self-reported)	0 0 0	− 0 0	0 0 +
	Volunteer officers	0 0 0	0 0 0	− 0 0
Community	Resettling in home community	0 0 0	− 0 0	0 0 0
	Settling in the national capital	0 0 0	− 0 0	0 0 +
	Higher reported rates of crime	0 0 0	0 0 0	− 0 +

Notes
*Number of statistically significant findings (at 10%) and their direction of magnitude (three outcomes were tested per dimension/per area of influence).
**Estimation compares the DDRR programme registrants against the sub-sample of programme non-participants.

Significantly, it was found that those respondents with a higher education level are reintegrating better socially and economically than those with lesser levels of education.[72] Most important, married respondents appear to represent a group that can be examined the most precisely within the framework of this study. The group of married respondents demonstrated a significant advantage in achieving reintegration success even though married former fighters appear to struggle in the political dimension.[73]

While research in Liberia yielded many important and nuanced findings with respect to the reintegration process, the extent to which DDRR has made a positive impact to date is more difficult to determine. Disaggregating the categories of ex-combatants for analysis into those who completed a course of reintegration training, those currently enrolled, those who had disarmed but had not yet enrolled in training, and those opting not to register but to reintegrate on their own revealed significant differences, by class, across the dimensions of reintegration. Pugel (2007a) identified that ex-combatants who registered with the NCDDRR were more likely to feel accepted within their chosen resettlement communities than those who chose not to formally disarm. When programme completers were compared with those ex-combatants who did not register for benefits, the completers, in addition to being accepted, were also more likely to be engaged in a livelihood-producing activity, including employment, school or home duties. Both findings were only weakly significant and subject to the methodological limitations and biases mentioned earlier in the chapter, but they provide a modicum of evidence that suggests that the DDRR intervention positively impacted the lives of many who participated.[74] The areas where success was observed also corresponded with areas addressed in the initial strategic framework.

Reintegration – a victim of altruistic culmination

Recently published guiding principles for UN peacekeeping operations (UNDPKO 2008: 26) unintentionally illustrate the disassociation between the DD and the R components and open the door for asking if the intervention tool is, indeed, overextended. The DPKO capstone document states that 'DDR is a critical part of efforts to create a secure and stable environment in which the process of recovery can begin'. The guidance proceeds to outline how UN peacekeeping missions 'are usually mandated to assist' in many of the security aspects of the DDR intervention, but when it comes to the critical reintegration process, 'other agencies … are responsible'. It should be recalled that the reintegration phase of a DDR programme is of a completely different character than the disarmament and demobilization processes. The first two stages typically focus on actors that were party to the conflict.[75] Disarmament and demobilization requires the establishment of an enabling environment – with an emphasis on security and restoring order. Access to various areas may be limited – even after a ceasefire and peace agreement – and meaningful security seldom emerges immediately after the deployment of a peacekeeping force. Ensuring a stable environment requires a concerted effort on behalf of interveners to secure and maintain the peace – at all costs. In the case of Liberia, while disarmament and demobilization were completed roughly a year after the ceasefire and violent crime was generally held in check, the burden of securing the peace as well as the cost of the un-forecasted programme over-subscription was debited against the long-term reintegration account (UNOWA 2005: 3).

Reintegration interventions require long-term investment and planning. Despite evidence recent shifts to 'collective' approaches, the focus in most DDR programmes tends to be on former combatants and less so on others in the community who are attempting to reintegrate (Muggah 2006). It should be recalled that in Liberia, as elsewhere, ex-combatants are not the sole community members who may have lost out during the conflict and forced to rebuild their lives. The combatant-centric approach raises an important question: can a reintegration process succeed if only a modest proportion of war-affected citizens' benefit? Liberia's conflict, for example, was devastating for an estimated 3.3 million citizens. Nearly one-third of the Liberian population is attempting to return home and regain their lives – but *only one in nine of the returnees will be a former combatant*. In light of these challenges, together with the stigmas attached to forced migrants and former combatants, there are questions as to whether it may be worth considering integrating reintegration efforts more efficiently with parallel aid programmes and partners.[76]

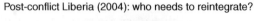

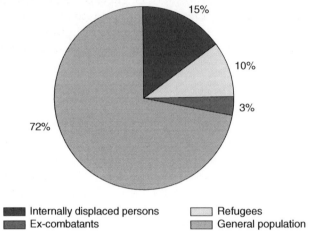

Post-conflict Liberia (2004): who needs to reintegrate?

15%

10%

3%

72%

| ■ Internally displaced persons | ☐ Refugees |
| ■ Ex-combatants | ▨ General population |

Figure 3.1 Quantifying the scope and magnitude of reintegration.

The reintegration component of the Liberian DDRR programme faced funding challenges throughout the course of the mission. The lack of funding has made it difficult for the implementers to execute the mission in accordance with the RBM outcomes stated in the original framework document. There is evidence that the Liberian reintegration programme was weakly constructed and poorly funded. Pugel (2006) found that there is a major risk of leaving behind a very vulnerable grouping of NCDDRR-registered ex-combatants – those who have disarmed and demobilized but have yet to receive training. This category of former fighters is the least educated, most agriculturally-oriented, and poorest of the four classes under investigation. While these fighters were found to have gained acceptance within their chosen resettlement communities and also demonstrated a commitment to breaking ties with their former factional leaders, they were also found to be more economically disadvantaged than those former fighters who chose to reintegrate on their own (Pugel 2007a). The group was also shown to have less faith in the democratic system than the category of ex-combatants that opted to self-reintegrate. Other research emphasizes the effect of funding and strategy shortfalls. In her study within the Liberian capital region, Jennings (2007, 2008) describes how unfulfilled expectations might have been mitigated if reintegration had been de-linked from the disarmament and demobilization phase of the DDRR programme. More important, however, the continued over-optimistic planning of reintegration outcomes too early in the intervention process has resulted in inflated expectations, delayed benefits, and broken promises for nearly 10 per cent of the beneficiary caseload.

As signalled in the introduction to this volume, DDR planners and practitioners may need to rethink reintegration. Indeed, DDR doctrine already calls for a transition from ostensibly security-related activities such as disarmament and demobilization to more developmental activities including reinsertion and reintegration. But bridging this gap in a planned and coordinated fashion has proven consistently challenging. A shift in programming focus and implementation may allow the international aid community to concentrate on collective, long-term and inclusive strategies targeting the majority of war-affected populations without compromising support for targeted ex-combatants.

Locating a way forward

Although the chapter has illustrated the empirical findings from the Liberia DDRR (2003–present) there is reason to believe that the general findings are applicable to other interventions. As other chapters in this volume amply show, the setting of objectives, outcomes of success and monitoring and evaluation mechanisms is regularly overlooked in DDR programming. Three important aspects of DDR programme design – baseline data collection, measurable outcomes and scope – are briefly reviewed here as a point of departure for locating a way forward.

Evidence-based policy and identifying measurable outcomes

There is growing interest in evidence-based policy in relation to development in general and DDR in particular (see Introduction, this volume). For example, the OECD *Paris Declaration* (2005)[77] emphasizes accountability and transparency and the importance of evidence-driven interventions. Determining the efficacy of future DDR programmes requires more unbiased research to inform and shape policy decisions. Owing to the fact that RBM is becoming more accepted (and expected) in donor circles, attention to measuring impacts and outcomes of DDR will likely grow. An important way for policy-makers and practitioners to ensure they develop accountable and effective DDR interventions is to develop quantifiable metrics that demonstrate real and relative efficacy. The essence of evidence-based policy-making is rooted in an unbiased, apolitical, rigorous research approach that results in quality policy options for decision-makers.[78] Employing a RBM strategy in a post-conflict environment requires the best available evidence for making decisions on the fate of a limited amount of funds.

There is value in collecting data that can be used to generalize to broader beneficiary populations. The compilation of comparable indicators tailored to local contexts can enhance learning across cases and potentially enhance programme efficacy. Accounting for heterogeneity[79] and adapting DDR interventions appropriately can be facilitated by the collection of reliable data. Critically, the still nascent DDR doctrine should seek to incorporate guidance for handling the 'political' dimension of reintegration. Acknowledgment of the political dynamics of integration of vulnerable groups has been explored at length in the refugee and IDP sectors[80] and lessons might be learned in the DDR field (see Chapter 7, this volume).[81]

Rethinking the scope of DDR

The challenges encountered during the Liberian DDRR intervention are analogous to those found in other countries. For example, in their review of DDR lessons learned Malan and Meek (ISS 2004: 12) observed a profound 'lack of clarity in reintegration planning ... execution remains the Achilles heel of DDR programmes'. Likewise, the complexities and long-term requirements of reintegration are often rushed during large-scale DDR missions (Specht 2006). A badly planned and executed reintegration strategy that fails to protect an individual's economic future can present as much of a threat to security as a poorly implemented disarmament and demobilization intervention. A common refrain among critics of DDR is the apparent disconnect between the disarmament and demobilization on the one hand, and reintegration activities on the other (UNOSAA 2005). One implication of these observations is that reintegration interventions are distinctly *not* sequential; i.e. a process that necessarily follows behind disarmament and demobilization. The reintegration intervention should be a parallel and mutually reinforcing process (IPA 2003: 8).

Another challenge facing DDR practitioners is the inflation of expectations by donor governments, senior UN officials and affected governments. While a DDR programme can potentially enable former soldiers and militiamen to obtain and maintain a temporary livelihood it cannot necessarily create, among other things, long-term employment capacities in the beneficiary country.[82] Rather, this more complex task is ultimately the responsibility of the host nation, donor consortia, the private sector and other sectoral programmes (see Chapter 6, this volume).[83] Rhetoric must be tempered with realism if the practitioners are to have any chance of winning the peace in the long run.[84]

Towards an alternative model for DDR

The time may be ripe to consider an alternative strategic model for future DDR interventions. Such a model should draw on the strengths of past initiatives and acknowledge the intrinsic limitations of programming interventions in a post-conflict setting.[85] In essence, the model should advocate the de-linking of reintegration programming (*not* planning) from disarmament and demobilization processes. Instead, reintegration could be pursued via institutions with a comprehensive and holistic approach to community integration and reintegration rather than missions lacking the requisite capacities (UN ECHA 2000). One way of reducing the scope of DDR as currently conceived is by substituting 'reintegration' with 'reinsertion' in order to refocus the programme away from long-term and open-ended commitments to short-term and fixed objectives. Reintegration could then emerge as a more deliberate intervention tool, or superseded by mainstream development programmes entirely.[86]

It is possible to hypothesize how an alternative model might have been implemented in the case of DDRR in Liberia. The essence of the alternative approach would be to focus on reintegration earlier and anticipate each phase of the post-conflict intervention appropriately so that practitioners could set feasible and achievable targets. A de-linked approach might have narrowed the first phase of the intervention from five years, 2003–2008 (includes reintegration outcomes) to two years, 2003–2005 (includes disarmament, demobilization and a reinsertion period). Crucially, reintegration planning would have formally begun in parallel with the initial security phase. In hindsight, it would be impossible to determine what timeframe might have been decided upon for the reintegration phase, but it would have been conceived as a long-term intervention. Just as important to the security phase, reintegration, too, must have feasible and achievable objectives. While disarmament, demobilization and reinsertion benefits can usually be programmed fairly precisely in a compressed planning cycle, the efficacy of the long-term process of reintegration demands thorough assessments and analysis of many confounding factors. Unnecessarily rushing through the process can be potentially detrimental not only in relation to wasted funding but also to the overall stability of a nation recovering from armed conflict.

De-linking reintegration from DDR does not necessarily imply that it not take place at all. To the contrary, there is considerable evidence that sustained investment in reintegration can generate important dividends. Rather, the proposal advanced here is that reintegration planning be administered in parallel with security promoting activities such as disarmament and demobilization. Reintegration should be conceived in such a way that it targets a more inclusive group – particularly communities of return rather than an exclusive focus on combatants themselves. A holistic approach to reintegration requires unified planning and direction. As noted above, ex-combatants in Liberia represent only a fraction of those citizens attempting to integrate or reintegrate after war – and a focus on former fighters at the expense of others may have undermined the potential for long-term reintegration success. The implication of the proposed model is that DDR assumes a defined and closed timeframe and that reintegration is approached as a separate intervention tool that is inclusive and long-term by nature.

Conclusion

Drawing on new research undertaken in Liberia, this chapter offers a critical review of the design and evaluation of DDR. Specifically, it focused on the limitations of DDR planning and assessment through examination of the case of Liberia – particularly in relation to mission scope, baseline data collection and the measurement of quantifiable outcomes. If the gap between outputs and desired outcomes is to be closed, consensus on bureaucratic roles and functions must be agreed upon lest 'mission creep' continue to degrade the efficacy of a given intervention. If realistic outcomes are not articulated in a consensual manner, DDR planning and programming will likely remain vulnerable to over-optimistic (and unfunded) goal-setting. In helping to locate a strategic focus for subsequent interventions, the chapter recommends rethinking the DDR enterprise. In proposing to de-link disarmament and demobilization from reintegration and run the interventions in parallel vice sequentially, it anticipates enhancing the quality and quantity of security promotion on the one hand, and renewed attention to development on the other.

There is growing interest in evidence-based policy in the security sector – including in relation to DDR. The adjustment of DDR missions to account for their security and development aspects may in fact facilitate the effective use RBM strategies and enhance accountability in the long-term. While limiting the scope of future DDR interventions is potentially crucial to enhancing effectiveness, adopting a more holistic approach to reintegration through the identification and formal incorporation of the economic, societal, political and psychological dimensions can potentially enhance inclusive programme design and implementation. Critical to the success of any DDR programme is understanding that without proper collection of baseline data, the efficacy of programmes will continue to be difficult to assess and quantify.

Notes

1 Interview with Ambassador Donald Booth (US Ambassador to Liberia) February 2006.
2 See, for example, the introduction of this volume for a review of the IDDRS (UNWG 2006) and the UN DPKO (2008) capstone principles.
3 As noted in the Introduction, the expansion of DDR operations around the world has generated a new burden on international peacekeeping operations, international donors and security and development agencies. It is incumbent on these supporters of DDR to issue precise guidance that provides for clear and achievable goals.
4 These findings concur with those of Patrick Barron (2007: 1) who observes in the case of Aceh that there is an urgent need to undertake consensus-building exercises in order:

> to develop a common understanding of reintegration; a stocktaking exercise, to evaluate what approaches have been effective and key remaining gaps ... and developing a medium and long-term strategy that outlines how reintegration programs should transition into longer-run post-conflict development approaches and institutional responsibilities.

5 Americo-Liberians accounted for less than 2.8 per cent of the entire population as reported by the Ministry of Planning and Economic Affairs (1977: 84–86) in Nelson (1984).
6 The first international intervention efforts began in 1990 with ECOWAS's observer force, the Military Observer Group (ECOMOG). Later, the United Nations Observer Mission in Liberia (UNOMIL) was established on 22 September 1993 by Security Council resolution 866. UNOMIL was to work with ECOMOG in the implementation of the Cotonou Peace Agreement. The mission operated until September 1997.
7 Taylor's rule was described as featuring 'poor governance, administrative malfeasance, corruption, intimidation, threats, torture, terrorist acts against his population and summary executions of civilians' (Levitt 2005: 216).
8 In order to remain technically correct, the discussion in this chapter will use DDRR

when referencing the Liberian national programme and DDR when referring to the general programmatic concept and implications across country cases.

9 'Rehabilitation' was discussed around the periphery of the mission, but was largely an unacknowledged component of the DDRR. The May 2004 planning documentation (UNDP 2004: 26) does reference 'rehabilitation' as a 'psycho-social' component that will be included in every economic reintegration funding proposal.

10 After extensive interviews with UNMIL and UNDP staff and senior management, the author learned that 'rehabilitation' was essentially a 'non-component' (never realized) for the Liberian DDRR programme. Initially designed to be a five-day programme in the cantonment area during demobilization, the programme was drastically cut when time in the camps were to be reduced.

11 There are a variety of monitoring and evaluation references available for understanding the importance of this activity in post-conflict development programming. For understanding the UNDP specific approach, see UNDP (2002). For a general understanding of monitoring and evaluation, readers may review the text Morse and Struyk (2006).

12 The UNDP, for example, acknowledged a 'paucity of impact assessment documentation for the reintegration efforts stretching over the past decade' (UNDP 2000).

13 As the Deputy Special Representative of the Secretary General (DSRSG) for the UNMIL mission for Operations and Rule of Law, Souren Seraydarian also led the DDRR section at all stages of the operation from planning to implementation. The DSRSG was assisted in developing the Strategic Framework by Kelvin Ong of the UN DPKO who until the end of 2007 was the acting chief of the DDR section in New York and Charles Achodo of the UNDP.

14 The Draft Interim Secretariat (2003: 40) presents in a single page the intervention logic and indicators that would be used to evaluate results in accordance with RBM management strategy. Five programme results are articulated and subsequently refined by measurable indicators. Result four, for example, is 'Ex-combatants are received into and contribute to the development of their communities'. Two of the five indicators supporting result five include 'Ex-combatants are accepted as active members of their communities' and 'Ex-combatants extend their social network beyond their ex-military circle and improve their perception of personal security'.

15 In UN nomenclature this reveals that ex-combatant-focused reintegration was selected as the initial primary approach to the intervention as opposed to the community-based reintegration approach that seeks to support ex-combatant reintegration through a wider societal effort targeting all members of a community as beneficiaries (UN 2006b: 159).

16 The 11 sites around Liberia included Buchanan, Ganta, Gbarnga, Harper, Kakata, Schefflin Barracks, Tappita, Tubmanburg, VOA, Voinjama and Zwedru.

17 Residual operations continued through the end of the year.

18 National Transitional Government of Liberia (NTGL 2004: 11).

19 Readers may review some of the scepticism surrounding the disarmament activities in the following articles: Nichols (2005) and IRIN (2004).

20 A status report was run by the JIU from the NCDDRR database especially for the UNMIL RRR study (Amara *et al.* 2006)

21 Nichols (2005) indicated reintegration that fears over financing surfaced as early as December 2004. An electronic news wire posted by IRIN (2007a), raised the issue of depleted funding lines and questioned the UN's capacity for fulfilling the promise of reintegration training to all who registered.

22 See, for example, IRIN (2007b).

23 While on fieldwork during the spring of 2006, the author observed that the USAID and UNDP programme implementers were running their respective programmes separate from each other. This 'independent' implementation was a source of frustration for both the UN mission and the beneficiaries on the ground. UNDP planners

recognized the need to coordinate with 'parallel programme partners' and established a plan do so early in the mission (UNDP 2004: 12).

24 Information on the CBR efforts can be found at http://www.lr.undp.org/cbr.htm. An initiative to support local inclusive governance (the District Development Committees) is a part of the CBR programme. A concept paper discussing the DDC initiative in Liberia recommends its institutionalization and was prepared by Charles (2006).

25 The *Operational Guide to the IDDRS* is an abridged handbook version meant to assist users. Downloadable versions of related documentation can be found at http://www.unddr.org. In 1999, the Lessons Learned Unit of the DPKO published a principles and guidelines handbook entitled *Disarmament, Demobilization and Reintegration of Ex-combatants in a Peacekeeping Environment*. While the handbook indicated a significant step forward, it was thin on operational guidance and lacked analytical depth.

26 Siegel (2000: 115) believes that one definition of mission creep 'is derived from situations in which the military moves from well-defined or achievable missions to ill-defined or impossible ones'.

27 Caramés *et al.* (2006: 9) also indicate that the start time of a DDR programme comes, on average, one year after the signing of a peace agreement. In Liberia the DDRR began less than four months after the signing of the CPA.

28 The Stockholm Initiative on DDR (2006), for example, highlights the UN's inability to properly address the long-term component of reintegration due to limited funding. The report highlights DDR programmatic challenges, 'particularly on the more ambitious reintegration components, which almost without exception have ended up under-funded and therefore either largely unimplemented or clearly incapable of bearing the weight of overly ambitious expectations' (MFAS 2006: 10).

29 The UN (as well as the EU and US) had observer status during the Accra CPA negotiations.

30 The imperative of 'do no harm' resulted from a project that began in 1994 from CDA Collaborative Learning Projects and included a number of international agencies, including bilateral donors, non-governmental agencies and agencies of the United Nations. The website states that 'the Project seeks to identify the ways in which international humanitarian and/or development assistance given in conflict settings may be provided so that, rather than exacerbating and worsening the conflict, it helps local people disengage'. See, for example, www.cdainc.com/dnh/.

31 See, for example, GoL (2003: 2).

32 Much work has been done to codify societal transformation in the post-conflict period. 'Theories of change' are well established in the field and draw upon programme evaluation literature for foundation. Readers are directed to Shapiro (2005) for further exploration.

33 The quality of the decisions made and the profile the senior management team will significantly influence the outcomes targeted for the implementation phase.

34 Inherent to RBM programme design is the requirement of understanding how to establish reasonable performance levels that will be evaluated as programme outcomes.

35 UNDP (2002) provides significant insight into the management strategy employed in post-conflict programming. The handbook notes that RBM has been gaining momentum within the organization since 1999.

36 Recent micro-level empirical research on DDR and post-conflict reintegration and reconciliation in Liberia has been conducted by Jennings (2007); Bøås and Hatløy (2006); Fearon *et al.* (2007) and SFCG (2005).

37 The project, which was vetted through the Inter-Agency Working Group on DDR, drew on the expertise of many groups and individuals with experience in the field and came complete with a very informative resource web-site for practitioners and researchers alike. A plethora of lessons learned, checklists, and tools can be found relating to many different countries and features of DDR.

38 Reintegration is the process by which ex-combatants acquire civilian status and gain sustainable employment and income. Reintegration is essentially a social and economic process with an open time frame, primarily taking place in communities at the local level. It is part of the general development of a country and a national responsibility and often necessitates long-term external assistance.

39

> 'Societal' ... refers to the relational capacities of a human being or of a community, the capacities for being able to live with others in community, the capacities for religious, ethnic, political plurality, the capacity for peace, partnership, friendship, solidarity etc. It also includes the capacity to forgive and to include as well as the capacity to become integrated and included. The 'societal' dimension is basic to any post-war rehabilitation and reintegration process.
>
> Lichem (2006)

40 While many discrete dimensions have been considered in this chapter, there also appears to be a number of confounding variables, (many yet to be determined) that may contribute to 'successful' reintegration outcomes.

41 'Peace-building' is defined in UNDPKO (2008: 18).

42 For more information on this study see the *Key Findings* at Pugel (2006) and the full report at Pugel (2007b). The first study supervised by the DDRR Programme and Policy Advisor, Mr Charles Achodo, for UNDP Liberia, was conducted in February and March 2006, approximately a year and a half after the disarmament and demobilization formally ended for most of the combatants, and was designed to provide an interim programme impact assessment.

43 For more information on this study see Amara *et al.* (2006). The second study was supervised by Mr Andrea Tamagnini, Director of UNMIL's Reintegration, Rehabilitation and Recovery section, and was meant to provide a situation analysis of ex-combatant reintegration.

44 The database for Liberia's NCDDRR is maintained by the UNDP and the Joint Implementation Unit (JIU). The database contains all registered former combatant data obtained through the intake forms gathered during the disarmament and demobilization process. The database also contains programme follow-up information for each individual as they proceed through the process.

45 This non-participation rate was actually found to be quite reflective of the population in Liberia. After two larger-scale nationwide, random sample surveys conducted by the author, non-participation rates were found to be 12 per cent and 11 per cent.

46 Quasi-experimental designs are very similar to 'experimental' designs in research, but they have one significant difference – quasi-experiments lack the element of 'random assignment'. For the Liberian studies, the common quasi-experimental 'non-equivalent-groups design' was considered appropriate, but it lacked the 'pre-test' element that is commonly paired in analysis with the 'post-test' group for comparison.

47 The author is most grateful for the assistance rendered by Macartan Humphreys and Jeremy Weinstein. Of note, the UNMIL RRR collaborated with the NGO PRIDE to conduct the study. PRIDE was also the lead NGO for Humphreys and Weinstein (2004).

48 On average, the surveys took approximately one hour to administer. Design of the cluster size for each survey took this logistical element into concern. So, for example in the UNDP study where 40 surveys were required per cluster, a team of five (one field team supervisor and four enumerators) had approximately two days to arrive and present themselves, collect interview intakes, and depart for next location. Importantly, both samples were nationwide, random samples, the number of clusters were a function largely of maximizing time and resources.

49 The author utilized a tool for selecting random geographic clusters that was provided by Macartan Humphreys.

50 The p-codes (place code) were provided by the Humanitarian Information Center

from a mapping project that was completed in 2005. The data lists all villages with a unique p-code that can subsequently be linked to many other sources of information. The database currently associates the following information as well: county, district, number of houses, percentage of displacement, percentage that have returned, presence and functionality of schools and health facilities, accessibility by car in wet and dry seasons. The database can be accessed at http://www.humanitarianinfo.org/liberia/mapcentre/reference/village_ws_maps/index.asp.

51 Field research in post-conflict environments is often challenged by a host of factors that inhibit a truly 'untainted' set of respondent cases. Experiences with bias in field research is cited by Humphreys and Weinstein (2007); Blattman and Annan (2008) and Justino and Verwimp (2006) to name but a few.

52 Field teams reported not feeling entirely secure in some locations in Margibi County, which resulted in an under-sampling of almost 50 per cent in those geographic clusters. Grand Gedeh County was another geographic location affected by weather. The remaining issues were geographically distributed and surfaced due to weather and timeframe constraints.

53 Similar challenges were encountered in studies undertaken in Ethiopia and Timor-Leste (see Chapters 6 and 7, this volume).

54 Some may have certainly hidden their past from the community and others might have simply been at work or away from their homes at the time of the survey.

55 While the Liberian Truth and Reconciliation Commission (TRC) mandate was enacted on 12 May 2005 by the National Transitional Legislative Assembly, it was not officially launched until 22 June 2006. The actual public hearings in Monrovia did not commence until January 2008. For more on the TRC see https://www.trcofliberia.org/.

56 Figure reported in the mid-term evaluation of the DDRR programme, Bugnion (2006: 8). Readers can compare this ratio with that of other country programmes as documented in Caramés *et al.* (2006).

57 Meek and Malan (2004) recognized the need to expand the post-conflict beneficiary set, as did the UNDP Practice Note on DDR (2006: 33), which recognized that 'not all of them will have borne arms'. The *Operational Guide to the Integrated Disarmament, Demobilization and Reintegration Standards* (UN 2006b) provides an exceptional generic framework for approaching DDR programme design within the context of an RBM strategy. Critical to the success of any programme is understanding that without proper collection of baseline data, the efficacy of programmes chosen for implementation will be difficult to assess and the policy community will indeed continue to rely on subjective and qualitative measures for future decision-making.

58 There are many accounts of the disarmament and demobilization process that was conducted in Liberia. Interested readers should refer to Paes (2005); Weiss (2005) and Nichols (2005) for more detail.

59 The mission in Liberia suffered from many administrative inadequacies. Readers may refer to Paes (2005) and Nichols (2005: 118).

60 Four months into the DDRR programme, the former warring factions had yet to provide a full accounting of their troops, their locations or the weapons under their control see IRIN (2004).

61 This criterion was recommended for inclusion into the programme by UN senior staff who had recently participated in the DDR in Sierra Leone. The purpose was to establish a standard threshold for accepting combatants without weapons. While the first phase of the disarmament operations emphasized weapons and ammunition turn-in for registration, subsequent phases allowed women and children associated with fighting forces to register without either weapons or ammunition.

62 The Government of Liberia (2004: 13) stated, 'Past experience has taught us that the RR strategy ensures that assistance is targeted to cover all needy populations in order to consolidate peace and community cohesion'.

63 Partial serial numbers of imprecisely identified weapons yield little value to those looking to track down the history of a particular weapon. Not all small arms information and trends went unrecognized, however. Readers can read more on cases of successful analysis by reviewing Nichols (2005) and Weiss (2005).

64 This oversight was eventually rectified by handwriting the option of 'GoL militia' onto the intake forms.

65 This category was introduced (by UN officials) to account for a number of armed combatants who were 'leftover' from the first stage of the Liberian civil war (1989–1996) but did not fight for the LURD, MODEL, or the government.

66 Disturbingly, the oversight in the registration process also negates its use as a viable sampling frame for researchers to refer to when attempting to obtain and recognize a representative sample population for study and evaluation when examination by faction is stipulated. More importantly, it becomes problematic for practitioners attempting to analyse or assess intervention efforts (disaggregated by faction) while the mission progresses.

67 The ten factors included the individual demographics: education level, home ownership, marital status, gender, age; captured wartime experiences in variables that described respondent participation: abducted or volunteer officer; and also considered community factors: whether they resettled in their pre-war home community, resided in the capital region, or lived in a community with a high incidence of crime.

68 For a more detailed discussion of the findings related to reintegration outcomes and influencing factors, readers may review Pugel (2007a).

69 Successful economic reintegration outcomes were assumed as: to be living above the poverty line, engaged in a livelihood-producing activity, and demonstrating a capacity for excess spending.

70 Importantly, all statistically significant indicators reacted in the same direction across the three outcomes designated as economic, providing a fair bit of confidence in the relationship between the factors under study and the dimension as a conceptual grouping.

71 A UNDP mid-point evaluation of the DDRR programme identified a monitoring deficiency.

72 The most significant finding of a factor correlated with successful reintegration outcomes – higher education levels – provides empirical evidence that reinforces what has been advanced in theory for some time now, that 'education drives economic growth and economic growth reduces poverty' (Nelson-Richards 2006: 14). While this finding is quite promising, we still know very little about the dimensions of post-conflict reintegration on the whole. We know even less when it comes to assessing reintegration as a function of DDR programme impact. The evidence in Liberia weakly indicated that the DDRR programme positively impacted the lives of those who completed the reintegration training – a finding that should be seen as optimistic but interpreted very cautiously. In the programme in neighbouring Sierra Leone, even though there were positively perceived macro-level reintegration outcomes, Humphreys and Weinstein (2007) also found that programme impact was elusive and could not uncover any substantial evidence of impact at the micro-level.

73 They were shown to be sceptical of the impartiality of the judges and were also found to maintain ties with former faction leaders at a higher rate than their comrades without partners.

74 A selection effect must also be considered in assessing the results of the study. Blattman argues that individuals who choose to partake in DDR are those who may be more socially integrated (or more likely to socially integrate) in the first place. For the case of Sierra Leone, Humphreys and Weinstein examined DDR entry and did not uncover any obvious selection effects. The qualitative analysis and results in Sierra Leone were very much akin to the responses in Liberia (Amara *et al.* 2006).

75 This point is very readily apparent in the Liberia case, as demonstrated by a formal

disbanding of the contemporary warring factions at the completion of the disarmament and demobilization period. The LURD, MODEL, and the ex-government of Liberia held a ceremony on 3 November 2004 at the Executive Mansion in Monrovia (UNMIL 2004).

76 The UN and the World Bank presently recognize three distinct approaches to reintegration interventions – short-term stabilization (or reinsertion, which is usually linked to demobilization), ex-combatant-focused, and community-based (UN 2006b).

77 The *Paris Declaration* was endorsed on 2 March 2005 with an eye to enhancing aid delivery effectiveness. See more at www.oecd.org.

78 There are numerous references discussing and defining 'evidence-based policy making'. See, for example, UNICEF (2008).

79 Humphreys and Weinstein (2006: 32) confirm that 'no single logic [sic] offers a complete explanation for revolutionary mobilization' and that 'distinct patterns of recruitment are apparent across different fighting factions'.

80 The UNHCR emphasizes the 4Rs framework in its operations – repatriation, reintegration, rehabilitation and reconstruction. The definition of reintegration within the handbook is defined as 'the ability of returning refugees to secure the necessary political, economic, legal and social conditions to maintain their livelihood and dignity'.

81 An example of a well-defined methodology that highlights the 'holistic' nature of integration is CARE's Household Livelihood Security (HLS) approach. The methodology recognizes that basic needs (food, shelter etc.) and social services (education, health services etc.) are inherently connected to the political/security environment. This rights-based approach to understanding vulnerability indicators is also appropriate for the micro-level researcher as the methodology focuses on individual outcomes. The tools provided through CARE's website complement the UN's RBM strategy approach and set a framework for rigorous research design. Readers can find more information at http://www.care.org. Tools that describe the methodology as well as current reporting that utilizes the approach in contemporary case studies can be reviewed.

82 This argument is made by Muggah (2005, 2006) in his discussion of the maximalist and minimalist approaches to DDR. DDR cannot substitute for large-scale development interventions which should be articulated in national development strategies, poverty reduction strategy papers (PRSPs), UN development assistance frameworks (UNDAFs) and bilateral development arrangements.

83 Forecasting a prognosis of economic stability (let alone growth) in a country that has been torn apart by civil war is a dangerous proposition and creates an untenable position for those responsible for programme delivery.

84 Based upon his experiences in the Democratic Republic of the Congo (DRC), Peter Swarbrick affirms that bringing economic stability to a post-conflict country is hard enough even when the mission is fully backed financially. When faced with the pressures of timetables and hordes of armed combatants, a 'workable system for re-integration … is in practice usually impossible' (Swarbrick 2007: 20).

85 Practically, the author advances this alternative model based upon an intimate understanding of the Liberian case and subsequent exchanges in formal and informal forums with practitioners and policy-makers familiar with the details of planning and implementing other African intervention programmes. Substantially, the model is also advanced as a result of building upon the findings of several UN agency working group forums on DDR and their subsequent proceedings UNICEF (2008); UNOWA (2005); UNDP (2006) and UNOSAA (2005). The literature on programme evaluation and post-conflict reintegration (as listed in the reference section) cements the bridge between high level policy and lessons learned and the critical insights provided by the usually unheard and unpublished field practitioner.

86 Barron (2007) makes a similar argument in his article on DDR in Aceh.

Bibliography

Amara, J., M'Cormack, F., Pugel, J. and Quee, A. (2006) *A Situation Analysis of Ex-* *combatant Reintegration in Liberia*. Monrovia: UNMIL RRR. December.

Anderson, M.B. and Olson, L. (2003) *Confronting War: Critical Lessons for Peace Practitioners*. Cambridge: CDA, Inc.

Barron, P. (2007) 'Getting Reintegration Back on Track: Problems in Aceh and Priorities for Moving Forward', *Conference on Aceh at Harvard University*, 24–27 October.

Berdal, M. (1996) *Disarmament and Demobilization after Civil Wars*. Adelphi Paper 303. Oxford: Oxford University Press.

Bøås, M. and Hatløy, A. (2006) *After the Storm: Economic Activities among Children and Youth in Return Areas in Post War Liberia – the Case of Voinjama*. Fafo report 523. Olso: Fafo.

Blattman, C. and Annan, J. (2006) 'The Consequences of Child Soldiering', *Households in Conflict Working Paper 22*. August.

—— (2008) 'On the Nature and Cause of LRA Abduction: What the Abductors Say', in T. Allen and K. Vlassenroot (eds) *The Lord's Resistance Army: War, Peace and Reconciliation*. Oxford: James Currey.

Bugnion, C. (2006) *External Mid-Term Evaluation Report of the Disarmament, Demobilization, Rehabilitation, and Reintegration Programme in Liberia*. 2 October.

Caramés, A., Fisas, V. and Luz, D. (2006) *Analysis of Disarmament, Demobilization and Reintegration (DDR) Programmes Existing in the World during 2005*. Barcelona: Escola de cultura de Pau. February.

Charles, M. (2006) 'Liberian Local Government Development Programme: Towards Decentralization', *A UNCDP/UNDP supported Concept Paper*. 9 June.

CPA (Comprehensive Peace Agreement) (2003) *Comprehensive Peace Agreement between the Government of Liberia and the Liberians United for Reconciliation and Democracy (LURD) and the Movement for Democracy in Liberia (MODEL) and Political Parties*. Accra, Ghana, 18 August.

Doyle, M. and Sambanis, N. (2006) *Making War and Building Peace*. Princeton: Princeton University Press.

Draft Interim Secretariat (2003) *Liberian Disarmament, Demobilization, Rehabilitation, and Reintegration Programme: Strategy and Implementation Framework*. Monrovia. October.

Fearon, J., Humphreys, M. and Weinstein, J. (2007) *Community-Driven Reconstruction in Lofa County Baseline Survey Preliminary Report*. Unpublished Report.

GoL (Government of Liberia) (2003) *Community Based Support in Reintegration and Recovery Process*. Project outline coordinated with UNDP Liberia. 15 December.

—— (2004) 'Government National Community Resettlement and Reintegration Strategy', June.

Humphreys, M. and Weinstein, J. (2004) *What the Fighters Say: A Survey of Ex-Combatants in Sierra Leone*. CGSD Working Paper no. 20, August.

—— (2006) 'Who Rebels? The Determinants of Participation in Civil War', Unpublished Paper, Columbia and Stanford Universities, July.

—— (2007) 'Demobilization and Reintegration', *Journal of Conflict Resolution* 51 (4): 531–567.

ICG (International Crisis Group) (2003) 'Liberia: Security Challenges', *Africa Report No 71*, November.

IPA (International Peace Academy) (2003) *Transforming War Economies: Challenges for Peacemaking and Peacebuilding*. Report of the 725th Wilton Park Conference, 27–29 October.

—— (2006) *Counting What Counts: Ten Steps toward Increasing the Relevance of Empirical Research in the UN System*. Meeting Note. New York, February.

IRIN (2004) 'Liberia: Where are the Weapons? Is Disarmament really Working?' 28 July. Online, available at: www.irinnews.org/report.aspx?reportid=50857.

—— (2007a) 'Liberia: Idle Fighters Cause Concern', 9 January 2007.

—— (2007b) 'Liberia: Donor fatigue threatening DDR process', 20 April. Online, available at: http://www.irinnews.org/Report.aspx?ReportId=71730.

ISS (Institute for Security Studies) (2004) 'Trends in DDR in Peacekeeping in Africa', in M. Malan and S. Meek (eds), *Identifying Lessons from DDR Experiences in Africa*. Monograph no. 106, October.

Jennings, K. (2007) 'The Struggle to Satisfy: DDR through the Eyes of Ex-combatants in Liberia', *International Peacekeeping*, 14(2): 204–218.

—— (2008) *Seeing DDR from Below. Challenges and Dilemmas Raised by the experiences of Ex-combatants in Liberia*. Fafo-report 3.

Justino, P. and Verwimp, P. (2006) 'Poverty Dynamics, Violent Conflict and Convergence in Rwanda', *Households in Conflict Working Paper 16*, April.

Kingma, K. (1997) 'Demobilization of Combatants after Civil Wars in Africa and Their Reintegration into Civilian Life', *Policy Sciences* 30.

—— (2002) 'Demobilization, Reintegration and Peacebuilding in Africa', *International Peacekeeping* 9 (2).

Levitt, J. (2005) *The Evolution of Deadly Conflict in Liberia*. Durham: Carolina Academic Press.

Lichem, W. (2006) *DDR Processes and Societal Development*. Address to the Conference on Post-Conflict Peacebuilding in Africa: Assessing DDR Process. Kofi Annan International Peacekeeping Training Center, Accra, Ghana. August.

Liebenow, J. (1969) *Liberia: The Evolution of Privilege*. Ithaca: Cornell University Press.

LNP (Liberia National Police) (2006) *Annual Crime Report and Statistics for 2005*. October.

Mayne, J. (2005) 'Challenges and Lessons in Results-Based Management', August. Online, available at: www.adb.org/mfdr/documents/Challenges-Lessons-Joh.pdf.

Meek, S. and Malan, M. (2004) 'Identifying Lessons from DDR Experiences in Africa: Workshop Report', Monograph No. 106, October. Pretoria: ISS.

MFAS (Ministry for Foreign Affairs of Sweden) (2006) *Stockholm Initiative on Disarmament Demobilization Reintegration*. Final Report. Online, available at: www.sweden.gov.se/siddr.

Morse, K. and Struyk, R. (2006) *Policy Analysis for Effective Development*. Boulder: Lynne Rienner.

Muggah, R. (2005) 'Managing "Post-Conflict" Zones: DDR and Weapons Reduction', in *The Small Arms Survey 2005: Weapons at War*. Online, available at: www.smallarmssurvey.org.

—— (2006) 'Emerging from the Shadow of War: A Critical Perspective on DDR and Weapons Reduction in the Post-Conflict Period', *Journal of Contemporary Security Policy* 27 (1).

NTGL (National Transitional Government of Liberia) (2004) *Joint Needs Assessment*, February.

Nelson, H. (ed.) (1984) *Liberia: A Country Study*. Washington, DC: American University.

Nelson-Richards, M. (2006) *Youth in Post-Conflict Africa: Community-Based Rehabilita-*

tion, Rebuilding and Reconstruction of Society. Paper presented at the Expert Group Meeting on Youth in Africa, Windhoek, Namibia. 16 November.

Nichols, R. (2005) 'Disarming Liberia: Progress and Pitfalls', in N. Florquin and E. Berman (eds) *Armed and Aimless: Armed Groups, Guns, and Human Security in the ECOWAS Region*. Geneva: Small Arms Survey.

Nilsson, A. (2005) *Reintegrating Ex-combatants in Post-Conflict Societies*. Paper commissioned by Sida to the Department of Peace and Conflict Research, Uppsala University. May.

Organisation for Economic Cooperation and Development (2005) 2 March *Paris Declaration*. Online, available at: www.oecd.org/.

Paes, W. (2005) 'The Challenges of Disarmament, Demobilization and Reintegration in Liberia', *International Peacekeeping* 12 (2).

Pugel, J. (2006) *Key Findings from the Nation Wide Survey of Ex-combatants in Liberia: Reintegration and Reconciliation February-March 2006*. Monrovia: UNDP, October.

—— (2007a) *Deciphering the Dimensions of Reintegration*. Manuscript.

—— (2007b) *What the Fighters Say: A Survey of Ex-Combatants in Liberia*. Monrovia: UNDP Liberia.

SFCG (Search for Common Ground) (2005) *Key Findings from 2005 Risk and Conflict Assessment: Liberia before Elections*. Online, available at: www.sfcg.org/programmes/liberia/programmes_liberia.html.

Shapiro, I. (2005) 'Theories of Change', in G. Burgess and H. Burgess (eds). *Beyond Intractability*, Boulder: University of Colorado. Posted: January. Online, available at: www.beyondintractability.org/essay/theories_of_change/.

Siegel, A. (2000) 'Mission Creep or Mission Misunderstood?' *Joint Forces Quarterly*, Summer.

Specht, I. (2006) 'Socio-Economic Profiling and Opportunity Mapping Pack', *Transition International*, handout.

Swarbrick, P. (2007) *Avoiding Disarmament Failure: The Critical Link in DDR – An Operational Manual for Donors, Managers, and Practitioners*. Working Paper 5. Geneva: Small Arms Survey. Online, available at: www.smallarmssurvey.org/files/portal/spotlight/disarmament/ddr.html.

UN (United Nations) (2006a) *Disarmament, Demobilization, and Reintegration*. Report of the Secretary General A/60/705.

—— (2006b) *Operational Guide to the Integrated Disarmament, Demobilization and Reintegration Standards*. Online, available at: www.unddr.org.

UN ECHA (Executive Committee on Humanitarian Affairs) (2000) 'Harnessing Institutional Capacities in Support of the DDR of Former Combatants', Final Report of the DDR Working Group, 19 July.

UNDP (UN Development Programme) (2000) *Sharing New Ground in Post-Conflict Situations: The Role of UNDP in Support of Reintegration Programmes*, January. Online, available at: http://www.undp.org/eo/documents/postconflict_march2000.pdf.

—— (2002) *Handbook on Monitoring and Evaluating for Results*. New York: UNDP.

—— (2003) *Community Based Support in Reintegration and Recovery Process*. New York: UNDP.

—— (2004) *Strategic and Operational Framework of Reintegration Support for Ex-Combatants* (3rd draft), New York: UNDP.

—— (2006) *Practice Note: Disarmament, Demobilization and Reintegration of Ex-combatants*. Online, available at: www.undp.org/bcpr/whats_new/ddr_practice_note.pdf.

—— (2007) *Liberia Evaluation of Results-Based Management at UNDP*. New York: UNDP.

UNDPKO (UN Department of Peacekeeping Operations) (1999) *Disarmament, Demobilization and Reintegration of Ex-combatants in a Peacekeeping Environment*. New York: UNDPKO.

—— (2008) *United Nations Peacekeeping Operations: Principles and Guidelines*. New York: UNDPKO.

UNHCR (UN High Commissioner for Refugees) (2004) *Repatriation and Reintegration of Liberian Refugees: January–February 2004*. Geneva: UNHCR.

UNICEF (UN Childrens Fund) (2008) *Bridging the Gap: The Role of Monitoring and Evaluation in Evidence-based Policy Making*. January. Online, available at: www.unicef.org/ceecis/evidence_based_policy_making.pdf.

UNMIL (UN Mission Liberia) (2004) 'Liberia's Warring Factions Disbanded as Disarmament of Ex-Combatants Ends', Press Report 142. Monrovia, 3 November. Online, available at: www.unmil.org/article.asp?id=95.

—— (2006) *Human Rights in Liberia's Rubber Plantations: Tapping into the Future*, May.

UNOCHA (United Nations Office for the Coordination of Humanitarian Affairs) (2004a) 'Liberia: Where are the Weapons? Is Disarmament really Working?', Integrated Regional Information Networks (IRIN). 28 July. Online, available at: www.irinnews.org/report.aspx?reportid=50857.

—— (2004b) 'Liberia: UN Confirms Disarmament will Restart on 15 April', Integrated Regional Information Networks (IRIN), 11 April. Online, available at: www.irinnews.org/report.aspx?reportid=49475.

—— (2007a) 'Liberia: Donor Fatigue Threatening DDR Process', Integrated Regional Information Networks (IRIN), 20 April. Online, available at: www.irinnews.org/Report.aspx?ReportId=71730.

—— (2007b) 'Liberia: Idle Fighters Cause Concern', Integrated Regional Information Networks (IRIN), 9 January.

UNOSAA (UN Office of Special Advisor on Africa) (2005) *Disarmament, Demobilization, Reintegration (DDR) and Stability in Africa*. Conference report, Freetown, Sierra Leone.

UNOWA (UN Office for West Africa) (2005) 'Seminar on the Challenge of Reintegration of Ex-Combatants in DDR Programmes in West Africa'. Final Communiqué presented in Dakar, Senegal, 8 April.

UNWG (2006) *Integrated Disarmament, Demobilization and Reintegration Standards (IDDRS)*. Online, available at: www.unddr.org/iddrs/.

Weinstein, J. (2002) 'The Structure of Rebel Organizations: Implications for Post-Conflict Reconstruction', Research Dissemination Note 4, Conflict Prevention and Reconstruction Unit, Washington DC: World Bank.

—— (2007) *Inside Rebellion: The Politics of Insurgent Violence*. Cambridge: Cambridge University Press.

Weiss, T. (2005) *Perpetrating Power: Small Arms in Post-Conflict Sierra Leone and Liberia*. ISS Monograph no. 116. June. Online, available at: www.issafrica.org/.

Wood, E. (2003) *Insurgent Collective Action and Civil War in El Salvador*. New York: Cambridge University Press.

4 Child combatants in northern Uganda

Reintegration myths and realities

Christopher Blattman and Jeannie Annan[1]

French foreign minister Philippe Douste-Blazy recently warned that the use of child soldiers is 'a time bomb that threatens stability and growth in Africa and beyond'. At a conference on child soldiers in Paris he announced that they constituted 'lost children' who were 'lost for peace and lost for the development of their countries' (BBC 2007). This lost generation metaphor has become a commonplace in discussions of child soldiers, who are presumed to return from war traumatized, stigmatized and broken. 'They are walking ghosts', mourns a recent *New York Times* (2006) editorial, 'damaged, uneducated pariahs'. While such alarming assertions attract much-needed attention and money to the reintegration of former child soldiers, the evidence to support these claims is weak at best. In fact, the evidence to support almost *any* claim relating to children affected by war is sadly lacking.

Studies of child soldiers – and indeed of ex-combatants in general – are few in number and largely case-based, drawing on testimonies from former participants.[2] While such studies yielded important insights for reintegration of young ex-fighters, the evidence base is alarmingly thin. With interview accounts, moreover, one worries that the most sensational rather than the most common experiences find their way into discourse. In the absence of representative data within and across conflicts, we have little sense of the proportionality and generalizability of any findings.[3] This chapter considers new evidence from Uganda on the impact of war on young recruits and considers what that evidence implies for the long-term reintegration of child and young adult combatants.

With or without evidence, concern for children trained to kill (and the society they return to) is more than warranted. What is worrisome is that alarmist claims and popular beliefs regarding young combatants appear to drive not only fundraising and advocacy but programme interventions as well. As this chapter will reveal, post-conflict programming for children and youth is (at least in Uganda) often based on popular myths, immediate needs, rules of thumb, and possibly mistaken assumptions about what sort of help ought to be provided – a state of affairs that governmental and non-governmental organizations delivering assistance in northern Uganda are the first to lament.

As it turns out, northern Uganda is an unusual but important place to evaluate the impacts of child and youth soldiering and the meaning of reintegration. Tens of thousands of civilians have been forcibly recruited by the rebel Lord's Resistance Army, or LRA, over two decades of war – two-thirds of them children under the age of 18. Only a small number of early LRA recruits were volunteers (many of whom became senior commanders in the force as time went by) and only a handful of these have returned from the bush. Thus virtually all ex-combatants in this region are former abductees, and DDR programmes have focused mainly on the reception and return of children and youth escaping from abduction.

While northern Uganda is seemingly a special case, it is one that allows us to assess with an unusual level of confidence and precision the very impacts of war and the meaning of reintegration for young recruits – a large and important class of ex-combatants. Because ex-combatants are usually a selected group – they are both self-selected and screened by the armed group – a comparison of their well-being to that of non-combatants can provide a misleading picture of their reintegration success. For instance, if they are poorer or socially dislocated post-conflict, it may reflect characteristics that led them to join the armed group in the first place, rather than the consequences of combat experiences. In Uganda, LRA recruitment was large-scale, involuntary, and (most important of all) indiscriminate – so much so that abduction appears to be a chance event. As a result, a comparison of abductees to non-abductees years after the fact allows a tragically accurate accounting of the long-term impacts of combat and the appropriateness of current programming.

To investigate these impacts, we conducted a large-scale and representative survey of nearly 1,000 households and youths in the war zone, including nearly 500 former abductees. The findings suggest a shift in our understanding of the impacts of war on children and youth and a change in our approach to their post-conflict reintegration. As will be discussed below, reintegration programming in northern Uganda has been greatly influenced by the fears of trauma, dislocation, and a 'lost generation' of youth. Thus NGO programming has tended to focus on reuniting families and providing psycho-social care – activities to minimize psychological trauma and social dislocation. Their economic and educational programmes have tended to remain small in scale. Several large post-conflict programmes by the government of Uganda address economic and educational needs, but have only recently begun to function.

Survey and interview evidence from northern Uganda paints a different picture, however – suggesting little aggression among former abductees, child or adult, and a range of distress symptoms. Rather, frequently occurring symptoms of distress are concentrated in a relative minority, especially those that experienced the most severe violence and those who returned to the least supportive family environments. There is little evidence of hostility and alienation. If anything, distressed youth are quiet and withdrawn rather than aggressive, and political engagement is actually greater on average among former abductees. Rather, the main impact of war appears to be substantially lower education levels, diminished productivity, and increased poverty and inequality, largely due to time away rather than psychological distress. The impacts are greatest for children, who are more likely to have had schooling interrupted.

The chapter concludes by discussing the extent (and the limitations) of generalizing from a sample of forcibly recruited young persons. We argue that while the precise impacts of war and reintegration gaps are likely to differ in other contexts, the main patterns we observe – that is, a concentration of high distress symptoms in a minority of former combatants, and a broad-based human capital gap between ex-combatants and non-combatants – seems likely to hold more generally. A large cross-country psychological literature testifies to the resilience of the majority of victims and perpetrators of violence. Moreover, all civil war combatants – child or adult, voluntary or involuntary – lose civilian education and labour market experience as a consequence of military service. Similar consequences of 'time away' are observed even among US soldiers.

If true, these patterns suggest that a shift in reintegration programming is needed. This may include a move towards more targeted psycho-social programmes (to those exhibiting the worst symptoms) and large and broad-based support for schooling (including adult education) and employment and enterprise development. As previous chapters of this volume have shown, DDR economic programmes are usually focused on keeping ex-combatants occupied after demobilization and breaking their ties to and networks with armed groups. This chapter makes clear that long-term reintegration is a major development and humanitarian concern, as well as a security one. The consequences of large human capital losses for post-conflict redevelopment are undoubtedly substantial. With so many young people affected, and since lost education and experience take time to re-accumulate (if they re-accumulate at all), in the absence of broad-based and sustainable economic programmes, the level and growth rate of income in conflict regions may be depressed for decades.

The war in northern Uganda

The conflict in northern Uganda has both spiritual and political roots. In 1988, a spiritual leader named Joseph Kony assembled the extremist remnants of several failed insurgent groups from the Acholi region of northern Uganda into a new guerrilla force, the LRA.[4] Locally Kony is believed to possess great spiritual powers, and his stated goal was to seek a spiritual cleansing of the nation. Kony's movement, however, was also rooted in a longstanding political grievance. In 1986, rebels from the south-west of the country led by Yoweri Museveni overthrew an Acholi-dominated government. Several guerrilla forces in the north initially resisted the takeover, but for the most part settled for peace or were defeated by 1988. The handful of fighters that would not settle for peace gathered under Kony to continue the fight.

Kony and the LRA are often portrayed in the media as an irrational religious group inflicting senseless violence on the Ugandan populace. A closer look at the rebel group, however, yields a more nuanced view; the LRA appears to be a political and rational organization, however evil and cruel their actions. The group's political messages have been relatively consistent and coherent, although poorly articulated. Moreover, violence against the citizenry has often been selectively and strategically employed to discourage collaboration with government forces. Finally, forcible recruitment and the torture and terrorization of abductees appear to have been a highly criminal yet effective means of recruiting an armed force in the absence of material resources and popular support.[5]

The poverty and unpopularity of Kony's movement limited his military options and ultimately accounts for the nearly total dependence of the LRA on the forcible recruitment of youth via abduction. Unpopular among their ethnically-Acholi brethren, from its earliest days the rebels looted homes and abducted youth to maintain supplies and recruits. The Acholi populace, after three years of such abductions and lootings, began to organize a local defence militia in 1991 with army assistance. To punish them for this betrayal, and to dissuade them from further collaboration with the government and army, Kony ordered the widespread killing and mutilation of civilians. Thus from 1991 onwards, Kony's war was waged not only against the government but against the populace at large. Abduction from 1995 to 2004 was large-scale and indiscriminate, with at least 60,000 youths estimated to have been taken by the LRA (Annan *et al.* 2006). The majority of these are adolescent males, though men and women of all ages are commonly taken.

The war would not likely have lasted these two decades, however, were it not for interference from neighbouring Sudan. In 1994 Sudan's government began supplying Kony with weapons and territory upon which to build bases. Sudan's support enlarged and invigorated a weakening LRA. Rebel attacks and abductions escalated dramatically after 1995, peaking in 2002 and 2003 when the Ugandan armed forces were permitted to enter the Sudan to engage the LRA and shut down their bases. It was during the height of violence and risk in 2002 and 2003 that the Ugandan government forcibly displaced the entire rural population of Acholiland to crowded camps. Many displaced voluntarily in order to protect themselves, but threat of force by the government and army compelled many others to leave their lands. Although displaced persons might be no more than a few kilometres from their lands, the army forbade them from venturing more than a kilometre or two from the camps. The primarily agricultural economy collapsed, impoverishing the populace.

By 2004, however, the rebels appeared weakened and abductions all but ceased. In 2006 an informal truce was reached, followed by peace talks brokered by the government of southern Sudan. While the talks continue, progress has been slow and at alternate times the talks have come close to breaking down. Moreover, since 2006 a process of 'decongestion' has sought to create smaller camps closer to people's homes, thus increasing access to land. Moreover, as violence has abated, households have begun to cultivate their lands again. With peace uncertain and potentially distant, however, most households remain (or maintain a foothold) in the camps to this day.

New evidence: the Survey of War Affected Youth (SWAY)

In northern Uganda, as in many other areas of armed conflict, the in
cupboard is bare. As a consequence, myths about the scale, nature and incidence
of abductions and war violence abound, with the more sensational images of the
former abductee often appearing to drive advocacy and programming. Even the
number of youth affected is essentially unknown. In the absence of hard data,
government and aid agencies based their DDR programming on immediate and
observable needs, rules of thumb, and possibly erroneous assumptions about
what sort of help ought to be provided.

To understand in more detail war experiences, their long-term impacts on
youth, and reintegration success, in 2005 and 2006 the authors conducted a
survey of young males living in the conflict zone (a survey of females is currently underway). Youth were drawn from a representative sample of roughly
1,000 households across eight sub-counties in the districts of Kitgum and Pader.
In order to be sure to capture youth who perished or migrated away over the
course of the conflict, respondents were selected based on their presence in the
household in 1996 – a year prior to the vast majority of violence and abductions,
and also a year most households remembered as the first election since 1980. In
the cases where youth had migrated from their home counties – 41 per cent
overall – they were tracked across the country and interviewed by local research
assistants. In this fashion 70 per cent of migrants and nearly all non-migrants
were found, for a total success rate of 85 per cent, or 741 males currently aged
14 to 30 (including 462 former abductees). Data were collected on unfound and
deceased youth from their surviving household members, and the estimates presented herein are re-weighted to account for observable patterns of attrition.[6]

The quantitative data were combined with detailed qualitative interviews with
community leaders, clan leaders, former rebel commanders, and dozens of youth
and former abductees. Furthermore, 40 of the surveyed youth were followed up
by the counselling psychologist multiple times for semi-structured interviews
with the youth and their family, friends and teachers. The focus of these in-depth
interviews was to obtain a better understanding of psychological and social challenges and resiliency. Finally, the results of the analysis, including policy recommendations, were reviewed with and commented upon by aid agencies,
psycho-social counsellors, and community leaders, as well as with several
groups of youth in the displacement camps surveyed.

Abduction experiences

In Uganda, a clear understanding of abduction experiences is central to understanding reintegration. The scale of abduction in the districts forming Acholiland was simply massive, including more than one in three male youth in the
areas surveyed. Numerically-speaking, virtually all LRA cadre were forcibly
recruited. A small number of volunteers were available in the early days of the
conflict (and, where they have survived, have since risen through the LRA

ranks). There are few accounts of youth voluntarily joining the rebels after 1990, however, and almost none after 1994. Youth were typically abducted by small roving groups of rebels conducting night raids on rural homesteads. Lengths of abduction ranged from a day to ten years, with half gone for at least four months. Only 20 per cent remained a year or more, and only 5 per cent remained more than three years.[7]

Young adolescents were disproportionately targeted by the rebels, with youths aged 12 to 14 five times more likely to be abducted than a youth of nine or 25. Somewhat unusually, child soldiers were not only the primary source of recruits, but the preferred ones. There are three main explanations for this focus on young adolescents. First, due to a demographic boom there were dramatically more adolescents in the population than young adults. A population-adjusted comparison of the abduction probabilities by age suggests that young adolescents were only twice as likely to be targeted as a young child or a young adult. Second, lengths of abduction were falling in age – young adolescents stayed more than a year on average, while young adults stayed only four months. The data suggest that the younger a youth the more likely he was to feel disoriented and fearful of escape or indoctrinated and loyal to Kony. Third, while young children were even more likely to be loyal and disoriented than young adults, they do not appear to have been effective as fighters, explaining the preference for adolescents older than 12 to those below that threshold.

Violence was an instrument of control in the LRA, and even short abductions involved exposure to significant brutality. The vast majority of abducted youth were tied, beaten, and abused in some fashion. Youth who failed to escape were trained as fighters and, after two or three months, were given a gun for raiding and abducting. Roughly one third of male abductees reported receiving a gun, including half of all those that remained at least two weeks with the LRA. A quarter of those taken for more than two weeks reported being forced to kill soldiers or civilians. Stories abound of abducted youth being forced to beat or even kill family and friends in order to bind them (if only by stigma) to the rebel group. Twelve per cent of abductees report being forced to beat someone close to them and 8 per cent report being forced to kill a family member or friend. Importantly, four-fifths of abductees eventually escaped, almost always during an unsupervised moment (such as in the heat of battle, or when sent for food and water). The remainder can, tragically, be assumed perished as relatively few remain with the LRA at this time. A blanket amnesty has been granted to all 'returnees' and, as discussed below, self-reported rates of acceptance by the family and community are high.

Existing DDR efforts

Given the forcible nature of abduction, and since the core of the LRA remains at large at the time of writing, demobilization and disarmament activities have been somewhat incidental to the post-conflict process so far.[8] As noted, virtually all returnees are escapees, with a smaller number captured or released. There were no large-scale returns or demobilizations. Rather, returnees have trickled in as individuals or small groups, often reporting to local leaders, army detaches, or heading straight home. Roughly half of our respondents went home without reporting to any authorities, abandoning any weapons in the bush (if they had any to begin with). The other half of respondents reported to an army detach or were picked up by the army in the bush. These youth were typically passed to a NGO-operated reception centre within a few days – usually after an interrogation by the armed forces for intelligence on the LRA. Demobilization and disarmament were thus incidental to the process of return, and current and past programming has focused predominantly on the 'R' in DDR – namely, reintegration. Reintegration programmes and service, meanwhile, are highly varied. Historically, local and international NGOs (with financial support from both bilateral and multilateral donors) provided the bulk of assistance. More recently, two major government programmes have begun to offer demobilization and reintegration packages.[9]

Non-governmental reintegration programmes

A principal instrument of reintegration is the reception centre – organizations run alternately by international and local NGOs that receive formerly abducted youth upon their return. The centres provide partial to full medical care for injuries sustained in the bush, family reunification, and 'counselling' – in reality group discussions and advice – led by local social workers. After a stay of a few weeks or months, a formerly abducted youth is sent home to his or her family with a few household items, such as a mattress and an extra set of clothes.

Within the camps, the follow-up and monitoring of vulnerable youth (including former abductees) is performed on a relatively modest scale. As of late 2005 and early 2006, roughly one in ten former abductees had received some follow-up care from an NGO.[10] The vast bulk of NGO activity in northern Uganda was directed at emergency support to the displaced population – food delivery, water and sanitation, and so forth. Non-emergency aid spending generally falls under the umbrella of 'psycho-social' care, where the objectives are the mitigation of psychological impacts of violence and the promotion of social acceptance. NGOs and NGO workers tend to view former abductees through a psychological trauma lens. Forms of support include support for clubs, school support, counselling, and assistance in starting a vocation or small business. Such assistance is overwhelmingly targeted at various categories of vulnerability: orphans, 'child mothers' and former abductees. The vast bulk is intended for youth under the age of 18.

Communities and families also sought to aid reintegration, often through traditional and Christian cleansing ceremonies. Traditional cleansing ceremonies are performed by elders to cleanse the youth from spiritual pollution, or *cen*, and are seen as appeasing the spirit with an animal sacrifice.[11] Five per cent of youth reported being haunted by spirits, or *cen*, with the large majority being the formerly abducted. The collective understanding of *cen* is that it can spread from one person to another, polluting a family or community. This has social implications on a youth with serious emotional distress (especially nightmares or flashbacks) since a community may be frightened of being polluted by him or her. Just under half of the formerly abducted males reported having a cleansing ceremony performed for them. Family members of the formerly abducted explained that it was important for them to know whether the youth killed anyone, primarily because they worried about spiritual pollution.

Government reintegration programmes

The Ugandan government's role in DDR has historically been much more modest than the NGO and community effort, but is beginning to expand. From a legal perspective, all rebels have been offered amnesty by the government via the Amnesty Act of 2000. The act exempts from punishment or prosecution all those who, since 1986, were actual participants in combat or who collaborated with or otherwise aided the perpetrators of war or armed rebellion, provided they report to the authorities and renounce their association (MDRP 2007).[12] The sole exception to the amnesty appears to be the senior leadership of the LRA, who have been indicted by the International Criminal Court (ICC) for their war crimes.[13] While not limited to members of the LRA, LRA ex-combatants (particularly former abductees) make up the bulk of expected and actual 'reporters'.

The general attitude towards the amnesty in Acholiland was initially one of indifference, as there seemed to be little to be gained from its receipt, and little to be feared by its absence. The significance of amnesty, however, recently began to change. In 2005, the Amnesty Commission began providing 'reinsertion packages' to all reporters (including registered former abductees) consisting of a substantial cash payment and several household items. By 2005 a backlog of 11,200 reporters had registered with the Commission but had not received any form of support. With financial support and technical assistance from the World Bank and the Multi-Country Demobilization and Reintegration Program (MDRP), by the end of August 2006 the Amnesty Commission delivered resettlement services and payments to these (and several hundred more recent) reporters (MDRP, 2007). The vast majority of former combatants had, by 2005, demobilized of their own accord. Thus, in order to pay out reinsertion packages, the names of former abductees were called over the radio to re-report, in many cases many years after their return.

The government also provides services to former combatants and their communities via the Northern Uganda Social Action Fund (NUSAF), a large peace, economic and community development programme serving all northern districts, including the LRA-affected region. Under NUSAF, communities or groups can apply for funds for a variety of projects and programmes, including conflict resolution services, vocational training, enterprise development and livestock restocking. Beneficiaries include, but are not limited to, former combatants. The programme is notable for being the largest initiative in the north aimed at promoting employment among vulnerable youth. Activities directed at youth only began in earnest in 2004 and 2005, however, and cover a relatively small proportion of the population. While it has been an important complement to reintegration programmes in the north, it has not been a substitute.

Challenges and lessons learned

Limits to the reception centre approach

Reception centres represented the first and most comprehensive attempt at large-scale reintegration of formerly abducted youth. They are widely credited with having played an instrumental role in the reinsertion of youth back into their families and communities. In addition to providing basic medical care, anthropologist Tim Allen (2005) emphasized their importance as 'liminal space' – a place for youth to begin their transition from the bush to 'normal' life. Social workers also seek to provide youth with counselling and advice-giving, individually or in groups. Perhaps most importantly, reception centres proved adept at locating the immediate and extended families of returned youth and arranging reunification.

In retrospect, the reception centre approach can be criticized on several grounds. First, one perhaps ought to question what is meant by 'reintegration' in the context of the mass displacement of the Acholi people. The life to which most youth return is bleak. Youth returning from abduction are sent to live with their families in cramped and crowded internal displacement camps. The vast majority live relatively idle and impoverished lives – at the time of the survey, 23 per cent of young males out of school had not found any work at all in the previous month, and even when 'employed' they found an average of just 14 days' work with gross earnings of less than two dollars per day. Water and sanitation in the camps are poor. Mortality rates are among the highest in the world, even compared to other complex emergencies (WHO 2005). Virtually all livestock have been lost to rebels and raiders, and by army decree there is no access to land more than a mile from the camp. Thus people are explicitly denied a livelihood. While the threat of rebel attacks makes people frightened to leave, their presence in camps is also demanded by the government army (under threat of imprisonment or death). These camps are therefore prisons in a very real sense. In this context, as pointed out by Allen (2005), reintegration could be regarded as the process of turning young men and women into good inmates or, as noted by Baaré (2006) 'as poor as the rest'.

A second challenge with the reception centres is their partial coverage. Although NGOs have long suspected that passage through such a centre is only partial, until now no data were available to indicate the proportion. The survey data suggests that, for those taken at least two weeks, only half pass through a reception centre. Rates are lowest for those taken for less than a month (roughly one-third) and highest for those abducted for more than a year (more than two-thirds). These figures are alarmingly low, especially given that passage through a reception centre is the primary means by which a youth receives NGO assistance and that, as we will see below, even short abductions seem to have substantial adverse impacts on education, health and livelihoods.

Challenges facing the amnesty programme

Of some concern is the government's payment of 'reinsertion packages' to former combatants via the Amnesty Commission. While the payout of reinsertion packages followed, and thus were not covered by, the survey, community meetings to present and discuss the survey findings coincided with the first payouts of reinsertion packages in 2006. The evidence on the amnesty programme is thus largely anecdotal, and awaits serious evaluation.

Reinsertion packages are generous by local standards, and are thus highly desired. Packages, however, have been paid out to former combatants slowly and in piecemeal fashion. In most cases the payouts come years after an abductee's return. More seriously, at the time of distribution, resentment of these packages was high among non-abducted youth and households. Those not abducted by the armed group have suffered a great deal due to war violence and displacement, and the public payment of relative generous packages to abductees (who may themselves have committed terrible acts against the community) years after the fact appeared to have rankled the community leaders and individuals interviewed by the authors. Upon revisiting communities 12 months later, discontent was no longer apparent. Nevertheless, the approach seems to carry with it serious risks.[14] For example, following several LRA attacks in Pader County, it was reported to the authors that community members were listening to a radio discussion about the Amnesty Commission packages given to former LRA combatants and they insisted that if the Amnesty Commission opened an office in their sub-county, they would 'burn it down'. They emphasized how unfair it was that the returnees – abducted or not – benefited from services while those who are merely victims were left with nothing. Similar sentiments were echoed in meetings in several communities, arousing by far the more intense emotions and discussion of any issue in the meeting.

Several additional issues plague the payout of reinsertion packages, and will continue to challenge any future DDR programmes planned or underway. First, the line between combatants and non-combatants is blurry because of the nature of recruitment and abduction (Jensen and Stepputat 2001). In particular, most abductions are short in length. One long-term abductee explained in apparent frustration,

> I would like to know why some formerly abducted who took a short duration in captivity, like 5 weeks, are now getting assistance but some like us who took over 10 years are not yet getting anything from the government.

These frustrations are often aggravated by a lack of transparency in the targeting, timing, and appropriateness of the packages. For instance, the same youth asked whether, 'in giving packages to us – the formerly abducted people – in the future, will there be any criteria or differences in giving these packages depending on the duration one took in captivity?'

Second, while joining the rebel group is almost always involuntary, those who remain with the group for a long time do exercise some agency, perhaps a great degree. For instance, 44 per cent of abductees taken longer than two weeks report having felt allegiance to Kony and the LRA at some time. Majorities were involved in looting, stealing and violence against civilians. One-quarter were forced to kill at sometime, often a civilian. The disproportionate targeting of aid to perpetrators over victims may lead to increased resentment. In particular, several former abductees explained that it is difficult to watch the top commanders rewarded. One youth who was with the LRA for ten years explained that,

> sometimes the thought comes as to why it is that we are not getting any assistance. Not even 50 shillings and yet the former LRA leaders who did more evil are being paid money and for us we are living like dogs. The government does not think about us but about those leaders.

Reintegration programme design: the wrong focus?

The chief problem with reintegration programmes in northern Uganda may be the focus on broad-based psycho-social assistance to the 'traumatized' former combatant. A survey-based assessment of the impacts of abduction suggests that the most pervasive and arguably largest impact is on education and livelihoods rather than physical or psychological trauma.

The LRA's recruitment tactics provide a unique if tragic opportunity to identify the lasting impacts of military service and the gaps to be filled by reintegration programmes. In most contexts, ex-fighters are a selected segment of the population, including those who chose to join, those screened by the armed group, and those more vulnerable to abduction. Thus a comparison of combatants to non-combatants confuses the impacts of abduction and combat experiences with pre-existing differences. In Uganda, however, not only was there no self-selection into the rebel group, but LRA abductions appear to also be independent of all of a youth's characteristics other than age (Blattman and Annan 2007). That is, there appear to be no differences in pre-abduction wealth, education, and orphaning between those youth that were abducted and those that weren't. Non-combatant youth of the same age and location as abducted youth can therefore be used as a comparison group, and the impacts thereby identified.

Psychological reintegration

Based on these comparisons, there appears to be little basis for the emphasis on disabling trauma. The survey and interview evidence suggest that on average formerly abducted youth appear similar in their mental health to youth in the area who have not been abducted. The majority of youth – both abducted and non-abducted – report low levels of psychological distress symptoms and high levels of pro-social behaviour. Frequent symptoms of distress are concentrated in a minority of abductees, especially those that experienced the most extreme violence.[15]

The predominant story of these youth is one of psychological resilience, with family acceptance and social support associated with the strongest resiliency among youth. Overall, family acceptance is remarkably high. Only 1 per cent of youth report that their family was unhappy or unwelcoming upon their return. Over 94 per cent of the youth report being accepted by their families without insult, blame or physical aggression. From a 23-year-old who was abducted for two months:

> When I just came home, I was really happy to be home. I couldn't realize whether people hated me or not. Life in the bush was not for people but for animals. I found life good at home. Both of my parents were alive. No neighbors said anything bad to me.

A minority experience frequent distress symptoms such as nightmares, flash-backs, withdrawal and hyper-arousal. These symptoms are often interpreted as spiritual haunting, or *cen*, and seen as both individually harmful and as poten-tially polluting to the family and community. Such serious distress appears to be closely associated to the degree of violence experienced and committed. From the survey data, each additional act of violence reported by a former abductee (out of 12 major types of incidents) is associated with a (roughly) 10 per cent increase in reported levels of distress (Annan 2007; Blattman and Annan 2007).[16] This link between violence and distress holds for non-abducted youth as well.

Social reintegration

The reception from the community, while typically strong and welcoming, was not quite so unanimous. While almost no one reported that their community blamed them for the things they had done, more than one-quarter of returnees said that they were insulted by community members upon return, or that community members were afraid of them. Even so, these insults and fear did not seem to deter their long-term reintegration: 94 per cent reported that they felt 'very' or 'somewhat' accepted by their community at the time. Moreover, there was no significant difference between the abducted and non-abducted in reported levels of 14 concrete forms of social support, suggesting that former abducted youth are able to find support within their communities.[17]

Where persecution of formerly abducted youth by the community takes place, however, it seems to take specific forms and follow regular patterns. First, alcohol is often part of the problem. Youth report that verbal abuse often comes from drunken community members. Further, arguments are often about scarcity of resources. Second, returnees were least accepted and sometimes persecuted by grieving parents and families whose children had not yet returned. Returnees explain that relatives of unreturned youth would angrily ask them why they returned when their children were not so fortunate. From a youth abducted for three years, 'When I returned, some people used very bad and unkind language because some of them whose sons and daughters were abducted but did not return felt bad that I returned'. Third, these insults seem to occur more frequently when there is rebel activity in the area. Unable to react against the LRA, the community seems to displace their anger onto the youth who have already returned. Fourth, children who return with some marks from the rebels such as any form of deforming injury or disability take quite some time to adjust because they are teased and constantly reminded of their experience. Those who exhibit abnormal behaviour that is labelled as spiritual pollution (*cen*) seem to be more stigmatized as well.

Finally, particular youth are targeted and insulted when the community knows or suspects they were involved in raids or killings, as this 18-year-old youth describes:

> I think they are talking like that because when I was abducted, the rebels beat me and asked me to show them where goats could be got. So I showed them the neighbor's goats because we didn't have goats of our own. So ever since I returned, the owners of these goats are on my case and some have very bad thoughts about me and I think some of them can even kill me. And I think that if it were possible, I should not continue staying in [my camp].

A social worker from a reception centre later disclosed that this youth was actually known to have killed some members of the community and that they had discussed several alternative living situations for him. He also described how recent attacks made the situation worse for him: 'In case you heard about the recent ambushes on the roads, they took place last week but its making life very hard for me. Because wherever people see me, they say, "Look at the murderer. There he is passing".'

Educational and economic reintegration

While psychologically and socially resilient on average, the survey-based analysis implies a large and broad-based impact of forcible recruitment upon education and earnings – impacts that come as a consequence of time spent with the rebel group in the bush rather than in school or acquiring employment experience. The average loss of schooling is roughly nine months, almost exactly the same amount as the average length of abduction. This schooling loss, while seemingly moderate, has a disproportionate impact on a youth's skills. Former abductees are also twice as likely to be illiterate, in part because the years of schooling missed by adolescent abductees – grades six and seven – are ones where students in Uganda typically learn to read and write. The economic consequences of this skill loss are substantial. Abducted youth are half as likely to be engaged in skill- or capital-intensive employment, and have one-third lower daily earnings. The education gap seems to account for nearly two-thirds of this earnings gap, followed by loss of experience and injuries.

The evidence suggests that these educational and economic gaps are not driven by exposure to violent trauma, but rather time out of civilian education and labour market experience. Longer abductions, not violent trauma experienced, are associated with the greatest gaps in education, skilled employment and wages. A decomposition of wages into the individual components of human capital suggest that the gap in education among abductees appears to account for roughly 60 per cent of the gap in wages and productivity. Since children and adolescents are more likely to have their education interrupted than young adults, the education and wage impact of child soldiering is greater than that for adults.

Qualitative evidence suggests that abducted youth are engaged in lower-productivity employment. Local labour markets could be characterized as an occupational ladder increasing in skill and resource requirements, which a youth gradually ascends through the slow accumulation of education and capital. One young man's experience is representative of that relayed by many youth:

> I began [my business] when I was still at home. I was making charcoal. But when people came to the camps, I started riding a boda boda [bicycle taxi] … I used to ride as a boda boda on all the roads but when the rebels started killing boda boda cyclists along the way. I left this job and then started studying.… [Later] the money that I had saved helped me to start this business.

By many accounts, abduction interrupts a youth's ascent up this ladder, or pulls him off one rung and places him on a lower one.

Abducted youth exhibit some catch-up over time. Among former abductees in our sample, the education and wage gap is smaller the longer a youth has been back since abduction, after controlling for potentially confounding factors such as length and age of abduction. However, the gap does not appear to close fully, suggesting that, in the absence of significant economic and educational interventions, abduction has led to a persistent gap, or inequality, between ex-combatants and non-combatants in the population.

Violence and alienation

A final concern relates to the way abduction and war violence may increase youth hostility, aggression and political alienation. There is comparatively weak evidence to support this view. Formerly abducted males were no more likely to have been in a physical fight in the past month, and there was no difference in reported attitudes towards spousal abuse. Overall, levels of violence are not high, and we observe little difference among abducted youth. As a technical school teacher explained, 'None of them [former abductees] has yet displayed any serious form of indiscipline like theft or physical fights'. Rather, 'it's the non-abducted students who are very stubborn [defiant]', he explained, 'There is always some fear in the formerly abducted students but this goes away say after the first year and after this, you can hardly differentiate the formerly abducted and the non-abducted'. In fact, fewer than 5 per cent of all youth reported behaviours and attitudes associated with hostility (such as cursing, taking things without permission, or getting angry for little reason). Former abductees were, however, somewhat more likely to self-report such behaviours. It is difficult to interpret such self-reported disparities in the absence of any evidence of differences in actions. It may reflect a willingness to admit to hostile feelings rather than real changes in behaviour.

As for political exclusion, preliminary results suggest that political engagement actually *increases* as a consequence of abduction. Formerly abducted youth were one-quarter more likely to vote in the 2005 referendum, and were twice as likely to report holding a community leadership position (Blattman 2007). Abduction has little relationship with other, non-political forms of participation such community group or committee membership, however. The principal determinant of this heightened political engagement, moreover, appears to be the degree of violence experienced – more violence is associated with a greater propensity to vote and be a community leader. Indeed, violence experienced while abducted appears to be the only war experience that is significantly and consistently related to political participation, and accounts for nearly all of the observed relationship between abduction and participation. Evidence presented in Blattman (2007) suggests that this link from violence to political action is most consistent with theories of 'expressive' participation, whereby youth are motivated to action by a desire to express frustration over adverse past experiences and right past wrongs.

Implications for peace-building and security

With new evidence at hand, it is worth considering whether child soldiers are indeed a time-bomb that threaten stability and growth as widely feared. In northern Uganda at least, the adverse impacts on growth are much more obvious than those on stability. There is no obvious evidence of violence or political alienation, and indeed the opposite may be true. The economic and educational gaps, however, appear large and seemingly persistent and with so many youth affected, the aggregate consequences for the region's income and growth are undoubtedly large. Of course, what may be more important for predicting future security risks is not an average increase in the propensity for violence, but rather an increased risk of violence among a very small group. After all, both Kony's movement and previous guerrilla movements in northern Uganda were begun by a small handful of distrustful and dislocated professional soldiers (Behrend 1999). What happens in a very small, statistically 'invisible' group may thus be more important than the average impact on the bulk of ex-combatants.

Related to this concern, a real risk is that the poverty and inequality that come about as a result of war and abduction increase the likelihood of future conflict.

Some scholars of civil war have suggested the idea of an economic 'conflict trap', where the adverse economic impacts of war make the outbreak of further conflict more likely. Some theorize that poverty leads to increased rebellion, as individuals may have relatively more to gain from soldiering than peace when economic opportunities are poor (e.g. Grossman and Kim 1995; Sambanis 2004; Walter 2004). Others argue that inequality, perhaps even that arising between combatants and non-combatants, leads to greater discontent and, ultimately, rebellion and turmoil (e.g. Gurr 1971). This study draws a fairly concrete link between participation in civil conflict and persistent poverty and inequality. The link from there to violence has yet to be made, however, and ought to be a focus of future research.

Implications for reintegration programme design and targeting

The evidence from male youth in Uganda suggests that more targeted psycho-social programmes and broad-based economic and educational recovery programmes are most appropriate.

Targeted, specialized, and culturally relevant psycho-social interventions

Psychologically, a minority of former combatants experience frequent symptoms of distress. Furthermore, a small number of youth continue to be harassed by community members or are estranged from their families. These youth seem to need more than what is offered through the current general psycho-social programmes and network of helpers and assisting them may take more specialized interventions than the wide-scale community-based programming that has been taking place. Moreover, these services need to be culturally-relevant and draw on local resources.

Culturally-appropriate individual or group symptom-reduction interventions are likely to be the most successful approach for some of the most extreme cases that have not improved with the available social networks and interventions (such as ceremonies, prayers or recreational activities). In northern Uganda there are currently a handful of diploma-level counsellors who have been trained in mental health interventions. Many are working in full-time positions in other capacities, however, and are only able to able to meet with their cases on occasion due to travel and time constraints. Building the capacity and reach of these counsellors as well as increasing the number of counsellors able to provide interventions would help to treat this population.

For those youth who continue to be stigmatized by the community, it is not clear that the current approach – broad-based community-sensitization meetings and public messages – will address the causes of the stigmatization. As discussed above, stigmatization and conflict are often between the youth and a specific handful of people over specific and persistent grievances. Rather than large-scale sensitization campaigns, family- and community-based conflict resolution interventions might better address the issues that are emerging.

Anecdotal evidence collected alongside the survey also suggests that resentment runs high in communities over the targeting of the formerly abducted for aid and assistance. While the survey and research design did not allow a formal evaluation of reintegration packages and programmes, above we noted post-survey interviews with individual youth, as well as community meetings with both youth and elders in eight camps, that suggest that the targeting of former abductees continues to upset and offend many community members. Stigmatization rather than reintegration may be the unintended consequence of such an approach to service delivery. As discussed below, targeting youth according to well-identified needs rather than combatant status may be less stigmatizing and more effective.

Broad-based economic and educational interventions

The survey and interview evidence suggest that formerly abducted youth exhibit a deficit of education and experience, and may need assistance to get back on track. In the current war economy, youth face an occupational ladder of entrepreneurial activities, ascending in skill and capital intensity. A best strategy may be to support them in this climb through programmes that increase their access to skills, equipment and working capital (i.e. start-up and operating funds). Official reintegration packages, providing cash and household items years after return, likely do little to help youth make up their losses and increase their productivity. Many NGO programmes appear to have done better, promoting skills training and micro-enterprises. Of course, there have been no evaluations of the success of these programmes, and so their actual impact upon economic development and reintegration is unknown.

Even if effective, however, the promotion of entrepreneurial activities is at best a short-term solution, and a partial one at that. The survey evidence suggests that most youth earn only a meagre income from the casual labour and odd jobs that form the basis of employment in camp economies. Increasing the supply of these services by scaling-up of vocational training and enterprise development programmes will soon run up against an inevitable constraint: a lack of demand. It is far from clear that camp economies can support more kiosks, more tailors, more charcoal production, or more bicycle taxis. The economics is simple: as these services increase, prices will fall, making such activities unprofitable for all.

The only real option for helping households generate a real income appears to be a return to the original productive base of the northern Ugandan economy: a combination subsistence farming, cash-cropping and livestock-rearing. Yet until recently there has been little or no government or NGO focus on returning people to the land, increasing agricultural productivity (through access to inputs or extension services), or re-stocking the cattle population of the north. Cattle stocks in particular are thought to have fallen from hundreds of thousands in the 1980s to nearly zero today.

Finally, in terms of closing the education gap, age-appropriate educational interventions will be required for adolescents and young adults. Understandably, the bulk of attention so far has been upon keeping primary schools open and running. These programmes do little to help the bulk of ex-combatants returning from conflict, and indeed little to help youth over 15 years of age more generally. These are an important group. The 11 per cent of youth who are illiterate are almost all unschooled young adults, and it has severely reduced their earning opportunities. At the time of writing, however, there were no fast-track literacy and numeracy programmes in operation in the north.[18] Most youth who missed out on primary school have no other option than to rejoin primary classes with children many years younger. The sole adult-oriented programme in existence, which uses the government adult literacy curriculum, serves the young adult population but uses methods and materials geared towards primary students. It also moves at the same pace as regular primary school – one year for each standard – a pace that few adults can afford given their financial, parental and social obligations.

Targeting based on needs rather than combatant status

The anecdotal evidence is strongly suggestive that targeting of former combatants as a group is counter-productive, primarily because it can be stigmatizing within the community. As an alternative, broad-based, inclusive support, as we have advocated for education and economic programmes, need not create categories or stigmatization, especially when they are both merit- and needs-based. Rather, targeting programmes to *all* war-affected youth based on well-identified needs rather than combatant status may be more effective and less stigmatizing than current categories of vulnerability, and yet still reach the most vulnerable by default. As discussed in Annan *et al.* (2006), the markers for vulnerability include serious injuries, illiteracy, low levels of education (i.e. less than three years), persistent unemployment, estrangement from families, severe symptoms of psychological distress, and conflicts with community members. Moving from a system of circumstantial categorization to one based on specific, easily identified, and acute needs promises more effective and less stigmatizing targeting of assistance.

How applicable are lessons from the Ugandan case?

Can such findings and recommendations be generalized beyond northern Uganda? In spite of the special circumstances in Uganda, evidence from other conflicts suggests that the general patterns we observe among Ugandan ex-combatants may hold true in other settings. For instance, the psycho-social resilience of the average youth is consistent with the idea that resilience is ordinary rather than extraordinary (Masten 2001). What is remarkable is that this resilience is 'ordinary' even in an area of such extreme violence, something that varies widely across different studies.[19] The relationship between increased exposure to violence and higher emotional distress is similar to other findings (Mollica *et al.* 1997). Moreover, the relationship between violence, long-term reintegration success, and political participation is consistent with evidence from post-war Sierra Leone (Bellows and Miguel 2006; Humphreys and Weinstein 2005). Finally, the economist Joshua Angrist (1990, 1998) has also found a large negative earnings impact from military service among white American youth drafted into the Vietnam War. As in northern Uganda, the source of this earnings gap appears to be time away from civilian education and work experience. While only a handful of data points exist, the similarity of findings in such disparate circumstances is striking. While levels of income, schooling and economic activity will change across contexts, what may remain constant is the relative gap between ex-combatants and civilians, the greater prevalence of economic and educational impacts relative to psycho-social ones, and the relevant channels of impact.

In the meantime, it is worth considering special features of the Ugandan case, to thereby understand whether larger, smaller, or completely dissimilar results could be expected in other contexts. There are several seemingly special features of the Ugandan case. First, we are dealing with the reintegration of conscripts rather than volunteers. While the results are most easily generalized to other instances of forcible recruitment, they may actually understate the consequences of voluntary participation in other unpopular armed groups. Popular discourse in Uganda holds that the abducted should not be held accountable for their actions. Parents of non-abducted children, for instance, frequently noted in interviews that it could just as easily have been their child that was taken, and most recognize the importance for their community of welcoming back the two-fifths of young males that were taken over the years. The remarkable community response observed in Uganda directly diminishes the social exclusion of abducted children, and indirectly may mute the economic, social and psychological impacts. That is, volunteer recruits, had they existed, might not have been so easily forgiven and reintegrated into the community. Globally one-third of child soldiers are thought to be forcibly recruited (ILO 2003). For the other two-thirds of child soldiers, who might not receive as warm a welcome after war, the treatment effects estimated in this chapter might be regarded as a minimum impact.

Second, the armed group was highly unpopular, poor and unskilled and few investments were made in training youth. Alternatively, had participation in the armed group offered social prestige, relevant training and experience, or a chance at enrichment, then we might have observed fewer gaps in the economic performance of former combatants. For instance, in the same study of US Vietnam veterans discussed above, Angrist (1990) found that African-American draftees experienced a net gain in long-term earnings. Angrist speculates that the effect may be due to a willingness by employers to hire black veterans over non-veterans after the war. Also, the training and experience available to black males in the US army may have been superior to the limited options available to them in a relatively unequal US labour market.

A third unique feature of the Ugandan case is that the majority of abductees were children at the time of abduction. This cruel focus appears to have come as a consequence of the LRA's dependence on forcible recruitment – under coercion, young adolescents appear to have made more dependable recruits due to their propensity to become indoctrinated or be more easily disoriented. Where rebel groups possess more resources or command greater respect or support, a higher proportion of the rebel group is likely to be adult. The evidence from Uganda suggests that the impacts of soldiering on adults will be less than that for child soldiers when the returns to education are greater than the returns to work experience. One reason is that wages and productivity in northern Uganda appear much more responsive to additional education than to additional work experience. Another is that work experience may also be more easily regained than education, especially where remedial education programmes are scarce. Children, who trade schooling for soldiering, may thus experience greater long-term economic losses than adults, who are more likely to miss out on work experience. In economies where the relative return to work experience is greater, however, the opposite could be true.

Before we can make any such conclusions and generalizations with confidence, however, there is an acute need for more research in more zones of conflict. Moreover, to understand which reintegration programmes have what impacts and unintended consequences, evaluations of DDR will be required. While research such as that reviewed in this chapter may help identify the gaps between combatants and non-combatants as a consequence of conflict, the ability of government and NGOs to fill these gaps – a key determinant of the allocation of reintegration resources – is still unknown. Moreover, the potentially adverse unintended impacts on combatants – whether stigmatization or other still hidden effects – compel us to ensure that DDR programmes are doing no harm. The aim should be to move from ad hoc to evidence-based policy in post-conflict reintegration, redevelopment and peace-building.

Notes

1 Christopher Blattman is an Assistant Professor of Political Science and Economics at Yale University. Jeannie Annan is based at the Yale University School of Medicine. Dr Blattman and Dr Annan are co-directors of the Survey for War Affected Youth in Northern Uganda (www.sway-uganda.org).
2 See Wessells (2006) for a thorough review of the literature on child soldiering.
3 Interviewing large, representative samples of former combatants has proven expensive, time-consuming and logistically challenging, and so even the few large-scale surveys of children and adults associated with armed groups have tended to be unrepresentative of ex-combatants within a particular conflict. Allen (2005) and ILO (2003), for instance, provide detailed and insightful analyses of combat and reintegration experiences, but are based on convenience or otherwise non-representative samples.
4 This history is based on Allen (2005); Behrend (1991, 1998, 1999); Doom and Vlassenroot (1999); Finnström (2003); Lamwaka (2002) and Omara-Otunnu (1987).
5 See Finnström (2003) and Dolan (2005) for a discussion of the political rhetoric and activities of the LRA. See Branch (2005); Vinci (2005); van Acker (2004) and Doom

and Vlassenroot (1999) for a discussion of the strategic use of violence in northern Uganda. Finally, see Blattman and Annan (2008) for a discussion of the logic of child recruitment.

6 The collection and analysis of these data are described in more detail in Annan *et al.* (2006) and Blattman and Annan (2007). Additional detail on psychosocial measures is contained in Annan (2007), and additional analysis of abduction experiences is provided in Blattman and Annan (2008).

7 Throughout this chapter, 'abduction' refers to any time forcibly spent with the rebels, regardless of length. Abductees thus include those taken for a few hours up to those absent for a decade.

8 The current size of the LRA remains unknown, with estimates ranging from a few hundred to a few thousand fighters. A very different DDR process than that which has taken place so far may be required should a peace agreement be reached and demobilization begun.

9 It should be noted that these programmes are distinct from the DDR Agreement (2008) discussed in Chapter 9 by Muggah and Baaré (this volume).

10 Such results are echoed by Allen and Schomerus (2006).

11 Baines (2005, 2007) and Harlacher *et al.* (2006) describe these ceremonies and their significance in detail.

12 A copy is available at www.c-r.org/our-work/accord/northern-uganda/documents/ 2000_Jan_The_Amnesty_Act.doc.

13 See Chapter 9 by Muggah and Baaré (this volume) for more on the ICC and implications for DDR.

14 There are many questions surrounding the use and appropriateness of the Amnesty Act, many of which have been addressed by Allen and Schomerus (2006).

15 See Annan (2007) for an in-depth discussion of the psychosocial impacts, including risk and protective factors.

16 This estimate controls for potentially confounding factors such as length of abduction. The experience or commission of violence is not exogenous, of course, so we must be cautious with a causal interpretation of the violence-distress link. For instance, if sociopathic tendencies lead some abductees to commit more violence as well as feel less remorse, we might underestimate the causal relationship between violence and distress. Other confounding factors may likewise lead our estimate to over- or understate the causal relationship.

17 Examples of social support include whether in the previous month someone lent you money or belongings, watched your belongings while you were away, comforted you when you were sad, gave you advice or counsel, and so forth.

18 In 2005 and 2006, an adult literacy programme was launched in Gulu with support from the International Rescue Committee. The programme, however, used a standard (children's) curriculum and required that as many years be spent in the programme as years of education received – that is, the programme did not provide fast-track opportunities for adults.

19 See, for example, Ajdukovic and Ajdukovic (1998); Dyregrov *et al.* (2002) and Dyregrov *et al.* (2000)

Bibliography

Ajdukovic, M. and Ajdukovic, D. (1998) 'Impact of displacement on the psychological well-being of refugee children', *International Review of Psychiatry, 10*(3), 186–195.

Allen, T. (2005) *War and Justice in Northern Uganda: An Assessment of the International Criminal Court's Intervention*. London: Crisis States Research Centre, Development Studies Institute, London School of Economics.

Allen, T. and Schomerus, M. (2006) *A Hard Homecoming: Lessons Learned from the*

Reception Center Process on Effective Interventions for Former 'Abductees' in North-ern Uganda. Washington, DC: Management Systems International.

Angrist, J.D. (1990) 'Lifetime Earnings and the Vietnam Era Draft Lottery: Evidence from Social Security Administrative Records', *The American Economic Review, 80*(3), 313–336.

Angrist, J.D. (1998) 'Estimating the Labor Market Impact of Voluntary Military Service Using Social Security Data on Military Applicants', *Econometrica, 66*(2), 249–288.

Annan, J. (2007) *Self-Appraisal, Social Support, and Connectedness as Protective Factors for Youth Associated with Fighting Forces in Northern Uganda.* Unpublished dissertation. Indiana University.

Annan, J., Blattman, C. and Horton, R. (2006) *The State of Youth and Youth Protection in Northern Uganda: Findings from the Survey of War-Affected Youth.* Kampala: UNICEF Uganda.

Baaré, A. (2006) 'An Analysis of Transitional Economic Reintegration', *Stockholm Initiative on Disarmament Demobilization and Reintegration Background Studies:* 17–54 Ministry of Foreign Affairs, Sweden.

Baines, E.K. (2005) *Roco Wat I Acholi: Restoring Relationships in Acholiland.* Kampala: Liu Institute for Global Issues, Gulu District NGO Forum, and Ker Kwaro Acholio.

Baines, E.K. (2007) 'The Haunting of Alice: Local Approaches to Justice and Reconcili-ation in Northern Uganda', *International Journal of Transitional Justice, 1*(1), 91.

BBC (2007) 'Child Soldiers Are a Time Bomb' [Electronic Version]. *BBC News.* Retrieved 5 February 2007, from www.news.bbc.co.uk/go/pr/fr/-/2/hi/europe/6330503.stm.

Behrend, H. (1991) 'Is Alice Lakwena a Witch? The Holy Spirit Movement and its Fight against Evil in the North', in H.B. Hansen and M. Twaddle (eds), *Changing Uganda. The Dilemmas of Structural Adjustment and Revolutionary Change.* London: James Currey.

Behrend, H. (1998) 'War in Northern Uganda', in C. Clapham (ed.), *African Guerrillas.* Bloomington: Indiana University Press.

Behrend, H. (1999) *Alice Lakwena & the Holy Spirits: War in Northern Uganda, 1985–97.* London: James Currey.

Bellows, J. and Miguel, E. (2006) *War and Local Collective Action in Sierra Leone.* Unpublished mimeo. UC Berkeley.

Blattman, C. (2007) *Violence and Voting: The Impacts of War on Youth Political Partici-pation in Uganda.* Unpublished mimeo. UC Berkeley.

Blattman, C. and Annan, J. (2007) *The Consequences of Child Soldiering.* Unpublished mimeo. UC Berkeley.

Blattman, C. and Annan, J. (2008) 'On the Nature and Causes of LRA Abduction: What the Abductees Say', in T. Allen and K. Vlassenroot (eds), *The Lord's Resistance Army: War, Peace and Reconciliation.* Oxford: James Currey.

Branch, A. (2005) 'Neither Peace nor Justice: Political Violence and the Peasantry in Northern Uganda, 1986–1998', *African Studies Quarterly, 8*(2).

Dolan, C. (2005) *Understanding War and its Continuation: the Case of Northern Uganda.* Unpublished dissertation. University of London.

Doom, R. and Vlassenroot, K. (1999) 'Kony's Message: A New Koine? The Lord's Resistance Army in Northern Uganda', *African Affairs, 98*(390), 5–36.

Dyregrov, A., Gjestad, R. and Raundalen, M. (2002) 'Children Exposed to Warfare: A Longitudinal Study', *Journal of Traumatic Stress, 15*(1), 59–68.

Dyregrov, A., Gupta, L., Gjestad, R. and Mukanoheli, E. (2000) 'Trauma Exposure and

Psychological Reactions to Genocide Among Rwandan Children', *Journal of Traumatic Stress, 13*(1), 3–21.

Finnström, S. (2003) *Living with Bad Surroundings: War and Existential Uncertainty in Acholiland, Northern Uganda.* Uppsala: Dept. of Cultural Anthropology, Uppsala University.

Grossman, H.I. and Kim, M. (1995) 'Swords or Plowshares? A Theory of the Security of Claims to Property', *The Journal of Political Economy, 103*(6), 1275–1288.

Gurr, T.R. (1971) *Why Men Rebel.* Princeton: Princeton University Press.

Harlacher, T., Okot, F.X., Obonyo, C.A., Balthazard, M. and Atkinson, R. (2006) *Traditional Ways of Coping in Acholi: Cultural Provisions for Reconciliation and Healing from War.* Kampala: Caritas Gulu Archdioceseo.

Humphreys, M. and Weinstein, J.M. (2005) *Disentangling the Determinants of Successful Demobilization and Reintegration.* Paper presented at the Annual Meeting of the American Political Science Association.

ILO (2003) *Wounded Childhood: The Use of Child Soldiers in Armed Conflict in Central Africa.* Washington, DC: International Labor Organization.

Jensen, S. and Stepputat, F. (2001) 'Demobilising Armed Civilians', *CDR Policy Paper.* Copenhagen: CDR.

Lamwaka, C. (2002) 'The Peace Process in Northern Uganda 1986–1990', in L. Okello (ed.), *Protracted Conflict, Elusive Peace: Initiatives to End the Violence in Northern Uganda.* London: Conciliation Resources and Kacoke Madit.

Masten, A.S. (2001) 'Ordinary Magic: Resilience Processes in Development', *American Psychologist, 56*(3), 227–238.

MDRP (2007) *Uganda.* Retrieved 1 June 2007, from www.mdrp.org/uganda.htm.

Mollica, R.F., Poole, C., Son, L., Murray, C.C. and Tor, S. (1997) 'Effects of War Trauma on Cambodian Refugee Adolescents' Functional Health and Mental Health Status', *Journal of the American Academy of Child and Adolescent Psychiatry, 36*(8), 1098–1106.

New York Times (2006) 'Armies of Children'. Editorial, 12 October.

Omara-Otunnu, A. (1987) *Politics and the Military in Uganda, 1890–1985.* London: Macmillan in association with St. Antony's College, Oxford.

Sambanis, N. (2004) 'Using Case Studies to Expand Economic Models of Civil War', *Perspectives on Politics, 2*(2), 259–279.

UNWG (2006) *Integrated Disarmament, Demobilization and Reintegration Standards (IDDRS).* Online, available at: http://www.unddr.org/iddrs/.

Van Acker, F. (2004) 'Uganda and the Lord's Resistance Army: The New Order No One Ordered', *African Affairs, 103*(412), 335–357.

Vinci, A. (2005) 'The Strategic Use of Fear by the Lord's Resistance Army', *Small Wars and Insurgencies, 16*(3), 360–381.

Walter, B.F. (2004) 'Does Conflict Beget Conflict? Explaining Recurring Civil War', *Journal of Peace Research, 41*(3), 371–388.

Wessells, M. (2006) *Child Soldiers: From Violence to Protection.* Cambridge: Harvard University Press.

WHO (2005) *Health and Mortality Survey among Internally Displaced Persons in Gulu, Kitgum and Pader Districts, Northern Uganda.* Kampala: World Health Organization.

5 The politics of demobilization in Afghanistan

Michael Vinay Bhatia[1] and Robert Muggah

There appears to be an emerging consensus on the normative parameters of DDR.[2] Notwithstanding the UN's preoccupation with enhancing national ownership, comprehensive frameworks and community inclusiveness, newly minted standards still cast DDR as a short-term stand-alone initiative rather than a long-term strategic interaction. Moreover, standards such as the IDDRS tend to emphasize enabling frameworks and bureaucratic structures rather than the dynamics of mobilization or the often dynamic requirements of peace-building. Such guidelines tend to focus more on the (admittedly vital) mechanics of programming than on projected outcomes. Likewise, as noted in the Introduction, conventional approaches adopted by international agencies frequently privilege economic incentives and the promotion of livelihoods and side-step tricky questions related to politics. This chapter contends that narrowly defined approaches to DDR can unintentionally sideline complex interests held by an array of stakeholders (from states to private entrepreneurs) thereby undermining their potential role to aid (or hinder) the enterprise.

Although not necessarily by design, Afghanistan's various DDR interventions were and continue to be intertwined with the dynamics of state-building and the state's effort to monopolize the use of legitimate force. DDR was connected to a series of strategic interactions associated more broadly with political reform, peace-building and security sector reform (SSR). In order to highlight aspects of these strategic interactions, the chapter adopts a critical perspective on two successive and connected DDR initiatives. These include the Afghanistan New Beginning's Program (ANBP) (2003–2005) which focused on government-designated Afghan Militia Forces (AMF) and the (ongoing) Disbandment of Illegal Armed Groups (DIAG) (2005–2008) initiative targeting remnants of various non-state militia groups. The findings of this chapter suggest that Afghanistan's recent DDR experience offer a challenge to certain basic assumptions governing conventional DDR programming. For example, the common conceptualization of commanders and combatants as homogeneous actors appears to be particularly inappropriate in the Afghanistan context. The failure to recognize the complex relationships between former combatants from their communities – an essential factor shaping mobilization – is lamentably common. As noted elsewhere in this volume, if DDR is to generate more positive dividends its supporters will need to extend their perspective beyond a rational choice and combatant-centric approach and better accommodate factors relating to real and perceived legitimacy, outreach and community peace-building.

The chapter is divided into three sections. Following a short overview of the contemporary Afghan armed conflict, the second section examines the ANBP DDR and DIAG interventions in more detail.[3] The third section assesses DDR through a number of critical lenses:

1 from above, as part of a broader interaction with state-building and peace operations;
2 from below in relation to the differentiated factors shaping the mobilization of armed groups; and
3 in relation to tactical diplomacy and public outreach.

The chapter reveals how DDR should not be pursued narrowly as an *economic* process of reintegration, but rather conceived as symbolic, diplomatic, political and legal processes linked to local, national and international conceptions of legitimacy. Ultimately, effective DDR in Afghanistan *necessitates* the parallel ascendance of state armed forces and their acquisition of a monopoly over the legitimate use of force.[4]

The chapter draws from a comprehensive review of ANBP, DIAG and the lived experiences of commanders and combatants. Specifically, the methodology includes semi-structured life history interviews with 345 combatants conducted by Michael Bhatia in Afghanistan between mid-2004 and mid-2005. Respondents were randomly sampled at different intervals of various DDR processes. Bhatia interviewed combatants during periods of demobilization, reintegration training and as part of the work of Mobile Disarmament Units (MDU) in selected communities. The methodology also included event monitoring through a review of press and media reports and key informant interviews with international and Afghan policy-makers and practitioners. Given the protracted nature of armed violence in Afghanistan, and the geographic scale of DDR activities, a quantitative survey was not considered to be an appropriate instrument for gathering comparable data.

Overview of conflict and combatant mobilization

The Soviet invasion of Afghanistan in late 1979 was preceded by a series of tribal and garrison rebellions against an indigenous Communist *Khalqi* party government. Afghanistan's ensuing three decades of protracted warfare have been described variously as being motivated by 'tribal', 'holy', 'civil', 'ethnic', 'proxy' and 'opium' factors. The Soviet withdrawal in 1989 triggered a host of unanticipated consequences including the acceleration of armed conflict between the state and competing politico-military parties. Indeed, the collapse of the Soviet-backed Najibullah government in 1992 heightened already existing intra-Mujahidin competition and also enhanced the power of local armed strong-men. While the rise of the Taliban from 1994 onwards brought a certain measure of stability in the south, ethnic persecution of the Hazaras increased. More recently, in late 2001, Operation Enduring Freedom (OEF) rapidly expelled the Taliban. But eight years later, the Government of Afghanistan (GoA) and the NATO-led International Security and Assistance Force (ISAF) continue to struggle to defeat the insurgency, reduce poppy production and secure the majority of the population from warlords, insurgents or criminals, whether inside or outside of the government.

Over the course of Afghanistan's three decades of warfare, armed groups were empowered by billions of dollars in financial, material and military assistance.[5] The Soviets, including at least 118,000 soldiers and secret police sent to Afghanistan, were responsible for providing extensive financial and military assistance to the GoA prior to their withdrawal in 1989. By 1990, the US and Saudi Arabia had provided between US$6–8 billion in financial and military assistance to the various Mujahidin parties.[6] Training was an integral component of external military assistance – from the USSR's training of the Afghan Army in the 1950s (and the decision by the Americans to forego military engagement) to Pakistan's early support of contra-state armed groups in 1973. External military and financial assistance served as start-up or venture capital allowing armed groups to enhance their influence over the economy, village and provincial politics and local consultative bodies (*shuras*). Rubin (2003) observed how 'once armed and funded, commanders can become economically self-sufficient by gaining control of customs posts, bazaars, and opium trafficking routes'.

Afghanistan's political landscape is complex. Contemporary political parties (*tanzims*) appealed at first to educated elites lacking a foothold in local or tribal political structures.[7] These early *tanzims* were formed in Kabul during the early 1960s and included the Jawan-e-Musliman (Muslim Youth) at Kabul University in 1968, the Jamiat-i-Islami in 1972 and competing Communist and Maoist groups (e.g. Khalq, Parcham, Shola-e-Jawid). Following the Soviet invasion, the Mujahidin resistance parties were divided into moderate, traditionalist, fundamentalist, communist and nationalist *tanzims*.[8] Moderate and fundamentalist groups are present among both the Shi'a and Sunni groups. More moderate and traditionalist *tanzims* were inspired more by (pre-conflict) community and locally-based (*qawm*) order. Many of these political parties played an intermediary role in funnelling arms to various armed groups. Arms and other entitlements were at first provided through the external representatives of the seven primary *tanzims* in Peshawar (Pakistan).[9] More centralized 'bureaucratic' parties gradually emerged from secular educated groups that lacked a strong sense of ethnicity (Tajiks) and amongst urbanized Pashtuns. After 1992, however, these *tanzims* were increasingly mobilized around ethnic politics (Giustozzi 2005). Yet, it is important to note that ethnic differences and inter-ethnic conflict were a consequence, and not a root cause, of conflict.[10] With the collapse of the Najibullah government (1986–1992), the professional officer corps, army and its weapons were rapidly absorbed into Mujahidin parties or integrated into the Uzbek warlord Dostum's Army of the North (Giustozzi 2004).

There is comparatively little reliable information on the overall numbers of formal and informal combatants in Afghanistan during the past three decades, much less since 2001. Admittedly flawed estimates generated by the International Institute for Strategic Studies (IISS) reveal that peak Afghan mobilization (i.e. 533,000 'active' combatants) occurred after the Soviet withdrawal (from 1989 until 1992). During this period, the Soviets, together with Western, neighbouring and Arab states accelerated their financial support for a host of armed groups. IISS data also reveals shifting (and at times misrepresentative) external classification of Afghan armed groups throughout the Afghan conflict.[11] Between 1989 and 1992, a diverse cluster of Mujahidin 'parties' (basically temporary, permanent and reserve combatants) began fighting against state 'militia forces'. From 1993 to 1999, a rash of 'factional' fighting ensued between militarized tanzims, particularly following the emergence of the Taliban in 1994. In 2000 and 2001, the newly formed multi-ethnic 'Northern Alliance/United Front' began clashing with the Taliban. With the collapse of the Taliban, 'strongmen' and 'commanders' militias' re-emerged (with the considerable provision of US assistance) from 2002 to 2004.[12] Afghan armed actors over the past three decades exhibit an extraordinary level of heterogeneity and include multiple Mujahidin parties, tribal militias, warlords, paramilitary organizations, a trained state officer corps, armed intelligence services, and both mono-ethnic and multi-ethnic armed groups and alliances.

Following the Taliban's collapse in 2002, the loosely affiliated commanders of the anti-Taliban coalition and Northern Alliance were formally integrated into the GoA. This was achieved through the creation of the *8-Corps Afghan Military Forces* (AMF) with a combined total of 84 military units.[13] The Bonn Agreement pronounced that:

> upon the official transfer of power, all Mujahidin [sic], Afghan armed forces and armed groups in the country shall come under the command and control of the Interim Authority, and be reorganized according to the requirements of the new Afghan security and armed forces.[14]

Formal military titles were provided to local commanders depending on their connections with Kabul. In other words, loose collections of local militia were converted almost overnight into a formal military structure. The AMF effectively legitimized many commanders and private militias by association. Former officers returned to their old posts irrespective of whether they were affiliated to the previous Communist governments or to the Rabbani government. Paradoxically, the formation of the AMF induced some individuals to become combatants for the first time. Likewise, AMF commanders used their positions to further acquire local legitimacy.

The architecture of the ANBP DDR programme in Afghanistan

The ANBP DDR initiative was one of several GoA attempts to regulate the tools and agents of armed violence. It is worthwhile recalling that there is a fairly long tradition of disarmament efforts in Afghanistan: previous voluntary arms collection initiatives had been launched by the Soviet-backed Najibullah government in the late 1980s. Likewise, forced disarmament was undertaken by the Taliban in areas under its control. More recently, tactical disarmament was pursued by OEF and ISAF forces. Disarmament, then, was long deployed as a strategic intervention to secure territory and control populations.

The ANBP DDR for its part advanced a relatively conventional approach to DDR (see Introduction, this volume). It sought to promote the surrender of weapons, sever the links between AMF commanders and combatants, and reintegrate ex-fighters into meaningful employment or a newly reconstituted security sector. The structure, approach and financing arrangements for the ANBP DDR programme also evolved gradually over five years of international donor conferences. Specifically, the 2001 Bonn Agreement established the Afghan Interim Authority (AIA), and placed all United Front and anti-Taliban militias and remaining Afghan army officers in Kabul under the authority of the GoA Ministry of Defence (MoD). The 2002 Geneva Conference set-out a five-pillar strategy for SSR and assigned lead donor responsibility and a division of labour.[15] The 2002 Conference on Rebuilding Afghanistan and President Karzai's Petersberg Decree created the Afghan National Army (ANA) and reasserted the demand for 'all Afghan military forces, Mujahidin [sic] and other armed groups [to be placed] under the control of the Ministry of Defense' (Government of Germany 2004). In early 2003, the AIA created a Disarmament Commission and a Demobilization and Reintegration Commission to develop a comprehensive strategy for DDR. Soon after, the 2003 Tokyo Donors conference established the key principles and procedures for subsequent DDR programming.[16]

International commitment to DDR deepened in the wake of the 2003 Tokyo Conference. With practical interventions on the ground lagging behind expectations,[17] the March 2004 Berlin Conference generated a pledge to enhance the size and capacity of AMF troop strength by June 2004 – regarded by donors as a necessary precondition of effective DDR on the ground. This pledge was bolstered by the 2006 London–Afghanistan Compact that broadened the definition of security to incorporate 'good governance, justice and the rule of law, reinforced by reconstruction and development' (Government of Japan 2006).[18] From a diplomatic perspective, DDR was to be overseen by a Disarmament Committee (in support of the Disarmament Commission and the Demobilization and Reintegration Commission), which was composed of coalition partners, ISAF, USA, Japan, UK and UNAMA.[19] With financial support effectively shored-up, DDR operations were quickly expanded.

It is important to recall that despite growing donor commitment, DDR interventions were not fully initiated until three years after the collapse of the

Taliban. The primary impediment to more rapid implementation appeared to be the desire by Japan to initiate more comprehensive defence reform prior to the rolling-out of practical DDR activities. To be fair, many donors felt that a professional MoD and armed forces and accountable public security sector was essential to avoid the emergence of security dilemmas between competing local armed factions (see Conclusion, this volume).[20] The reform of the MoD and related security services was also considered essential to promote Afghan – or national – 'buy-in' and 'ownership' over future DDR activities.

The ANBP DDR programme was from the beginning designed explicitly to deal exclusively with former AMF personnel. Thus, in the wake of ministerial reforms, the pilot phase was initiated in late 2003 and targeted approximately 6,000 former combatants based in Kunduz, Kabul-Parwan, Paktia and Mazar-i-Sharif; and later Kandahar and Bamiyan (Curran 2003). A full-scale national programme was launched in early 2004. It should be recalled that parallel security promotion interventions were undertaken alongside DDR. For example, the removal of heavy weapons – particularly anti-aircraft missiles and armour – from Kabul was determined to be an immediate priority for ISAF.[21] Nevertheless, many AMF commanders at first adopted a 'wait and see' attitude toward the ANBP DDR initiative. In some instances, commanders sought to delay their involvement in the process as long as possible, so as to leverage their capacities to influence the electoral process and their own involvement in public office. Some commanders contended that compliance with the government's DDR order would leave them open to revenge attacks from local rivals along with reducing their capacity to negotiate lucrative provincial or national government appointments.[22]

Not unlike other DDR processes reviewed in this volume, disarmament constituted the first stage of the ANBP DDR intervention. The disarmament phase involved weapons collection, weapons verification and in certain cases on-site disposal/destruction[23] or transfer of useable weapons to the central government. It required commanders to submit lists of combatants who were paired with either small arms or heavy weapons. One of the more innovative features of the disarmament process was the creation of mobile disarmament units – or MDUs. These MDUs literally went to combatants rather than requiring the combatants to assemble in cantonment sites.[24] Either before or after surrendering their weapons, combatants were required to participate in disarmament ceremonies. Combatants were then provided with medals and certificates signalling an end to their military service and formal acknowledgment of their contribution to the 'nation'.

Former AMF combatants were also typically required to enter a demobilization process.[25] Eight regional centres were established as headquarters for disarmament and demobilization – in Kabul, Gardez, Jalalabad, Kandahar, Herat, Kunduz, and Mazar-i-Sharif and Bamiyan. Each site also maintained a Regional Verification Committee (RVC) composed of MoD officials, who established the accuracy of the lists and set-up the 'disarmament schedule ... to achieve regional balance in order to ensure ongoing stability' (UNAMA

2004a). At these centres, former fighters received reintegration advice, a lecture on mine awareness, registration for elections and bio-metric identifiers and were requested to pledge to abide by a code of conduct for good citizenship.[26] The pledge did not fully convey the fact that future mobilization would be considered a criminal act or that any future decision to pick up the gun would be considered illegal. Nevertheless, when the demobilization process was completed, the combatant was provided with an assistance package (i.e. 130 kg of wheat, oil, salt and other staples) and a *shalwar kameze* (i.e. traditional Afghan clothing). Food items rather than a cash grant were provided after commanders were found to be confiscating cash. Due to the extended travel distances and expenses of transport, many combatants nevertheless sold their demobilization package on the open market, potentially depressing local prices.

The disarmament and demobilization processes did not conform to a transparent and orderly flow as anticipated by proponents of the ANBP. As early as 2002, prospective participants were selling their weapons on local markets. One report claimed that: 'Northern Alliance soldiers have become players in one of the world's biggest and most unregulated weapons markets, perpetuating the region's war machine' (Buchbinder 2002). An arms smuggler claimed that: 'we mostly buy the arms from soldiers who are not paid their salaries'.[27] Likewise, evidence emerged that commanders demanded that soldiers hand over either the entirety or a portion of their US$200 'reintegration' payment (AFP 2004a). Commanders claimed that since they had provided the original weapons to combatants they deserved a share of the entitlements on offer.[28] Moreover, during the reintegration phase, commanders manipulated information on DDR to extract further payments from participating rank and file.

Despite the many challenges presented by disarmament and demobilization, the ANBP DDR programme advanced a threefold approach to reintegration. It focused on:

1   literacy assistance, emergency employment and food;
2   reintegration assistance and job training; and
3   a specialized commanders' programme.

The first phase included a literacy programme on the basis of findings that more than 80 per cent of all demobilized soldiers (as of September 2004) were unable to read or write.[29] Likewise, the World Bank's National Emergency Employment Program (NEEP) was initiated around the same time to issue reinsertion funds for immediate employment (cash for work and wage labour) for roughly 10,000 ex-combatants.[30] These reintegration activities were also open to combatant dependents.[31] In addition, 'vulnerable' families of ex-combatants received winter food packages and, along with former fighters, some were given temporary placements with local businesses. The ANBP DDR programme issued a number of options for reintegration designed to promote training and employment.[32] The vast majority of participating ex-combatants opted for the agricultural package (43 per cent) followed by vocational training (23.7 per cent) and small business grants (26 per cent).[33] This was not especially surprising since from the beginning, DDR planners exerted a strong agricultural bias. They by and large harboured a strong presumption that combatants were linked to village-level agricultural economies. It followed that investment in rural livelihoods offered a sustainable source of subsistence and informal income. It is worth noting, however, that the agricultural 'package' consisted primarily of the transfer of commodities rather than transferring skills or building-on existing agricultural knowledge and practice.

Overall, ex-combatants reported a considerably high level of dissatisfaction with the quality and quantity of reintegration assistance. This was at least partly attributable to their conviction that they were *owed* jobs rather than merely training. For example, an ANBP sponsored survey revealed that almost half (48 per cent) of DDR participants indicated that small business assistance was 'not good'. Likewise, a considerable number of participants claimed that they were dissatisfied with their small business support (38 per cent reporting that it was 'not good' and 60 per cent claiming that it was 'mediocre') (Winderl 2005: 18–21). They were also largely dissatisfied with other support packages, especially de-mining training and farming support. Although a con-siderable proportion of participants voiced satisfaction with skills training (71 per cent claiming it was 'very good'), interviews with those receiving skills training revealed that many advocated for greater access to micro-credit funds in order to open shops. As described by one ex-combatant: 'DDR always promises things and we get nothing.... No one gives us a job.... We are all so disappointed.'[34] By early 2005 there appeared to be an over-supply of trained de-miners, with substantial competition for employment after training (ANBP 2005a). At the conclusion of the programme in 2005, the ANBP initiated a Reintegration Support Project to train Afghan civil servants to provide re-integration 'advice' to combatants.

Unsurprisingly, the reintegration of ex-combatants appeared to be more chal-lenging than either disarmament or demobilization. Several years after DDR, evidence of 'successful' political, social or even economic reintegration was dif-ficult to find. While a considerable proportion of the more than 60,000 combat-ants participated in reintegration training, less than 25 per cent of participating combatants claimed to 'have found a long-term and sustainable activity'.[35] Records from the ANBP DDR programme indicate that some 18 per cent did not participate in any form of reintegration at all – opting instead for spontaneous settlement. Some observers attribute the 'failure' of reintegration to the ex-combatants' limited civilian skills and the absorptive capacity of areas of return. But as discussed in more detail below, the narrow conceptualization of Afghan combatants as mono-skilled (with few possibilities for alternative livelihoods) and an undifferentiated approach to addressing mid-level commanders were also partly to blame.

Meanwhile, the Commander Incentive Programme (CIP) and Senior Com-manders Programme (SCP) also encountered challenges in providing reintegra-tion support. Dealing with commanders was never going to be a straightforward task. As noted by Rubin (2003): 'the most difficult and challenging problem will be the mid-level commanders. Many of them have grown wealthy through the use of their forces to commandeer property and prey upon trade, including the drug trade'. Other analysts highlighted the challenges accompanying the reintegration of village-level commanders.[36] The commanders' programme provided training to 320 commanders and 150 MoD generals, and a salary of US$1,200 per month, which was generally considered to be an insufficient substitute for the amount the commanders were likely capable of earning while under arms. Moreover, funds were issued exclusively to senior commanders with no similar programme for low and mid-level commanders raising the ire of many not receiving support. In order to supplement cash transfers, partnerships were simultaneously launched with the Ministry of Education to encourage teacher training and with the Ministry of Communication to provide training in communication systems. But the relatively low salaries provided to teachers (US$50 per month) diminished the attractiveness of these options to commanders. As a result, the CIP and SCP came under intense criticism.[37]

If measured by numbers alone, the ANBP DDR intervention appears to have registered certain important dividends. For example, the programme collected, destroyed and secured an unprecedented number of ammunition, weapons and explosive rounds. In 20 months (from 2004 until late 2005) and for US$141 million, 259 AMF units were demobilized, over 63,380 AMF members were disarmed and demobilized with 53,415 (84 per cent) of them finishing a reintegration programme. A total of 106,510 weapons were collected; with 38,099 light weapons and 12,248 heavy weapons handed over to the Afghan MoD, and 56,163 weapons destroyed. The Steering Group on Anti-Personnel Mine and Ammunition Stockpile Destruction Project surveyed 30 tonnes of ammunition, destroyed 15.8 tonnes and 512,845 mines for a total cost of US$16 million (UNDP 2006). The Panjshir Valley alone was estimated to contain 305 containers of surplus, with another 1,900 truckloads of ammunition and weapons gathered from caves and fields.

As important as these outputs were, the primary flaws in the ANBP DDR approach limited its outcomes. The absence of a permanently standing DDR steering committee – which was later rectified with the creation of a DIAG steering committee – seriously impeded progress. The lack of political buy-in and coherence limited senior commander involvement. Also, in the rush to secure strategic buy-in from commanders on the ground, DDR programmes unintentionally formalized their fighting forces and militias – they were basically left intact and integrated into government security forces. Alternatively, commanders avoided DDR altogether, presenting a token force for disarmament and demobilization while abstaining from reintegration. At a more operational level, the absence of sufficiently attractive remuneration for mid-level commanders reduced their incentive to participate in DDR and increased their willingness to join thriving private security companies (PSC) proliferating in Kabul. Ultimately, reintegration programmes were not designed (or evaluated) to anticipate the future (re)mobilization of participants into other armed groups. This kind of contingency planning would have required a more expansive and multi-phased intervention.

Other external factors also contributed to limiting DDR effectiveness. The presence of other opportunities for (profitable) armed employment – including the coalition-driven war economy – meant that individuals could opt out of the DDR programme at each phase. Predictably, demobilized soldiers without a range of alternate income opportunities could opt for working with a PSC or in the poppy economy. But the prevailing assumption that exclusively economic factors determined and sustained mobilization neglected the broader motives of status, authority and protection derived from membership of one armed group or another. Thus, it could be credibly argued that the challenges of the ANBP DDR programme were connected not just to structural flaws, but also the profound inability of the international donor community or the Afghan government to elaborate a coherent plan to promote security and minimize security dilemmas.

Architecture of the DIAG programme in Afghanistan

Beginning in early 2005, the UNDP-administered DIAG intervention was aimed to shore-up the (admittedly modest) gains of the ANBP DDR programme.[38] Explicitly linked to the ANBP process, DIAG was designed to contend with non-state militias that existed outside of the AMF structure and deal with 'high risk' spoilers. These militias were widespread and menacing: as many as 2,000 armed groups (consisting of an estimated 125,000 potential fighters) were reportedly dispersed throughout the country following the DDR of AMF forces although only 200 of them were considered to constitute any kind of threat (Barron 2005). The objectives of DIAG were described by the ANBP (2006) as:

> a process intending to eradicate the influence of illegal armed groups in Afghanistan, thus allowing the consolidation of peace, rule of law and prosperity in the country. By voluntarily surrendering their weapons, disbanding and severing link with armed groups, ex-commanders and government officials linked with groups will demonstrate their support to the Government to build a safe and prosperous Afghanistan.

Although ostensibly targeting non-state militia, DIAG also included a number of 'beneficiaries' from previous DDR efforts. In fact, many of the irregular militias targeted by DIAG were headed by former-AMF commanders previously demobilized by the ANBP DDR process. In certain cases, commanders had only demobilized their peripheral or reserve forces, and not those members held in highest esteem.[39] In fact, many of these more senior members had separately (and often informally) been integrated into state officialdom (e.g. as governors and police chiefs) or pursued a role in parliament.

In order to be successful, the UN deemed that the DIAG intervention required a coherent normative framework to guide the process.[40] As with the ANBP DDR programme, the DIAG initiative was bolstered by a series of international donor support conferences.[41] Unlike the ANBP DDR process which was driven by international actors and support from the MoD, DIAG was and continues to be primarily led by the GoA and a new DIAG Commission.[42] Although supported by the UNDP and certain donors,[43] many aspects of the DDR programme are overseen by the central government together with provincial councils and governors. In Kabul, for example, the DIAG Commission is led by the second Vice-President Karim Khalili and the Commission Vice-Chairman Masoum Stanikzai and overseen and executed by the Ministry of Interior (MoI), MoD and NDS.[44] The DIAC Commission includes a 'participatory' coordination mechanism (known as the DIAG Forum), a DIAG international consultative group and DIAG provincial committees to guide the process with representatives of the provincial governments.

From June 2005 onwards, DIAG was expected to proceed in three phases:

1   voluntary entry to the programme prior to the parliamentary elections (with possibilities for disqualification);
2   the identification of commanders and requests for commander participation with support of NDS and other national security bodies; and
3   potential forceful disarmament of non-participants (Ibrahimi 2006).

But before embarking on full-scale DDR, DIAG supporters were adamant that a legal precedent be established for the disarmament phase. While they sought to respond to local demands for disarmament and proposed community development projects 'in exchange' for arms, they also reserved the option to use force. Following the establishment of national firearms legislation, the possession of weapons without a license in Afghanistan was determined to be a criminal offence.[45]

The DIAG DDR process adopted a decentralized implementation process at the provincial level, with governors made responsible for executing the programme and chairing various DIAG committees supported by elected Provincial Councils. The 2005 election of Provincial Councils (essentially a provincial legislature) provided an additional mechanism through which to coordinate and exert pressure on local commanders. Afghanistan government-led delegations from Kabul visited provinces to oversee the surrender of weapons thereby fortifying the connection between the Kabul central government and the provinces and communities. The number of weapons to be submitted by each commander was negotiated between provincial DIAG committee and individual commanders.[46] But this process also experienced a degree of moral hazard. Because weapon surrenders were negotiated between the parties and transparent records of commander stockpiles are unavailable, the amount of weapons submitted by each commander varied considerably.[47] Intriguingly, the majority of the commanders and militia leaders surrendering weapons had already participated in the original ANBP DDR programme, perhaps highlighting the potential value of successive DDR campaigns in the country.

Over time, the DIAG provincial committees sought to broaden local support to enhance the handing-over of arms. This was achieved through regular meetings with tribal elders, mullahs, district and Provincial Governors, Provincial Councils, and local with the end goal of inducing participation by local commanders (and intensifying local stigmas against arms possession).[48] After undertaking localized disarmament, District Development Councils (the Afgan district body used for identifying and prioritizing local development needs) identified potential community development projects. Despite much fanfare, however, DIAG community projects were few and far between[49] and outputs were dismal. Development projects were launched in three districts of Kapisa following the participation of ten leaders of IAGs and the surrendering of only 141 weapons (UNDP 2006b).

The challenges associated with forcefully disarming commanders through the DIAG DDR process were daunting. Beginning in May 2006, the government began issuing notifications to commanders demanding that they surrender their weapons and disband armed groups within a month. The selection of target provinces appeared to be partially based on popular demand and support, as demonstrated by community protests against predatory commanders in each of these locations (ANBP 2006c). For example, in 2005, thousands of Takhar civilians protested against commanders (many of whom held positions in the upper/lower house of parliament or as senior police authorities at the provincial level) who avoided dismantling their private militias and instead redistributed weapons to their supporters. The province was subsequently targeted by DIAG in June 2006.[50] The early outputs were disappointing. By early July 2005, in Kapisa province, some 45 Jihadi commanders had submitted just 251 weapons (only 94 of which were actually functioning), with more than 20 commanders failing to submit weapons at all (ANBP 2006d).

One of the primary weaknesses of DIAG appeared to be its lopsided structure and narrow conceptualization as a disarmament programme with sporadic development incentives. Interventions were effectively negotiated between DDR Commission representatives, and to some extent provincial governors and commanders but were less able to address the interests of combatants, commander networks and local structures. Likewise, incentives for disarmament – including development projects or infrastructure schemes – were often negotiated only *after* disarmament was achieved. The DIAG programme soon became equated, erroneously, with disarmament and to a lesser extent demobilization, throwing up obstacles to local buy-in. Consequently short-term outputs (weapons returned) were limited and long-term benchmarks (dismantling a commander's links to local combatants) seldom occurred. As of writing, despite some early gains, the DIAG programme appears to have stalled, partly due to the government and international community's renewed focus on the counter-insurgency.

Reconsidering DDR in Afghanistan

It is difficult to imagine a more challenging environment for DDR than Afghanistan. The interconnected challenges were recently described by the government of Afghanistan (GoA 2006) to include, *inter alia*:

(i) the growing insecurity and insurgency centred in four southern provinces, fueled by persistent cross-border support; (ii) the largely unfulfilled aspirations of many Afghans for increased economic opportunities and more accessible social services; (iii) the slow progress in eliminating the scourge of narcotics production that is fueling the ongoing insurgency and undermining efforts to improve governance and reduce corruption; and (iv) the difficulties of building capacity in the public sector that is needed to effectively manage the country's development.

Not only is Afghanistan situated in a paradigmatically bad neighbourhood wedged as it is between Tajikistan, Uzbekistan, Pakistan and Iran, but the country also features a multiplicity of armed groups, protracted armed conflict due to an escalating Taliban–AGF insurgency, an expanding poppy-driven economy and escalating violence amongst competing local commanders. It also appears that many localized armed groups continue to 'reinvent' themselves as private security actors.

From the beginning, DDR was expected to be undertaken in parallel with the creation of new Afghan national army. However, despite episodic investment, robust SSR initiatives were seriously under-resourced by the international community and ISAF-contributing countries. Not only does Afghanistan exhibit one of the lowest foreign troop to population ratios of any recent multilateral peace-support intervention,[51] but political progress in reforming and reconstituting legitimate Afghan national police, judicial and army structures was repeatedly postponed. The twin objectives of training and deploying 18,000 Afghan army forces by late 2003 fell behind due in part to the desire to create a multi-ethnic force de-linked from the Mujahidin and Northern Alliance factions.[52] Moreover, the absence of an accountable, rights-respecting and responsive police and judiciary increased popular discontent and alienation from the government. Thus, at the outset of both the ANBP and DIAG DDR initiatives, Afghanistan faced the dilemma of mass demobilization without a corresponding increase in the national army or police resulting in a classic security dilemma.

A related and significant challenge was the inability of donors to effectively align and coordinate their interventions. As described by Sedra and Middlebrook (2005: 8): 'inadequate donor coordination ... has had a particularly adverse impact on Afghanistan's security sector reform process due to the multi-sectoral donor support scheme erected to facilitate international assistance', wherein 'responsibilities for each of the five pillars of the reform process [were divided] among the five main states funding the security sector'. Likewise, as in other cases of SSR, 'a narrow focus on professionalizing the armed forces at the expense of efforts to strengthen the rule of law and role of civilians in managing and monitoring the security sector would be counter-productive and potentially dangerous' (Hendrickson 1999: 27).

Having reviewed both the history of armed conflict in Afghanistan and two successive DDR initiatives, the following sections seek to re-situate the debate on DDR in the country. It examines contradictions and dilemmas of the DDR process in Afghanistan from several perspectives:

1   from below, in relation to differing armed group composition and combat-
     ant motives;
2   from above, in relation to aspirations of those promoting peace-building and
     state legitimacy; and
3   programmatically, in relation to negotiating DDR and managing
     expectations.

It is in comparing and contrasting how international actors, local armed groups
and the local population view DDR and mobilization that their perceptions can
be critically assessed. By disaggregating armed groups (and the role of family
and customary authority in driving certain forms of mobilization), the section
then considers whether the Afghan government's efforts to establish a monopoly
over the legitimate use of force are perceived to be legitimate.

Competing perceptions of DDR

The ANBP and DIAG DDR programmes are described by donors, government
officials, commanders and ex-combatants in contradictory ways. This is not
entirely surprising: the unprecedented variety of actors virtually guarantees a
diverse interpretation of the purpose, outputs and outcomes of DDR. External
observers, particularly the media and human rights organizations, often miscon-
strued ANBP's objectives (including DIAG), typically describing them as a disarmament campaign rather than as the DDR of the AMF or militia. Former AMF
combatants, for their part, often described DDR as an entitlement that they were
owed. At the same time, commanders frequently interpreted DDR as either a
reward or a threat to their right of rule in spite of their frequent rejection by local
communities. Meanwhile, the coalition, donor nations and many local PSCs
continue to rely on these same commanders for counter-insurgency and security
promotion operations.

Despite these many interpretations, at least three narratives emerge in
describing the ANBP DDR and DIAG processes. They can be summarized in
terms of DDR as *reward*, as economic *reintegration* and as *threat*. Adopting a
rewards perspective, certain outsiders and donors described DDR as compensation for the Mujahidin's role in the anti-Soviet struggle. In advancing a reintegration optic, other donors and multilateral agencies emphasize the importance
of providing ex-combatants with meaningful skills and options for employment
(in order to promote a more productive economy). Alternatively, DDR is construed as a deterrent to prevent potential spoilers from undermining stability and
security. For its part, the ANBP DDR incorporated all three narratives while
DIAG tended to focus more on the latter with commanders described as spoilers.
Specifically, ANBP DDR proposed that the DDR programme return combatants
to civilian life through peace-building and stabilization and to 'honourably
decommission the AMF so that the new [ANA] becomes the sole military
defence force for Afghanistan'.[53] Afghan government officials generally stressed
the importance of economic reintegration[54] even as participating commanders

adopted a reward frame.[55] But while commanders emphasized their legitimacy due to their own anti-Soviet and anti-Taliban action, international observers often stressed how these groups were primarily involved in the factional contest for power, and not in the fight against terror or local crime.[56]

DDR from below

In Afghanistan, there is no generic armed group 'type' or one fixed or static motive guiding combatant behaviour. While this may appear obvious, the chapter finds that by assessing DDR from below a much more nuanced understanding of the dynamics shaping armed group formation and combatant mobilization can emerge. DDR programmes launched in Afghanistan have not sufficiently accounted for the complex realities of mobilization. A narrow focus on presumed greed – whereby combatants are treated as undifferentiated rational utility-maximizers – neglects crucial issues such as the role of state and local legitimacy or community reliance on commanders for protection. As such, the conventional approach adopted toward DDR underplays the diverse motives of combatants.

It should be clear that all Afghan armed groups are neither ideologically-driven Islamists nor warlords or tribal militias. Instead, there are a wide variety of armed groups differentiated by their composition, organization, activities, varied internal distribution (and management) of weapons and aspirations (see Table 5.1). By rendering a distinction between government officers and *jihadi* commanders, the ANBP and DIAG DDR processes did not substantively differentiate between types of armed groups or combatants. This is not to say that typologies were not established. For example, the DIAG DDR process differentiated prospective participants according to threat and involvement in criminality and their community legitimacy (e.g. the tribal police [*arbaki*] are in example of the latter).

Depending on their type, armed groups are linked to and guided by different sources of authority. For example, a community militia is tied to the *qawm-e-mesharam* (local elders) and is based on community consent and is generally limited to local protection. Local strongmen can acquire enough power to either rise autonomously or to dominate the *qawm-e-mesharam*, and hold a direct relationship with combatants. By way of contrast, contemporary militarized *tanzims* are primarily bureaucratic organizations propagating a specific ideology. Most armed groups in Afghanistan are fluid and dynamic, combining features of each type. Moreover, an armed group can evolve from one type to another over time. Thus, different types of armed groups dominate in different regions, with different constellations of community militias, strongmen, government-armed groups (official and informal militias), foreign forces and political-military parties operating in each region. Acknowledging the fluid character of distinct armed groups is essential to understanding mobilization (and future demobilization) strategies.

Each type of armed group also relies on different assets to mobilize combatants. Community militias acquire combatants through communal institutions

Table 5.1 Ideal-type armed groups in Afghanistan

Type of armed group	Source of authority	Composition	Activities	Weapons ownership	Internal weapons distribution
Tanzims (political-military party)	Organization and indoctrination, charisma	Detribalized, delocalized and ideologically-oriented	Contest for national power or regional autonomy	Party stockpiles with central distribution	Mix of heavy weapons, infantry, specialized units
Warlords and strongmen	Charisma, force and patronage	Both community members and other de-localized elites	Contest for regional, provincial or local power and autonomy	Individually-owned weapons and commander stockpiles	Relatives, close affiliates and *nezmi has* given 'special' weapons for predation and internal enforcement
Community militia	Tradition and charisma	Local community members	Local protection and predation; autonomy	Individually-owned weapons	Combatants possess similar weapons

and drawing on local legitimacy; strongmen can acquire combatants through the selective application of force and incentives, but also by manipulating and dominating a given community of elders. In this way they are able to assume a degree of legitimacy and extend their influence. The resilience of local *qawm* and religious authorities also affects the forms of non-material resources (e.g. honour and shame) available for mobilization. Particularly in the case of community militias, fighting networks are closely intertwined with other non-fighting social networks and practices. Combatants can distinguish between illegitimate and legitimate mobilization. In some cases, they choose 'who' can demand mobilization, whether commanders, communities or political military parties. During interviews, de facto power was perceived differently than institutional or *de jure* power. A particular commander's short-term acquisition of power – his ability to overpower community elders and local authorities – does not necessarily alter community and individual perceptions of their actions. Strikingly similar practices – a demand for mobilization, the implementation of a family rotation system, or the demand for payment in substitute for mobilization – are perceived in different ways depending on who's asking and the perceived legitimacy of the mobilizer.

The typical outsider's conceptualization of Afghan combatant motives is predominantly focused on (the pursuit of) economic livelihoods. A 2001 UNDP, World Bank and Asian Development Bank report on demobilization adopted an 'alternative livelihoods' and economic framing of mobilization, describing the

> rise of a war-fed political economy with military activities offering employment opportunities to many fighters especially young men. The commanders use their tribal and ethnic bases to mobilize support, but recruitment and conscription of fighters largely depends on cash payments and promises of financial rewards.
>
> (UNDP *et al.* 2001)

Likewise, the UNDP (2004a) recommended a voluntary demobilization programme focusing on decreasing the economic incentives for mobilization.[57] As noted above, however, these approaches seriously misjudged the complexity guiding group and individual behaviour.

Just as there is no generic 'armed group' there is no prototypical combatant in Afghanistan. Interviews revealed a diverse array of life-narratives and histories of involvement in conflict, whether as temporary combatants, community militia members, local strongmen or in-service with political-military parties. As revealed in Table 5.2 a cursory summary of these interviews reveals the absence of consistently dominant motives across time and space. Key themes emerging from the interviews highlight the significance of family, tribal and customary institutions in mediating (demanding, supporting or rejecting) mobilization; the role of mobilization for family protection; the significance of forced combatant mobilization in the north-east and the multiple and often interlocking forms of authority in conditioning mobilization. All told, the factors influencing mobilization must be more broadly conceived than (political) ideology, greed or grievance. Economic motives were exclusive factors for only a select group.

It is vital to recall that individual behaviour is socially embedded and likely responds to the social construction of 'correct' mobilization. The authority of elders, coercion and the requirements of protection all played significant roles. But perceptions of legitimacy (of the actor demanding mobilization) are perhaps stronger predicators than the aforementioned factors. Combatant interviews can reveal their 'dominant motives' over time and highlights how motives are geographically and temporally contingent. For example, elder authority was regarded as more important in Ghor, Paktia and Kandahar than in other regions of Afghanistan. While elder authority was restricted for the protection and policing of communities in Paktia and for the creation of the *arbaki*, it was invoked for a broader range of mobilization in Ghor and Kandahar. In contrast, there was a striking absence of descriptions of elder and community authority in the northeast of Afghanistan, with family authority emerging as the dominant social relationship shaping mobilization.

Determining 'why people fight' is a complex proposition in the Afghan context. In fact, the question can be divided into at least four sub-components: whether to ideologically participate in fighting (support the jihad or the communist regime); whether to join a particular party (and which party to join); when to actually fight, participate in a particular operation, and become an active combatant; and whether to continue as an active combatant (sustained mobilization). Combatant mobilization in Afghanistan cannot therefore be reduced to a binary equation – whether or not to fight – but rather involves a series of *calculi*, endogenous influences and individual choices. A host of factors need to coalesce in order for an Afghan to be prepared to become an 'active combatant'.

One of the flaws in the conceptualization of reintegration in the ANPB DDR programme was the interpretation of combatants as a homogeneous category rather than as possessing multiple livelihoods and income streams. As a consequence, reintegration was understood in terms of substituting an exclusive occupation of 'soldiering' with another exclusive, singular occupation. For example, combatants are often viewed as young and under-skilled, consisting of 'unemployed, landless young people with no marketable skills or experience but fighting' (UNDP *et al.* 2001: 11). In fact, interviews with combatants, as well as any number of reports, revealed that many combatants possessed a range of livelihood skills. As described by a combatant, 'among armed people we have a lot of people with good economic conditions and skills, while there are many others with no income at all, with many of them disabled and unable to do anything'.[58] For the vast majority of combatants interviewed, mobilization and military service either played little role in their broader economic decisions or were simply one part of a broader economic strategy. For many – if not for most – 'soldiering' is only one of several skills, coinciding with farming, animal husbandry and other specialized tradecrafts. Some combatants regularly travelled to Iran to engage in wage labour, with some acquiring skills as master bricklayers

Table 5.2 Combatant backgrounds by province and region

Location (number of interviewed combatants)	Ghor (34 combatants)	Paktia (41 combatants)	Kandahar (37 combatants)	Northeast region (56 combatants)	Jalalabad (29 combatants)	Hazarajat (40 combatants)
Schooling	50% studied in the local mosque or madrassas	25% had some form of schooling	14% had some form of education	Majority up to fourth class	50% had some form of schooling	25% had some form of schooling
Prominent livelihoods	Farmer, shepherd, street labour, driver, shopkeeper	Woodcutting, farmer, street labour, driver	Day labour, farmer, fruit trade, transport, shopkeeping, poppy harvesting, transport	Farmer, street labour, carpenter, civil servant	Small business, street labour (in Pakistan)	Wage labour, farmer shepherd, carpet-weaving, teacher
Labour migration	Labour migration to Iran, Faryab and Heart	Many went to Pakistan as refugees or as temporary labour migrants; smaller number involved in labour migration to Saudi Arabia, Gulf and Iran	Migration to Quetta or Peshawar. Significance of internal displacement due to insurgency, and relocation to Kandahar from Kabul and Urozgan	Majority relocated to Pakistan as conflict displaced; labour migration to Iran and Tajikistan; internal displacement to Takhar during Taliban	Conflict-induced displacement and labour migration	Substantial labour migration from Daikundi and Shahristan
Average age of first mobilization	18.8	18	18	17.1	17	19.2
% recruited under 18	47%	40%	49%	59%	55%	43%
% recruited at or under 16	30%	30%	37%	49%	38%	35%

Period of first recruitment:

Jihad-period	38%	45.8%	47%	24%	41%	43%
Civil war	17.6%	12.5%	17%	42%	24%	17.5%
Taliban	17.6%	8.3%)	0%	27%	14%	27.5%
Bonn process	26.4%	33.3%	36%	1%	28%	12.5%
Prominent motives by period: Jihad	Jihad, religious/ elder authority, grievance, force	Family selection, grievance, economic incentives, Jihad, religious authority	Family, religious and elder authority, grievance, economic incentives, family/ group belonging	Grievance, force, protection, family/ elder authority; economic incentives	Family authority, ideology, entitlements, protection, force	Ideology, grievance, elder authority, economic incentives
Civil war	Grievance, protection, elder authority, economic incentives	Economic incentives, elder authority	Elder authority, family belonging, protection, economic incentives	Force, protection, family authority	Economic incentives, force, protection	Economic incentives, protection, elder authority
Taliban	Protection, force, economic incentives, grievance	Economic incentives, family selection	Economic incentives	Grievance, group belonging, force	Economic incentives, group belonging, grievance, elder authority	Ideology, grievance, elder authority, economic incentives
Bonn	Elder authority, economic incentives–force, protection	Elder authority, protection, economic incentives, grievance	Economic incentives, elder authority, family/ group belonging, grievance, protection	Economic incentives, group belonging, force, protection	Economic incentives, group belonging and protection	Economic incentives, protection, elder authority

and craftsmen, and were able to accrue income to send home in the form of remittances. Remobilization therefore will not be singularly dependent on the availability of economic opportunity as seductive as this 'choice' may be.

Examining DDR from above

International actors and senior representatives of the Afghan government exhibit a combination of pragmatism and idealism in their approach to promoting the legitimacy of the current government of Afghanistan. Early on, the profound fear of alienating the Northern Alliance and the prominent tribes of Kandahar, Jalalabad and Helmand, led to a (pragmatic) strategy of US and Afghanistan government financing local commanders to fight the Taliban. The subsequent 2001 Bonn Conference effectively institutionalized the power of these same commanders in government. These allied commanders exerted significant influence over most major political events from the emergency *Loya Jirga* to the 2004 parliamentary elections. The coalition war-fighting strategy directly shaped the post-Taliban peace and state-building strategy. From the vantage point of the tribes, the consequence of this assistance, particularly the style of its delivery, was at the expense of locally-credible community decision-making bodies. Drawing on proxy allies may be an effective short-term strategy that requires less force and fewer soldiers. It may also temporarily co-opt otherwise rebellious actors. But it can also serve to undermine sustainable grassroots peace-building and civil society.

As signalled in the Introduction, DDR is typically understood to take place after the (formal) cessation of hostilities. A key goal is to build confidence and trust between parties through a staged and negotiated standing-down of the factional armed forces. These preconditions were only partially applicable in the Afghanistan context. In fact, the 2002 Bonn Agreement was not so much a peace agreement as a power-sharing agreement, with the exclusion of the then defeated Taliban. As a governing compact it included conditions for disarmament. However, the Mujahidin groups and commanders continued to enforce a popular narrative of participation in jihad and against the Taliban as justifying their presence in parliament and government ministries. Likewise, the use of armed violence to achieve these goals continues to be justified. The dilemmas of achieving short-term peace through co-option as opposed to long-term peace-building were clear cut and widely understood in Afghanistan. These tensions, far from disappearing, affected every stage of the post-Bonn period.

It is worth questioning whether the basic preconditions for DDR exist in Afghanistan. As noted by Cooper and Pugh (2002) the 'presence [of international military contingents] and their coercive techniques, if privileged over issues of accountability and justice, can foster the erosion of politics and an increase in violence'. Rama Mani (2003) has also recounted how:

> decisions made in Bonn and at the Emergency Loya Jirga [ELJ] favoured 'negative' peace over 'positive' peace. That is, the Bonn Agreement and the

ELJ focused on stopping hostilities and securing agreement, however minimal, between parties through a power-sharing deal. In the process, the parallel need to identify and institute the necessary structural, systemic and institutional changes to consolidate peace and avert a relapse into conflict were overlooked.

According to Rothchild and Roeder (2005: 12–13): 'the dilemma of power-sharing emerges from the gap between the promises needed to initiate the transition and the performance necessary to consolidate peace and democracy'. Thus, many of the differing conceptions and inconsistencies in DDR programming in Afghanistan can be traced not reservedly to narrow conceptualizations of reintegration, but more critically to the strategic dilemmas engendered by the Karzai administration and the coalition's military strategy, including the co-option of warlords and the continued employment of local PSCs and militias.

The effectiveness of DDR resides in large part in its perceived legitimacy and the legitimacy of its proponents. Noted above, there are of course multiple sources of legitimacy in Afghanistan. Due to its connections with the Soviet military and successive factional governments, the central government of Afghanistan suffered a major erosion of its capacity to monopolize the legitimate use of force within its territory. Likewise, the post-Bonn Afghan government faces severe challenges in its capacity to exert military dominance and a monopoly over the legitimate use of force. Afghans have long felt that the state and its institutions are compromised through affiliation with and support of foreign governments (and their concomitant resort to repression). In contrast, the now demobilized AMF units and local militias derived legitimacy from at least three sources: their capacity to provide local protection; their national service;[59] and in their anti-Taliban/anti-Soviet activity.[60]

Afghanistan regularly confronts tensions from those who have 'legitimacy without power' and 'power without legitimacy'. The dominant armed parties following the end of hostilities may not be recognized by key segments of the population, while traditional leaders were gradually overpowered by a new warlord class. A 2004 Afghanistan Research and Evaluation Unit (AREU) report described how:

the situation [in Afghanistan] is complicated by the fact that some individuals were given *de jure* positions based on their *de facto* power and use the latter to influence the *de jure* structures according to their interests at both the central and local levels.

For example, many commanders were conferred with the titles and trappings of state power due to their military clout and connections rather than meritocratic procedures.

Preventing future mobilization depends in part on the state's ability to define, regulate and contain legitimate and illegitimate force. The state will need to actively seek to transform community and individual understandings of and incentives for mobilization. This can be achieved by enforcing rights and protecting the population – namely by consolidating the rule of law. The Afghan government only began to legally define the terms of mobilization and arms ownership from 2004 onwards. It did this by, *inter alia*, enforcing DDR, banning child soldiers and police under the age of 17, outlawing armed forces and banning firearms and explosive possession without a license.[62] The extension of the central government's authority is not singularly dependent on resources or even power, but also on *perceived* legitimacy – the population's view of its regulations, activities and intermediaries. The dissemination of legislation banning militias was the first genuine challenge to the legitimacy of illegal armed groups. Disarmament and demobilization ceremonies, oaths of fidelity to the Afghan state and certificates commemorating past service all seek to demonstrate to the combatant the end of (illegitimate) mobilization.

Even so, the legitimacy of the new Afghan National Army is under threat from within and without. The acquisition of legitimacy is constrained by government corruption, as well as by local perceptions that it is deployed instrumentally as a counter-insurgency force. The Karzai government recognizes that the current insurgency features domestic and foreign-backed fighting forces. To counteract this, the GoA seeks to negotiate with the Taliban through the Peace through Strength (PTS) Commission while simultaneously restraining coalition air strikes, detention and search-and-seizure operations. Owing to the comparatively modest size of the Afghan army and foreign NATO/US forces, the ANA *requires* the consent of the population. A mass rebellion – indicated by the invocation of tribal elder authority and religious authority at the community and national level against the government and the coalition – would quickly overwhelm a fractured government and the 30,000-strong NATO force. In the future, the GoA may only be able to enhance its legitimacy through incremental and participatory legal reform; restrained and accountable use of government power; credible consultation with local communities and authorities (informal and formal); the provision of security; and the arbitration of local disputes.

Contradictions in DDR programming are thus not exclusively rooted in the conceptualization of the ANBP/DIAG strategies but more fundamentally in the military tactics adopted by the Karzai government and coalition forces. The creation and deployment of non-state militias to instil security or for use against the insurgency carries a price. Delays in the launch of various DDR and disarmament interventions were attributed partly to the fact that 'America still needs many of these armed groups to maintain security and fight Al Qaeda; and Afghanistan has yet to figure out how to reintegrate a generation of men who have known no other job than war' (Baldauf 2003). Even so, strategies can change. By mid-2004, the coalition began to reconsider commanders as threats and deploying over-flights to deter their movement and activity. But despite the common view that DDR initiatives should be locally-owned and led, the Afghanistan government's role in inspiring and sustaining local militias is seldom discussed. Whilst the government seeks to establish a legal monopoly over the use of force – through the drafting of laws and strengthening of enforcement capacities – its *de jure* aspirations are undermined by de facto practice.

The implications of contracting militia and PSCs for DDR are seldom critically examined. In Afghanistan, the very presence of PSCs has reduced the incentives of certain actors to disarm. Currently, the UN Protection Force (UNPO/UNPF),[62] USPI's road militias,[63] the Afghan Highway Police,[64] the Afghan Security Guard,[65] the Afghan National Auxiliary Police (ANAP)[66] and PSC militias offer regular wages.[67] Commenting on the ANBP, the ICG (2005) stressed the importance of keeping 'pace with the evolving nature of Afghanistan's militia structures, many of which have found a new lease on life as police forces or private militias associated with governors or district administrators'. As observed above, the Afghan government and coalition partners were complicit in bolstering the reach of both militia commanders and PSCs, although 2007 licensing regulations began to reduce their influence. The paradox was that by empowering their local allies militarily and economically, they also facilitated their resistance to government control and DDR initiatives.[68]

There is a fine balance in Afghanistan in reconciling short-term needs and long-term outcomes. While ensuring security remains an overwhelming priority, the recruitment of militia and PSCs can bolster the position and influence of commanders. Allowing them to retain their weapons and side-step DDR lends credence to commander's claims of providing security. They also sustain commander capacities to provide patronage and salaries to their combatants. The continued existence of PSCs threatens even the modest gains of DDR. The proposed creation of a locally-recruited ANAP, for example, has the potential to undermine the DIAG process by re-igniting tensions and schisms between Pashtun and other ethnic groups. According to one international official involved in the latter programme: 'ANAP is a problem for DIAG because we are essentially reconstituting militias and setting back DDR' (Wilder 2007). The creation of ANAP has also fuelled the perception, especially among non-Pashtun ethnic groups, that the Karzai government is rearming Pashtun militias in the south while the DIAG programme is trying to disarm non-Pashtun militias in the rest of the country.

Enhancing legitimacy and encouraging participation

The final sections highlight two critical programmatic aspects of the DDR process in Afghanistan: the role of vertical diplomatic linkage and the continued necessity of improved public information and outreach functions. Both are central to challenging the legitimacy of local commanders, which in turn plays an instrumental role in shaping a soldier's decision to mobilize and thus the likelihood of sustainable demobilization.

Although DDR is typically advanced to enhance stability in the short to medium term, it can also be interpreted as a vertical diplomatic initiative intended to bolster higher order state-building objectives. For example, the interim director of ANBP, regional office managers and representatives of various MDUs regularly negotiated with intransigent commanders. These commanders alternately concealed the extent of their forces, participated incrementally, or delayed disarmament as part of a 'wait and see' strategy. As such, representatives of the ANBP DDR programme and the MDUs played both a national and tactical-level *diplomatic* function as much as pursuing technical objectives. They were involved in a constant process of negotiating compliance with commanders and local authorities, particularly in relation to the number of weapons to be surrendered and the number of combatants to be demobilized and reintegrated. Likewise, the DIAG DDR programme made use of a Steering Committee that both identified dissident militias for forcible disarmament and allocated funds for development projects amongst communities that were receptive to disarmament.

Effective DDR requires the ability of donors and the Afghan government to coordinate and apply incentives and pressure against local commanders. For commanders, however, there were substantial incentives for retaining armed groups. Rank and file combatants, however, constituted real power against competitors and a bargaining chip with which to negotiate national and provincial positions. They also guaranteed protection for their constituencies, and constituted sources of power, authority, status and income provided via AMF (at least until September 2004). In order to successfully undertake DDR, the GoA needed to counter these incentives. Incentives to encourage compliance with DDR included *inter alia* participation in elections, the provision of reintegration assistance, and community development grants.[69] Deterrents or punishments included the threat of armed action, exclusion from reintegration assistance, labelling as an IAG or 'warlord' and de-certification from the elections. Karzai's presidential decree of 7 September 2004 and the electoral certification/decertification process was critical for the acceleration of DDR in mid-September, when 1,400 men were disarmed in one week, 10 per cent of that disarmed in the previous ten months.

The ANBP programme was conceived from the beginning as a technocratic exercise with DDR defined in narrow terms. A lesson from Afghanistan is that technocratic interventions, while inherently limited in their reach, can be enhanced through renewed investment in diplomatic and domestic outreach. But such engagement requires both horizontal and vertical coordination if it is going to be effective. The centrality of politics must therefore be acknowledged. For example, in order to strengthen its reach and relevance, the ANBP Director deliberately nurtured an international network in the form of a working group to shore-up the support of the USA, Japan and the Karzai government, thus strengthening the role of his regional officers and adding additional clout to the programme. Through agonizing negotiations, the ANBP and DIAG DDR programmers managed in some instances to encourage a degree of engagement from below. While no panacea and carrying risks, such vertical engagement can enhance the dividends of DDR.

DDR and public outreach

Public outreach is critical for the government's shaping of local conceptions of legitimate and illegitimate mobilization. It also enhances transparency. As noted by Cooper and Pugh (2002: 53), DDR and SSR should be a

> transparent and open process ... demilitarization may only be possible as a consequence of publicity and verification because, in politically tense circumstances where engendering trust between adversaries is an incremental process, highly visible activities are necessary to preclude subterfuge and accusations of cheating.

Public information campaigns can play a critical role in DDR programmes by emboldening local calls for the disarmament of local factions. By appealing to families and local villagers, pressure can be placed upon commanders and soldiers to follow through on their commitments.

Public information campaign needs to be focused on building community support for demobilization and on informing the population of legislation governing armed group formation and weapons possession. Family or community pressure can induce either mobilization or demobilization. For example, a selection of soldiers from Kunduz described how family pressure supported demobilization, with combatants arguing that 'none of my relatives wanted me to have a weapon' and that 'my brother once told me.... You will not have a good future with this weapon. When ANBP started I remembered what my brother told me, and I gave the weapon to DDR' (UNAMA 2004a). In Afghanistan, however, sophisticated and sustained public information and outreach campaigns were largely neglected. Rather, the ANBP's public information section exhibited a tendency to focus externally, rather than internally. The emphasis was not so much on Afghans and the local media, but reaching out to external donors, UN agencies and the international press corps.

The outcomes of such local neglect can generate far-reaching consequences.[70] For example, a DDR client survey revealed that 94 per cent of all combatants had 'no knowledge of the DDR process prior to demobilization' and that these combatants were dependent on information from the radio (Radio Azadi/Radio Liberty), their commanders and the BBC as the 'main sources of information' (Winderl 2005: 3). Surprisingly few ex-combatants mentioned the commanders as a source of information. However, the 'ANBP discovered during the initial stages of the DDR process that although commanders were regularly briefed on DDR activities, they did not always relay accurate information to their subordinates' (ibid.: 10). The absence of a sustained and strategically timed outreach campaign by DDR planners allowed commanders to continue to monopolize information and secure their authority over combatants and their communities. Commanders wilfully distorted key components of successive programmes in order to dissuade them from participating. This was consistently observed during disputes over the allocation of US$200 to each soldier. Following the three pilot projects (in Gardez, Mazar and Kandhar) in 2003, for example, this practice discontinued due to the confiscation of reintegration funds by many commanders.

In ideal circumstances, a public information campaign would inform communities and combatants about the timing, laws, logistics and activities of the DDR programme. Combatants would be provided with precise details of their reintegration package. These activities could serve to build local consent among the local population (placing pressure on commanders to fulfil their commitments) and also undermine the commanders position as the exclusive source of information. Following DDR, commanders would no longer be permitted to present themselves as being officially part of the government. In those cases where the commander still remains dependent on a local *shura* or community of elders, through issuing legislation and making public statement, the government could re-empower a community to check the activities of a commander.

DDR success or failure?

Assessing the legacy and effectiveness of DDR in Afghanistan is a challenging enterprise. Of course, success cannot be determined exclusively by the quality of programme design and execution or the number of guns collected or fighters demobilized. The overarching security and political dynamics must also be taken into consideration. It is clear that coalition forces, donor governments, the Afghan administration, PMCs, militia and armed groups and a host of local actors played a significant role in shaping DDR outcomes. Although a critical review of ANBP DDR and DIAG interventions is warranted, withering criticism is to some extent misguided.[71] There is some evidence that the various DDR programmes served an important role in shifting the 'balance of power' away from regional warlords toward the Karzai government.[72]

There are a number of different quantitative and qualitative benchmarks to determine the effectiveness of DDR outputs and outcomes. One obvious output metric relates to the real and relative reductions in the number of arms and armed groups in circulation. For example, the ANBP and DIAG DDR initiatives appeared to contribute to a reduction in the overall stock and availability of weapons (particularly heavy), munitions and ammunition throughout the country despite concerns over limited weapons returns[73] and the poor quality of surrendered arms.[74] The significant amounts collected may nevertheless represent only a fraction of those weapons circulating in rural and border areas: by mid-2006, estimates of illegal arms in the country varied from 100,000[75] to 1,000,000.[76] Likewise, the UN estimated that there were approximately 750,000 ex-combatants in Afghanistan as of 2002 and repeatedly revised its estimates downwards throughout the course of ANBP DDR (from 200,000 to 100,000 to 60,000). The decrease in numbers appeared to be more a simple exercise in creative accounting than representative of the actual numbers of those disarmed, demobilized and reintegrated.[77] As noted by Denny's (2005) 'numbers are notoriously fluid in Afghanistan'. Moreover, a reduction in the numbers of small arms and certain munitions does not necessarily correlate to a decrease in violence and insecurity for the Afghan population. Neither does a quantitative decrease in the number of militias. Numerical measures of success are in large part ephemeral.

Qualitative measures of success are even more difficult to determine. The primary benchmark of DDR 'success' should be sustained demobilization or the severing of the bonds between former commanders and combatants. Specifically, the goal is

> to break the historic patriarchal chain of command existing between the former commanders and their men and to provide the demobilized personnel with the ability to become economically independent – the ultimate objective being to reinforce the authority of the government.[78]

The DIAG DDR strategy determined that:

> success will not be defined by the collection of weapons alone, but the actual disbandment of illegal armed groups – as demonstrated by the cessation of their illegal activities – and advances in citizens' security, good governance and the rule of law.

Oddly, while recognizing this, the DIAG programme focused almost exclusively on commanders (and only symbolically on communities), rather than on the combatant–commander–community linkages. There is some evidence from combatants that commanders' power has expanded (rather than contracted) in the post-Bonn period. Combatants disarmed in Imam Sahib in Kunudz province, for example, asserted that their 'local commanders have more weapons and more money than in years before, so they may force us to take up arms again if they are not addressed' (IRIN 2003b).

Sustained demobilization is inextricably linked to the relative legitimacy of the government in relation to commanders, the political parties and the community. The state's monopoly on legitimate force is strengthened when it is able to *define* and *enforce* the laws determining the use of force and the carrying of arms. Demobilization is ultimately achieved when it is perceived by the population to be illegal and illegitimate. But the process of delegitimizing illegal armed groups only began after 2004 with the creation of the DIAG programme. The DIAG Steering Committee began the process of determining whether government officials, electoral candidates and others had really severed ties with armed groups. Provided representatives of the donor community and the Afghanistan government remain committed to this process and aware of the gaps and limitations of previous efforts, there is a prospect for long-term success. However, a history of distracted international engagement (most particularly following the Soviet withdrawal) and the recurring focus on short-term interventions are grounds for pessimism.

Conclusion

DDR is inevitably a complex, convoluted and politically-charged activity. The experience of DDR in Afghanistan emphasizes the limits of what can realistically be achieved in a context where state-building, peace-building, counter-insurgency and counter-narcotics operations converge. This chapter explored the ways in which DDR effectiveness depends in large part on a wider cluster of activities associated with the consolidation of state institutions, including SSR. Sustained demilitarization, demobilization and reintegration are dependent not exclusively on the design and implementation of ANBP DDR or DIAG alone, but on the broader outcomes of state-building in the country. DDR is thus a strategic interaction and must be conceived as such throughout.

Achieving DDR success requires investment in enhancing both diplomatic coordination and local outreach. Harnessing the capacities of donor governments, international military contingents and national ministries from above and reducing their dependence on militias (or PSCs for counter-insurgency operations) is critical. The strategic use of public information programmes from below to increase stigmas and local pressure against local commanders is also critically important. Ultimately, enhancing state legitimacy and its monopoly on the use of legitimate force is a sine qua non of DDR effectiveness.

Most of all, this chapter contends that effective DDR will require a better understanding of the dynamics shaping combatant mobilization and the formation of armed groups if it is to be effective. Envisioning combatants as economically-motivated and exhibiting limited skills can reproduce DDR programmes that focus narrowly on livelihood substitution. This chapter stressed the importance of recognizing and building on the heterogeneity of militia groups – from the commanders to the rank and file. An important lesson is that strategies to demobilize and reintegrate combatants must acknowledge their varied endowment sets and coping mechanisms but also the real and perceived 'legitimacy' of actors involved in DDR. Interventions designed to sever ties between commanders and combatants from below must also be accompanied with legal and practical enforcement and monitoring mechanisms.

Ultimately, the ANBP and DIAG processes provide an important if limited entry-point for addressing spoilers. Considerable numbers of weapons and munitions were collected and destroyed and tens of thousands of former combatants were demobilized and reintegrated. However, there is a clear risk that the growing insurgency in Afghanistan may push DDR down the list of donor priorities and will spur a push for rearmament among northern commanders. Until 2007, in their pursuit of military victory over the Taliban, the NATO coalition forces neglected the degree to which popular support for the insurgency is located in local disenfranchisement and repulsion of corrupt commanders, public security institutions and government officials. Moreover, so long as official and visible positions are occupied by individuals preoccupied with local disputes, the government's capacity to enhance its legitimacy will be compromised.

Notes

1 The ANBP hospitably allowed Bhatia to accompany their disarmament and demobilization teams. Gurpawan Singh, Vikram Bhatia, Peter Babbington, Basil Massey, Paul Cruickshank and Steven Feller were particularly responsive to his innumerable requests. Interpretation was provided by two Afghan citizens who endured long hours and harsh living conditions. Field research grants for projects related to this article were provided by the Small Arms Survey, the Marshall Aid Commemoration Commission and the British Committee on Central and Inner Asia. Robin Poulton, Stina Torjesen and Gordon Peake all eruditely critiqued the first draft. Robert Muggah generously and repeatedly redrafted the first manuscript, greatly enhancing its clarity. Without his assistance, this chapter would not have been completed.

2 See, for example, UN Inter-Agency Working Group on Disarmament Demobilization and Reintegration (no date: 6) 'Briefing Note for Senior Managers on the Integrated Disarmament, Demobilization and Reintegration Standards'.

3 The two initiatives in Afghanistan (ANBP DDR and DIAG) were different in approach and composition. There are four potential components of DDR: surrendering weapons (disarmament), severing the links between commanders and combatants (demobilization), reintegrating combatants (reintegration), and/or building community pressure against armed groups. The ANBP DDR was a demobilization programme often misunderstood as a mass disarmament campaign. Commanders were only required to submit a weapon per soldier, and not their entire stockpiles. DIAG is a mass disarmament initiative described as a demobilization effort. While described as focusing on 'illegal armed groups', no attention is given to the relationship between commanders and soldiers. The ANBP DDR was deadline-oriented; while DIAG is event and certification-focused. DDR was combatant and individual demobilization and reintegration oriented; DIAG is commander and weapons-oriented with no focus on combatants and with development assistance only provided to communities.

4 For Weber,

> the modern state is a compulsory association which organizes domination. It has been successful in seeking to monopolize the legitimate use of physical force as a means of domination within a territory. To this end the state has combined the material means of organization in the hands of its leaders, and it has expropriated all autonomous functionaries of estates who formerly controlled these means in their own right. The state has taken their positions and now stands in the top place.
>
> See Connolly (1984: 37)

5 This occurred even as the government security forces steadily disintegrated due to mass defections.

6 See, for example, Kartha (1999: 61–62, 66–68, 77, 82); Rubin (1995: 22, 30); Kenzhetaev (nd); Galster (1990: 58–190) and Harpviken (1997: 280).

7 The Sunni tanzims included: Hizb-i-Islami Hekmatyar; Ittihad-i-Islami; Jamiat-i-Islami; Mahaz-i- Milli (NIFA); Harakat-i-Inqilab-i- Islami; Hizb-i-Islami (Khalis); Jabh-e-Nijat-i-Milli (ANLF). Communist political-military parties included Khalq and Parcham (later Watan party). Shi'a political-military parties included: Hizb-e Wahdat (1988–); Shura-ye Inqelab-e Ittifaq Islami (1979–); Sazman-e Nasr; Pazdaran-e-Jihad/Sepah-e-Pazdaran; Harakat-e Islami; Sazman-e Fallah Islami; Sazman-e-Mujahidin-e-Mustazaffin; Hizbollah.

8 For a typology of armed groups, see Harpviken (1997) and Roy (1990).

9 There are substantial challenges to determining the precise number of small arms and light weapons in Afghanistan prior to the disarmament campaign. Estimates vary considerably, and range between 500,000 to ten million (Musah and Thompson 1999).

10 'The origin of the war is not ethnic, and the solution will not be ethnic, but the conduct of the war is ethnic, which has had corrosive effects on the potential for national reconstruction' (Rubin *et al.* 2001: 8–9). Likewise, 'ethnicisation was therefore an unintended and counter-productive result of regionalization, rather than a strategy of mobilisation' (Dorronsoro 2005: 258).

11 For example, it observes conflicts between Afghan 'state' forces against a unified 'mujahidin' (1978-1989), instead of a diverse and frequently violently fractious Mujahideen during this period.

12 The primary commanders cited in the post-Bonn period included the Paktia and Khost commander Padsha Khan Zadran, the self-titled 'Emir of Herat' Ismail Khan, Hazrat Ali of Jalalabad, Gul Agha Sherzai of Kandahar; Abdul Rashid Dostum of the northern Junbish party; and Marshall Fahim of Jamiat's Panjshiri. Zadran, Sherzai and Ali each received substantial financial assistance from Operation Enduring Freedom thereby permitting them to reenergize their flagging militias.

13 Specifically, 30 of 32 AMF divisions and the MOI were said to be dominated by Northern Alliance affiliated generals directly after 2002 (Rashid 2002a: 15). There were considerable differences in the size of the regional corps, with General Ludin claiming that the 3rd Corps possessed only 4,200 soldiers; while Ismail Khan was believed to possess a 30,000 soldier army (Rashid 2002b: 14).

14 See, for example, http://globalsecurity.org.

15 For example, police reform (Germany); judicial reform (Italy); counter-narcotics (United Kingdom); DDR (Japan); and military reform (USA).

16 The principles were that DDR be government-led; include international observation; ensure enhanced ANA training to coincide with disarmament; and reintegration training linked to reconstruction (Government of Japan 2003).

17 An ANBP pilot programme was initiated in October 2003, and was expanded across the country only by February 2004.

18 With a total cost of US$141 million, the primary ANBP donors were Japan (US$91 million), the United Kingdom (US$19 million), Canada (US$16 million), USA (US$9 million) and the Netherlands (US$4 million).

19 In practice the group met only sporadically.

20 Indeed, the AFP (2003) reported that the 'militias were reluctant to hand over their weapons to a ministry dominated by a rival faction'. Finally, in February and August 2003, President Karzai pushed for reforms in the Ministry of Defense, with the goal of both broadening the ethnic composition of the officer corps (away from domination by Tajiks affiliated with the Northern Alliance) and increasing professionalism more generally (Sarwan and Karokhel 2003).

21 In December 2003 the Ministry of Defence sought to remove militia and heavy arms from Kabul, particularly in the Paghman, Pul-i-Charki and Panjshir cantonment areas.

22 Ultimately, a number of commanders became governors and were transferred to major civil positions (Ibrahimi 2004).

23 Many weapons were shredded at Pul-i-Charki by Halo Trust. Communication with Robin Poulton, 1 April 2008.

24 Japan and UNAMA Military Observers participated in an International Observer Group (IOG), which accompanied the Mobile Disarmament Units.

25 Combatants typically travelled considerable distances (with minimal travel assistance) to receive their assistance and were potentially required to transit through an opponents territory.

26 See, for example, http://www.undpanbp.org/programactivities/demobilization.htm.

27 Later, during the demobilization and reintegration phase, there were further revelations of some corruption in the process, to include the selling of disarmament certificates and falsification of numbers by commanders, to both provide income and to conceal their primary combatants. In February 2005, the ANBP suspended demobilization and reintegration in Herat following allegations that some 300 soldiers

purchased forged documents for $100 apiece. See Xinhua News Agency (2005) and IWPR (2002).

28 There were over 40 complaints from combatants in the first part of the pilot project phase in Kunduz (IRIN 2003a).

29 Press Briefing by Manoel de Almeida De Silva Spokesman for the Special Representative of the Secretary-General and by UN agencies, 9 September 2004.

30 The NEEP included vocational training for 100–300 ex-officers and AMF commanders and 2,500 ex-combatants, with these individuals primarily trained for road reconstruction (World Bank 2004).

31 Over 24,500 'wives and female family members of former soldiers have received or are scheduled to receive additional education and income generation opportunities in development projects'. See, for example, http://www.unddr.org.

32 These included agricultural packages, on-the job-vocational training, small businesses, teacher training, community-based de-mining and the Afghan National Army or 'wage-labor employment as a bridging activity', see Winderl (2005: 5).

33 Other choices included de-mining (1.4 per cent), ANA (1.4 per cent), ANP (0.2 per cent), contracting team (0.9 per cent) and teacher training (0.8 per cent) (Winderl 2005: 5).

34 Interview with Combatant #235, Khanabad (June 2005).

35 The Client Satisfaction Survey was founded on interviews with 2,785 combatants carried out by caseworkers in the ANBP's field offices, with the majority of interviewees from Parwan, Herat, Kabul, Kandahar, Balkh, Logar, Kunduz, Bamiyan, Paktia and Baghlan. Meanwhile, only 1,000 participants submitted weapons without participating in demobilization or reintegration, another 7,500 participants did not select a reintegration option, and another 1,465 dropped out of the reintegration programme (Winderl 2005).

36 According to Vikram Parekh, previously of the ICG and currently of UNAMA, the ANBP had limited ability to both understand and implement DDR at the village level, arguing that 'it is essential that all commanders, including "sargroups" [team leaders] in the villages, are brought into the process; otherwise, militia leaders will retain the capacity and networks to mobilize new recruits' (IRIN 2004).

37 According to Dennys (2005):

> there are several thousand of these Commanders who have a higher drop out rate than the soldiers. The international community's failure to find the money necessary to run a full and effective commanders' programme means that the commanders who are now causing the greatest local problems are these low level commanders ... These low level commanders also keep alive the informal networks that sustain the more senior commanders, in keeping access open to smuggling routes, retaining party or ethnic loyalties or spheres of influence and thereby strengthening regional power holders as well.

38 The ANBP programme was exclusively focused on the DDR of the AMF leaving thousands of militias and hundreds of thousands of combatants still mobilized.

39 The DIAG programme revealed the degree to which the distinction between the AMF and these irregular was titular rather than substantive.

40 This was accompanied by the creation of a comprehensive database, the establishment of various commissions, and the articulation of a public information strategy.

41 The first conference tasked with the support of the DIAG program was the 2006 Tokyo Conference on Consolidation of Peace in Afghanistan. A year later, the June 2007 Tokyo Conference on Disbandment of Illegal Armed Groups for the Stabilization of Afghanistan, sought to elaborate additional forcible disarmament tactics, and attempted to the coordinate new Afghan national police (ANP) deployments with DIAG efforts. See, for example, the *Co-Chair's Summary, The Conference on Disbandment of Illegal Armed Groups (DIAG) for the Stabilization of Afghanistan:*

Coordination with Police Reform, 21 June 2007: http://www.mofa.go.jp/region/middle_e/afghanistan/summary0706.

42 This was composed of representations from Afghan government security and reconstruction ministries.

43 For example, donors from Japan, UK, Canada, USA, Netherlands, Italy together with the EU military forces (Coalition and ISAF) and UNAMA all shored-up the effort.

44 Further membership includes a wide variety of government ministries (National Security Council (NSC), Ministry of Rural Rehabilitation and Development (MRRD), Ministry of Agriculture and Irrigation, Ministry of Finance, Ministry of Information and Culture, etc.).

45 Previous attempts to establish a licensing system were uneven and largely the product of Provincial Reconstruction Team initiative – with the USA PRT supporting these efforts in Gardez but with local security commanders unable to agree on a procedure in Jalalabad. Though seeking voluntary compliance, the resort to forceful disarmament were tested almost immediately in Helmand in April 2005 following clashes between Commander Khano of LashkarGah and the local police during a (voluntary) arms collection effort (IRIN 2005).

46 The listing of a commander as a Government Official Linked to an Illegal Armed Group (GOLIAG) required the consent and agreement of the DDR Commission, the NDS and representatives of the international community. Of the 130 officials below the rank of governor, only 13 names were agreed upon both by the NDS and international community (ANBP 2005b).

47 For example, communities in Khost collected some 15 metric tonnes of weapons and ammunition for submission to the ANBP, while commanders in other areas provided considerably fewer. While 45 commanders in Kapisa submitted less than 100 functioning weapons, nine militia leaders submitted some 750 light and heavy weapons and 42 metric tonnes of ammunition in Ghazni.

48 For example, in Nangarhar, a DIAG workshop for 350 junior and senior commanders in early 2007 was sponsored by the provincial PRT, and involved participants from UNAMA, ANBP and the provincial council (ANBP 2007).

49 Select examples include canal cleaning in Kapisa and a still delayed micro-power plant in Farkhar.

50 Even so similar popular protests against commanders occurred in Kandahar, but had little effect in inducing further DIAG initiatives.

51 The success of DDR is certainly hindered by the absence of a large international observer presence (whether civilian or military, UNAMA MLOs, ISAF or Coalition). The numerical scarcity of a reliable neutral partner further made commanders unwilling to disarm. Indeed, according to Berdal (1996), 'outside involvement in several African countries has shown that the higher rates of demobilization occurred in countries with the largest ratio of observers to combatants, and with multilateral monitors who had a broad mandate'.

52 Sedra (2006: 95) describes:

> a slide towards expediency that has stripped the SSR model of its intrinsically holistic vision. Programmes to advance the transparency and democratic accountability of the sector, while situating it within a clear legal framework, have been superseded by a singular focus on training and equipping the country's fledgling security forces.

53 For example, Deputy Defence Minister Attiqullah Baryalai declared that: 'Mujahidin will not be demobilized until job opportunities are created for them'. See, for example, http://www.undpanbp.org/FAQ/faq.htm.

54 An interview with interim foreign affairs minister Abdullah Abdullah in February 2002, revealed an economic conceptualization of mobilization: 'The minute some rural development activities are established, nobody will bother to enlist in militias.

Becoming a soldier in Afghanistan should be an honorable and professional job' (IRIN 2003b).

55 A Faryab commander criticized the DIAG process on the following terms: 'This programme is completely unfair because the government wants to get our weapons for nothing … The mujahedin acquired these weapons at the cost of their lives and they will not lose them for free' (Ibrahimi 2006). Likewise, in early February 2006, Dostum's *Aina* television network indicated that youth group, elders and provincial officials:

> complained bitterly about the fact that representatives of the jihadi fighters, who sacrificed their life in the battle against terrorism, were sidelined. Jihadist rhetoric – and its use to protest disarmament – remains most pronounced in the Panjshir valley, where the most sustained and entrenched resistance to DDR occurred.

Jowzjan Aina television as cited in Rally in North Afghanistan Protests Against New Government Makeup (BBC 2005).

56 For UNAMA (2004): 'the DDR project's aim is the phasing out of militias in order to create the Afghan National Army and police forces, as well as to promote greater security throughout the country by minimizing the influence of armed factions'.

57 An Afghan Interim government planning document further echoed the belief that: 'young people often enlisted because it was the only option for survival' (AIA: 5–6).

58 Note IRIN (2003c) that observes: 'Guns for Jobs would be vocational training, basic education, micro-credit for skilled workers, supply of tools and equipment for skilled workers and course graduates, and job introductions'. Likewise, Noble (2002) writes that:

> many of the soldiers interviewed had skills already, owned a shop or farm. For these soldiers rather than basic training, financial support in the form of micro-credit, material support in the form of tools and/or equipment and assistance in finding jobs if appropriate would be better. All of the soldiers interviewed say they would gladly give up their weapons if they knew a stable life awaited them.

59 The creation of the ANA and the formalization and reform of the MoD – emphasizing professionalism and national service over party affiliation – removed the ability of erstwhile AMF units to situate themselves as national units.

60 The proposition of a right to rule and retain arms due to anti-Soviet and anti-Taliban action is evident in the parliament's deliberations over press freedom and a potential amnesty from war crimes prosecution.

61 Press Briefing by Manoel de Almeida e Silva, Spokesman for the Special Representative of the Secretary-General and by UN agencies, 9 September 2004.

62 The UNPU was a 2005 police unit, most of which has previously belonged to AMF Division 1 but who avoided DDR. As both a unit and as individuals, their primary loyalty and unit of affiliation remains their commander.

63 USPI is responsible for security for the Louis Berger project sites between Kabul, Kandahar and Herat, and hired over 15,000 armed guards for these compounds and workers, and also began its own highway police. In recruiting these guards, USPI directly went to local commanders and is not believed to have a vetting system for these commanders.

64 The AHP was a migration location for commanders seeking to maintain armed forces, filtering soldiers into police uniforms (Dennys, 2005: 6).

65 These include extra-ANA Afghan forces utilized by the coalition. In the case of Paktia, the coalition Afghan forces, referred to locally as the 'campaign', were recruited through a loose network of family and tribal connections, recruited largely through the Ahmadzai tribe. In Khost, the coalition created a local militia called *Falak* (and later the Khost Provincial Corps), which was utilized for operations against the Taliban/AQ in partnership with coalition forces (Ahmed Rashid 2004).

66 In late 2006, the Afghan National Auxiliary Police Force was recruited through local tribal elders to provide static security in villages and at checkpoints. It remains unclear the degree to which this new locally recruited unit is being used.

67 In 2005, the UNPU was paid US$150 per month (plus US$5 per day when on patrol). At that time, they earned more than the ANP trained through German Police Project (US$120) or even those passing through the Regional Training Centers (US$42 per month). All payment rates gathered through interviews by the author with UNPU and ANP policemen.

68 But many of these partnerships lack a clear statutory framework regarding the authority of local militias, their regulation and the limits on the use of force. The scale and distribution of monetary support for informal militias outweighed that provided to develop formal state security forces, further empowering the social and interpersonal networks underpinning these militias.

69 A June 2007 report describes the following:

> Tools and levers available to the government: Political: political negotiation and public opinion, including its expression in the new parliament and provincial councils, can help pressure reluctant leaders at all levels to conform to legal requirements and actively support DIAG; Economic: Economic resources may not be committed as a precondition or direct reward for IAG disbandment, but development will be encouraged in areas where DIAG has contributed to a secure and stable environment.

> Social: Community leaders, including elders, religious leaders, and teachers, have in many areas voiced their desire for IAG disbandment. The support of such figures can be cultivated in other areas, and their social authority used to encourage complicated with DIAG; Public information: The use of media resources to provide a unified information campaign will be an important tool for DIAG. National campaigns will help establish an understanding of DIAG and reinforce popular support, while local campaigns will address issues specific to particular provinces or district.

> Law enforcement: Legislation and degrees will allow the government to prosecute IAG leaders and members. Penalties such as fines, custodial sentences, and seizure of assets will provide powerful incentives for compliance and deter reversion to illegal activity.

> (GoA, 'Strategy for DIAG': 7)

70 Anecdotally, ANBP's exceptional posters were evident only in abundance in ANBP offices – a chronic problem in UN operations – but tragically missing from rural communities and market towns. This became all the more striking when compared to the broad availability and presence of election information posters (produced by the JEMB and UNOPS) and candidate posters (often of the local commander or his national figurehead).

71 For example, ANBP DDR was criticized for 'ignoring irregular tribal forces' (BICC 2007). However, these militias were addressed by the succeeding DIAG programme. Some of these criticisms were products of the misunderstanding of the focus of each programme.

72 Communication with Robin Poulton, 1 April 2008.

73 At a DIAG press conference of May 2006, a delegation from Takhar complained that only 600 of 36,000 weapons in Takhar had been collected, revealing the continued mobilization of grassroots support for disarmament in that province (ANBP 2006e).

74 Accordingly, 7,000 of the 20,000 DIAG weapons submitted were considered old and unusable (Ibrahimi 2006). However, Poulton rightly noted the ability of Afghans to rebuild old weapons. Communication with Robin Poulton, 1 April 2008.

75 See IRIN (2006a).

76 In 2006, MOD officials estimated that there were one million weapons remaining in the northern provinces (Ibrahimi 2006).

77 An early planning document asserted:

> The exact number of combatants ... is unknown. For planning purposes however regular forces, those that are uniformed and/or under the clear command and control structures, and with livelihoods tied to the military establishment, are currently estimated at some 75,000 men. While another 100,000 irregular militia combatants and war veterans dispersed throughout the country also require assistance of some kind. Although others have taken part in the conflict, including those who joined quickly organized *lashkars* or tribal military forces, these one-time unpaid combatants will be encompassed within community development programmes and be absorbed into jobs as overall economic growth takes place, and will not benefit from demobilization and reintegration.
>
> (AIA undated: 5/6)

78 Crucially, the ANBP DDR programme was never mandated to disarm the population or provide direct population, but rather to 'assist AMF military personnel to transition from military into civilian occupations' (ANBP 2006b).

Bibliography

Afghan Interim Authority (AIA) (undated) 'Security, Demobilization and Reintegration Framework and Future Programme', 5–6.

AFP (2004a) 'UN Stop Paying Demobilized Soldiers After Extortion Revealed', 7 March.

AFP (2004b) 'Afghan Disarmament Programme to Begin on October 25: UN', 1 October.

ANBP (2005a) 'Weekly Summary Report: 13–20 November 2005', 20 November.

ANBP (2005b) 'Weekly Summary Report, 23–30 October 2005', 30 October.

ANBP (2006a) 'ANBP Fact Sheet on DDR Completion', 1 July.

ANBP (2006b) 'Weekly Summary Report, 4–10 June 2006', 14 June.

ANBP (2006c) 'ANBP Newsletter', Issue No. 4, December.

ANBP (2006d) 'Afghanistan: Kapisa – More Commanders Should Voluntarily Surrender Weapons', 6 July.

ANBP (2006e) 'DIAG Press Conference', 14 May.

ANBP (2007) 'ANBP Newsletter', Issue No. 6, February.

Baldauf, S. (2003) 'Afghans yet to Lay Down Arms: A Deadly Skirmish between Warlords last Week Points to the Perils of slow Disarmament', *Christian Science Monitor*, 14 October.

Barron, P. (2005) 'Afghanistan Struggles to Keep Warlords off the Ballot', *Christian Science Monitor*, 8 September.

BBC (2005) *BBC Monitoring Service*, 1 February.

Berdal, M. (1996) 'Disarmament and Demobilization After Civil Wars', *Adelphi Paper No. 303*. Oxford: Oxford University Press.

Bhatia, M. (2007) 'Legacy, Legitimacy and Demobilization', *International Peacekeeping*, 14(1): 90–107.

Bhatia, M. and Sedra, M. (2008) *Afghanistan, Arms and Conflict: Armed Groups, Disarmament and Security in a Post-War Society*. London: Routledge.

Bonn International Center for Conversion (BICC) (2007) 'Security Sector Reform in Afghanistan', accessed online on 12 July.

Buchbinder, D. (2002) 'Guns offer Past Profit for Afghans: Poor Soldiers are Key Players in a Massive Unregulated Weapons Market', *Christian Science Monitor*, 6 August.

Connolly, W. (ed.) (1984) *Legitimacy and the State.* Oxford: Basil Blackwell.

Cooper, N. and Pugh, M. (2002) *Security-sector Transformation in Post-conflict Societies.* London: The Conflict, Security and Development Group, King's College, February.

Curran, B. (2003) 'Afghan Commander Hands over Fighters for Demobilization', AFP, 23 October.

Dennys, C. (2005) 'Disarmament, Demobilization and Rearmament?: The Effects of Disarmament in Afghanistan'. Japan Afghan NGO Network, 6 June.

Dorronsoro, G. (2005) *Revolution Unending: Afghanistan: 1979 to the Present.* London: Hurst.

Doyle, M. (2000) 'Peacebuilding in Cambodia: Legitimacy and Power', in Cousens, E. and Kumar, C. (eds) *Peacebuilding as Politics: Cultivating Peace in Fragile Societies.* New York: International Peace Academy/Lynne Rienner.

Galster, S. (ed.) (1990) *Afghanistan: The Making of U.S. Policy, 1973–1990.* Vol. 1. Alexandria: Chadwyck Healey/National Security Archive.

Giustozzi, A. (2004) 'The Demodernisation of an Army: Northern Afghanistan, 1992–2001', *Small Wars and Insurgencies*, 15(1), Spring.

Giustozzi, A. (2005) 'The Ethnicisation of an Afghanistan Faction: Junbesh-I Milli from its Origins to the Presidential Elections', *Crisis States Working Paper* 67.

GoA (Government of the Islamic Republic of Afghanistan) (2006) 'Afghanistan National Development Strategy: Sector Summary Report', November.

(GoA DIAG) Government of Afghanistan Disbandment of Illegal Armed Groups. Online, available at: www.diag.gov.af/.

Government of Germany (2006) 'Berlin Declaration', 1 April.

Government of Japan (2006) 'Co-Chairs Summary: The Second Tokyo Conference on Consolidation of Peace in Afghanistan (DDR/DIAG)', 5 July.

Government of Japan (2003) 'Tokyo Conference on Consolidation of Peace (DDR) in Afghanistan – Chair's Summary', 22 February.

Harpviken, K. (1997) 'Transcending Traditionalism: The Emergence of Non-State Military Formations in Afghanistan', *Journal of Peace Research*, 34(3).

Hendrickson, D. (1999) 'A Review of Security-Sector Reform', *CSDG Working Paper.* London: Conflict Security and Development Group, King's College.

Ibrahimi, S. (2004) 'Army Develops Despite Militia Disarmament Issues', *IWPR ARR* 37, 29 September.

Ibrahimi, S. (2006) 'Afghan Disarmament a Never-ending Process', *IWPR ARR* 15, 12 May.

ICG (International Crisis Group) (2004) 'Elections and Security in Afghanistan', Media Release, 30 March.

ICG (2005) 'Getting Disarmament Back on Track', *Asia Briefing* 35, 23 February.

International Institute for Strategic Studies (2006) *Military Balance 2006.* Oxford: Oxford University Press.

IRIN (2003a) 'Reintegration of Disarmed Combatants Begins', 9 December.

IRIN (2003b) 'Afghanistan: Kabul Calls for Jobs for Former Combatants', 26 February.

IRIN (2003c) 'Interview with Disarmed Combatant', 27 October.

IRIN (2004) 'Disarmament Accelerated as Elections Approach', 21 September.

IRIN (2005) 'Afghanistan: Warlord Attacks Provincial Disarmament Team', 14 April.

IRIN (2006a) 'Afghanistan: where the Gun Still Rules', 7 June.

IRIN (2006b) 'Afghanistan: Former Militia Leaders Surrender Arms', 6 March.

IWPR (Institute for War and Peace Reporting) (2002) 'Taleban Buying Up Smuggled Guns', *IWPR ARR* 34, 1 November.

Kartha, T. (1999) *Tools of Terror: Light Weapons and India's Security.* New Delhi: Institute for Defence Studies and Analysis.

Kenzhetaev, M. (undated) 'Arms Deliveries to Afghanistan in the 1990s', *Moscow Defense Brief.*

Mani, R. (2003) 'Ending Impunity and Building Justice in Afghanistan', *AREU Issues Paper*, 31 December.

Musah, A. and Thompson, N. (1999) 'South Asia: Drugs, Guns and Regional Conflict', in Musah, A. and Thompson, N. (eds) *Over a Barrel: Light Weapons and Human Rights in the Commonwealth.* London/New Delhi: Commonwealth Human Rights Initiative.

Noble, C. (2002) 'Conflict Prevention Needs in Afghanistan', Japan Center for Conflict Prevention, 20 January.

PAN (Pajhwok Afghan News) (2004) 'Takhar Residents took to Streets against Armed Men', 2 October.

Pusher, I. (2003) 'UN Aims to Disarm Afghan Fighters', *Christian Science Monitor*, 2 December.

Rashid, A. (2002a) 'Afghanistan: Still Waiting to be Rescued', *Far Eastern Economic Review*, 21 March.

Rashid, A. (2002b) 'Afghanistan: Warlord, Profiteer, Ideologue Chief', *Far Eastern Economic Review*, 23 May.

Rashid, A. (2004) 'Karzai Seeks to Accelerate Pace of Militia Disarmament in Afghanistan', *EurasiaNet*, 29 June.

Rothchild, D. and Roeder, P. (2005) 'Dilemmas of State-Building in Divided Societies', in Roeder, P. and Rothchild, D. (eds) *Sustainable Peace: Power and Democracy After Civil Wars.* Ithaca: Cornell University Press.

Roy, O. (1990) *Islam and Resistance in Afghanistan.* 2nd edn. Cambridge: Cambridge University Press.

Rubin, B. (1995) *The Search for Peace in Afghanistan.* New Haven: Yale University Press.

Rubin, B. (2003) 'Identifying Options and Entry Points for Disarmament, Demobilization and Reintegration in Afghanistan'. New York: Center on International Cooperation, New York University.

Rubin, B., Ghani, A., Maley, W., Roy, O. and Rashid, A. (2001) 'Afghanistan: Reconstruction and Peace-building in a Regional Framework', *KOFF Peacebuilding Reports*, January.

Sarwan, R. and Karokhel, D. (2003) 'Demobilization Moves Closer: Defense Ministry Changes to Unblock Countrywide Disarmament Scheme', *ARR* 73, 27 August.

Sedra, M. (2003) 'Confronting Afghanistans Security Dilemma: Reforming the Security Sector', *BICC Brief 28.* Online, available at: www.bicc.de/publications/briefs/brief28/content.php.

Sedra, M. (2006) 'Security Sector Reform in Afghanistan: The Slide Towards Expediency', *International Peacekeeping*, 13(1), March.

Sedra, M. and Middlebrook, P. (2005) 'Beyond Bonn: Revisioning the International Compact for Afghanistan', *Foreign Policy in Focus*, November.

Thruelsen, P. (2006) 'From Soldier to Civilian: Disarmament Demobilization Reintegration', *DIIS Report 7.* Danish Institute for International Studies.

UNAMA (2004a) 'Afghan Update', No. 6, May.

UNAMA (2004b) 'Afghan Update', No. 5, March.

UNDP (2005) 'Disarmament and Reintegration Commission Joins Secretariat', 10 October.

UNDP (2006a) 'Development Projects to be Launched in Two Districts of Kapisa', 17 October.

UNDP (2006b) '189,163 Landmines and 10,071 Tons of Ammunition Destroyed in Afghanistan', 13 August.

UNDP (2006c) 'Nine Commanders Voluntarily Surrender Weapons in Nangarhar', 10 May.

UNDP–World Bank–Asian Development Bank (2001) 'Afghanistan: Demobilization: Towards a Programme for the Reintegration of Ex-Combatants', Draft Sector Report, December.

UNWG (2006) *Integrated Disarmament, Demobilization and Reintegration Standards (IDDRS)*. Online, available at: www.unddr.org/iddrs/.

Wilder, A. (2007) *Cops or Robbers: The Struggle to Reform the Afghan National Police*, AREU Issues Paper, July.

Winderl, T. (2005) 'Client Satisfaction Survey: Initial Assessment of Client Satisfaction for the Afghanistan's New Beginning's Program', 5 April.

World Bank Group (2004) 'Afghan Ex-combatants and Poppy Growers Receive New Livelihoods', 28 August.

Xinhua News Agency (2005) 'Fraud Discovery Leads to Suspension of Disarmament in West Afghanistan', 27 February.

6 What the Timorese veterans say

Unpacking DDR in Timor-Leste

Gordon Peake[1]

Introduction

In Timor-Leste, DDR extended far beyond ex-combatants in active service when conflict ended. Only one DDR programme targeted those fighting when hostilities ceased in 1999. Three other interventions also reached out to all those who played an active role during the two decades of resistance against Indonesia and whose actions contributed to the establishment of the first new state at the dawn of the twenty-first century. This chapter considers three interconnected issues relating to DDR in Timor-Leste: first, the limitations of what DDR can be realistically expected to achieve; second, the relevance and impact of DDR 'best practices' in shaping outcomes; and third, the challenge confronting technical projects in addressing fundamentally subjective and wider-reaching grievances. In doing so, it poses the question of whether a discrete cluster of programmes can ever genuinely reintegrate people in the long-term. DDR in Timor-Leste partly succeeded in negating a potential security problem and providing short-term assistance. Where it failed manifestly is in providing former fighters with a longer-term framework for socio-economic advancement, a sobering conclusion for those who praise the far-reaching potential for DDR to achieve wider goals.

This chapter examines the outcomes of four DDR interventions designed to assist veteran combatants. It does not restrict the analysis narrowly to fighters at war's end. Specifically, two DDR programmes were internationally designed and managed while the other two were led primarily by institutions of the new state (with international funding support). The first of the two international initiatives consisted of a conventional short-term reinsertion programme known as FRAP (FALINTIL Reinsertion Assistance Program) intended to help assist cantoned fighters return to civilian life. The second, led and managed by UNDP, was wider in scope and ambition and took a 'community-based' approach. This was known as the RESPECT programme (Recovery, Employment and Stability Programme for Ex-Combatants and Communities in Timor-Leste). The third consisted of two national initiatives managed by the presidency and the national government respectively. A series of presidential commissions certified and registered individuals who played a role in the struggle against Indonesia. Fourth, a department of the government was created dedicated to veterans' issues.[2]

Although the DDR programmes adopted a wide definition of 'combatant' in Timor-Leste, their approach and outcomes are similar to initiatives adopted elsewhere. In spite of the importance attached to them by donors, evidence of the positive effects of DDR, henceforth referred to as *veterans' assistance programmes*,[3] remain comparatively thin. The chapter finds that whatever credible achievements there may have been, they steadily evaporated over time. Many veterans that participated had themselves long forgotten the nature of assistance they were provided. The chapter echoes the circumspection of other contributors to this volume and reaffirms the need for some deflation of anecdotal claims of success. It also leaves open the question of whether this well-intentioned technical process can generate a meaningful outcome during a complex, dynamic and multifaceted process of political reform. As one senior official from the latest UN peacekeeping mission in Timor-Leste commented: 'if we cannot do this here, in a small country with a comparatively benign political environment, then how can we even contemplate working in somewhere like the [Democratic Republic of] Congo'.[4]

In one sense, this chapter recites a familiar story of over-optimistic programming and sub-optimal outcomes. But it is also a tale of dashed dreams, the hard realities of independence and the challenges of being old and under-appreciated in a new nation. This chapter considers these interconnected issues in some detail. It asks how technical assistance programmes can solve issues that are inherently subjective, personal and idiosyncratic. Since independence in 2002, the inflated hopes of many veterans to assume a meaningful involvement in development have not materialized. Although the research for this chapter sought to probe socio-economic issues of veterans relating to specific interventions, respondents constantly veered away from specifics and towards a wider malaise related to fundamental questions of identity and place in the new dispensation. The performance of Timor's leaders was lamented and there was a general sense of being 'left behind'. A central question emerging from this chapter, then, is whether and how any technical response can ultimately redress ostensibly emotional and individual issues.

The chapter proceeds in four sections. Following a brief overview of the context in which DDR programmes were executed, the second section sets out the methodology employed to assess them. Leavened through all subsequent sections is the voice of veterans themselves drawn from focus groups undertaken around the country's 13 districts. The third section examines the characteristics of separate DDR processes undertaken in Timor-Leste during the UN transitional administration and post independence period. International programmes focused, initially, on providing immediate assistance to recently demobilized combatants. Subsequent programmes adopted a wider definition of combatant and expanded the focus beyond the individual to the community.[5] But this wider categorization of the 'beneficiary group' resulted in the setting of unclear goals, and less sure-footed implementation. Taken together, the section reveals the limited long-term outcomes of these programmes allied with frustration in the delayed disbursement of tangible government assistance. The fourth section discusses the views of veterans in more detail. A conclusion rounds up

Table 6.1 Summary of DDR programmes

	Duration	Implementing agency	Funding sources	Cost ($ million)
FRAP	2001–2002	International Organization for Migration (IOM)	World Bank, USAID, Canada	2
RESPECT	2003–2005	United Nations Development Programme	Japan	4
Presidential Commissions	2002–2005		United Nations, Ireland, Norway, Sweden USAID, United Kingdom	
Department of Veterans' Affairs[6]				

the analysis and suggests the need for greater appreciation of the limited role and outcome of programming within a wider, dynamic process of societal change and related modesty on the part of donors and international organizations as to what such programmes can achieve.

Difficult beginnings: the challenge of state-building in Timor-Leste

Timor-Leste is not simply Asia-Pacific region's newest country. It is also the poorest. Experiencing a significant demographic 'youth bulge', unemployment is estimated at 40 per cent, per capita gross domestic product is US$520 a year and few sustainable industries exist to absorb a rapidly growing labour pool (Center on International Cooperation 2008). According to UN agencies, half the population still has no access to safe drinking water. Revenue from oil and gas in the Timor Sea has yet to fill government coffers, and much is being siphoned-off by corruption. Even when and if it does, the government suffers from a technical or human capacity deficit. In the last three years, it has been unable to execute its budget. Much of the optimism that greeted independence has faded.

The country remains politically fragile, especially after a severe descent into armed violence in mid-2006. The 'crisis' – as the events are known – has complex origins. Its proximate cause was the dismissal of one-third of the Timorese defence force, itself led by (former) resistance leaders – the F-FDTL (FALINTIL-Forsa de Defesa de Timor-Leste). A series of follow-on events awakened incipient tensions between soldiers from Timor's eastern and western regions. The police force also fractured along similar east–west lines and various factions began fighting with elements of the defence force. The breakdown in order led to high levels of gang violence. Reports at the time indicated that some

37 people were killed and many houses destroyed (Rees 2006). More than 150,000 Timorese – 15 per cent of the entire population – sought refuge as internally displaced persons (IDP) in makeshift camps. Two years on, most remain too fearful to return and remain scattered throughout the city and outlying districts (ICG 2008).

Within the space of a few months, many of the national institutions established by the UN and subsequently handed over to the government unravelled. In addition to the triggers noted above, the escalating rates of armed violence were also motivated by a complex brew of elite-driven political tensions, latent state weaknesses, high rates of youth unemployment and associated poverty. An unstable macro-economic environment exacerbated a sense of political disappointment and ethnic resentment. These and other events forced the UN to cancel plans for their withdrawal, and return in greater number. The UN Integrated Mission in Timor-Leste (UNMIT) is the fifth UN mission on the half-island since 1999, and the third since independence in May 2002.[7] Then Secretary-General Kofi Annan observed that the magnitude of the tasks facing UNMIT meant it was 'likely to stay for many years'.[8] Overall, the current state of Timor-Leste is far from the halcyon state that many veterans fought for. Outbreaks of armed violence remain likely. Indeed, in February 2008, a renegade soldier tried to assassinate the country's senior leadership, seriously injuring Timorese president, Jose Ramos-Horta.

Timor-Leste's former combatants are known by the sobriquet of 'veterans' [*veteranos*]. The label confers almost mythical status in Timor-Leste. Veterans occupy a central role in the national consciousness and are formally recognized in the new state's constitution.[9] As one long-standing observer of Timor-Leste politics observes: 'the role of the veterans dominates the country's political equation from the capitol to villages' (Rees 2004: 6). All told, they number approximately 56,000 – far more than the estimated 1,900 serving in 1999 when the insurgency waged against Indonesia ended with a vote for independence that occurred three years later. The veterans are remarkably heterogeneous, encompassing diplomats and activist exiles, jungle fighters and clandestine agents [*clandestinos*]. Widows and orphans of fallen fighters also legitimately claim the title 'veteran'.

Although independence has arrived for the veterans, it has done so at a cost. Few of the anticipated entitlements promised to them emerged. All but one of the veterans interviewed as part of the research for this chapter indicated they felt worse off and struggled to pay for basic necessities such as food and clothing for themselves and their family. Ultimately, the issue of the veterans – including their sustainable demobilization and reintegration – is inextricably tied to the challenges of building a new state. This is the real difficulty facing veterans in Timor, something far more wide-ranging and existential than perhaps any targeted programme can meaningfully address. The condition of the veterans is fundamentally connected to the dynamics of unfulfilled state-building and security sector reform. Owing to the deep emotional, imaginative and deeply subjective undertones of the national project, there are legitimate questions over whether DDR is in fact the right tool and whether it should be advertised as such.[10]

Investigating veterans' issues

The basic empirical claims of this chapter are derived from focus group and survey-based research conducted in Timor-Leste in summer 2007. In this sense, the chapter adopts a qualitative and representative approach in contrast to the quantitative survey and incident-based assessments undertaken in Sierra Leone, Liberia, Uganda or Colombia. The centrepiece of the research included a combination of six meetings conducted in six districts spread evenly throughout Timor-Leste together with key informants in other districts.[11] The methodology replicated the approach adopted by Muggah and Bennett in Ethiopia (Chapter 7, this volume), and sought to gauge the extent of economic, social and political 'reintegration' following demobilization, while simultaneously examining the efficacy of international and Timor-Leste veterans' assistance programmes that touched them, namely FRAP and RESPECT, the Presidential Commissions and Department of Veterans' Affairs.

The sessions combined focus groups (103 people) followed by participants completing a survey questionnaire.[12] The State Secretary for Veterans Affairs, Ministry of Labour and Community Solidarity, arranged the focus groups by sending a letter out to the district administrator in each targeted district, the highest ranking local government official. The district administrator then posted the notice and used informal information networks to advertise the meeting and a wide cross-section of veterans were encouraged to voluntarily attend. The focus group sessions were designed to be representative, though certain biases were unavoidable. Because the information emanated from the district administrator, those with close temporal and political linkages stood a greater chance of learning of the meeting than others. While such an approach is inherently self-selecting, there is reason to believe that those participating in the sessions were generally representative of the various groups that claim the title veteran. They included members of FALINTIL, widows and orphans of resistance fighters, former clandestine activists and current members of the country's new defence and police organizations.[13]

The decision to adopt a focus group approach generated opportunities and constraints. On the positive side, focus groups provided a useful means to attain insights into the priorities, concerns and aspirations of the FALINTIL veterans who were demobilized. The approach enabled direct contact between the evaluator and quite a few beneficiaries, allowing for follow-up and more unstructured dialogue. The questionnaires also allowed specific questions to be shared across groups so as to enable (limited) comparisons to be made. But, as noted above, the focus groups – and the nature in which veterans were assembled – also revealed certain limitations. The approach may have led to over-representation of certain veteran groups, as well as other spatial demographic and socio-economic biases.[14] Most participants came from the town in which the district administration office was located. Because of poor communication linkages, it was difficult to let participants in the countryside know of the meeting. Even if the news did travel, poor transport linkages prevented attendance. Travelling to the towns in which the focus groups were conducted would have necessitated an arduous day-long journey.

Supplementing the focus group and survey was a series of detailed key informant interviews. These interviews were targeted at individuals involved in the design, implementation and evaluation of veterans' assistance programmes, as well as senior Timorese government officials and parliamentarians.[15] As no centralized database or resource centre exists, efforts were made to track down documents relating to veterans' issues.[16] There was considerable unevenness in the amount of material available from each intervention. For example, there have been extensive evaluations of, and material relating to, the FRAP programme and presidential commissions, but much less on the Department of Veterans' Affairs and the UNDP RESPECT programme.[17] Interviews were also needed in order to glean a more candid sense of programming than emerged from project documents and evaluations, which were often tempered in their critiques because of fears relating to career repercussions.[18]

Two methodological challenges emerged during the course of the focus group interviews. They serve as a note of caution for future research in Timor-Leste and perhaps other post-conflict contexts. The first is related to the wariness among respondents of researchers – otherwise known as 'survey fatigue'. There was profound disgruntlement expressed by focus group participants at being used for another round of interviews that would 'change little' on the ground. In each focus group location, at least one participant was able to recount 'promises' given by previous researchers that largely went unfulfilled.[19] A member of the focus group in Liquica observed how:

> Various groups from national level came to see us asking for data related to veteran issues, such as government commission, president's commission, international agencies and NGO as well as local ones. Many activities had being conducted and yet no result is at hand for us. We were promise by these groups on the result of activities conducted previously in order to facilitate the process of working out planning of programs and activities for us in the future. Everything remains a promise and we remained living in such poor living condition as veterans. What else do you want from us now?[20]

A deep sense of ennui pervaded the six focus groups and was reflected in turnout and participation. In five of the six locations, fewer participants than expected attended the meeting. Many wondered what the point of the exercise was and were wary following claims made by previous researchers that the information provided would positively impact their lives. The research team strove to make clear that this research would not necessarily be followed up by international agencies or the government of Timor-Leste. Broadly, the team's candour was appreciated, as was the US$10 incentive paid to participants.[21] The fact that one veteran said about the payment that it was 'more tangible than anything else I've received' might be somewhat hyperbolic but somewhat revealing of the poor economic straits of many.

The second methodological issue that emerged was how little was recollected of programmes that concluded just a few years previous to the author's visit. This recall bias raises questions as to whether evaluations are conducted too soon after the event as to allow for a credible judgement on outcome. In some focus groups, participants admitted they could not recall what had been provided to them. For example, one participant in the eastern city of Los Palos in Lautem District had to remind fellow participants that he had indeed participated in the FRAP reinsertion programme. Of course, such poor recall is a commonly detected feature of many DDR programme evaluations. Information often has to be drawn out through gentle prodding, triangulation and other key informant methods. That said, the hazy recollection's reinforce the impression of limited outcomes.

An inadvertent result of examining interventions too soon after they are concluded may be that premature findings can reinforce a policy tendency in the literature to believe that DDR programmes 'work'. For example, the evaluation of the FRAP programme occurred just a few months after its conclusion. Although the evaluation was broadly complementary, and detected marked impact, was it administered too soon to detect any real 'impact'? Donors appear to be reluctant to undertake longitudinal assessments. From a bureaucratic perspective, it reflects the ways in which interventions are financially structured: most DDR interventions normally budget for a single evaluation. In a world of competing priorities, evaluating a long dormant veterans' assistance programme is likely low down on the list. However, an inadvertent consequence of early evaluations is that they may strengthen a conventional wisdom that DDR is more effective than it actually is. Whatever the case, hastily launched evaluations render even more difficult the already daunting challenge of discerning cause and effect in a dynamic, fluid, and often conflict-affected, environment. This is especially so in the case of DDR, which is often linked with other ongoing poverty-reduction programmes and within the context of wider economic development. Moreover, processes of attitudinal and institutional change can often ebb and flow in different directions. Can any assessment tools capture the complexity of DDR?

DDR processes in Timor-Leste

A central theme animating this volume is the role of context in shaping the motivations and mobilization experiences of former combatants. Acknowledging the way that politics and conflict inform actor agency, and the heterogeneous characteristics of former fighters, are of pivotal importance in shaping their receptivity to DDR. Before turning to the veterans' assistance programmes in Timor-Leste, this section revisits various aspects of the 24-year war and the resistance movement.

After more than two decades of Indonesian occupation, the people of the former Portuguese colony of East Timor voted for independence in 1999. Following three years of UN transitional administration, the Democratic Republic of Timor-Leste came into being on 20 May 2002. A major challenge facing the international community and the new republic was the 'veteran issue'. Throughout the Indonesian occupation, the East Timorese resistance front, known as Forças Armadas da Libertação Nacional de Timor-Leste (FALINTIL) led an armed struggle for independence against the Indonesian army. An estimated 56,000 people who fought in and/or clandestinely supported the resistance campaign claim the title of 'veteran'. This accounts for approximately 5 per cent of the current population.

The struggle for independence took many forms. It was waged by the gun, the conference dais and through awareness-raising political campaigns. In addition to fighting from the forests of Timor-Leste, Timorese diaspora waged a diplomatic campaign to force the international community to restore Timor-Leste's short-lived independence. In constructing a broad front to oppose the Indonesian occupation, Timor's politicians and fighters found a unity of purpose lacking in 1975 as Portugal hastily and chaotically withdrew from its former colony. Several political parties emerged during that period with opposing visions for the future. For example, the FRETILIN party (Frente Revolucionaria de Timor-Leste Independente) argued for immediate independence with the support of its FALINTIL militia, while other parties such as UDT and ASDT were significantly more cautious and favoured autonomy within neighbouring Indonesia.

These differences over political end-state turned violent as a civil war began in August 1975. By November, FRETILIN was in the ascendancy and declared unilateral independence.[22] It would be a short-lived 'state'. Two weeks after a national flag was raised, and with the tacit consent of Australia and the United States who feared a FRETILIN-run Timor-Leste would become a communist outpost in the South Pacific, Indonesia invaded and duly annexed the territory. Many members of Timor's political elite immediately left the territory, most relocating to Portugal or Lusophone Africa. During the early years of the occupation, FALINTIL controlled a significant portion of the country but as Indonesian control strengthened in the late 1970s, the fighters were eventually pushed east, and their activities underground. Their tactics changed to that of a 'hit and run' guerrilla force.

Broadly speaking, the resistance adopted a three-pronged approach: armed, clandestine and diplomatic. FALINTIL constituted the armed front and sustained a guerrilla war against the Indonesian army, while the clandestine front supplied the fighters with food, intelligence, weapons, ammunition and hiding places. The diplomatic front, based primarily in Lisbon and Maputo, focused on keeping Timor-Leste on the agenda of the UN and lobbying other government. Jose Ramos Horta, Timor-Leste's current president, and the second since the restoration of independence, personified the diplomatic campaign.

Some of the internal conflict that characterized late colonial and independence era politics endured, both within FRETILIN, and between FRETILIN and other groups. (The effects of these earlier tensions still affect post-independence Timor-Leste's political dynamics.) However, the trend was towards unifying the resistance and presenting a broad, non-partisan front. The driving force behind this unity is often credited to resistance leader, Jose Kay Rala 'Xanana' Gusmao. Part of the invigoration meant removing FALINTIL from a direct political association with FRETLIN and placing it under the framework of a broad resistance movement. Timor-Leste is thus somewhat remarkable as appearing to have the normal chronology of a political movement in reverse: split, then unity. At the same time, the resistance placed greater emphasis on the 'diplomatic struggle', compelled by a recognition that armed struggle alone could not alone pave the way to independence. Gusmao remains a central figure in Timorese politics. He would become the first president and, since 2007, served as the Timorese prime minister, a politically more powerful post.

An end to conflict but not violence

Although there appeared to be the trappings of a unified national struggle, the subterranean guerrilla nature of the conflict meant that this was not exactly the case. The influence of a clandestine intelligence and support network leveraging village or regionally-based loyalties meant there was little truly 'national' about this 'national liberation' struggle. This made sound strategic sense but had the effect that, when conflict ended, there was no definitive account of who did what and when.[23] As in many conflicts, there is a problem of attribution and verification. Even with prominent commanders, facts are disputed about who did what, to whom and with whom (Rees 2004).

A combination of persistence in the jungle and on the lobbying front brought Timor-Leste to global consciousness during the late 1990s. Within the context of a national reform movement occasioned by the Asian economic crisis and war-weary, Indonesia proposed a referendum to offer the people of East Timor a choice between autonomy and independence in January 1999. FALINTIL fighters emerged from the forest and voluntarily cantoned themselves in five sites (Martin 2001). The Timorese leadership took the decision based on fears that any Timorese group being seen as under arms could negatively distort international sympathy. The UN conducted the 'popular consultation' in late August 1999, with 78.5 per cent of voters opting for independence. Pro-Indonesian militias immediately launched a campaign of violence in which the Indonesian authorities were complicit (Cohen 2003). In addition to large-scale casualties (estimated at 1,400) the territory was physically devastated. Over half the population fled their homes (CAVR 2005).

Under intense pressure, Indonesian president B.J. Habibie agreed to an international security presence to quell the violence and restore order. On 15 September 1999, the UN Security Council authorized an Australian-led peacekeeping force to restore peace and security under Chapter VII of the United Nations Charter. In October, the UN Transitional Administration in East Timor (UNTAET) was established under Security Council Resolution 1272 to administer the territory for a transitional period. UNTAET was endowed with state-like discretionary authorities and, along with Kosovo, the most comprehensive mandate in the history of UN peacekeeping.

The forgotten fighters

During the lead-in to the referendum and amidst the chaos that followed, the estimated 1,900 FALINTIL fighters remained outside the fray. Despite provocations from the Indonesian army and requests from Timorese for assistance, they remained loyal to the political leadership and opted not to become involved. Following the arrival of the Australian peacekeepers, the five groups reassembled in one site near the mountain town of Aileu, 50 miles south of Dili. Then, as the International Crisis Group (ICG 2006) put it, 'the world seemed to forget them'. Donors and humanitarian organizations baulked at dealing with the issue of demobilizing men under arms, fearing political repercussions.

Although operating under one of the most expansive resolutions in UN peacekeeping history, UNTAET interpreted their mandate to mean that the veteran issue was beyond their remit.[24] Some UNTAET policy-makers also lacked an appreciation of community esteem for FALINTIL, seeing the Timorese resistance as party to a civil war rather than as a victorious liberation movement enjoying wide popular support.[25] To the cantoned fighters, their fate seemed down the (admittedly long) priority list of former resistance leaders in the chaotic time of political transition. Cantoned far from Dili, living in atrocious conditions without adequate basic necessities such as food, shelter, clothing and medical care, calls from observers about the potential security risks of leaving armed men in such conditions generally went unheeded (Rees 2003).

In part, the fighters were ignored because there was no real strategic thinking among UN or Timorese politicians as to what to do with them. But the impending threat of violence from cooped up and desperate men – 'spoilers' in the vernacular – moved the issue up the political agenda. Reacting (too late with the benefit of hindsight) to the deteriorating conditions, UNTAET commissioned a team from King's College, London to examine the issue alongside the question of what future security sector architecture the future state of Timor-Leste should possess. Following their recommendations the decision was taken to integrate roughly one-third of the cantoned – 650 in total – into a newly-created defence force while the remainder would receive social and economic reintegration assistance from International Organization for Migration (IOM) under the auspices of FRAP.[26] The demobilization of FALINTIL was combined with the creation of the Forca Defesa de Timor-Leste (FDTL) in early February 2001. The force was renamed Falintil–FDTL during the constitution drafting process.[27]

The decision as to who was transitioned into the FDTL was mired in politics and caused considerable acrimony. Bureaucratically, the decision was based on technical requirements of experience, health and capability. However, subjective criteria appeared to play a more important role. The selection process for those integrated was not transparent: all decisions regarding who would become part of the army were taken alone by the FALINTIL high command and Xanana Gusmao, without reference to a clear selection process or criteria. The decision to exclude the majority of FALINTIL from the new defence force provoked fury among those left out. Some of those denied entry vented their frustration by rampaging through the camp, destroying their possessions, and leaving before the IOM assistance programme could get underway.

FALINTIL Reinsertion Assistant Program (FRAP)

The first programme in Timor-Leste to focus on former fighters is likely the only one that conforms to the archetypal DDR paradigm. FRAP was the consolation prize for those not selected for the F-FDTL and intended to provide a 'soft-landing' to counter the challenges of returning to civilian life. It was a relatively short programme with implementation designed in December 2000 and the whole programme implemented and wrapped up in just 12 months.[28] The intervention was implemented by the IOM and funded by the World Bank and USAID.

FRAP was relatively modest in aim, and described by one architect as a 'political process with a political aim: to prevent FALINTIL from becoming problematic'.[29] From the beginning, veterans were thus conceived as a 'problem' to be solved. FRAP demobilized the remaining 1,308 serving combatants, and provided training and monetary benefits. The programme provided ex-combatants with transport from the cantonment site to their community, a transitional safety net consisting of US$100 a month for five months and a reintegration package worth approximately US$550. The majority of recipients chose to receive the assistance to buy either small vending kiosks or work the land by buying buffalo.

An extremely comprehensive independent evaluation of FRAP conducted in 2002 found that the programme was largely successful. It achieved its overall and primary objectives regarding the social and economic reintegration of demobilized FALINTIL. It was lauded for generating discernible benefits that contributed to security and stability – stated objectives of most DDR initiatives. According to beneficiary-surveys administered by the evaluator, FRAP recipients reported general satisfaction during the course of the evaluation. With the benefits of a year's hindsight, some recipients even remarked that the 'consolation prize' was much better than joining the defence force. The evaluator made a shrewd point in his conclusion: at the most fundamental level, the raison d'être of FRAP was to 'assist the reinsertion (and reintegration) of FALINTIL veterans' (McCarthy 2002: 102). To phrase it another way, the intervention was not intended to be a solution to the wider veteran problem.

Five years on, asking broadly the same set of questions to FRAP beneficiaries elicited very different answers. Despite the earlier assumptions of FRAP supporters, in the absence of any significant economic development, the programme was popularly perceived as being 'a solution to the veterans problem'. The US$500 was long spent and many of the kiosks supported under the programme had long since closed down. Participants in three of the focus groups noted that the buffalo they purchased had died. Of the 11 participants in the focus groups demobilized during FRAP, all signalled that they felt less wealthy than before and were unable to buy food or clothing for themselves and their families more easily since leaving. In short, the impact of FRAP was negligible several years after the programme ended.

In part this should not surprise – the aim of the assistance was to rapidly and consciously defuse a potential political problem of spoilers. FRAP was explicitly not conceived as a spur for wider development (McCarthy 2002: 55). The vocal criticism of FRAP benefits are also clearly blended in with a general sense of embittered disgruntlement relating to the insufficient attention, assistance and legitimacy bestowed upon FRAP beneficiaries, and veterans in general. Nevertheless, this does not disclaim the fact that even the narrowly conceived outcomes (i.e. reintegration) are slight. This is not a direct criticism of IOM – the agency was scrupulous not to advertise the programme as anything other than a short-term transitional assistance effort – but it is counsel that evaluations may be carried out too rapidly to adequately gauge real outcomes. They also indicate that, despite efforts, DDR programmes are often construed by recipients as offering more than is actually programmed for.

The President's Commissions

The 1,308 FALINTIL veterans that received assistance from FRAP and the 650 who joined the F-FDTL were a small segment of a much wider group that played a part in the resistance. As Taur Matan Ruak, then Commander of FALINTIL and now Commander of the F-FDTL observed:

> If we were to recognize all those who supported our struggle, we would have to extend this recognition to most of the population, as all have, at some point in time and in their own way, participated in the liberation of our nation.
>
> (Meden 2002)

Many of those described by Ruak as supporters were not actively serving fighters. If serving FALINTIL felt somewhat excluded, the 'veterans' that served previously in FALINTIL or were active in the large clandestine network that provided intelligence and material assistance had been ignored almost entirely. The issue of entitlement for widows and orphans had not been addressed at all.

But who were these 'veterans'? On one hand, the answer was straightforward since commanders and other long serving members in a tight-knit community generally knew exactly who their comrades were. But from a bureaucratic perspective, answering the question definitively was more difficult. Moreover, owing to the clandestine nature of the resistance, it was hard to identify who was a veteran and who was merely being opportunistic. There was also a wider, more emotive veterans issue at play. One of the founding mythological narratives of the new state was the role of the resistance in securing its arrival.[30] But the relatively modest-sized FRAP programme had ended with many veterans still facing profound difficulties in adjusting to the social and economic aspects of the new civilian life.

While the FRAP process continued between 2001–2002, the question of how to provide adequate support to all veterans became an increasingly prominent political issue and one with the potential to unleash renewed violence. In the run up to Timor-Leste's independence in 2002, a number of associations 'purporting to represent veterans' interests began actively registering members, staging public rallies, and undertaking military-style drills' (Bowles 2006). With threatening rhetoric and militaristic posture, some of these grouping appeared to set themselves up in direct opposition to the F-FDTL (Rees 2004: 50–51). The cause of the 'veterans' was sufficiently malleable and emotive to serve as a political rallying-cry. Although some observers claimed that comparatively few 'veterans' were actually involved in these staged protests, it was difficult to ascertain with clear certainty who was or was not a veteran.[31] Owing to the fact that veterans themselves were part of a resistance movement operating under occupation, the subterranean nature of their activity meant no records could safely be kept.

To defuse a potentially incendiary situation, the government in line with its responsibilities under article 11 of the nascent constitution, adopted a number of policy initiatives. The first step was to establish an Office of Veterans' Affairs within the Ministry of Labour and Solidarity. The aims of the office were to formally recognize the individuals who played an essential role in the resistance, focusing in particular on the clandestine movement and the armed resistance. Following a formal acknowledgment of governmental responsibility, the office would coordinate and facilitate initiatives regarding veterans and assist families of dead fighters.[32]

Around the same time, President Gusmao created three commissions tasked with providing a definitive answer to the question of who was or was not a 'veteran'. The Comissão para os Assuntos dos Antigos Combatentes (CAAC), was responsible for identifying ex-combatants during the period 1975–1979.[33] The Comissão para os Assuntos dos Veteranos das FALINTIL (CAVF) was tasked with identifying veterans in subsequent years. Finally, the Comissão para os Assuntos dos Quadros da Resistencia (CAQR) was also enabled to identify and register members of the clandestine networks.[34] Their aim was to create a database of 'legitimate' veterans with the goal to publicly recognize and financially compensate individuals and families that played a role in the resistance.[35]

All told, this was a two-year process, exhausting in its complexity and necessarily incremental in its approach to crosschecking and verifying information, especially as regards deceased veterans.[36] Testimony and registration took place in public, with people registering in front of friends and neighbours, a means of mitigating community approbation and to prevent bandwagoning. The process was also national. With the exception of one international assistant, the process was entirely Timorese-directed, staffed and administered. This fact alone stands as a rejoinder to the frequent claims that Timorese lack governance capacity. Evaluations of the process record that commission staff were well organized, dedicated and hard working, with little indication of financial impropriety (Democratic Republic of Timor-Leste 2004: 5). In total the commissions registered more than 74,925 registered veterans of which 18,377 were deceased and 56,548 living (Democratic Republic of Timor-Leste 2004: 2). Of the living veterans, 13,025 were registered but excluded from benefits because they served less than the three-year stipulated minimum. This left 43,523 potential beneficiaries.[37] An Estatuto dos Combatentes da Libertação Nacional was passed by the national parliament on 2 March 2006, giving the state a legal obligation to provide veterans' benefits.[38] The statute provides for four different categories of pensions, which range in value from US$255–285. For purposes of recognition, the law creates a number of orders for veterans of the armed, clandestine and diplomatic fronts, as well as the founders of the resistance and martyrs of national liberation.

The Department of Veterans' Affairs

Although the creation of a dedicated office, a statute and the formal categorization of veterans highlighted the priority attached to the issue by the government, considerable challenges remain. Growing frustration among former resistance fighters without meaningful opportunities for training, employment and social services as well as access to education, health and credit and the slow roll-out of benefits, generated widespread discontent. Interviewees outside Dili commented that they received little information about the office, and were unaware of its activities.

A major constraint to the government's activities was logistical in nature. Its small office (of uncertain capacity) was tasked with disproportionately large issues. Fulfilling the bureaucratic and financial reporting requirements to manage the various programmes supported by international donors and humanitarian agencies slows down implementation considerably.[39] Related, interviews with personnel in the office suggested few were aware of DDR 'best practices' in addressing veteran issues. Material generated in donor countries did sit in some offices, but gave the impression of being more adornments than well-thumbed tomes. Despite the country's small land mass, communications beyond the capital are not easy and information is either frequently miscommunicated or not communicated at all. There is no island-wide postal system and, although the cellular network is comprehensive, many have insufficient credit to make calls. Moreover, the administrative architecture to enact quick disbursement of assistance or even rapid relay of basic information from the centre is simply not present.[40]

The disbursements of pensions are a case in point. Although funds exist to finance pensions, the delivery of monies to the registered veterans requires a substantial investment in administrative capacity building. Even though enabling legislation is developed, a host of administrative problems hamstring disbursement. For example, Timor-Leste's banking system is under-developed – the financial architecture is simply not in place to disburse pension entitlements. Although veterans received symbolic recognition for their sacrifice for the country's independence – a series of commemorative medals were minted and awarded in 2006 and 2007 – the actual financial settlement has yet to reach them. The basic precondition for implementation – the enactment of implementing regulations – is still absent. The delay causes deep frustration for the veterans. As one senior figure from Baucau commented:

> A medal is merely a symbol and yet it does not respond to our real needs in our daily life. We cannot get money out of that medal; we cannot get materials to build our broken house and other essential things for living; we cannot eat that medal. Medal does not change our lives! What we need is the good will of the government and leaders of this country to make some thing happen to change our lives.[41]

Community-based DDR: the UNDP RESPECT programme

One of the largest international programmes to reintegrate veterans was initially budgeted at some US$12 million, a sum subsequently revised down to US$4 million. Developed and managed by UNDP, the programme was called the Recovery, Employment and Stability Programme for Ex-combatants and Communities in Timor-Leste or RESPECT. It was designed to support identified 'vulnerable groups', including ex-combatants, widows, unemployed youths and others, with employment, skill development and other livelihood opportunities. This programme was significantly wider in scope and ambition than its FRAP predecessor. Instead of a narrow concentration on individual veterans, the programme was framed in terms of providing employment assistance to communities, with a concentration on providing 'work-fare' to veterans and enhancing the absorptive capacity of areas of return.

The RESPECT programme deliberately adopted a human security-centric approach. Set against the background of public disorder in 2002 widely perceived to be tied to veterans' issues, the programme identified under-employment and lack of employment opportunities for Timorese as a clear and present threat to the stability of the country. RESPECT was designed to assist with a variety of inter-linked projects whose overall aim was to provide both short and medium to long-term employment and sustainable livelihood opportunities to these people. Community participation was a leitmotif of the programme. Commitment and engagement of communities in RESPECT process (such as targeting of beneficiaries, identification, designing, planning and implementation of micro-project activities and management of infrastructure) was considered crucial to promote sustainable employment opportunities for their most vulnerable members, including ex-combatants, widows, disabled people and others.

Mid-term programme documents made bullish claims about its accomplishments. Without any evidence presented to back up core assertions UNDP (2004) claimed:

> Selected communities have their social facilities rehabilitated for more sustainable livelihood opportunities, and increased capability to maintain those

facilities; the skilled labour force has been expanded both quantitatively and qualitatively. Micro-enterprises have made an impact on local economies and employment creation in a long run and ex-combatants and other vulnerable groups displaced through conflict will be reintegrated in economic and social terms and local governments have an increased capacity in planning, facilitating, and supporting community development activities through a participatory approach.

The document rounded off these breathtaking accomplishments by claiming 'UNDP believes that at least two-year framework seems appropriate for RESPECT's impact on the community to be visible' (UNDP 2003).

Other, less invested, sources are more sceptical of the outcomes of RESPECT. Key informant interviews with members of international agencies involved in the margins of the programme suggested a range of flaws from conceptualization to delivery that severely impaired intended impact. Former programme staff noted that the sheer complexity and ambition of the intervention prevented it from achieving all of its goals. In the haste to disburse large sums of money in such a short time, especially when the project relied in large part on proposals received from local communities, there was (albeit anecdotal) evidence that projects were approved with wildly over-estimated costs.[42] Perhaps more important, an overly complicated programme design meant that there was never a clear elucidation of its goals or benchmarks; there was minimal government 'buy-in' and input; local leadership structures were bypassed; and there were consistent allegations of nepotism and cronyism.[43] To compound this, there was no clear definition of the 'target' group (whether individual veterans or an ill-defined 'community'). There were also difficult personal relations between some UNDP staff and national 'partners'.[44]

The respected Timorese NGO Lao Hamutuk raised strongly-worded concerns about the RESPECT programme. For example, they singled out the minimal process of socialization and communication of RESPECT objectives and processes to communities, a lack of coordination of the RESPECT structure with local leadership structures especially at the village level, lack of grassroots community participation in decision-making, limited participation of women in the project, the weakening of the position of the government as a result of funds controlled by UNDP and the lack of community freedom to determine other priorities since RESPECT had pre-determined three development sectors before the implementation of the programme (Lao' Hamutuk 2004).

In the aftermath of the RESPECT programme, few were aware of its activities or its benefits. In the focus groups, veterans suggest that very few benefits appeared to percolate downwards to them. The acronym was unfamiliar to many in the focus group meetings. Participants said that they had heard of the programme, but did not know for certain what it entailed. (Indeed, the only tangible remnant of the programme appeared to be UNDP Respect stickers which can be seen on the otherwise bare walls of government offices.) The programme's minimal yield led to it being wound up sooner than anticipated. Interestingly, and somewhat shockingly for a programme with such a large budget, no public evaluation was ever undertaken.[45]

The RESPECT programme raises a number of red flags with respect to the difficulties of running a programme with 'community' beneficiaries without adequate legitimacy and poor execution. It raises more fundamental questions concerning who is in charge of implementing the programme. Documented observations are few and far between – interviews with UN staffers suggested written criticism was muted given that the programme had the enthusiastic support of the SRSG and Resident Co-ordinator of UNDP Sukehiro Hasegawa. Some years later, their recorded comments in private correspondence and interviews were more scathing, suggesting that many involved in the programme had little experience of any kind in veterans-directed programming. One long-time observer said perhaps unfairly that the staff consisted of 'inexperienced development generalists'.[46]

Veterans' say

In contrast to other contributions to this volume, the political context in which DDR-type activities were administered was the end of a liberation war. Timor-Leste's DDR processes also proceeded in line with a UN transitional interregnum and subsequently under the purview of an independent, albeit weak, state. In this instance, brand new governmental institutions had to be created, posing immediate challenges for international administrators but also national staff unversed in the vagaries of public administration and budgeting. As the crisis of 2006 tragically exemplified, the state-building process is an exceptionally challenging one.

In such circumstances, the mythology of resistance confronts the pragmatic challenges of state-building and for the real and relative position of fighters in the new dispensation. A number of the leading members of the resistance have transitioned swiftly into the state's political elite. As well as Horta and Gusmao, many members of the government and parliament derive their legitimacy from the status conferred by past service to the revolutionary cause. Individuals involved in the resistance occupy the majority of seats in parliament. The dominant political parties in Timor-Leste, FRETILIN and CNRT (Congresso Nacional da Reconstrução de Timor) root their legitimacy in past deeds done. The leadership of the F-FDTL is also drawn from FALINTIL.

At the same time, the transition from fighter to politician is reserved for a small minority. More challenging is the position and role of the majority, many of whose 'good years' are well behind them. Participants in the focus groups focused more on emotional grievances than direct socio-economic concerns. A major issue related to the sense among interviewed veterans that Timor's politicians were besmirching an idealized sense of past unity. Rancour, disagreement and debate – inevitable in a democratic polity with regular elections – alarmed some of the veterans interviewed, particularly those who felt 'left behind' and economically disadvantaged.

Despite the continued sense of 'unity', there are now serious cracks in relations between the 'veterans' that constitute Timor-Leste's political elite. Tragically, these tensions were laid bare in the middle of three bloody months in
2006, which saw elements of state security institutions collapse, and the fledg-
ling nation lurch dangerously towards civil conflict. Aside from the veteran
leaders who climbed the political ladder, many veterans feel forgotten. Simply
put, the veterans felt their lives were mortgaged to the resistance and that they
had not yet been rewarded. The primary target of their ire is not primarily international agencies but rather a political elite they blame for neglect, and alighting
attention upon them only when it is politically expedient. One participant in the
Baucau focus group summed up the situation thus:

> What we know in this society is that our leaders do not recognize us and yet
> continually using our name 'veterans' for their interest. We became victims
> of this independence for the benefit of other opportunist people. This is the
> reality that makes most of us veterans feel sad in this environment of
> independence. The worst thing that happened in relation to veterans' issue is
> that people are using our names to benefit their interest.[47]

At the grassroots, there is a combination of anger at being ignored and baffle-
ment that a leadership that found strength in unity is so divided.[48] The sense of
let-down is palpable. Although such feelings are understandable, these growing
pains of transition are not peculiar to Timor-Leste. In other states, the transition
from resistance leader to political leader has been equally difficult. Leaders are
thrust into office with high expectations and are often overwhelmed by the challenges confronting them.

There is also a pervasive sense that those who did not contribute to the
struggle are reaping the rewards of independence. Some prominent independence-
era politicians are considered 'autonomistas' or those who supported solutions
less than full independence.[49] Often well educated, there is a sense that these
figures are reaping the rewards of a victory won by veterans. Running a state
and dealing with an international bureaucracy requires skills that many focus
group members did not have or could not acquire because their 'best years' were
spent on service. One admitted that he had 'lost the opportunity to go to school
in order to be intellectually formed'.[50] In effect, the perception is that veterans
are being left out of a victory they won for others. For example, a veteran participant lamented how:

> The people who prefer to integrate to the Republic of Indonesia they
> laughed at us by stating that 'why should you struggle for independence as a
> nation, the only way to reach to a better life is to integrate to Indonesia'.
> They said that we just spent time for struggling that will be in vain.
> However, once reach to independence, those opportunists who wanted
> integration now occupy the government to rule us and we remain to suffer
> now.... When we were struggling for independence in the forest, we ran up

and down to hide of the pursuing of the Indonesian military but after the independence came over other people who had no dream for independence who got benefit from that.

Veterans contend that they are not adequately recognized in decision-making processes from the official to the community level. Less than half of all respondents during the focus groups (45 per cent) considered themselves to be actively involved and able to use their status to transcend political differences. All but one voted in the 2007 presidential and parliamentary polls. Many of the former combatants exhibit close relationships with their communities, as well as cross-district linkages with some asserting that they maintain a measure of influence and stature within society. Emblematic of government neglect was the failure to locate and respectfully inter the bones of dead fighters still in the forest. Three years after submission of the report, a proposal in this regard has not been enacted. One focus group respondent noted how:

> I feel embarrass and sad with the low effort of the government to [*sic*] ... identifying the place and collecting the neglected and forgotten bones of our fellow veterans and ex-combatants spread through out the country. Many of our friends departed veterans and ex-combatants were not touched and found yet by their family members and relatives. There should be an extra effort by the government and together with community to do this work to be able to response to the needs of the family and relatives. Even though some family members and relatives had received medal on behalf of them, therefore until now their where being is still unknown.[51]

Veterans were also concerned with their generally poor socio-economic status in the wake of independence. One focus group respondent observed how:

> our lives now are more and more misery since we are not able to earn even US$1 a day. With this terrible lives and day by day we are getting old and then die. I will not enjoy anything from this country.[52]

Another echoed this, saying:

> we live like animals. For time being, we have no houses; we just occupy illegally the houses and lands left by the Indonesians. Therefore, we ask the government to provide us houses to live. In addition, we have no more capacity to earn money through cultivating land since we get old now.[53]

The continued impoverishment of veterans and their exclusion from political engagement in the national project is a potential tinder-box. Although some individual veterans were involved in the 2006 crisis, veterans *en masse* generally refrained from joining-in the violence. Part of the reason for this is likely because they were not themselves organized into a potent lobbying force – understandable as they are not a unified group and the term encompasses a wide range of individuals and circumstances. But there is a persistent feeling that silence accords few benefits. As one commented, perhaps rhetorically, 'if we had taken up arms and caused trouble, would we be listened to more'?

Conclusion

Timor-Leste's veterans do not much resemble the 'ex-combatant' often reproduced in the DDR literature or in best practice manuals. Not only do they consider themselves 'victors' of a liberation struggle and deeply wedded to a longer-term project, Timor's veterans are a wide-ranging group in terms of age, qualification, affiliation and years of service. In the case of widows and orphans who participated in veteran assistance programmes, it is apparent that some did not even serve at all, a further distinction from the commonly held definition of 'ex-combatant'.

The four separate veteran assistance programmes launched in Timor-Leste achieved some important dividends. Five years after independence, there is now a comprehensive and credible database of the nearly 75,000 living and deceased veterans from the armed and civilian fronts. This is accompanied by an inclusive veterans' statute and associated legislation, and the launch of recognition ceremonies. Unlike many cases presented in this volume, returning veterans enjoyed a good social status and were initially welcomed by their communities. From a strategic perspective, veterans and ex-combatants do not constitute a serious organized security threat as they have become in other post-conflict societies. Whether their quiet tolerance in the face of adversity is achieving the recognition they believe they deserve is another question.

This chapter finds that the outcomes of many veteran assistance initiatives are modest. Just one of the surveyed combatants claimed to be 'better off' after reintegration, an indication of how ephemeral policy and political successes are from the vantage of the disadvantaged. More so, the discontent of many veterans, although undoubtedly linked to wider socio-economic discomfort (and bearing in mind the caveat in the methodology section that those attending the groups were disproportionately from lower income brackets) is as much emotive and grievance-based as it is rooted in poverty. The feeling is that of unfulfilled promises and lives mortgaged for a struggle that has provided comparatively little in return.

This, perhaps, was the strongest sense to emerge from meetings in tumbledown government buildings symbolic of how little reach and impact the new state has on many lives. The dilapidation of the tenements is emblematic of the challenge of building a meaningful state that can deliver on the aspirations of its people. This failure of the state-building process was at the heart of the crisis of 2006. Few of its symptoms have been addressed. Despite the restoration of a workaday sense of law and order by UN police officers from more than 40 countries, many of the basic pathologies of the crisis remain. Violence following the formation of the new government illustrates how tenuous the 'peace' can be.[54] The new government – led by Xanana Gusmao – faces profound challenges.

Timor-Leste struggles with deep-seated social, economic and governance problems. Given the essential challenges confronting Timor-Leste, the veteran issue is one of many and not considered the most pressing. The national identity that unified most communities during the resistance is easily overshadowed today by the current development challenges.

Given the comparatively small size of Timor-Leste as compared to other larger and more complex situations, the case raises wider issues about both the remit of DDR and its programming outcomes. If the medium-term effects are so slight, should so much hope be invested in it? Can DDR programmes be connected to other parallel development interventions? Can such programmes respond to individual and often idiosyncratic concerns? This chapter presented a critique of overly technocratic approaches to DDR. Over the past decade, the UN, multilateral agencies, donors, think tanks and NGOs have issued a succession of guidelines, handbooks and principles for DDR programmes (Douglas *et al.* 2004; SIDDR 2006). In frequently dizzying detail, these manuals and handbooks offer guidance on how to 'do' DDR as if it amounted to little more than a technical exercise. But such manuals give few insights into the feelings of individuals. Research among Timor-Leste's veterans suggests that their grievances are motivated as much by psychic concerns relating to inclusion and social status as by economics. While these issues may be hard to grasp in practice, they are too important to be ignored.

Notes

1 This chapter is based on research commissioned by Bradford University's Centre on International Cooperation and Security. The research forms part of a wider project on DDR and Human Security: www.bradford.ac.uk/cics/ddr.

The views and opinions expressed in this chapter are those of the author. Although, the author was/is undertaking work for the AFP while researching the information for this chapter, the views and opinions in this paper do not represent the official views of the AFP.

2 The Department for Veterans Affairs is housed within the Ministry of Labour and Community Solidarity. The department has its own Secretary of State for Veterans' Affairs (the equivalent of a junior minister).

3 The actual term DDR is almost unknown in Timor-Leste, except among members of the United Nations and World Bank set-up that have worked in post-conflict countries elsewhere. The phrase 'veterans' and 'development' are common parlance.

4 Interview, Dili, 2 October 2007.

5 Extensive Timor-Leste government programmes concentrated on mapping categories of veteran and developing financial assistance packages.

6 As there was no certainty of data, this section is left blank.

7 In order, these missions were UNAMET (United Nations Assistance Mission to East Timor) 1999, UNTAET (United Nations Transitional Administration in East Timor) 1999–2002, UNMISET (United Nations Mission of Support in East Timor) 2002–2005, and UNOTIL (United Nations Office in Timor-Leste) 2005–2006.

8 'Would it have made a difference if the UN had stayed longer, if we had not drawn down our forces too quickly? This is something that I must assess'.

9 Article 11 states that the state acknowledges and values the former resistance, and shall ensure protection for widows, orphans and the disabled.

10 I owe thanks to Preston Pentony for making this observation.

11 The six districts were: Aileu, Baucau, Bobonaro, Liquica, Lautem and Manututo.

12 The survey instrument was based on one used by Muggah and Bennett. The survey was pre-tested with a set of veterans in the capital, Dili, and modified so that the questions fit more cleanly with the context. For example, one set of questions – which asked participants to use stones to determine wealth ranking was eliminated because it caused bewilderment and veterans felt demeaned when the question was explained to them.

13 Methodology reviews of previous veteran focus group research in Timor-Leste observed that over-bearing former commanders dominated focus groups. This problem did not repeat itself in these focus groups. One problem that did arise in two focus groups – in Manatuto and Lautem – was that participants were not able to answer questions, no matter how simply phrased the prompts were.

14 Those veterans with gainful employment may not have been able to attend at such short notice. Likewise, individuals with links to the administrator's office may have received notice of the focus group – thus distorting the objectivity of their situation. Also, in a rural society with poor roads and communication, there may have been an urban-bias.

15 Many of the individuals involved in the design and implementation of the DDR programmes in Timor-Leste have since moved on. When this occurred, telephone interviews were conducted.

16 Some existed on the Internet, but most was provided by personal contacts from material that existed on their hard drives.

17 Somewhat surprisingly for a programme of its size and duration, no independent evaluation exists, or would be released. Interviews with some participants and observers of RESPECT were used to supplement focus group material.

18 The distinction between written documentation and personal opinion was most noticeable in views on the UNDP RESPECT programme.

19 This remark is a generalized phenomenon in Timor-Leste, reflecting the very low capacity of government and utter inability of government to execute its budgets. Weak state capacity will always undermine good intentions and what 'promises' may have been given.

20 Focus Group meeting, Liquica, 15 August 2007.

21 Paying a US$10 incentive for focus group participation is commonplace in Timor-Leste. The payment is designed to offset travel costs and given in lieu of providing a meal.

22 The independence of the self-proclaimed Democratic Republic of Timor-Leste was recognized only by the former Portuguese colonies of Angola, Cape Verde, Guinea-Bissau, Mozambique and Sao Tome e Principe.

23 The Timor-Leste Truth and Reconciliation Commission determined that some 102,000 Timorese suffered conflict deaths during the occupation; their report records a brutal occupation with large incidences of arbitrary detention, torture, forced displacement and gender-based violence (CAVR 2005: 44–47).

24 Interview with senior official in UNTAET, 21 October 2007.

25 Conflict, Security and Development Group (2003) 2.E.2.

26 See, for example, McCarthy (2002).

27 Six hundred and fifty FALINTIL joined the new defence force. Although the acronym FALINTIL is appended to the title of the new defence force and intended to signify a teleology between the past and the present, the link is not necessarily that strong (Rees 2004). While it is true that one-third of the members of FALINTIL in Aileu were funnelled into the defence force, the majority of the 1,500 strong F-FDTL did not play any direct role in the resistance. Many were simply too young. As a consequence, many veterans regard F-FDTL as an illegitimate inheritor of the mantel. The disgruntlement is borne from frustration at the perceived favouritism exercised by the F-FDTL candidate in selecting candidates.

28 FRAP was implemented by the IOM, and funded by the World Bank with a grant from the Post-Conflict Fund and USAID.

29 Interview, Dili, August 2007.

30 Mimicking the insignia on Mozambique's flag, a Kalashnikov rifle is on the state's coat of arms.

31 According to McCarthy (2002: 101), just a small number of veterans were involved in these groups.

32 This office will be considered in the following section.

33 Also known as the Commission for Assistance of Former Combatants.

34 Also known as the Commission on Cadres of the Resistance.

35 The World Bank, UNDP, USAID, AusAid, Ireland, the UK, Norway and Sweden supported the CAAC-CAVF and CAQR. The total cost of the commission activities was about US$2.2 million, with approximately half of this cost borne by the World Bank through grants from the Post-Conflict Fund.

36 For details of the methodology see CAAC-CVVF (2004).

37 Survivors of the deceased are also entitled to benefits (Bowles 2006).

38 A Statute for National Liberation Combatants.

39 The office provided details of the projects that it knew of currently underway although, perhaps emblematic of the capacity challenges it faces, and no database of activity exists. Thus, this is not necessarily a complete list. Programmes include the delivery of seeds, agricultural equipments and coffee grinding machines, in cooperation with Ministry of Agriculture, Forestry and Fisheries and FAO; physical treatment and mental health programmes in cooperation with Ministry of Health and UNIFEM; forestry work and training for gardeners; (Câmara Municipal de Lisboa). Information provided by Office of Veterans' Affairs.

40 For example, the office prepared six letters of introduction for the research team, which would be sent out with a weekly 'milk run' from the capital. Only three of the letters reached their intended source.

41 Interview, Baucau, 27 August 2007.

42 Several other donors have already complained that this makes it more difficult for them to hold local organizations to realistic project costs.

43 Email correspondence with UN official, 10 November 2007.

44 Email correspondence with UN official, 10 November 2007.

45 An 'internal learning document' apparently was compiled but would not be released. Interview, Dili, 31 July 2007.

46 Interviews, Dili, 21–22 October 2007; private correspondence with UN official 14 November 2007.

47 Interview, Baucau 20 August 2007.

48 Interview, Aileu 17 August 2007; Liquica, 18 August 2007.

49 Directly translated as 'supporters of autonomy', the phrase is used to describe Timorese who worked with Indonesia or were educated in Indonesia.

50 Interview, Baucau, 20 August 2007.

51 Interview, Manututo, 17 August 2007.

52 Interview, Liquica, 17 August 2007.

53 Focus group, Aileu, 12 August 2007.

54 In riot protests in Dili and major cities, where FRETILIN supporters protested the results, an estimated 400 houses were torched, a UN convoy ambushed, and hundreds of civilians were displaced in the ensuing violence (Center on International Cooperation 2008).

Bibliography

Baaré, A. (2005) 'An Analysis of Transitional Economic Integration', Working Paper, Stockholm Initiative on Disarmament, Demobilization and Reintegration.

Bowles, E. (2006) Unpublished paper (copy with author).

Carames, A., Fisas, V. and Luz, D. (2006) *Analysis of Disarmament, Demobilization and Reintegration Programmes existing in the World during 2005.* Madrid: Escola de Cultura de Pau.

Center on International Cooperation (CIC) (2008) *Annual Review of Global Peace Operations 2008.* Boulder: Lynne Rienner.

Chappell, D. (2005) 'Africanization in the Pacific: Blaming Others for Disorder in the Periphery?', *Comparative Studies in Society and History* 47 (2).

Cohen, D. (2003) 'Intended to Fail: The Trails Before the Ad Hoc Human Rights Court in Jakarta', New York: International Center for Transitional Justice.

Commission for Reception, Truth and Reconciliation in East Timor (CAVR) (2005) *Chega! Final Report of the Commission for Reception, Truth and Reconciliation in Timor-Leste.*

Conflict, Security and Development Group (2003) *A Review of Peace Operations. A Case for a Change.* London, King's College, 2003. Section 2.E.2.

Democratic Republic of Timor-Leste (2004) 'Final Report of the Activities of the Commissions for the Issues of Former Combatants and the Commissions for the Issues of the Veterans of Falintil (CAAC-CAVF)'.

Douglas, I., Gleichmann, C., Odenwald, M., Stenken, K. and Wilkinson, A. (2004) *Disarmament, Demobilization and Reintegration. A Practical Field Guide.* Bonn: GTZ.

Forman, S. (2007) 'The Failings of Security Sector Reform in Timor-Leste', in Center for International Co-operation, *Annual Review of Global Peace Operations 2007.* Boulder: Lynne Rienner.

Fox, J. and Soares, D. (2001) *East Timor: Out of the Ashes: The Destruction and Reconstruction of an Emerging State.* London: Hurst & Co.

Fraenkel, J. (2004) 'The Coming Anarchy in Oceania? A Critique of the "Africanisation of the South Pacific" Thesis', *Journal of Commonwealth & Comparative Politics*, 42 (1), 1–34.

Hood, L. (2007) 'Missed Opportunities: The United Nations, Police Service and Defence Force Development in Timor-Leste, 1999–2004', in Scheye, E. and Hills, A. (eds) *Managing Insecurity: Field Experience of Security Sector Reform.* London: Taylor and Francis.

International Crisis Group (ICG) (2006) 'Resolving Timor-Leste's Crisis', Asia Report No. 120, 10 October.

International Crisis Group (ICG) (2008) 'Resolving Timor-Leste's IDP Problems' *Asia Report* No. 120.

La'o Hamutuk (2004) La'o Hamutuk Bulletin Vol. 5, No. 5–6. Online, available at: www.laohamutuk.org/Bulletin/2004/Dec/bulletinv5n5.html.

McCarthy, J. (2002) 'FALINTIL Reinsertion Assistance Programme: Final Evaluation Report', Dili, IoM.

Martin, I. (2001) *Self-Determination in East Timor: The United Nations, the Ballot, and International Intervention.* Boulder: Lynne Rienner.

Meden, N. (2002) 'From Resistance to Nation Building: The Changing Role of Civil Society in East Timor', Dili: World Bank. Online, available at: www1.worldbank.org/devoutreach/winter02/article.asp?id=141.

Muggah, R. (2005) 'No Magic Bullet: A Critical Perspective on Disarmament, Demobilization and Reintegration and Weapons Reduction during Post-Conflict', *The Commonwealth Journal of International Affairs*, 94 (379).

Muggah, R. and Bennett, J. (2007) *Making a Difference? A Beneficiary Impact Assessment of the EDRP*, Addis: EDRP/World Bank.

Paddock, R. (2006) 'Bloodied East Timorese Hope the UN Will Return', *Los Angeles Times*, 5 June.

Peake, G. (2008) 'Veterans Say: Assessing the Human Security Impact of DDR Programmes in Timor-Leste', *CICS Working Paper*, Bradford: Centre for International Cooperation and Security.

Peake, G. and Marenin, O. (2008) 'Their Reports are Not Read and their Recommendations are Resisted', *Police Practice and Research.* 9(1): 59–69.

Peake, G., Gormley-Heenan, C. and Fitzduff, M. (2004) *From Warlords to Peacelords: Political Leadership in Conflicted Societies.* Derry/Londonderry: INCORE.

Pouligny, B. (2004) *The Politics and Anti-Politics of Contemporary Disarmament, Demobilization and Reintegration Programmes.* Paris: CERI.

Rees, E. (2003) 'The UN's Failure to Integrate Falintil Veterans may cause East Timor to Fail', *Online opinion*, September, available at: www.onlineopinion.com.au.

Rees, E. (2004) *Under Pressure: FALINTIL Forcas de Armadas de Timor-Leste – Three Decades of Defence Development in Timor-Leste*, Geneva: DCAF.

Reilly, B. (2000) 'The Africanisation of the South Pacific', *Australian Journal of International Affairs*, 54(3), 2000, 261–268.

Scheye, E. and Peake, G. (2005) 'To Arrest Insecurity: Time for a Revised Security. Sector Reform Agenda', *Conflict, Security and Development*, 5 (3).

Smith, M. and Dee, M. (2003) *Peacekeeping in East Timor: The Path to Independence.* Boulder: Lynne Rienner.

Stockholm Initiative on Disarmament, Demobilization and Reintegration (SIDDR) (2006). Online, available at: www.sweden.gov.se/siddr.

UK Department for International Development (DfID) (2005) 'Fighting Poverty to Build a Safer World: a Strategy for Security and Development', London: DFID.

UN (2006) Independent Special Commission of Enquiry for Timor-Leste, Geneva: OHR.

UNDP (2003) 'RESPECT' Project overview document (copy on file with author).

UNDP (2004) RESPECT mid-term evaluation (copy on file with author).

University of Bradford (2006) *DDR Framed from a Human Security and Pro-Poor Perspective: Literature Review and some Key Challenges.* Bradford: CICS.

UNWG (2006) *Integrated Disarmament, Demobilization and Reintegration Standards (IDDRS).* Online, available at: http://www.unddr.org/iddrs/.

World Bank (2004) *Veterans: Pensions and Other Compensation in Post-Conflict Countries.* Washington DC: World Bank.

7 Context matters in Ethiopia

Reflections on a demobilization and reintegration programme

Robert Muggah and Jon Bennett with Aklu Girgre and Gebru Wolde

Introduction

Ethiopia's latest round of demobilization and reintegration was undertaken in comparatively unusual circumstances. Because it followed on the heels of an inter-state armed conflict with Eritrea rather than a civil war, former soldiers were popularly regarded as heroes to be celebrated rather than former enemies to be feared. Moreover, the damage caused by the war was more or less restricted to the border areas with Eritrea, with comparatively limited damage to the national economic and social fabric.[1] As it was a relatively short and brutal conventional war between organized armies, recruits were not away from their homes and land for prolonged periods of time. Such an experience stands in stark contrast to most other protracted armed conflicts in Africa that are largely internal, waged by irregular forces and highly destructive to households and communities.

This chapter considers how specific ethnic and socio-cultural features specific to the Ethiopian context shaped the process and outcomes of a demobilization and reintegration programme. Although there are of course ethnic variations across administrative units (or *woredas*), in the highland areas from which most recruits were drawn there is also a significant level of homogeneity.[2] In addition to the persistence of comparatively robust kinship networks, there is also strong respect for authority – whether directed toward the state or customary leadership – as well as a widespread celebration and expression of civic identity. These endogenous factors appeared to play a decisive role in facilitating DDR and contributing to its effectiveness.

The sheer scale and dimensions of Ethiopia's demobilization and reintegration programme were staggering. More than 148,000 Ethiopian veterans of varying age and experience were directly involved in aspects of the demobilization, reinsertion and reintegration processes from 2000 to 2003. Not unlike other such interventions, the process was intensely political and politicized and not a reservedly 'technical' exercise. From the beginning, the initiative was designed to explicitly reinforce the legitimacy of the ruling authorities by delivering entitlements to deserving veterans and a 'reward' to specific constituencies, including communities of return. Those veterans and communities that did not receive support inevitably resented the fact that they were bypassed. Whether real or imagined, differentiated assistance can exacerbate tensions that in turn affect various aspects of DDR.

Drawing on fieldwork undertaken in 2007, this chapter examines the successes and failures of a central component of Ethiopia's post-war reconstruction efforts, the Emergency Demobilization and Reintegration Project (EDRP). The chapter does not offer a comprehensive overview of all aspects of the EDRP, but rather a general treatment of the extent to which the EDRP achieved its 'maximalist' objectives: reduced national expenditures in defence and enhanced spending on health, education and welfare. The chapter also considers whether the EDRP achieved more minimalist outcomes – including the economic, social and political reintegration of veterans. The analysis is based on a participatory impact assessment of veteran livelihoods[3] and considers the endogenous and exogenous factors influencing reintegration outcomes. The chapter also reflects on the extent to which lessons emerging from the reintegration of veterans can be extended to other 'post-conflict' priorities, including the generation of durable solutions for displaced populations. Taken together, the analysis privileges a 'voice from below', drawing as it does on evidence from the field.

A war of attrition

Ethiopia's war with Eritrea displays long and seemingly contradictory roots. Despite a history of common struggle to overthrow the 1974–1991 Derge dictatorship,[4] tensions between the leaders of Ethiopia and Eritrea escalated rapidly during the 1990s. All-out war erupted from May 1998 to June 2000. The two-year armed conflict was a product of a combination of grievances arising from competing claims over territory, taxation and revenue generation and political antagonisms. The trigger was a bitter dispute over small sections of Ethiopia and Eritrea's common border.[5] Given the satisfactory relations between the Eritrean and Ethiopian governments in the early 1990s, historical disputes over the delineation of this 620-mile border had previously been sublimated. They came to a head, however, when Eritrea sent its army to expel Ethiopian troops stationed in Badme and claimed the area as Eritrean.

The human costs of the short war were nothing short of breathtaking. Approximately 100,000 soldiers were directly killed on both sides of the border, tens of thousands more died of 'external' or excess causes and over 360,000 people were internally displaced. The vast majority of these casualties – as much as 90 per cent – were located in the Tigray region and a smaller but significant number in Afar (HRW 2007). The legacy of the armed conflict on 'national' identities and political relations was also considerable: Ethiopia deported tens of thousands of persons identified as Eritrean, while Eritrea did the same with persons identified as Ethiopian living within its territory. The legacy of mistrust continues to keep relations between the two countries at a razor's edge.

The international community moved swiftly to separate and offer mediation between the warring parties in mid-2000. After the signing of a Cessation of

Hostilities Agreement between Ethiopia and Eritrea in mid-June 2000,[6] Ethiopia agreed to withdraw its troops to pre-war positions. Both sides agreed to the establishment and deployment of an international UN peacekeeping force (UNMEE) to monitor the agreement and patrol the physical area separating the two armies.[7] The political settlement dealt primarily with the formal separation of the belligerents' forces, demarcation of the border,[8] and competing claims for compensation. The issue of the wartime expulsion of tens of thousands of people on grounds of their purported nationality or national origin was quietly overlooked by the international community in the war's aftermath.[9] By early 2008, however, the remaining 700 peacekeepers working for UNMEE were withdrawn owing to apparent obstruction from Eritrea.[10] The possibility of renewed armed conflict remains.

The macro and micro-level aftershocks of the conflict, including rising military expenditures, were severe.[11] On the one hand, the armed forces of Ethiopia predictably grew rapidly before and during the cross-border war. Between 1998 and 2000, Ethiopia's land forces increased by an estimated 120,000 to more than 352,000 (IISS 2002). Likewise, military expenditure escalated from approximately US$215 million (2003 dollars) in 1997 to well over US$719 million (2003 dollars) by 1999. International donors and the Ethiopian government agreed that it was necessary to rapidly downsize the army after the war and to redress highly skewed public expenditure (Muggah and Bennett 2007). Meanwhile, on – or under – the ground, some two million anti-tank and anti-personnel mines were believed to have been laid in the area bordering Eritrea from 1998–2000. The UN estimated that these put the lives of some 400,000 people at risk. Indeed, in Tigray region and, to a lesser extent, in Afar, landmines in agrarian areas are purported to be the primary factors that prevented the remaining internally displaced persons (IDPs) from returning home and becoming 'self-sufficient'. In these regions, mines killed almost 600 people and wounded over 700 between 2001 and 2004, and civilians continue to be maimed and killed on a monthly basis.

The past and lingering effects of the conflict also generated destructive impacts on the local economy. On the one hand, internal displacement led to widespread productivity losses. Approximately 10 per cent of the total population of Tigray was displaced, which in turn distorted agricultural production, livestock rearing and animal husbandry practices, formal and informal livelihood patterns, and access to homes and belongings. Cross-border petty trade – an important source of income in the border areas – including the selling of vegetable, spices, livestock and locally-brewed beverages came to a halt. Access to hard cash was thus dramatically reduced. Although the presence of the two countries' respective militaries accounted for some economic activity (especially the acquisition of livestock and investment in local infrastructure), people living around the border areas experienced a deepening and widening of poverty (White 2005). It would take some years for the local economy to recover, and demobilized soldiers returning to these border areas faced particular problems in regaining a livelihood (World Bank 2003).

Enter demobilization and reintegration

In late June 2000, the Government of Ethiopia (GoE) approached the World Bank to assist with a comprehensive post-war recovery programme. The government's expectation was that an International Development Assistance (IDA) loan could re-balance the national economy while simultaneously accommodating the needs of veterans. The loan was designed to account for a host of connected challenges. Specifically, the intervention was designed to address the real costs of the demobilization and reintegration of excess personnel (so-called 'new regulars' and 'militia'), emergency humanitarian needs, rehabilitation and reconstruction of infrastructure and stabilization of the economy to re-start the reform agenda. The total package comprised three discrete emergency operations and amounted to some US$700 million in total.

From the beginning, the international donor community sought to ensure that interventions were harmonized or aligned with other aid packages and ongoing programmes. For example, the IDA support was expected to complement the activities of international stakeholders, in particular the UN and Organisation of African Unity (now African Union) who, together with the US and the European Union (EU), took the lead in facilitating the peace process. The IDA loans were designed in such a way as to improve the prospects for macro-economic recovery by facilitating the reallocation of public resources away from defence to more productive sectors, including public health, education and social services – or welfare-related – spending. Put another way, the IDA loan constituted a form of direct budgetary support, reflecting the desire of donors to enhance national ownership and extant state capacities.

This chapter considers the experience of only one component of the overall package of post-war assistance – an EDRP undertaken by the GoE. Funded through the overall IDA agreement (with a small symbolic contribution from the GoE) the EDRP targeted more than 148,000 Ethiopian veterans at a cost of approximately US$174 million.[12] More precisely, the EDRP goal was to contribute towards macro-economic stability in Ethiopia through a set of discreet objectives:

- to help an estimated 133,000 able-bodied veterans and 17,000 disabled veterans rebuild their lives and resume productive economic activities;
- to rehabilitate about 17,000 disabled veterans through the provision of medical services; and
- to facilitate the reallocation of public resources to priority social and infrastructure investments by reducing defence expenditures.

The EDRP was undertaken in two phases over a three-year period. The first phase (November 2000–June 2001) was conceived as a pilot; this involved the demobilization and reintegration of approximately 17,000 disabled and 42,000 able-bodied veterans (those who joined the army last, and those who had large families to support). The second phase (July 2001–December 2003) was designed to accommodate a larger share of the veterans – the demobilization and reintegration of a further 90,000 able-bodied veterans.

With financial and technical support from the World Bank, the GoE developed a comparatively well articulated definition of demobilization, reinsertion and reintegration. Outlined in programme documents and progress reports,[13] demobilization included formal discharge, registration and health screening (including HIV/AIDS) and transport to area of return. Each veteran received cash coupons that could be redeemed in subsequent phases. Reinsertion included a standard subsistence support cash grant of ETB 2,000 (US$210) for all veterans. Reinsertion and reintegration constituted the largest financial outlay of the EDRP. Implemented at the regional level, and targeted according to data collected on the socio-economic profile of the veterans (gathered from the demobilization centres) and locally available economic opportunities, grants were made available for a 'menu' of assistance options.[14] Severely disabled soldiers also received targeted medical rehabilitation assistance, including specialized housing and access to newly-constructed prosthetic and orthosis centres.

The demobilization and reintegration processes were managed primarily by state bureaucracies rather than external agencies such as the UN or NGOs. Moreover, allocated funds were regularly folded into other service providers of 'entitlements' for veterans rather than being issued as one-off monetary transfers. For the most part, finances and disbursement were managed by local authorities and through selected regional project units responsible for identifying suitable opportunities and schemes for returning veterans. There was also a significant financial investment in capacity building within the local and regional administrations and absorption of EDRP funds into reconstituting local infrastructure.

As noted in the Introduction and other chapters in this volume, reintegration is often understood to consist of a *process* by which veterans and ex-combatants acquire civilian status rather than a de facto outcome.[15] Immediately following disarmament, demobilization and in certain cases reinsertion, reintegration is acknowledged as a crucial element of the overall post-conflict reconstruction and recovery process.[16] Reintegration is also considered to be a national responsibility, even if directly supported by multilateral and bilateral donors. But reintegration is frequently narrowly defined, focused exclusively on former soldiers and measured according to specific dependent (economic) variables such as income and employment. As signalled in other chapters of this volume, however, reintegration as an outcome clearly consists of more than simply the restoration of income to pre-mobilization levels. It also features social, cultural, psychological and political elements. While the resumption of gainful employment is an engine of productive integration, it is equally important to access social networks and ensure a healthy political connectivity.

More recently, scholars and practitioners have outlined a broader set of parameters of reintegration. For example, investments in reintegration are expected to engineer *'acceptance'* of veterans by their families and neighbours on return (see Chapter 2, this volume). There are similar expectations that former soldiers will be *'de-linked'* from their former command and control as a result of reintegration (see Chapter 5, this volume). Likewise, they may expect reintegration to contribute to the proclivity of veterans to *'associate'* with non-combatants in community-based organizations and cooperatives or participate free of discrimination in municipal and federal elections (Chapter 3, this volume). In other words, the gauge of effective reintegration extends beyond sustainable income and includes an array of factors that shape sustainable livelihoods and minimize the threat of their becoming spoilers or predatory in communities of return.

Impact assessment methods

The expectation of the participatory impact assessment was to generate a summative *ex post* impact review through a multi-method approach, including participatory field research. A participatory survey, described in greater detail below, formed the centrepiece of the assessment. Basic socio-economic and demographic data was also derived from a review of macro-economic figures supplied by the World Bank and the Ethiopian Ministry of Finance and Economic Development (MoFED). Instead of ascribing standardized criteria to measure impact and change, however, the assessment drew primarily from 'emic' indicators[17] thus consciously involving stakeholders in determining the overall effects of the EDRP, rather than relying on a priori externally-derived variables.

The participatory survey aimed to determine the extent to which the EDRP contributed to the economic, political and social reintegration of regular, new regular and militia veterans as many as six years after their demobilization. The challenges of isolating pathways of 'effectiveness' so long after the end of a DDR intervention are studiously detailed by Peake (Chapter 6, this volume). Crucially, the assessment sought to generate a stratified review of regional variations (among veterans in Tigray, Amhara, Oromiya and SNNP) and veteran characteristics (between rural, urban, disabled and female beneficiaries). Drawing on a local partner[18] and eight academic staff recruited from the regions under investigation, a survey protocol was developed and tested. Three basic participatory tools were used – wealth-ranking (to measure economic reintegration), pair-wise ranking (to gauge social reintegration) and livelihood timelines (to assess political reintegration).

The participatory beneficiary assessment adopted a proportional size sampling (PSS) strategy and focused on regions and administrative units at the municipal (*woreda*) level exhibiting the highest concentration of 'returned' veterans. As such, focus groups were gathered in six regions (Tigray, Oromiya, Amhara, SNNP, Dire Dawa and Harare) and 15 *woredas*. It is of course important to acknowledge the limitations of participatory methods.[19] In addition to being non-generalizable, there are potential biases in such an approach. For example, an element of self-selection of individual veterans was inherent in the way participants were chosen by local civil servants, a challenge also noted in the case of Timor-Leste (see Chapter 6, this volume).[20] There may also have been an urban bias towards choosing veterans from areas within less than a few hours walking distance of the designated town; thus veterans' views emanating from more remote areas were not necessarily captured. The risks of 'reactivity' – where the presence of an outsider influences the behaviour of respondents – were also present. These challenges were offset through the transparent communication of the aims and expectations of the research, triangulation, continuous dialogue with respondents and, where appropriate, the passing on of expressed grievances to responsible authorities.

What the veterans say

A primary aim of the assessment was to determine the extent to which veterans themselves felt that they were adequately reintegrated. Tables 7.1 and 7.2 provide an indicative summary of the priorities accorded to specific entitlements by urban and rural veterans across regions. They summarize the core entitlements issued by the EDRP and their relative importance in all 15 sampled *woredas*. A simple scoring system was introduced in order to determine the relative importance accorded by veterans to different entitlements.[21] While providing only an illustrative overview, the tables nevertheless highlight the way different categories of veterans determine priorities across different regions. They emphasize the heterogeneity of experiences by category and location.

The findings reveal a degree of variation between regions and former combatants in how specific inputs were received and used. This suggests that a uniform approach to reinsertion and reintegration that awards blanket entitlements is unlikely to speak to the differentiated needs and requirements of veterans – a conclusion echoed by other authors in this volume. While this specific exercise did not examine in detail the 'quality' of entitlements, it does however highlight that entitlements were not uniformly perceived or appreciated. Genuinely sustainable reintegration has economic, social and political implications, all of which are overlapping. Moreover, it seems that in the case of Ethiopia's EDRP, successful reintegration was as much a function of the absorptive capacity of

Table 7.1 Ranking the 'importance' of EDRP entitlements: rural veterans

	Financial support	Training	Medical support	Urban/farm land	Other
Tigray	High	Above average	Above average	Below average	Below average[22]
Amhara	High	Below average	Below average	High	Below average[23]
Oromiya	High	Below average[24]	Below average	High	Low
SNNP	High[25]	Low	Above average	Above average	Low

Table 7.2 Ranking the 'importance' of EDRP entitlements: urban veterans

	Financial support	*Training*	*Medical support*	*Residential housing*	*Other*
Tigray	Above average	Below average	Below average	High	Below average[26]
Amhara	High	Below average	Below average	High	Below average[27]
Oromiya	High	Below average	Above average	High	Above average
SNNP	High[28]	Below average	Low	High	Above average

areas of return and the endowment sets of former soldiers as the quality and quantity of entitlements provided.

Ethiopia's reintegration experience

While generally achieving a number of its core objectives, the EDRP yielded mixed results. Overall, it appears that four years after the end of the demobilization process, income and asset holdings have deteriorated to varying degrees despite the fact that many veterans consider themselves to be 'empowered' and 'accepted' by their families and communities and not unduly discriminated against by political authorities. Urban veterans in particular appear to have slipped into lower income quintiles despite the assistance offered through the EDRP. On closer inspection, there appear to be a combination of endogenous (e.g. external factors) and exogenous (e.g. entitlement-specific) factors shaping reintegration outcomes.

The comparative experience of urban and rural returnees is particularly important in revealing the role of endogenous factors. The differentiated outcomes suggest that the endowments of veterans, the absorptive capacities of areas of return and reintegration and the macro-economic and environmental climate played a significant role in shaping reintegration outcomes. While there are ethnic and cultural variations across regions, there is a significant level of ethnic homogeneity in the predominantly agricultural and pastoral areas from where most rural recruits were drawn and eventually reintegrated. Factors such as robust kinship networks and persistent respect for authority played a decisive role in facilitating EDRP activities and outcomes. Moreover, because rural veterans were often away for only short periods and were from relatively well structured military units, social capital in areas of return remained largely intact.

The origins of veterans and their respective endowment sets heavily influenced reintegration outcomes. One reason attributed by veteran respondents to this was that returning soldiers tended to own land prior to their mobilization while urban veterans were generally landless. While there is evidence of social pathologies and dysfunctions emerging among certain clusters of rural veterans, they are considered by respondents to be more the exception than the rule. Nevertheless, a significant number of those recruited from urban areas were from the lowest income groups, and their reintegration challenges were inevitably compounded by comparatively lower levels of education, as well as financial, capital and social assets to their (civilian) neighbours.

It should be recalled that virtually all land in Ethiopia is government-owned, and that the GoE allocates user rights, including for resettlement, while private ownership is limited. According to key informants working in the civil service, continued government ownership serves a welfare function: it prevents uncontrolled urban migration and fragmentation since 'peasants' are reluctant to lose existing land rights by migrating to towns. It also limits wild land speculation, alienation and acquisition by 'foreign' capitalists. However, the practice of concentrating land policy in the hands of government officials may also generate tensions, particularly among pastoralist societies, when official land-use designation may not necessarily correspond with people's historic sense of land ownership. Varying tax regimes between administrative regions impede the pastoralists' freedom to trade, which further accentuates tensions.

By contrast, those originally recruited from (and returning to) urban areas faced greater ethnic heterogeneity, less obvious solidarity and social linkages, and higher labour inflexibility and standards of living. Although the EDRP included vocational training, with some attempts toward encouraging 'job placement', the programme was unable to effectively counter the chronic underemployment among veterans reintegrated into urban centres. What is more, the inability to secure legitimate land title for urban veterans lessened their capacity to use it as collateral to invest in and administer meaningful micro-enterprises.

The role of endogenous macro-economic and climactic factors in influencing reintegration outcomes cannot be discounted. Whilst measures were taken by GoE officials and the World Bank to avoid inducing inflation through the phased provision of monetized assistance to veterans, overall national inflation rose during the period of the demobilization and reintegration programme. Although it is likely that certain EDRP inputs may have contributed to expanding local-level commercial activity and stimulated markets, this remains uncertain. Crucially, Ethiopia was also affected by a severe drought from 2002 to 2003 which severely disrupted cereal and pulse crops and intensified food insecurity in certain areas, including those in which veterans sought to integrate.

With respect to EDRP entitlements, the assessment revealed how the predictability of assistance was almost as important as the amount received. Veterans were promised a range of benefits and privileges by the Ethiopian government in the wake of the conflict contributing to rising expectations. In some instances veterans borrowed from local money-lenders against the promise of future income and earnings. But a considerable proportion of rural and urban veterans spent their initial cash assistance – the so-called 'transitional subsistence support' – on consumer goods and debt repayment rather than productive assets as anticipated by programme planners. The promise of sustained financial support for veterans contributed to moral hazard. When promised assistance failed to materialize in a consistent or regular fashion, veterans found that their situation deteriorated. Moreover, when training in financial management or enterprise development was provided *after* they spent their entitlements, they had little incentive to continue the course without the means to invest.

Finally, political realities and constraints at local levels in the administration of entitlements were not always taken into account by EDRP planners. The portfolio of entitlements available under the EDRP appeared to assume that veterans would receive preferential access to land, jobs and materials necessary to quickly regain or acquire improved livelihoods, and local political institutions would recognize and uphold that preferential access as part of a medium-term assistance package. This was not always the case. For example, in some regions – notably Tigray – veteran associations continue to thrive while in most other regions they were implicitly discouraged. Newly displaced populations found it difficult to access the Productive Safety Net Programme (PSNP) resources. Previously, inhabitants of a *woreda* only received access to food aid after being resident for three years; and *woredas* that were not included in the PSNP when it was introduced in 2004, were unable to join the programme at a later stage.

The raising of expectations may have resulted from over-optimism in Addis Ababa (and lack of full consultation and adherence from local government) or from comparatively weak needs assessments at the outset of the programme. Information asymmetries between EDRP implementers coupled with poorly managed expectations among veteran beneficiary groups in some cases undermined the credibility of the demobilization and reintegration programme. Despite the reportedly smooth transfer of resources from federal to regional levels,[29] veterans were confused over what they were entitled to receive from national and *woreda*-level authorities. According to long-serving public servants and to veterans themselves, information on the entitlement portfolio was often poorly or partially transferred from local authorities (whether EDRP representatives or bureaucrats from line ministries) to demobilized and reintegrated veterans. Persistent grievances among many veterans participating in the focus groups appear to be compounded by poor lines of communication and rumour that continues between veterans across all four regions.

From reintegration to durable solutions

On reflection, it appears that many of the challenges associated with reintegrating former soldiers are broadly analogous to those associated with identifying durable solutions for forced migrants – particularly IDPs.[30] Both groups are regularly implicated in war and post-conflict situations, as both perpetrators and victims of violence. They are widely perceived to be dislocated from the mainstream and are frequently targeted by comprehensive programmes intended to promote their sustainable reintegration into society. But despite their obvious similarities, there is comparatively little inter-agency or academic exchange of knowledge on the subject.

What do former-combatants and forced migrants have in common? First, they are frequently involved in a host of interventions administered by a disparate collection of humanitarian and development agencies. Often coordinated by the DPKO, UNDP and the World Bank, disarmament, demobilization, reinsertion and reintegration programmes are expected to transform soldiers into productive civilians. Likewise, the UN High Commissioner for Refugees (UNHCR), UNDP, the World Bank and a number of UN and non-governmental agencies often assist refugees and internally displaced people to achieve a 'durable solution' such as repatriation, resettlement or return and to ensure that they are adequately 'protected' and self-reliant (Muggah 2006).

While those administering DDR and durable solutions often work autonomously from one another, there are a few instances where they actively collaborate. For example, throughout Africa and the Balkans, DPKO, UNDP, UNHCR, the International Organization for Migration (IOM) and the World Bank often work together (and with governments) to ensure that 'foreign' ex-combatants residing outside of their countries of origin are separated from refugee or IDP camps and repatriated back home. Because of international jurisprudence and human rights concerns, such activities are frequently intensely political and may entail criminal proceedings (see Chapter 10, this volume). Predictably, there is comparatively less focus on their sustainable reintegration into civilian life.

Regardless of whether there is cooperation or not, both DDR and durable solutions seek to enhance the well-being of potentially vulnerable populations. DDR and durable solutions generally only proceed in post-conflict contexts. They are designed as temporary processes – usually with a host government acting as the coordinating authority – issuing sequenced assistance with predictable linkages to development in the long-term. Both sets of activities involve a complex assortment of actors with varying mandates and competencies. In some cases, a 'natural' or organic ordering of responsibilities and division of labour has emerged. In the disarmament phase of an operation, DPKO, and to a lesser extent UNDP, are frequently involved. Owing to their comparative advantages, but also mandate constraints, the World Bank and others are often more engaged in demobilization, reinsertion and reintegration. In the case of durable solutions the recent inter-agency 'cluster approach' allows different agencies to assume sectoral responsibilities according to their competencies.[31]

For a host of reasons, ranging from the extremely complex environments in which they are established to the dilemmas associated with unpredictable assistance and inter-agency cooperation, DDR and durable solutions seldom meet the expectations set by their proponents. It is doubly important, then, to learn from potentially 'successful' cases of either DDR or durable solutions.

Conclusions

DDR in Ethiopia was broadly successful when compared to similar operations undertaken elsewhere in Africa. The country did not relapse into conflict following the EDRP,[32] the process was accompanied by comparatively little social unrest, and there is no obvious evidence that criminality escalated in areas of integration. A compelling feature of the EDRP was its reintegration strategy – an approach that consciously drew on international and domestic best practice and borrowed from contemporary 'development' thinking. A (positive) fiscal impact of demobilization appears to exist. The EDRP appears to have coincided with a concomitant shift of government expenditures from the defence sector to other social and economic development priorities. Specifically, defence expenditure dramatically decreased from 12.8 per cent of GDP in 2000 to 3.6 per cent of GDP by 2004. Over the same period, social expenditures increased from 15 per cent to 27 per cent of the government of Ethiopia's recurrent expenditure (Muggah and Bennett 2007).

One overarching lesson relates to measurement of success. The EDRP, not unlike other DDR programmes, did not adequately articulate its objectives, benchmarks or indicators of success. As a result, it was unlikely that researchers would be able to measure the precise outcomes of reintegration, or at least to what extent they accorded with the aspirations of project planners. While the Ethiopian government deserves some credit for having demonstrated a willingness to learn lessons from the participatory beneficiary assessment, the absence of clear criteria or baseline data from which to measure impact became a serious constraint. Nevertheless, some important lessons for forced migration scholars and experts emerge.

At the outset, the EDRP is a reminder that reintegration should be conceptualized holistically as having economic, social and political features. Genuinely successful reintegration requires improvements in all three areas and not just in relation to economic livelihoods as is often assumed. There are also important linkages between various elements of reintegration. For example, real and relative declines in income and asset distribution can lead to changes in social status and relative acceptance at the family and community levels. It is therefore important to stress both 'economic' and 'social' aspects of the reintegration process – and the relationships between them.

It should also be recalled that fluctuations in the macro-economic climate – inflation, commodity prices and the like – will invariably influence the behaviour and decisions taken by demobilized and reintegrating veterans and the communities to which they return. Other factors at the micro-level also matter; for example, in rural areas there were comparatively more robust social connectivity and market networks, and an economy less affected by labour migration, housing pressure and unemployment as was the case in urban areas. Sustainable reintegration thus requires a focus on strengthening the absorptive capacity of areas of return.

As such, the expectations of donors and government planners of what can realistically be achieved in such contexts must be commensurate with the (endogenous) capacities and endowments of the target group. The vast majority of participating veterans heralded from income-poor households. They had comparatively low levels of employment, education and marketable skills prior to their recruitment into the armed forces. Farmers and agricultural labourers mostly returned to their former occupations (and land), whereas urban soldiers ('self-selected' and often poorly-educated) had fewer pre-existing assets.

Finally, if reintegration entitlements are to be made more effective, it is important to ensure the proper 'sequencing' of financial benefits in line with training and vocational support. In many cases, cash assistance was provided – and spent – before enrolment in training/vocational courses; and veterans were not adequately informed or advised of how best to utilize their benefits. Few had any experience of managing finances on the scale provided or expertise in making long-term investment decisions. There are high risks and trade-offs associated with providing 'lump sum' payments to veterans without sufficient financial management skills.

Notes

1 There were in fact fairly concentrated economic consequences resulting from 10 per cent of Tigray's population being displaced – though data remains scarce.
2 This is especially the case in Tigray: more than 40 per cent of all regular veterans, 'new regulars' and 'militia' participating in the demobilization and reintegration were from this region. Amhara and Oromiya are obviously less ethnically homogeneous, followed by Addis and SNNP where there is a high level of ethnic heterogeneity.
3 In mid-2007, the authors led a Beneficiary Impact Assessment of Ethiopia's EDRP. The assessment adopted a participatory focus group approach measuring the influence of the EDRP on veteran reintegration in four regions and 15 *woredas* of Ethiopia. In this they were helped by a team of national experts from Development Studies Association (DSA).
4 Eritrea subsequently gained independence from Ethiopia in 1993 after having been part of the latter since 1962.
5 Ethiopia annexation of Eritrea in 1962 and the establishment of administrative boundaries blurred the 1902 colonial boundary notably around Badme, Tsorona-Zalambessa and Bure.
6 See, for example, http://www.usip.org/library/pa/eritrea_ethiopia/eritrea_ethiopia_12122000.html.
7 The United Nations Mission in Ethiopia and Eritrea (UNMEE), formed in 2000 to monitor the ceasefire, was reduced by 2007 from 4,200 to 1,700 troops, and its monitoring activities along the demilitarized 25-kilometre Temporary Security Zone remain severely restricted (UNSC 2007: 2).
8 Ethiopia's rejection of a border demarcation ruling, issued in April 2002 by the Permanent Court of Arbitration's Boundary Commission, caused renewed tensions between the two states. Ethiopia eventually accepted the ruling on 29 March 2007.
9 See, for example, Buffoni and Ehetemariam (2001).
10 See, for example, DPKO (2008).
11 See, for example, Geda (2004).
12 The only other DRPs that remotely compare include the demobilization of more than 350,000 Ethiopian soldiers (and rebels) following the collapse of the Derg in 1991 and activities supported by the Multi-Country Demobilization and Reintegration Programme (MDRP) in nine countries of the Great Lakes of Africa.

13 See for example, the following EDRP reports: Fourth Quarter and Annual Progress Report, January–December 2004; Fourth Quarter and Annual Progress Report, January–December 2003; Fourth Quarter and Annual Progress Report, January–December 2006; Progress Report No. 2, April–June 2001; Progress Report No. 4, January 2001–January 2002; Progress Report No. 5, January 2002–March 2002; Progress Report No. 11, July 2003–September 2003; Completion Report (English), Amhara Region, June 2004; Completion Report (Amharic), Tigray Region; Completion Report (Amharic), Oromiya Region; and Completion report (English), SNNP Region.

14 These included, for instance, the provision of seeds, fertilizers, tools, apprenticeship schemes (for rural veterans) and specialized equipment, schooling and vocational training (for urban veterans).

15 See, for example, UNWG (2006) which defines reintegration as:

the process by which ex-combatants acquire civilian status and gain sustainable employment and income. Reintegration is a social and economic process with an open-time frame, primarily taking place in communities at the local level. Though often treated in isolation of national development interventions, reintegration is part of the overall recovery-reconstruction process and a national responsibility, and often necessitates long-term external assistance.

16 See, for example, Muggah (2006, 2005); Gleishman *et al.* (2004).

17 Emic data is from the perspective of an insider, produced by the participant informed only by their perspective or frame of reference. It is likely to occur in a natural setting and be only minimally affected by the researcher or the research setting. This contrasts with etic data, which is from the perspective of an outsider, imposed from a frame of reference, probably that of the researchers. See Paffenholz and Rychler (2007).

18 Development Studies Association (DSA), based in Addis Ababa.

19 For example, because it involves the collection of household data and includes family names and a 'social map' of who lives where, with whom and owns what, participatory approaches can generate risks for respondents. It is crucial, then, that transparency, consent and judgment are used at all times.

20 Because more than three years had passed since the end of the EDRP, there were also challenges in locating appropriate civil servants in selected regions to identify past participants in the programme. Many had since moved on to new positions, moved away or changed their contact address and were thus difficult to locate. This challenge was also noted by Peake (Chapter 6, this volume) in his review of DDR programmes in Timor-Leste.

21 Each focus group was requested to list all the entitlements they received as part of the EDRP. Most lists counted between eight and ten entitlements – divided here into 'financial support', 'training', 'medical support', 'urban/farm land' and 'other'. Each FG then undertook a pair-wise ranking exercise to determine how individual groups prioritized EDRP entitlements. Focus group participants were then aggregated by region and overall entitlements ranked according to regional priorities – with appropriate weighting according to the number of respondents. Entitlements were then ranked for the region according to 'high' (number 1 or 2 priority), 'above average' (3 or 4), or 'below average' (5 or 6) and 'low' (7–10).

22 In Tigray, the 'other' category for rural veterans included 'grain support' and 'guard employment'.

23 In Amhara, the 'other' category for rural veterans included 'micro-credit'.

24 According to the EDRP Oromiya report, approximately 4 per cent of the veterans received 'skills training'. Training was provided in micro-business such as woodworking, business management, accounting, computer and sewing repair, electronics, mechanics and other areas.

25 In SNNP, 'financial assistance' was frequently conflated by rural veterans with 'pension scheme'.
26 In Tigray, the 'other' category for urban veterans included 'association and capital relief', 'accommodation support' and various forms of retail venues and irrigable land.
27 In Amhara, the 'other' category included 'opportunities for education'.
28 In SNNP, 'financial assistance' was separated by urban veterans into 'cash grants' and 'pensions' both of which scored highly.
29 The issues of EDRP management, bureaucratic organization, budget administration and related performance were outside the mandate of the assessment and thus not examined by the team.
30 See Muggah (2008) for a review of these relationships in the Ethiopian experience.
31 See, for example, Muggah (2007) for a review of the cluster approach.
32 Although the recent Ethiopian-led intervention in Somalia is arguably a continuation of the previous conflict with Eritrea by proxy (see Muggah 2008).

Bibliography

Adekanye, J. (1997) 'Review: Arms and Reconstruction in Post-Conflict Societies', *Journal of Peace Research* 34 (3): 359–366.
Ayale, D. and Dercon, S. (2000) 'From the Gun to the Plough: the Macro- and Micro-level Impacts of Demobilization in Ethiopia', in Kingma, K. (ed.) *Demobilization in Sub-Saharan Africa: the Development and Security Impacts.* New York: St. Martins Press.
Buffoni, L. and Ehetemariam, T. (2001) *Report on the Joint UNICEF/Women's Association of Tigray Study of Ethiopian Deportees/Returnees from Eritrea Living in Tigray* (unpublished).
CDA (Collaborative for Development Action) (2007) *An Approach to DAC Guidance on Evaluating Conflict Prevention and Peacebuilding Activities.* Paris: OECD-DAC.
Colletta, N., Kostner, M. and Wiederhofer, I. (1996a) *The Transition from War to Peace in Sub-Saharan Africa.* Washington, DC: World Bank.
Colletta, N., Kostner, M. and Wiederhofer, I. (1996b) *Case Studies in War-to-Peace Transition: the Demobilization and Reintegration of Ex-Combatants in Ethiopia, Namibia and Uganda.* Washington, DC: World Bank.
Geda, A. (2004) 'Does Conflict Explain Ethiopia's Backwardness – Yes and Significantly', paper presented at UN-WIDER Conference, Finland.
Gleishmann, C., Odenwald, M., Steenken, K. and Wilkinson, A. (2004) *Disarmament, Demobilization and Reintegration: A Practical Field and Classroom Guide.* Frankfurt: GTZ, NODEFIC, PPC and SNDC.
Human Rights Watch (HRW) (2007) The House Committee on Foreign Affairs: 'The Human Rights Situation and Humanitarian Situation in the Horn of Africa', 3 October.
IDMC (International Displacement Monitoring Centre) (2006) 'Ethiopia: Government Recognition of Conflict IDPs Crucial to Addressing their Plight'. Online, available at: www.internal-displacement.org/8025708F004BE3B1/(httpInfoFiles)/45DF6AD3E2E2D A3DC12573840037E3ED/$file/Ethiopia+-October+2007.pdf.
IISS (International Institute for Strategic Studies) (2004) *The Military Balance.* Oxford: Oxford University Press.
Isima, J. (2004) 'Cash Payments in Disarmament, Demobilization and Reintegration Programmes in Africa', *Journal of Security Sector Management* 2 (3).
Kingma, K. (2002) 'Demobilization, Reintegration and Peacebuilding in Africa', in

Newman, E. and Schnable, A. (eds) *Recovering from Civil Conflict: Reconciliation, Peace and Development.* London: Frank Cass.

Muggah, R. (2005) *Listening for a Change! Participatory Evaluations of DDR and Arms Reduction Schemes.* Geneva: United Nations Institute for Disarmament Research.

Muggah, R. (2006) 'Emerging from the Shadow of War: A Critical Perspective on DDR and Weapons Reduction in the Post-Conflict Period', *Journal of Contemporary Security Policy*, 27 (1).

Muggah, R. (2007) 'The Death-knell of '4R': Rethinking Durable Solutions for Displaced People', *ODI Humanitarian Practice Network* 36. Online, available at: www.odihpn.org/report.asp?id=2860.

Muggah, R. (2008) 'Comparing DDR and Durable Solutions: Some Lessons from Ethiopia', *Humanitarian Practice Network* 43, Spring.

Muggah, R. and Bennett, J. (2007) *Making a Difference? A Beneficiary Impact Assessment of the EDRP.* Addis: EDRP/World Bank.

Paffenholz, T. and Rychler, L. (2007) *Aid for Peace: A Guide to Planning and Evaluation for Conflict Zones.* Geneva: Nomos.

Spear, J. (2006) 'From Political Economies of War to Political Economies of Peace: The Contribution of DDR after Wars of Predation', in *Contemporary Security Policy* 27 (1): 168–189.

Tegegn, M. (1992) 'Demobilization and Employment of Combatants: Two Perspectives', in Doornbos, M. *Beyond Conflict in the Horn: the Prospects for Peace, Recovery and Development in Ethiopia, Eritrea and Sudan.* London: James Currey.

United Nations Security Council (UNSC) (2007) *Progress report of the Secretary-General on Ethiopia and Eritrea*, 30 April. Online, available at: daccessdds.un.org/doc/UNDOC/GEN/N07/323/19/PDF/N0732319.pdf?OpenElement.

UNDPKO (2008) 'Over 700 Blue Helmets Relocated Out of Eritrea', *DPKO Press Release.* New York.

UNWG (2006) *Integrated Disarmament, Demobilization and Reintegration Standards (IDDRS).* Online, available at: http://www.unddr.org/iddrs/.

US Department of State (2007) *Ethiopia Country Report on Human Rights Practices for 2006*, March. Online, available at: www.state.gov/g/drl/rls/hrrpt/2006/78734.htm.

White, P (2005) 'War and Food Security in Eritrea and Ethiopia', 1998–2000 *Journal of Disasters* 29 (1): 92–113.

World Bank (2003) *Integrated Safeguards Data Sheet: Ethiopia.* Washington, DC: World Bank.

8 (Dis)integrating DDR in Sudan and Haiti?

Practitioners' views to overcoming integration inertia

Robert Muggah, Desmond Molloy and Maximo Halty

Introduction

In post-conflict contexts where UN peacekeeping missions are established, humanitarian and development donors, policy-makers and practitioners are increasingly advocating for *integrated missions*. Motivated by a desire to ensure that development, humanitarian and peacekeeping agencies are mutually supportive and managed, integration is described as 'the new reality' for multidimensional peace operations (Campbell 2008; Cravero 2005).[1] Proponents of the integrated model are convinced that a system-wide approach to UN intervention in post-conflict contexts can, by increasing predictability and lowering transaction costs associated with poor coordination, reduce the likely resumption and prolongation of armed violence.[2] There appears to be a growing conviction that integrated approaches to DDR can enhance the work of the two primary UN contributors to this activity – peacekeeping operations mandated by the Security Council and UNDP.[3]

While few observers dispute the desirability of integration in principle, there is still considerable disagreement over what it practically entails. A vast array of strategic and bureaucratic constraints impede its emergence on the ground (Campbell and Kaspersen 2008). In the two countries where integrated approaches to DDR were piloted – Haiti and Sudan – interventions stalled. The reason for this is tied as much to prevailing political and security conditions on the ground as with the routine institutional challenges of integration. In spite of supportive normative guidance issued from headquarters, the two instances where integration was purposefully advanced revealed comparatively little agreement on how integration should be defined, much less how it might be practiced.[4] At least in the cases of Haiti and Sudan, the new reality of integration has been a bitter pill. This chapter considers a range of practical obstacles to integrated DDR in both countries and finds that alternative approaches, eschewing prescriptions from above, may in fact encounter comparatively less resistance from below.

A number of important lessons can be gleaned from the experiences of the UN Mission in Sudan (UNMIS) and the UN Stabilization Mission for Haiti (MINUSTAH) in their execution of integrated approaches to DDR. In both cases, weak political leadership within and outside the UN, turnover at the senior policy level in-country, the absence of clear direction from headquarters, competing cognitive framings of DDR among policy decision-makers, donors, project managers and other practitioners, together with confusion over financing mechanisms, all contributed to integration inertia.[5] As part of a broader effort to promote system-wide integration led by headquarters, UN agencies concerned with DDR in Sudan and Haiti were pushed to integrate at the level of implementation. In both cases, they confronted a host of barriers linked to competing agency mandates and bureaucratic interests. Despite optimism among diplomats and senior UN officials in New York and Geneva regarding the prospects for integration, it did not easily materialize.

This chapter considers the rationale and attendant obstacles confronted by those responsible for promoting integrated DDR interventions in Haiti and Sudan. Based on field research[6] and grounded experience in the field[7] it tests the outcomes of integration in two pilot countries selected by DPKO and UNDP. The analysis draws from a combination of key informant interviews, participant observation and 'lived experience' and reviews the ways in which UN institutions, policy-makers and practitioners at the country level reacted to the integration imperative. As such, it highlights how local realities on the ground and individual agency can shape DDR outcomes independently of international standards mandated from above.

To integrate or not to integrate?

The drive for integrating UN missions arose from, among other factors, a long-standing concern with strengthening civil–military relations in the context of peace-support operations. Certain donors were convinced that the slippage of post-conflict countries (back) into widespread violence had as much to do with incoherent and uncoordinated UN stabilization and recovery efforts as with structural factors in the countries themselves (UN 2004).[8] The former Secretary-General Kofi Annan referred to these coordination dilemmas euphemistically as a 'gaping whole' and regularly lamented the absence of inter-agency cooperation. The impetus to integrate was also motivated to a lesser extent by debates over how best to close the relief–development gap in both humanitarian and post-conflict recovery contexts. In the context of major UN-wide reforms launched in 1999 and subsequently ratcheted up in 2005,[9] integration came to be regarded as the bellwether of improved coordination and, ultimately, aid effectiveness (de Coning 2007; UN 2005).[10]

Oddly, there is still considerable ambiguity concerning what integration actually means and how it can be achieved. As noted by Campbell (2008: 3–4) integration can encompass a set of 'organizational processes' that can result in improved coherence. In her view, integration is a means rather than an end. The UN (2005) refers to integration as an 'ideal' – as the 'guiding principle for the design and implementation of complex UN operations in post-conflict situations and for linking the different dimensions of peace-building ... into a coherent support strategy'. Presumably this coherent support strategy will enhance overall effectiveness of multidimensional peace support operations. Others in and outside the UN system understand integration as an 'end' – as the product of a coherent vision and a set of processes that lead to functional management and programming.

From the outset, integration was pursued as a UN-centric exercise. The concept gathered steam after an initial spate of donor-driven reforms and peace-support experiences in the 1990s. The early focus was on linking-up multidimensional peace operations and UN country teams by consolidating country-level UN leadership,[11] centralizing technical support, rationalizing joint planning, implementing inter-agency programmes and developing unified compacts between the UN system and host governments. At the level of planning and programming, the integration of humanitarian, development, peacekeeping and fiscal priorities was encouraged in Common Country Assessments (CCA) and UN Development Assistance Frameworks (UNDAF) and even Poverty Reduction Strategy Papers (PRSPs).[12] As noted in the Introduction to this volume, early experimentation reinforced the conclusion that the form of integration should follow its function and that static blueprint templates were to be avoided (UN 2006; IAWG 2005).

These early initiatives encountered a host of growing pains. Whilst officials at the headquarters-level celebrated the promise of enhanced coherence[13] brought about by integration, there were fierce disagreements at the country-level over how to convert rhetorical plans into practice. Was integration expected to promote joint planning and prioritization, joined-up programmes, or both? What were the budgetary and financing implications? Senior-level political appointees quickly found it difficult to translate these aspirations into concrete directives.[14] Meanwhile, UN programme managers and practitioners complained that the parameters of integration were unclear, that the 'benefits' had not adequately been communicated and that few guidelines were issued to support the process.[15] Likewise, tensions surfaced between UN agencies over competing mandates and priorities, particularly in resource-scarce circumstances. Some actors appeared to resist integration altogether owing to the way it encroached on their 'turf'. Such was the gravity of these turf wars that Campbell (2008: 3) concluded pessimistically that although 'integration reforms have made some contribution to … the integration and coherence of the UN system, they have largely fallen short of their immediate goals and overall objectives'.

Integrating DDR in the field

Notwithstanding lingering disagreements over what exactly DDR is expected to achieve, there is a consensus among military and development actors that it plays a pivotal function in transition and peace-support operations. In fact, there is a widespread – if statistically unfounded – conviction that DDR is causally associated with preventing renewed war in fragile post-conflict contexts, reducing victimization and insecurity and promoting durable reintegration of ex-combatants. Nevertheless, donors and practitioners alike are stubbornly convinced that the anecdotal evidence is firm: despite examples of some failure, DDR exerts a net benefit for societies emerging from war. The belief that DDR contributes to a meaningful 'security guarantee' persists: by facilitating the disarmament of some, it reduces their likely involvement in future instability (Barnett 2005).

The UN has long played a lead role in DDR. It launched its first mission in 1989, in Central America, and has since undertaken or supported DDR in dozens of countries (see Introduction, this volume). Lessons emerging from mid-term and final evaluations of past DDR operations emphasize the importance of improving predictability and coordination[16] among political actors and implementing agencies (Stockholm Process 2006). These same concerns are echoed in multilateral donor debates in relation to improving 'coherence' and 'alignment' in the setting of donor priorities. To be sure, the sheer range and variety of state and UN actors and budget lines involved in DDR, and the frictions that can ensue, seemed to make a coherent approach imperative.

DDR was considered to be the perfect candidate for integration because its activities were necessarily embedded in peace-support operations and spanned multiple thematic sectors, agencies and contexts. Its various components theoretically spanned the so-called security–development nexus. Undertaken in the context of broader reforms and recovery operation, DDR was expected to organically combine strategic and socio-economic imperatives to bridge the gap between war and peace. Described in the Introduction, a UN inter-agency working group on DDR composed of more than 16 UN departments, agencies and non-governmental agencies was established in 2004 to promote conceptual and bureaucratic clarity.[17] By 2006, the group crafted operational guidelines – the IDDRS – to define a 'common and integrated international approach to support national DDR efforts'.

The IDDRS were at first greeted with considerable enthusiasm by UN agencies and donors and a desire to translate them immediately into action. A two-pronged approach was adopted to promote integration. First, in order to generate favourable conditions for integration, representatives of DPKO and UNDP encouraged donors to adopt recommendations in UN Security Council resolutions endorsing unified or, better, integrated, missions.[18] Second, DPKO and UNDP headquarters strongly advocated for the piloting of integrated DDR units/section within UN country missions in two countries – Sudan and Haiti. Though the IDDRS initially only recommended that planning be 'joined-up', many of its supporters expected that conjoined decision-making mechanisms could readily convert (unified) policy prescriptions into practical interventions and thus enhance predictability on the ground.

Revisiting the DDR integrated unit in Sudan

The case for an integrated approach to peace-support and DDR in Sudan was firmly embedded in international legal norms, including UNSC Resolution 1590.[19] The preconditions for DDR were also theoretically enshrined in the 2005

Comprehensive Peace Agreement (CPA)[20] ending Sudan's brutal two-decade civil war in the south between the Sudan People's Liberation Army (SPLA) and the Sudanese Armed Forces (SAF).[21] As soon as UNMIS was established by the UN Security Council, an integrated UN DDR unit – comprised of DPKO personnel and UNDP together with UNICEF – was rapidly set up to move the process forward.[22] The integrated UN DDR unit was itself established on the back of a UN DDR coordination unit funded in 2004 by UNDP during the early stages of the peace negotiations and in anticipation of the CPA.

The institutional infrastructure laid out by the CPA in support of DDR was relatively straightforward. In following best practice for conventional DDR, two national commissions were established in 2005 and 2006 to oversee the DDR of an estimated 100,000 ex-combatants in the north and south of the country.[23] By early 2006, an Interim DDR Programme (IDDRP) was agreed in principle by the parties to the CPA in order to address the specific reintegration needs of child soldiers, women associated with fighting forces and disabled ex-combatants (collectively labelled Special Needs Groups, or SNGs) for demobilization and reintegration. It was anticipated that by addressing the estimated 15,000 SNGs, this could build the necessary confidence to expand the programme into a full-fledged DDR of the larger caseload of ex-combatants associated with the SPLA, SAF and other armed groups. The CPA determined that the full phase of DDR should begin at the end of 2007 with a view to assist the parties in a process of 'proportional downsizing'.[24]

The ground realities were far more complex than anticipated by the drafters of original UN Security Council Resolutions and the CPA. For one, neither the Sudanese government in Khartoum nor the Sudanese People's Liberation Movement (SPLM) in Juba displayed much serious appetite for supporting a full-fledged DDR process (Muggah 2007b, 2006).[25] Owing to persistent political uncertainties related to contentious provisions in the CPA (i.e. power-sharing, oil wealth-sharing, and a referendum on succession in 2011), both parties were instead intent on strengthening their respective armed forces. In many ways, the interim period provided a means to shore up their political legitimacy and military presence while allowing for the shedding of excess and burdensome personnel. In some respects, neither party envisioned DDR as legitimate demilitarization, but rather an efficient means of 'right-sizing' their militaries. Given the persistent tensions over wealth sharing and the impending referendum, many observers close to the process feared a return to grinding low-intensity conflict.[26]

The newly integrated DDR unit was expected to set up shop in an extraordinarily complex and volatile environment. Military analysts and practitioners close to the process recognized from the beginning that DDR could only proceed within the broader ambit of serious reforms to the security sector. Security sector reform (SSR) was recognized to be a highly complex and contentious process in its own right, particularly given the directives issued by the CPA to form joint integrated units out of a multiplicity of SPLA factions, pro-Khartoum militia, pastoral self-defence groups and other armed groups (OAGs), many of whom had been deliberately excluded from the peace process.[27] The inadequate burcaucratic capacity to implement rapid military and police reforms, particularly in southern Sudan, presented a major impediment to serious efforts to undertake DDR. Likewise, the contentious issue of civilian disarmament was exempted from the CPA. The absence of consensual and detailed guidance for SSR,[28] DDR and civilian disarmament necessitated especially robust and determined political leadership from the UN – leadership that appeared to be lacking.

Against this backdrop, tensions rapidly emerged within the integrated DDR unit. In part because of a lack of clarity over *how* to proceed and competing cognitive framings over *what* DDR was expected to achieve, DPKO and UNDP staff were slow off the mark. Their inability to generate consensus over the best way forward prevented the unit from providing clear direction to its government partners. The lack of clear definitions of roles and responsibilities for DPKO and UNDP staff, especially in relation to each other, undermined the capacity of the DDR unit to provide clear support to the mission leadership regarding a coherent UN strategy on DDR. The new unit lacked capacity to forge either vertical or horizontal integration.

The lack of clear definitions of roles and responsibilities – spelled out in operational terms for DPKO and UNDP – undermined the articulation of a coherent UN strategy. Many within UNMIS assumed that DPKO would assume the lead in policy decision-making and overall coordination, with UNDP overseeing technical support for programming. Instead, a scramble for operational and financial control of the programme ensued, while the critical dimensions of political guidance and policy development were largely forgotten. It took more than two years of negotiations to create an operational MoU between DPKO and UNDP. This agreement did not lead to the unification of the two staffs, encourage a unified set of reporting procedures,[29] generate a consolidated fund, or ensure that UNDP employees were given the same priority as UNMIS staff.[30] A high-level review mission was sent to Sudan in February 2007 to uncover why integration had failed to materialize. By the end of the year, their report led to a number of personnel changes, a new leadership team and, at least in theory, a joint vision on the way forward.[31]

Reflections on the integrated DDR section in Haiti

As in Sudan, the MINUSTAH mission also adopted an integrated approach to DDR in-line with UN Security Council provisions, particularly UNSC Resolution 1542. Whilst senior policy-makers in New York advocated for an integrated approach, the newly-integrated DDR section of MINUSTAH was launched without formal guidelines or protocols to guide the process. The nascent integrated DDR section anticipated that in the absence of formal protocols, it could initiate a programme based on informal commitment, good will and the elaboration of shared objectives.[32] Given the high expectations at the outset of the initiative, UN policy-makers in New York, the DSRSG/Resident Representative in-country and the chief of the integrated DDR section all expected that institutional adaptations would follow incrementally as a product of (informal) inter-agency negotiation between DPKO and UNDP.

Even as the bureaucratic details of integrating country planning on DDR began to emerge, field-level planners and practitioners were coming to the conclusion that the preconditions for DDR in Haiti did not exist. Unlike in the case of Sudan, there had been no clear 'armed conflict' in Haiti – at least not according to standards widely in use by international agencies such as the International Committee of the Red Cross (ICRC). Rather, a state of general disorder, criminality and communal violence emerged in the wake of President Aristide's ouster in early 2004 (Muggah 2005a). In Haiti, there were no clearly defined armed groups demonstrating a political commitment to disarmament or demobilization, much less actors motivated by a coherent political agenda.[33] Likewise, there was no formal peace agreement to give political space for the DDR process. Instead, there was only an interim transitional government lacking in local legitimacy to oversee its various components. In the absence of a unitary command for either the former Armed Forces of Haiti (FADH) or the various predatory gangs, the Integrated DDR Section of MINUSTAH began establishing contacts amongst the armed groups and negotiating with their local leadership on a case by case basis.[34] With growing pressure from diplomats and senior UN policy makers to demonstrate results, efforts to develop a coordinated inter-agency DDR process to support national capacities came under strain.[35]

In line with UN resolutions, a conventional approach to DDR was rapidly elaborated by the newly-installed National Commission on Disarmament and the integrated DDR section. Owing to the volatile political realities in 2004 and 2005 and the increasingly shrill demands from representatives of the erstwhile FADH for back-pay from the mid-1990s, the initial focus of the section was on the former armed forces, including elderly soldiers not ostensibly involved in the violence plaguing the streets of Port-au-Prince. In fact, many of these veterans had already been demobilized, albeit unsuccessfully, by the US army and IOM in the mid-1990s.[36] The DDR section also focused to a lesser degree on Haiti's disparate criminal gangs, many of whom displayed competing allegiances with political elites, organized criminals and members of the pre-and post-Aristide regimes (Kovats-Bernat 2006).

While the DDR section focused primarily on FADH at the early stages, gangs were wreaking havoc in the slums surrounding the capital. Despite the section's preliminary efforts to establish contact in 2005 and 2006, many within the UN and interim government were doubtful whether these latter groups would participate in a voluntary DDR process. Complicating matters, the Préval administration was also simultaneously negotiating unilaterally with select gang leaders soon after the 2006 elections. Although MINUSTAH leadership – notably the SRSG – was kept informed of these negotiations, information did not always trickle down to the rest of the mission. Certain practitioners felt that these political negotiations militated against a transparent DDR process managed according to international standards.[37] In the absence of agreed strategic framework and an agreed way forward for effective integration, cohesion through coordination or national ownership, the Section began to fragment.[38]

International observers were soon conscious that this was no ordinary DDR process. Despite pressure from above to deliver DDR, the situation on the ground defied conventional approaches.[39] The country's estimated 170,000–210,000 weapons and 15,000 gang members and FADH troops were highly dispersed and not subject to clear command and control (Muggah 2005a). In the face of competing pressure from the UN Security Council, the SRSG and Western donors to show results in the form of visibly cantoned combatants and collected weapons, the integrated DDR section struggled to market an unconventional alternative. Although its first proposal adopted elements of a conventional DDR programme (e.g. emphasizing the formal cantonment of ex-soldiers and some gang members), it also highlighted a community-centred strategy to reduce violence, expanding on lessons drawn from a modest intervention piloted by UNDP in 2003.[40]

In the absence of basic prerequisites for DDR and political will within the interim government of Haiti, the programme failed to launch. The chief of the DDR section lamented the inability of the UN Brazilian-led peace-keeping force to exert a credible deterrent on the ground.[41] Without the threat of sanctions or punitive measures, armed groups operated with impunity throughout Port-au-Prince. Many quickly assumed roles that the pro-Lavalas gangs[42] occupied under Aristide prior to his ouster while others joined private security companies. Their legitimacy, while to some extent limited at the outset, was enhanced by the absence of government services, police or UN programmes. Meanwhile, elements within the government itself appeared heavily invested in the proliferating armed groups. To make matters worse, the National Commission established to advance DDR seemed not to share the same philosophy or approach as that supported by the DDR section.

The deteriorating security environment in Haiti hindered access to affected communities. With fears of potentially doing more harm than good[43] the DDR section proceeded cautiously and focused on the execution of small-scale quick impact projects. It was hoped that a softly-softly approach might foster positive relationships with affected communities thereby creating an opening for more concerted engagement. At the same time, the DDR section sought to establish pilot 'committees for the prevention of violence and for development'[44] to enhance 'protective factors' and resilience, an approach that drew heavily from earlier pilots and international best practice on dealing with gangs.[45]

In a politically-charged environment – with echoes of more than a decade of UN failure ringing loudly[46] – the DDR section came under fire from within and without. The section's inability to demonstrate convincing progress on virtually any front led to considerable alarm and resentment among donor governments and international non-governmental organizations (Muggah and Krause 2006).[47] A revised approach to DDR[48] was introduced and adopted by DPKO in early 2006. But despite (unprecedented) agreement within the DDR section on its theoretical and practical moorings, severe disagreements persisted over its methodology at the level of middle management. This further strained interpersonal and professional relations, impacting on the capacity to develop coherence and appropriate coordination. These strains grew ever more intense in the subsequent months.[49]

As the security situation continued to deteriorate, the international community and the newly-elected government of Haiti pursued a crack-down or 'mano dura' policy from mid-2006 to early 2007. In response to audacious criminal activity in Port-au-Prince, President Rene Préval and an increasingly proactive MINUSTAH force commander sought to create an enabling environment that permitted the piloting of DDR operations with an estimated 350 gang members. But the government just as quickly balked at the potential consequences of the new UN-led strategy. Despite increasing bilateral donor support, the newly appointed National Commission for DDR[50] was wary that the creation of community committees for violence reduction could challenge the authority of otherwise weakened and under-resourced municipal government structures.[51] With tacit support from the new Executive, the Commission stonewalled progress on the new DDR strategy.

The competing pressures from above and below led to a decision to re-allocate tasks within the DDR section. More pragmatically, it was determined that the new five-pronged approach could be more effectively executed by a new division of labour. Specifically, it was determined that DPKO would oversee DDR tasking while UNDP staff would focus on community security promotion and related capacity building. An internal review in March 2007 described this process more derisively as a process of 'disintegration'.[52] Alternatively, it could be argued that the conditions for an ideal-type integrated operation simply did (and do) not exist.

Beginning in 2006, DPKO and UNDP in New York undertook a joint review to evaluate the effectiveness and challenges facing DDR integration in Haiti and Sudan. The review aimed to assess options for developing more coherent and joined-up programmes and to issue recommendations for more effective implementation of integration in peace-support contexts. The review found that DDR personnel in the two missions exhibited surprisingly common concerns. These reflected their frustration with the dynamic political environment, their different corporate cultures, logistical and administrative obstacles and misunderstandings and limited guidance from their senior management. The review also found that in both cases, staff were not aware that a range of potentially straightforward solutions existed to resolve these problems.

The review issued a number of recommendations to overcome inertia on the ground. In order to enhance DDR integration and establish clear lines of command, the review recommended that the operational and administrative arrangements should include, *inter alia*, a single leadership team of the chief (DPKO) and deputy chief (UNDP) and the formation of a single management team together with heads of the primary sub-units. The review also recommended clear reporting lines with a distinction between administrative and financial reporting. Likewise, it suggested that a financial management unit be established for large programmes (e.g. Sudan) with the financial management functions being met through existing structures in the mission support division or UNDP country office for smaller programmes (e.g. Haiti). Finally, the review noted that all unit staff, regardless of their funding, should be considered part of the integrated mission and provided with equivalent administrative and logistical support.

Unified, integrated or joined-up

Achieving genuine integration, if it can be achieved at all, requires a clear and shared understanding of what it actually entails in practice. There are still ongoing debates within the UN over whether integration constitutes an enabling framework for planning and prioritization, a mechanism to promote coordination or the de facto merging of administrative, operational and budgetary polices and programmes.[53] There is even less agreement as to whether these forms of integration will improve programming in the short to medium-term. Any progress in moving the integration agenda forward, as with any process of norm habituation and internalization more generally,[54] requires clarity over core concepts, and understanding of the division of labour and a process to support capacity. Whether integration will achieve improved predictability and achieve economies of scale remains an empirical question.

The cases of Sudan and Haiti highlight the ways in which DPKO and UNDP conceptualize DDR differently. Within DPKO (military and civilian) DDR planners often adhere to a narrow reading of the peace agreement and the mechanics of the process because they are statutorily obligated to do so. They tend to focus primarily on the technical aspects of disarmament and demobilization, including arms collection, registration and the cantonment and discharge of ex-combatants, as these are the tasks for which they have a budget and resources. In addition to sticking to the letter of UNSC resolutions and peace agreements, they also tend to reproduce standardized operational procedures that, while in most cases effective for the task at hand, allow for comparatively little contextual adaptation. Owing to institutional rigidity and their technocratic focus, such interventions tend to skirt past the micro-political dynamics of DDR – including the competing interests of donors, international agencies, host governments, officers and even rank and file ex-combatants.

Meanwhile, development agencies such as the UNDP, the World Bank and UNICEF tend to adopt a comparatively more comprehensive approach to DDR. Their focus is primarily on the (reinsertion and) reintegration of ex-combatants (and their dependents) and the enhancement of the absorptive capacities of areas of return – areas for which they feel they exert a comparative advantage. Theirs is described in the introduction to this volume as a maximalist approach – one that envisions DDR as a means of alternately re-setting macro-economic priorities, kick-starting the recovery process or even promoting absorptive capacities in areas of return. In particular, UNDP tends to emphasize participatory, bottom-up and adaptive approaches to DDR, having experimented in dozens of countries with community-centred violence reduction, weapons collection and reintegration programmes since the mid-1990s.[55] But because the approach is open-ended, flexible and vague, the real dividends are exceedingly difficult to measure.

The fact that there are many competing conceptions of what is, and is not, DDR has implications for how programmes are ultimately planned, executed, monitored and evaluated. It also affects how the division of responsibilities between agencies is determined (see Introduction, this volume).[56] In both Sudan and Haiti, DPKO assumed responsibility for disarmament and demobilization (DD) while UNDP and other development agencies supported reintegration (R). This led to a presumption of linearity wherein DD proceeded 'before' R, and was largely independent of it. This conventional wisdom is problematized in the IDDRS wherein DDR is described as an indivisible, and highly political, process. Likewise, the IDDRS emphasizes that approaches to DDR must be jointly defined – rather than defined separately by individual agencies. In practice, applying the joint vision is a political process in and of itself.

In Sudan, the UN DDR unit recognized that the tendency to divide labour according to ascribed roles and a linear bias would have to be reversed. Indeed, as noted in previous chapters on Sierra Leone, Liberia, Timor-Leste and Afghanistan – 'who' is disarmed, demobilized and reintegrated and 'when' they are disarmed are defining factors for achieving effective outcomes. Whether in Sudan, Haiti or elsewhere, the design and negotiation of the entire DDR programme, including the shoring-up of political support and commitment from the various parties, are amongst the most important components of the enterprise. Ensuring that DPKO and UNDP adopt a common strategy and reference point, and that interventions are conjointly implemented, is also integral. In Sudan, however, despite agreement in principle between DPKO, UNDP and UNICEF on an initial joint programme, no further political and policy development work was carried out to bring the various CPA parties to the table.

The diverging conceptual approaches to DDR necessarily influence the bureaucratic ordering of integrated missions. Thus, in addition to the considerable challenge of getting various armed groups, governments and agencies to agree to a common plan of action, there are divergent inter-agency understandings that hamper the establishment and administration of a genuinely integrated UN DDR unit/section. A key difficulty relates to the recruitment and secondment of UN personnel from competing organizations. In most cases, they are unaware of the distinctions between integrated, unified or joined-up operations. Many do not know who they are expected to report to. Attempting to forge coherence and team unity when members observe multiple and separate reporting lines is no simple task. From a public management perspective, the incentives are mis-aligned. Since individual responsibilities (and related performance assessments) are intimately wedded to pre-determined reporting lines, the tendency toward disintegration can prove irresistible.

Another closely linked, and widely acknowledged, obstacle to integrated missions relates to financing. In virtually all cases, the funding of DPKO-led DDR is determined by a UN Security Council resolution and mediated by the budget committee and the Comptroller of the UN. As such, disarmament and demobilization activities are frequently funded with resources appropriated and controlled by the UN Secretariat. By way of contrast, UNDP often arranges its budgets according to annual development planning processes and voluntary bilateral contributions executed either directly by the agency (direct execution, or DEX) or through the government of the country in question (national execution, or NEX). In both Sudan and Haiti, additional 'preparatory' funding was provided by UNDP's Bureau for Crisis Prevention and Recovery (BCPR) for direct execution by the UNDP Country Office, though this simply reinforces the bifurcated funding streams.

While distinct funding lines should not present a problem in principle, in practice they generate contradictions and programming silos. Because two sources of funding existed and were channelled through two different mechanisms for parallel tasks, the integrated unit/section encountered difficulties in 'delivering as one' as prescribed by UN guidelines.[57] If both the UN and voluntary donors were to agree on a single funding mechanism through a single DDR executing entity with singular oversight over contracting, it is likely that a more holistic and comprehensive management approach could emerge on the ground. In fact, such a mechanism was drafted between UNDP and DPKO in Haiti in December 2005, though it was ultimately vetoed by stakeholders outside the country.[58] As noted above, however, the joint review mission discovered that part of the problem was that personnel were not aware (or not advised) about how the rules and regulations could be applied.

Given these many challenges, legitimate questions arise as to whether full integration is conceptually and practically feasible or even desirable. Indeed, it could be that the political and structural bureaucratic constraints to re-aligning incentive systems are simply too compelling to achieve coherence (Campbell and Kaspersen 2008). Though loathe to publicly counsel against the integration orthodoxy and aware that full operational integration is not practically feasible, certain practitioners quietly recommend more pragmatic approaches. They argue that a more appropriate approach would be to focus on developing a clear definition of 'integration' as the development of a common strategic DDR plan in line with the Secretary-General's definition. Alignment with the Secretary-General's position would then require all parties to agree and formally sign on to a joint programme. Each agency would then adopt its own set of deliverables for which they would be responsible.[59] Likewise, all agencies would manage their human and financial resources allotted to the task(s) according to their own procedures and management arrangements.

As noted in the Introduction to this chapter, the current emphasis within the UN is to deliver as one. A looser definition of integration was at first heretical to decision-makers in New York and Geneva, though it now appears that planners are more prepared to embrace 'joint programming' as opposed to a more fundamental merger of operations.[60] But we contend that the operative word in this formulation is not necessarily 'one', but rather 'as'. The outcome of this inter-pretive shift is not especially radical: institutional collaboration should be pursued where possible, but not at the cost of institutional identity. The main objective of integration should be to act, *in practice*, as a cohesive whole rather than to intertwine programmes at all levels. From the vantage point of the field, acknowledging the practical limits of integration, while maintaining its essence, is likely the most effective path to reaching that most elusive of international assistance goals: better results.

Conclusion

The recent experiences of UNMIS and MINUSTAH are a reminder of the ways in which post-conflict environments present exceedingly challenging contexts for any intervention, not least integrated approaches to DDR. In both Sudan and Haiti the drive for integration did not facilitate flexible programming or a coher-ent strategy for international and national authorities. Likewise, as shown in both contexts, conventional approaches to DDR designed to formally address the needs of ex-combatants and their dependents were not necessarily the most appropriate. In Haiti, more than in Sudan, the DDR section disintegrated shortly after its presumed integration. In both countries, DPKO and UNDP did not adopt joint structures or procedures for planning and implementing DDR, but rather resorted by default to more flexible interventions tailored to the realities on the ground. As argued elsewhere in this volume, conventional DDR may be superseded by second generation 'community-oriented' processes focused on putting arms beyond use[61] and emphasizing broader objectives of SSR.

At a minimum, the lesson from UNMIS and MINUSTAH is that DDR must acknowledge the heterogeneity of armed group interests together with the often legitimate (and competing) bureaucratic opportunities and differentiated con-straints of agencies involved in the process. While the IDDRS offer a tentative DDR doctrine, they do not issue concrete options for integrating planning and programming. This may in fact be an implausible objective. Perhaps more opti-mistically, the case of UNMIS and MINUSTAH reveal that alternative approaches emphasizing *coordination* may be more effective than full-scale integration. At the very least, a renewed focus on clarifying the expectations of integration, the division of labour and the nature of financing will vastly enhance DDR effectiveness.

Notes

1 In fact, as early as 2000, the UN described integration as:

> the guiding principle for the design and implementation of complex UN peace-keeping operations in post-conflict situations and for linking the different dimen-sions of peace-building (political, development, humanitarian, human rights, rule of law, social and security aspects) into a coherent strategy.
>
> (UNSC (2000))

2 Collier *et al.* (2003) claim that half of all countries relapse into war within five years of a conflict ending. This claim has been challenged by Suhrke and Samset (2007) who ague that the likelihood is far less.

3 This view is bolstered by recent findings from the Human Security Report (2006) that highlight the signal contribution of UN peace-keeping operations in reducing the number of conflicts globally, although they provide comparatively little evidence to support this claim.

4 The UNWG (2006) in referring to integration describes a process of *joint strategic planning* not *joint implementation.*

5 Campbell and Kaspersen (2008) identify a range of barriers to 'integration' within the UN more generally. They single out the structural disconnect of UN agencies (e.g. administrative policies, human resource systems and accountability mechanisms) and the inherent complexities of war to peace transitions as the chief obstacles though offer limited practical recommendations on how to overcome such challenges.

6 See, for example, Muggah and Krause (2006); Muggah (2007b) and Muggah (2005a).

7 Desmond Molloy served as the Chief of the integrated DDR Unit in Haiti (2004–2007) and initially Reintegration Coordinator and subsequently Chief of the DDR section in Sierra Leone (1991–2004) while Maximo Halty served as the Deputy Director of the integrated DDR unit in Sudan (2005–2007). Robert Muggah has undertaken research for both the unit in Haiti and the section in Sudan since 2004.

8 See, for example, Human Security Report (2006) and Collier *et al.* (2003).

9 The 2005 *Report on Integrated Missions* was commissioned by the UN and proposed the idea that form should follow function:

> when developing strategic and operational plans, designing missions structures and selecting key personnel for integrated missions, the desired function (i.e. what overarching strategic objectives the mission is supposed to achieve, and the activities needed to get there) should determine the structure.

See for example Campbell (2008: 3).

10 Campbell and Kaspersen (2008: 2–3) describe a series of ad hoc UN reforms intended to improve the efficiency and effectiveness of UN agencies during the deployment of peace-support operations. Key supporting texts include UN (1997) and UN (2006) and others.

11 This included an effort to promote greater synergies between the UN Resident Coordinator and the UN Humanitarian Coordinator, actors previously criticized for operating autonomously (UN 2006).

12 In Sierra Leone, for example, the DDR section played an active role in developing the CCA and UNDAF. Other frameworks include Consolidated Appeals (CAPs) and Results-Focused Transitional Frameworks (RFTFs).

13 Certain analysts discriminate between different categories of coherence – as 'agency', 'whole-of-government', 'external' and 'internal/external'. Conversation with Robert Picciotti, February 2007.

14 Many complained that the relatively short-term political horizons of senior UN officials also limited their preparedness to take risks or generate unnecessary tension. Indeed, the frequent movement of high-level actors such as Special Representatives of the Secretary General (SRSGs), Deputy SRSGs (DSRSGs), Resident Coordinators, Country Directors and Deputy Country Directors, all generated integration inertia.

15 It is important to emphasize that the IDDRS were not officially launched until 2006, at least a year after the DDR operation was initiated in Haiti and around the same time as the mission in Sudan.

16 de Coning (2007: 9) notes how 'coordination' is a multifaceted concept and can entail 'developing strategies, determining objectives, planning and sharing, information, division of roles and responsibilities, and mobilising resources'.

17 It is worth noting that the UNDP prepared, separately, a Practice Note on DDR to support its own management and programme officers better perform in the field. It claims to offer 'UNDP practitioners guidance on the potential role of UNDP within different DDR scenarios and provides advice on developing integrated programmes with other UN agencies as well as national and international partners (UNDP 2006: 5–6).

18 There is in fact considerable confusion in the UN system over what constitutes 'unified', 'integrated', 'joined-up' or 'coordinated' missions. The UN Secretary-General released a *Note of Guidance on Integrated Missions* that describes the concept as follows: 'An integrated mission is based on a common strategic plan and a shared understanding of the priorities and types of programme interventions that need to be undertaken at various stages of the recovery process'. The integrated missions concept thus refers to a type of mission where there are processes, mechanisms and structures in place that generate and sustain a common strategic objective, as well as a comprehensive operational approach, among the political, security, development, human rights, and where appropriate, humanitarian, UN actors at country level (de Coning 2007).

19 Sudan's DDR programme was in many ways fully IDDRS-compliant. Examples included ensuring that preparatory work was undertaken conjointly *before* the signing of the peace agreement, that capacity-building and national ownership was taken up by national commissions and that the focus was *first* on the forgotten groups, including women associated with fighting forces, children, and the disabled combatants. Likewise, there was agreement on a joint UN programme/policy toward DDR and that the establishment of the integrated Unit were consistent with guidance set out by the IDDRS. The problem was that the IDDRS did not indicate the administrative and procedural guidelines to the expected merging of two different organizational structures, staffs and funding mechanisms.

20 The CPA was signed on 9 January 2005.

21 For a description on historical and contemporary dynamics of Sudan's north–south war, consult www.smallarmssurvey.org/sudan.

22 From the beginning, however, donors and UN agencies registered confusion about the institutional and bureaucratic nature of the integrated DDR unit. Many referred to it casually as the UNMIS DDR unit or the 'joined-up' office, further problematizing understanding on the ground.

23 This was the initial planning figure of the UN DDR unit in mid-2006, but there is to date no formal agreement between the GoS and the GoSS regarding the overall caseload.

24 See CPA, Chapter 7, para 7.1.

25 For example, the Government of South Sudan only signed the IDDRP in January 2006, and the (northern) Government of Sudan in May 2006, while the National DDR Coordination Council met for the first time in early 2007.

26 See, for example, Young (2007) and the work of the Human Security Baseline Assessment (HSBA) at www.smallarmssurvey.org.

27 Correspondence with DfID advisers and Norwegian military personnel, January–December 2007.

28 There was an initial promising attempt to coordinate support for SSR for both parties by the aid troika (i.e. US, UK and Norway). These donors established a joint International Military Assistance Team (IMAT) and successfully opened an office in Khartoum in February 2006. Very soon after its launch, however, the office was aggressively shut down by the Khartoum authorities, and the team forced to leave the country.

29 This is spite of the fact that the legal and human rights departments of UNDP and DPKO were officially informed of the process in early 2007.

30 In fact, UNMIS staff are routinely prioritized on domestic flights, which means that

the UNDP staff are regularly left behind while the DPKO staff board the planes. This is partly because UN member states that fund 'operational costs' of peacekeeping operations are reluctant to finance activities for agencies that are otherwise subject to voluntary funding, including UNDP.

31 Moreover, the MoU was finally signed on December 2007.

32 Indeed, this had transpired in Sierra Leone several years earlier wherein a unified approach was adopted by UNAMSIL and UNDP between 2001 and 2004. For example, UNAMSIL DDR section and UNDP recovery section worked successfully in close collaboration from 2001–2004 in delivering Stopgap programmes, the community-based arms for development programme and the development of arms control legislation. See, for example, Chapter 3 (this volume).

33 Muggah (2005a: xiii) noted that:

> there are at least a dozen distinct types of armed groups in possession of varying numbers and calibres of small arms and light weapons: OPs, *baz armés*, *zenglendos*, ex-army (FADH), former paramilitaries (Revolutionary Armed Forces for the Progress of Haiti – FRAPH), the ex-Presidential Guard, prison escapees, organized criminal groups, self-defence militia, private security companies, civilians, and politicians. Each of these groups draws on a rich vein of local support. The alliances among these groups are fluid, and motivations stem from a complex combination of predatory and protective behaviour – itself firmly tied to local interests.

34 This placed an unsustainable workload on the section and militated against cohesion of the evolving strategy.

35 Despite efforts to generate coordination through an *ad hoc* Committee on DDR appointed by the government and related consultations with UN agencies, NGOs, ICRC, national civil society organizations, the Sectoral Table on Police and Disarmament of the Interim Collaborative Framework, donors, the transitional government of Haiti, and certain elite, the discussions were fraught.

36 A large number of representatives of the FADH claimed, not without some legitimacy, that they were owed pensions and compensation for being 'unconstitutionally' demobilized in the mid-1990s.

37 The possibility of dismantling the gangs by drawing members into a transparent process of disarmament was undermined. Appeasement (and allegedly, payment) of influential gang leaders by the new government strengthened the position of gangs *vis-à-vis* the community and resulted in increasing predation and criminal activity in August to December 2006. This mirrored the impact of the impunity assumed by the Revolutionary United Front (RUF) leader Foday Sankoh in Sierra Leone's Lomé Accord in 1999. Authors' observation.

38 See, for example, de Coning (2007), who identifies coherence, coordination and national ownership as requisites for the implementation of an integrated strategy.

39 Extreme pressure was placed on the Integrated DDR Section to 'deliver', despite the clear absence of basic prerequisites for a voluntary process; agreement, a facilitating legal framework, identifiable caseload, credible deterrent and national ownership. The Chief Integrated DDR section was, in fact, instructed to drop the word 'prerequisite' from his vocabulary altogether.

40 See, for example, Muggah (2005a) for a review of the BCPR-UNDP community violence reduction strategy established in 2003.

41 These concerns should of course be placed within the wider context of the use of force in peacekeeping missions. The Force Commander at the time noted that he would not use force against civilians when the 'cause' of violence appeared to be deep-seeded and linked to structural issues such as poverty and under-development.

42 Lavalas (or 'the flood') was the political party that Aristide built to promote development in impoverished areas. It was also used to attract armed supporters following his dismantling and sidelining of state security institutions.

43 On initial probing to move the DDR process forward, the DDR section met with a group of 57 child armed gang members in one volatile quarter of Port-au-Prince in December 2004. Within six weeks, five of these children were killed by gang leaders, ostensibly because their interest in the DDR process led to a questioning of their loyalty. This was a horrifying lesson to the DDR section of the potentially disastrous impact of moving too fast to implement DDR. This led to significant caution and risk averseness in developing future contacts.

44 Community committees were made-up of locally-elected representatives (elderly, youth, women, local leaders, business interests). Community violence prevention committees were expected to enhance opportunities for development in specific areas. Communication with Daniel Ladouceur, January 2008.

45 UNDP's community-based DDR and community violence reduction pilot project was implemented in the disadvantaged neighbourhood of Carrefour Feuille in Port-au-Prince from 2003–late 2004.

46 See, for example, Muggah and Krause (2006) for a review of the previous six UN peacekeeping missions in Haiti since the late 1980s.

47 Whilst acknowledging the difficult security context, bilateral donors exerted considerable pressure on the Integrated DDR section and demanded results.

48 The five-pillared approach to DDR in Haiti included:

   1 the disarmament, demobilization and reintegration of gang members;
   2 capacity building for community-based violence reduction;
   3 a focus on vulnerable youth;
   4 a focus on vulnerable women; and
   5 the development of arms control legislation.

49 According to insiders, interpersonal stresses were aggravated by a lack of horizontal and vertical communication in relation to how integration might proceed. Against a backdrop of dynamic political and policy-level change, those responsible for implementing programmes lacked clear directives, backing and support.

50 The newly appointed national commission for DDR (unlike the previous mechanism installed in 2005) was empowered to represent government policy rather than the disparate agendas of various politically active individuals. Problematically, government policy regarding armed violence remained something of a mystery to the international community. It appeared to combine vocal support for the DDR programme with covert appeasement of specific gang leaders.

51 Local government was simply not present in many of the more volatile quarters of Port-au-Prince and Gonaives, the second city. The local government elections, in mid 2006, created thousands of posts for which there was no infrastructure or resources, including salaries.

52 Muggah (2007b) also presented the question of disintegration rhetorically.

53 According to DPKO officials, these issues are increasingly discussed in the UN, however, including through workshops and regular meetings between the DSRSG/RC/HC and others.

54 See, for example, Finnemore and Sikkink (1998).

55 Muggah (2007b) notes also how the discourse and labelling of both DPKO and UNDP differ, often profoundly. For example, UNDP plans and implements its programmes within existing politico-administrative boundaries recognized by states, while DPKO tends to adopt a sector-specific approach in designating areas of operation and deployment.

56 The division between DD for DPKO and R for UNDP is considered by many to be a root cause of integration inertia. If DPKO (as in Liberia, or many other circumstances) decides by itself to open (cantonment) camps and pay civilians for returning single cartridges, DDR loses all focus and may cause more harm than good. See, for example, Chapter 3, this volume.

57 As noted by de Coning (2007: 10) the Report of the High-Level Panel on UN System-Wide Coherence called for 'delivering as one'. It also describes the strategy adopted by UN country teams in pursuit of coherence. See, for example, www.undg.org.

58 A March (2007) Integrated Mission Assessment reported that a formal MoU between both agencies was not required and that more flexibility within the MINUSTAH mission and UNDP could have resolved the issue. But owing to the pressures emerging at HQ in New York over the 'oil for food' scandals, UN financial managers were displaying considerable level of risk adversity regarding 'flexible' local contracting arrangements.

59 DPKO (2007) recommends that 'partnership operational references' could be developed in this regard.

60 The shift in semantics is not as esoteric as it sounds. Indeed, analogous challenges have plagued the forced migration community – particularly the UN High Commissioner for Refugees (UNHCR) and partner agencies – in their efforts to advance a collaborative or integrated response to promoting 'protection' and 'care and maintenance' in the case of internal displacement. In order to circumvent these difficulties, the UN inter-agency standing group proposed a 'cluster approach' as an alternative, though even these efforts have been plagued by criticism due to their UN-centric approach. The earlier plan – a 'collaborative approach' – collapsed relatively soon after it was proposed in the late 1990s. See, for example, Muggah (2007a).

61 See, for example, Molloy (2004).

Bibliography

Action Aid (2006) 'DDR and Police, Judicial and Correctional Reform in Haiti: Recommendations for Change' (mimeo).

Barnett, R. (2005) 'Constructing Sovereignty for Security', *Survival*, 47(4): 93–106.

Barbara, W. (1997) 'The Critical Barrier to Civil War Settlement', *International Organization* 51: 335–364.

Campbell, S. (2008) 'Integration's Challenge: Incoherence and (Dis)Integration in UN Post-Conflict Intervention', *International Peacekeeping* 14(3).

Campbell, S. and Kaspersen, A. (2008) *Confronting Integration: The UN's Integration Reforms and their Barriers* (mimeo).

Cravero, K. (2005) 'Statement by Kathleen Cravero, UNDP Assistant Administrator and Director, Bureau for Crisis Prevention and Recovery', *NUPI Conference on Integrated Missions*, 30 May. Online, available at: www.nupi.no/IPS/filestore/Kathleen Cravero-Oslo-Revision3.pdf.

Collier, P., Hoeffler, A., Elliot, L., Hegre, H., Reynal-Querol, M. and Sambanis, N. (2003) *Breaking the Conflict Trap: Civil War and Development Policy*, Oxford: Oxford University Press and the World Bank.

De Coning, C. (2007) 'Coherence and Coordination in United Nations Peacebuilding and Integrated Missions', *Security in Practice* 5, Oslo: NUPI.

DPKO (2007) *Report on the First Workshop for Chiefs of DDR Sections in Missions*, Brindisi: UNLB, 25–29 July.

Eide, W., Kasperen, A., Kent, R. and von Hippel, K. (2005) *Report on Integrated Missions: Practical Perspectives and Recommendations*. Online, available at: www.nupi.no/IPS/filestore/ReportonIntegratedMissionsMay2005.pdf.

Finnemore, M. and Sikkink, K. (1998) 'International Norm Dynamics and Political Change', *International Organizations* 52 (4): 887–917.

Human Security Report (2006) *War and Peace in the Twenty First Century*, Oxford: Oxford University Press.

IAWG (Inter-Agency Working Group on DDR) (2005) *Operational Guide to the Integrated Disarmament, Demobilization and Reintegration Standards*, New York: UN.

Kovats-Bernat, C. (2006) 'Factional Terror, Paramilitarism and Civil War in Haiti: The View from Port-au-Prince (1994–2004)', *Anthropologica*, 48 (1).

Molloy, D. (2004) 'The Gender Perspective as a Deterrent to Spoilers: DDR in Sierra Leone', *Conflict Trends*, Autumn.

Muggah, R. (2005a) 'Securing Haiti's Transition: Reviewing Human Insecurity and the Prospects for Disarmament, Demobilization, and Reintegration', *Occasional Paper* 14, Geneva: Small Arms Survey. Online, available at: http://www.unddr.org/countryprogrammes.

Muggah, R. (2005b) 'No Magic Bullet: A Critical Perspective on Disarmament, Demobilization and Reintegration (DDR) and Weapons Reduction in Post-Conflict Contexts', *International Journal of Commonwealth Affairs*, 94 (379).

Muggah, R. (2006) 'Reflections on Disarmament, Demobilization and Reintegration in Sudan', *Humanitarian Practice Network*, 35, November. London: ODI.

Muggah, R. (2007a) 'The Death-knell of "4R": Rethinking Durable Solutions for Displaced People', *Humanitarian Practice Network*, 39, London: ODI. Online, available at: http://www.odihpn.org/report.asp?id=2860.

Muggah, R. (2007b) 'Great Expectations: (Dis)integrated DDR in Sudan and Haiti', *Humanitarian Exchange* 38, London: ODI. Online, available at: http://www.odihpn.org/report.asp?id=2878.

Muggah, R. and Krause, K. (2006) 'The True Measure of Success? Considering the Emergence of Human Security in Haiti', in T. Shaw, S. MacLean and D. Black (eds). *Human Security: A Decade On*, New York: Lynne Rienner.

Small Arms Survey (2006) 'Armed Groups in Sudan: The South Sudan Defence Forces in the Aftermath of the Juba Declaration', *Issue Brief* Number 2, October. Online, available at: www.smallarmssurvey.org/files/portal/spotlight/sudan/sudan.html.

Stedman, S., Cousens, E. and D. Rothchild (eds) (2002) *Ending Civil Wars: The Implementation of Peace Agreements*, Boulder: Lynne Rienner.

Stockholm Initiative (2006) *Stockholm Initiative on Disarmament Demobilization Reintegration*. Online, available at: www.sweden.gov.se/sb/d/4890.

Suhrke, A. and Samset, I. (2007) 'What's in a Figure? Estimating Recurrence of Civil War', *International Peacekeeping* 14 (2).

Swedish National Defense College (2006) *Overview of Operations of Integrated DDR Section in Haiti*, Stockholm: SNDC.

UN (1997) *Renewing the United Nations: A Programme for Reform*, A/15/950, New York: UN, 14 July.

UN (2004) 'A More Secure World: Our Shared Responsibility', *Report of the Secretary General's High-level Panel on Threats, Challenges and Change*, New York: UN. Online, available at: www.un.org/secureworld/.

UN (2005) *Investing in the United Nations: For a stronger Organisation Worldwide, Reform at the United Nations*, New York: UN. Online, available at: www.un.org/reform.

UN (2006) *Note of Guidance on Integrated Missions: Clarifying the Role, Responsibility and Authority of the Special Representative of the Secretary-General and the Deputy Special Representative of the Secretary-General/Resident Coordination/Humanitarian Coordinator*, 17 January.

UN (2007) *Joint Review of the UN Integrated Assessment Team of the Pilot Integrated DDR Program in Haiti*, March (mimeo).

UNDP (2006) *Practice Note: Disarmament, Demobilization and Reintegration of Ex-Combatants.* Online, available at: www.undp.org/cpr/whats_new/ddr_practice_ note.pdf.

UN Security Council (2000) *Report of the Secretary-General: The Role of United Nations Peacekeeping in Disarmament, Demobilization and Reintegration,* S/2000/101, 11 February.

UNWG (2006) *Integrated Disarmament, Demobilization and Reintegration Standards (IDDRS).* Online, available at: www.unddr.org/iddrs/.

Young, J. (2007) 'Emerging North-South Tensions and Prospects for a Return to War', *Working Paper* 7, Geneva: Small Arms Survey.

Negotiating reintegration in Uganda
Dealing with combatants during peace processes

R. Muggah[1] and A. Baaré

Contemporary peace-support operations and post-conflict recovery interventions regularly include prescriptions for DDR. While the contours of such activities may feature in peace agreements and UN resolutions, they are often poorly understood, contested and motivated by short-term imperatives. This may be due to a lack of awareness of DDR on the part of key parties and mediators. Alternatively, it may reflect a rational tactical decision. Either way, the origins and parameters of DDR in relation to peace agreements are hardly given. Concerns over how DDR might affect sovereignty are central to the discussion. Moreover, mediators may harbour contrasting ontological understandings of what DDR is expected to achieve. Mediators themselves are not necessarily supposed to sanction 'progressive' outputs, but rather help parties reach agreement to their mutual satisfaction.[2] Plans for DDR may therefore appear fragmented and poorly constructed even when facilitated by the most experienced negotiating teams.

In order to help craft legitimate and credible DDR programmes in the post-war period, mediators should be well-informed about the history, principles, approaches and desired outcomes of the process. To assist specialists in this task, this chapter examines the process of integrating DDR into a fragile peace agreement between the Ugandan government and the Lord's Resistance Army (LRA) between 2006 and 2008. The chapter focuses primarily on the competing conceptual 'frames' applied by different stakeholders during the negotiations rather than the outcomes of the process. It then teases out a number of general trends and patterns in the ways that various actors interacted.[3] It finds that in addition to being largely under-conceptualized and carefully balanced against competing priorities, DDR is interpreted in heterogeneous ways by different actors. These competing framings can profoundly (and negatively) affect the way various aspects of the process – particularly reintegration – are negotiated and ultimately planned and executed. The chapter closes with a number of general recommendations for mediators and practitioners to better prepare for DDR during peace negotiations.

Dealing with reintegration

There is a widespread perception that approaches to DDR are becoming increasingly professionalized and standardized. A doctrine is gradually emerging –

encapsulated by the IDDRS (UNWG 2006) – and lessons are appearing to be learned.[4] There is a belief that for better or for worse, security and development priorities are effectively fusing at the normative level (Duffield 2007). Bureaucratically, this fusion is expressed in the UN's growing penchant for integrated missions, the production of associated guidelines, the increased funding for DDR from multilateral and bilateral aid donors and the expanding involvement of the World Bank and UNDP in related activities.

But the reality in New York and Geneva is that there are considerable (if at times unacknowledged) disagreements over what DDR is intended to achieve and the role and function of reintegration in particular.[5] As noted in the Introduction of this volume, security actors tend to view DDR more narrowly – a minimalist perspective – as a means of preventing the onset of renewed conflict, containing belligerents and spoilers and reigning in the tools of violence. Development actors often adopt a broader perspective – a maximalist perspective – a means of redressing structural contradictions in defence and welfare spending and expanding the livelihood opportunities of an economically productive sector of the population. These disagreements are not esoteric but fundamentally affect the conceptualization and design and execution of DDR.

In places such as Khartoum and Port-au-Prince, however, the realities are even more complex. On the one hand, the practical challenges of integrating DDR missions – fusing the planning and activities of security and development actors – has not been adequately thought through (see Chapter 8, this volume). There are the usual challenges of security providers (e.g. DPKO) receiving funds from assessed UN Mission budgets while development actors (e.g. UNDP) must raise their own from agency or voluntary contributions, often in competition with others. There are also the persistent difficulties of ensuring multi-year commitments for complex long-term operations, facilitating collective action between disparate (and frequently fractious) partners,[6] and ensuring government ownership of DDR when such governments may be unable or unwilling to support the process.

There are other more insidious challenges. When DDR is undertaken in the context of ongoing tensions – including counter-insurgency operations as in Colombia and Afghanistan – security actors may seek to promote development as means of winning hearts and minds (see Chapters 1 and 5, this volume). While this in itself is not necessarily detrimental to DDR, the selective provision of reinsertion and reintegration assistance can (unintentionally) intensify grievances and undermine perceptions of DDR legitimacy (see Chapter 10, this volume). By way of contrast, in the context of post-conflict situations such as Nepal, Rwanda or Ethiopia, development actors may be unable to provide sufficient reintegration assistance or adequately link discrete interventions for ex-combatant beneficiaries with wider sectoral programmes, also undermining the effectiveness of DDR in the long-term.

There is growing debate in certain circles as to whether DDR should 'de-link' reintegration altogether (see Conclusion, this volume). Donors and practitioners are beginning to ask tough questions about the feasibility and ethics of providing limited resources to generate 'sustainable livelihoods' for ex-combatants. They question whether modest packages – in many cases a few weeks of vocational and micro-enterprise training, seeds, tools and a phased grant – can do much more than temporarily stay a return to violence, much less break the command and control of former armed groups. Others ask whether more targeted 'area-based' assistance – provided through existing (or planned) and mainstream development programmes – would be more appropriate. While such debates raise more questions than they answer, they nevertheless signal an unease in some camps of the limitations of reintegration as presently conceived.

Multiple framings of reintegration

Despite growing enthusiasm with DDR, reintegration is singularly under-conceptualized in policy, research and practice. Although long recognized as poorly managed and financed (Stockholm Initiative 2006; Brahimi Report 1999), there have been few attempts to generate a coherent and comprehensive understanding of what reintegration actually means, how it might be implemented and appropriate indicators and means of monitoring them over time. This lacuna is only recently being explored in the context of impact evaluations, regrettably long after DDR may have been originally conceived and executed.

There is frequently a discrepancy between how mediators and practitioners conceive of DDR in general and reintegration in particular. Mediators may privilege ways to promote peace while practitioners must contend with the routine demands of executing programmes.[7] More importantly, mediators may be more interested in disarming armed groups as a requisite first step to securing a stable peace agreement. Practitioners, on the other hand, may be less preoccupied by linkages between discrete phases. Of course meaningful reintegration is only feasible 'after the shooting stops'[8] – but it is also the case that shooting may stop if reintegration is effective. Either way, these observations may be incidental: as the cases of Liberia and Sierra Leone's peace agreements amply demonstrate, reintegration may be an after-thought, if considered at all. In some cases it may be thrown out as a secondary concession – in the words of one senior practitioner: 'give him what he wants and he goes away.'[9]

The discrepancies between mediators and practitioners illustrated above serve to demonstrate that DDR is framed in varying ways by different stakeholders.[10] Although constructive ambiguity is to some extent unavoidable and potentially desirable, mediators must be conscious of this fact and its potential to generate obstacles later on.[11] The following section considers these competing frames in more detail, disaggregating them into at least four categories. Specifically, international donors tend to adopt an 'economic' or 'livelihoods' bias to reintegration. Meanwhile, host governments and armed groups – particularly those engaged in or bound by ceasefires and peace agreements – may envision reintegration as a means of extending their authority and legitimacy 'from above'. By contrast, certain commanders and senior officers use reintegration instrumentally as a means of shoring up legitimacy 'from below'. Finally, rank and file combatants often regard reintegration as a 'reward' or 'entitlement' owed to them in the context of peace agreement. Recognizing the heterogeneous framings of reintegration is crucial for mediators and practitioners.

Reintegration as economic development and livelihoods

According to international donors and UN agencies, the state of the art definition of reintegration is encapsulated in the IDDRS. The standards envision reintegration as:

> the process by which ex-combatants acquire *civilian status* and gain *sustainable employment and income*. Reintegration is essentially a social and economic process with an open time-frame, primarily taking place in communities at the local level. It is part of the general development of a country and a national responsibility, and often necessitates long-term external assistance (italics added).[12]

Not to be confused with reinsertion[13] – essentially a short-term transitional grant provided to ex-combatants during the demobilization period – reintegration is often cast as an economic process linked to gainful employment and acquisition of a stable income. This economic bias is pervasive in negotiation strategies, DDR proposals or programme-documents (pro-docs), evaluations and academic studies (see Chapter 6, this volume). The economics-first approach casts ex-combatants as homogenous actors subject to rational expectations – essentially *homo-economicus* that will respond to incentives in a predictable fashion.

A counter-narrative is quietly emerging that subtly challenges this focus on economic restoration and productivity above all else. A more nuanced approach conceives of reintegration in relation to sustainable livelihoods and human rights promotion. In this revised framework, reintegration has political, social, economic and even psychosocial dimensions (Baaré 2006). It also potentially takes into account reparations and reconciliation (see Chapter 10, this volume). It acknowledges that the extent to which ex-combatants can be economically productive depends on other factors – including the macro and micro-economic context in which reintegration takes place, the social and political dynamics shaping the mobilization of armed groups, perceptions of justice and the real and the relative endowments of ex-combatants. Nevertheless, a rational choice model stubbornly persists whereby 'interests' are still mechanistically conceived and amenable to a combination of carrots and sticks.

The fact remains that reintegration is only partially considered by donors and development agencies during peace negotiations. In Sierra Leone, Liberia and the Cote D'Ivoire, for example, the peace agreement described DDR, and reintegration in particular, in oblique terms.[14] Even after agreements on disarmament and demobilization are hammered-out at the negotiating table,[15] reintegration is sidelined. Some observers describe this gap between pre-negotiation and predeployment as the 'little red box'.[16] In Haiti, for example, the shape and character of reintegration emerged only after the launch of a large-scale fundraising exercise and the mandating of DDR in various UN Security Council Resolutions. As a result, the concept featured well into the 'peace process' and was nominally highlighted in the international financing mechanism. Although there is not necessarily a need for a single definition of reintegration, it is crucial that mediators and negotiators are conscious of the many ways it can be interpreted.

Reintegration as legitimacy from above

In the context of peace negotiations and the aftermath of armed conflict, DDR is one of many processes designed to secure the peace and extend the authority of the state. It is in some ways an instrument of military 'hard power' in contrast to softer measures such as the extension of democratic governance and social welfare functions. While disarmament and demobilization are expected to deal with legitimate ex-combatants, contain would-be spoilers and regulate the tools of violence, reintegration is designed to bolster the transition and guarantee the peace. DDR – coupled with SSR – is a compelling expression of a state's aspiration to (re)monopolize the legitimate use of force.

From the perspective of national governments, their armed forces and senior commanders, then, reintegration is a mechanism to expand their authority from above and enhance their legitimacy. These processes may be reinforced by donors, UN agencies and the World Bank who place a premium on ensuring that DDR is executed through national institutions – national commissions, inter-ministerial or departmental committees and task forces. The shoring-up of governmental capacities through direct budgetary support and capacity-building is expected to empower governments so that they might own the process.[17] In fractured and fragile contexts, DDR is ultimately channelled through potentially compromised state entities, even if the trade-offs are recognized from above.

It should be recalled, however, that there is seldom a common understanding of DDR or reintegration among the many national stakeholders likely involved in peace negotiations. In southern Sudan, for example, in addition to the Sudanese Peoples Liberation Army (SPLA) there are more than 50 different organized armed groups (OAGs) involved or (more likely) excluded from the comprehensive peace agreement (CPA) signed in 2005.[18] Many of them exhibit conflicting allegiances and interests that confound a unified perspective. Likewise, in the Democratic Republic of Congo, there are at least 20 separate groups involved in the multi-donor demobilization programme (MDRP).[19]

Reintegration as legitimacy from below

From the perspective of senior commanders and officers of both national armies and armed groups, the experience of DDR can be alternately profitable and traumatic. Not only do certain figures run the risk of being politically disenfranchised and potentially criminally prosecuted, they potentially lose a lucrative source of status and rent. From Afghanistan to Timor-Leste, for those not integrated into newly reconstituted security organs, the process of reintegration can be conceived as a demotion. By virtue of their relatively close proximity to peace negotiations and the processes of military re-organization, senior commanders are acutely conscious of the losses they are likely to endure. In certain cases, they may act to spoil negotiations and DDR planning if it does not suit their collective or personal interests. In other instances, armed groups may hold-out – as in the case of southern Sudan[20] and Uganda – until the terms of negotiations are altered or the political situation alters in their favour.

In such circumstances reintegration can actively be manipulated and distorted. Reintegration is therefore conceived as a means of shoring up legitimacy from below – demonstrating the ability of commanders to care for those under their charge. Reintegration therefore confers legitimacy on commanders who themselves may serve as intermediaries between donors and soldiers in order to control access to related entitlements. They may also actively manipulate the communication of rights and benefits to ensure their continued authority. In other cases, commanders may (informally) assume control of the reintegration process by selecting particular (typically male) candidates, taking a cut from reintegration benefits, and staging protests or resistance to enhance their stature and authority.

Reintegration as an entitlement

Rank and file combatants exhibit a wide assortment of concerns as they confront a reintegration process. These range from their likely role in the new military or policing dispensation to putting food on the plates of their families. Their inclination to engage in the process may depend in large part on the mechanisms by which they mobilized to begin with: those who were recruited by force may exhibit different preferences than those who were not. Likewise, those who have more resilient endowments and skill-sets may opt to integrate spontaneously on their own, while those with less education or social capital may be more inclined to access any entitlements on offer. Most DDR programmes, however, lack adequate baseline data or robust studies of the prospective caseload until after the intervention is launched. Though DDR programmes are often preceded by a pilot to allow for analysis of a discrete cohort and accompanied by registration to track progress and adjust benefits over time, such data is seldom adequately analysed or reflected in programme design (see Chapter 3, this volume).

A major factor affecting combatant perspectives of reintegration relates to the nature of the conflict, the peace agreement and the way the DDR process is communicated. Specifically, where combatants are demobilized and reintegrated in the context of a cross-border war as in Ethiopia and Eritrea – they may regard themselves (and be widely perceived) as victors – rewarded with a range of benefits for their services to the state or an armed group (see Chapter 7, this volume).[21] In other cases, as when an unsteady peace is realized with no clear winner – as in Nepal – disarmament and demobilization may be cast as an entitlement for simply keeping the peace (Buxton *et al.* 2006). In those scenarios where justice is imposed from without – as in the Republic of Congo – the entitlements on offer may be more unevenly perceived whereby former combatants cast their benefits as legitimate compensation while communities envision the process more negatively as a reward for war-mongering (Muggah 2004). Depending on how the DDR process is communicated (and interpreted) and the extent to which the process is manipulated these conflicting interpretations can generate renewed grievances as the Liberian experience amply shows.

All four of these framings were present during the negotiations of a peace agreement in Uganda in late 2006 and early 2008. While the peace process was (and continues to be) an immensely fraught exercise, lessons can be learned by disaggregating the process by which specific protocols for DDR were negotiated and understood. There are inevitably risks that accompany any academic treatment of real-time processes. As such, this chapter seeks not to appraise the merits or outcomes of the process so much as the strategies deployed by various actors throughout. Before turning to the negotiations per se, however, it is important to put them in context.

A simmering war in Uganda

Ugandan society was torn apart by an assortment of armed groups before and after the installation of Museveni's National Revolutionary Movement (NRM) in 1986. One of the most resilient was the Lord's Resistance Army (LRA) – a group that neither held firm territorial gains (as did the SPLA in southern Sudan) nor established alternative government structures (as did the NRM during its conflict against the Obote and Okello regimes). While it is not possible to do justice in describing the internal conflict between the NRM and the LRA here, it is of course crucial for negotiators to develop a detached and impartial overview of the competing narratives and frames that various warring parties and stakeholders bring to the table.

The NRM was widely supported by the international community when it came to power in the 1980s following decades of horrific rule under Amin and Obote. Donors had effectively labelled the country a de facto failed state and their posture toward the NRM's charismatic new leader was one of patience and understanding. Notwithstanding simmering tensions in the north of the country, in keeping with the good practice of the era, donors were prepared to 'work around conflict' rather than 'on it' (Goodhand 2001). By the early 1990s Uganda had adopted one of the continent's most advanced development frameworks and was feted for taking on the prescriptions of the aid community. At the time, the growing conflict inspired by a rebel group in the north was considered a residual grievance that would eventually fade away as the country spread the dividends of its new economic growth.

Meanwhile, the LRA, and its supporters in the Ugandan diaspora, contend that the period of NRM ascendancy was also one of fading (international and domestic) interest in their cause. Many in the aid community ignored the so-called 'root causes' that shaped grievances among the northern Acholi tribes. The NRM's disregard for power-sharing arrangements agreed in the 1985 Nairobi Agreement[22] was followed-up with hard-handed 'pacification' in the north and east.[23] It seemed that the donor community was prepared to accept semi-military rule by the NRM as the price for stability. By the mid-1990s, however, as news of the scale of its abductions and killings emerged, the LRA was designated an international pariah.[24] It was only a decade later that the full magnitude of the horrors unfolding in northern Uganda was made public.[25] A 'dual approach inclusive of both military activity and peace negotiations' was the modus operandi pursued by the NRM government and the international community (Uganda Conflict Action Network 2005: 2). Attempts to mediate repeatedly failed (Afako 2003).

In 2002–2003 a botched attempt by the Ugandan armed forces to defeat the LRA demonstrated that the latter's estimated 1,000–3,000 fighters exhibited capabilities far beyond the expectations of most outsiders.[26] Throughout 2004 and 2005 peace talks mediated by Betty Bigombe generated renewed hope but these too eventually collapsed.[27] Meanwhile, the ensuing military stalemate precipitated negotiations in Juba, Sudan, in 2006. But the LRA's practice of forcibly recruiting children and targeting civilians had led the Ugandan government in 2003 to refer senior members of the LRA to the newly established International Criminal Court (ICC) (see Chapter 4, this volume). Indictments of the LRA leadership, the first by the ICC, followed in 2005 and likely contributed to undermining meaningful negotiations.[28] The spectre of the ICC serves as a double-edged sword. On the one hand, it complicated ongoing mediations and held up negotiations in Juba. At the same time, it could be argued that the ICC also encouraged the LRA to come to the table in Juba in the first place.

The Juba process

It took military threats combined with an offer of third-party intervention from the nascent government of southern Sudan,[29] to bring the warring parties to the table for formal negotiations in July 2006.[30] The 'Juba process' as it is often called made good on a commitment by the SPLM/A to help address the northern Ugandan conflict after achieving its own peace settlement.[31] The latest round of mediation have gone further in bringing to (near) end one of Africa's most protracted civil wars than any previous effort by international and Ugandan brokers. Predictably, the political demands of nurturing the agreement were extremely high. The process involved furious spurts of 'in camera' negotiations but also protracted walkouts, repeated breakdowns, procrastination and lengthy stakeholder consultations in and outside of Uganda. On the security front a semblance of de facto peace came about in the worst affected areas when the LRA moved its troops out of northern Uganda and eastern Equatoria. The immediate security dividends of the Juba process were thus dramatic and tangible[32] (Brown 2007).

The negotiations revolved around several basic agenda items.[33] The Final Peace Agreement (FPA) was expected to include seven *protocols* on:

1   the *cessation of hostilities* and its six addenda;
2   *comprehensive solutions* covering agreements on political issues and root causes of the conflict;

3   *accountability and reconciliation* dealing with the core political-legal issues relating to the creation of a national alternative to prosecution of LRA leaders by the ICC;
4   *a permanent ceasefire* which would be linked to a protocol on;
5   *disarmament, demobilization and reintegration*;
6   *implementation and monitoring mechanisms*; and
7   *implementation schedule.*[34]

It is important to note that the signing of the FPA and the initiation of DDR are inextricably linked to action in relation to the ICC. Although the political process repeatedly stumbled, with support from former Mozambican president Chissano, negotiations were revived and two key protocols were signed between May and June 2007.[35] Between August 2007 and January 2008 consultations were undertaken in Uganda but the LRA continued to experience internal disarray and launched periodic walk-outs. The international community initially remained divided and gradually lost patience in the southern Sudanese-led mediation process.[36]

The intervention of the government of southern Sudan and the increasing international support over time were informed by at least two strategic considerations. First, as a 'power mediator', it saw in negotiating an end to the LRA an important advantage to securing its own sovereignty and international legitimacy. Even so, the external recognition accrued by a negotiated outcome was nevertheless secondary to the likelihood such an agreement might contribute to improved security afforded by a southern neighbour free of the LRA.[37] Put another way, a peaceful northern Uganda was indelibly linked to a secure and economically prosperous southern Sudan.[38] Second, the international community saw in their (uneven) support to the government of southern Sudan a way of managing the tricky politico-legal situation presented by the LRA. It allowed them to describe the process as an 'African solution for African problems' while holding out on making a final decision on the issue of the ICC arrest warrants. International actors could justify their continued involvement by claiming that they were adhering to the principle that the Rome Statute could allow national prosecution instead of prosecution by the ICC.[39] Instead of being accused of 'negotiating with terrorists' (and perpetrators of war crimes) they could now talk of pursuing the (domestic) arrest and trial of the indictees as a diplomatic objective. Ultimately, international support to the Juba process was conditional on meeting specific 'international standards' and this would invariably affect the way negotiators engaged with DDR.

Negotiating DDR in Juba

Formal agreement on a comprehensive DDR protocols was a major achievement of the Juba negotiations. By the end of February 2008 the government of Uganda and the LRA signed the 'Agreement on Disarmament, Demobilization and Reintegration'.[40] The agreement actively drew from the UN IDDRS as the primary standard for parties in undertaking *disarmament and demobilization*.[41] For *reintegration* the DDR protocol alludes to non-UN solutions and the potential for Ugandan experience and existing recovery and reintegration programming to bridge the gap.[42] The DDR protocol commits the Ugandan government to *adapt* its reintegration policy and includes a sub-section on reintegration programming.[43]

In many ways, the DDR protocol reflects the existing stakeholder architecture that accompanied the Juba process – including specific security and development agencies, local parties and, to a lesser degree, combatants.[44] Its contours are also a product of the negotiations that preceded its formulation. During the early stages of negotiations, for example, the focus of the various groups was on establishing basic conditions for a cessation of hostilities and formal negotiations such as the separation of forces. Negotiations were informed in large part by predominantly 'security' concerns of the Ugandan government and the LRA leadership. The cessation-of-hostilities agreement provided avenues to demobilize 'non-essential members of the LRA in the care of specialized humanitarian agencies'. To the international aid community, the expression 'non-essential' appeared at first to exclude the rights of abducted persons, particularly women and children, within the ranks of the LRA. Some donors were privately wary of appearing to appease the LRA leadership and not securing reciprocal commitments in return.[45]

On closer inspection, the above-mentioned clause appeared to partially satisfy potentially conflicting frames. Specifically, the military objectives of the Ugandan government were to reduce the presence of the LRA in northern Uganda and assemble them within designated areas. The LRA, on the other hand, sought to prolong full command and control within the assembly areas to which they had agreed to relocate. The release of women and particularly children up front, while a priority of donors and the Ugandan government, was not a tenable negotiating position given the former's central role in the LRA's fighting forces. Despite the efforts of mediators to promote early release of children and inject more palatable wording, the LRA stuck to 'non-essential' – several steps below the 'international standards' recommended by third-party mediators.[46]

The cessation-of-hostility agreement's focus on security arrangements and assembly was a natural response to the demonstrated military capabilities of the LRA.[47] But reintegration priorities were also directly and deliberately woven into negotiations on security. Subsequent protocols, for example, covered the integration of LRA forces into Uganda's security forces, as well as basic commitments to recovery and reintegration of former LRA and other war-affected groups.[48] The trade-offs made by negotiators must be understood in the context and immediate opportunity structure *at the time*. The international aid community tends to adopt a system analysis of security, rights and livelihoods in its approach to DDR. A byproduct of this perspective is that the bar for DDR and reintegration has been raised since the 1990s (Baaré 2006). The standards by which DDR was to be measured during the Juba negotiations were elevated even higher by negotiators owing to the spectre of the ICC. There was a clear danger of perfection becoming the enemy of the good. Meanwhile, national authorities, armed groups and civil-society representatives envisioned an approach to DDR grounded in local realities. At the heart of the negotiation strategy of Juba the agreement was not appeasement but patience to achieve a model of 'national and cultural justice without impunity' that would ensure justice would be pursued, but not by the ICC.

Still, patience cannot necessarily solve all contradictions arising during tense negotiations. In the DDR protocol, for example, progressive language is included that draws explicitly from Resolution 1325 on *Women, Peace and Security* and the *Paris Principles* and *Guidelines on Children Associated with Armed Forces or Armed Groups*.[49] However, the final agreement reflects a compromise between many competing framings.[50] Incentives for the parties to agree to the progressive DDR language proposed by the negotiators may reflect political opportunism: it was well understood that the agreement should reflect the international frame of DDR as much as possible because international movement on the ICC issue was deemed more likely with DDR protocols that met international standards.[51] There is a moral hazard inherent to the architecture of the negotiation process: progressive language achieved in the framing of the DDR protocol does not change the fundamental fact that throughout the negotiations the LRA refused to release anyone (forcibly or otherwise) recruited into its ranks. Nor does it resolve the fact that the LRA made progress on the DDR protocol contingent on parallel movements on the ICC indictments.[52] While a patient strategy may have yielded peace on paper, it is only with seeing through the implementation of the accords that a final assessment can be meaningfully rendered.

The Ugandan case signals the way in which expectations of international and local actors toward DDR are shaped by context and can be potentially reconciled. But this reconciliation comes at a cost. From the perspective of state representatives and senior commanders, 'security arrangements' may trump other concerns, including those of the most vulnerable rank and file urging for a quick peace deal. In the Uganda case, it is not yet clear whether the range of perspectives on DDR improve outcomes on paper and in practice. From the perspective of the international aid community, the economic reintegration of the 'dangerously poor' – themselves predominantly male ex-combatants – is a core objective. But donor expectations of what DDR can realistically deliver have increased exponentially due to the extension of donor activities as third-party intermediaries in relation to conflict prevention, peace-building and poverty reduction (Baaré 2004).[53] The role of the ICC indictments on LRA commanders in shaping DDR processes and outcomes also reduce the possibilities for alternative deals – including temporary amnesties, exile or impunity as part of a negotiated agreement.

Implications for negotiation and programming

Despite the principled commitment to DDR demonstrated by the UN Security Council, operational UN agencies, host governments and even warring parties, the process is fraught with challenges. These challenges are present during negotiations on DDR, particularly when trading-off ostensibly 'progressive' objectives and standards against immediate security concerns and the practical intricacies of reaching a mediated settlement. The expectations of what DDR – including reintegration – can achieve must therefore be carefully thought through and adjusted to what is practically feasible. This section issues a number of basic recommendations for mediators and practitioners in the context of peace negotiations.

The Ugandan experience highlights how negotiators and mediators came to recognize the heterogeneous interpretations of DDR and reintegration. Despite the prevalence of a strong security and livelihoods bias from above, mediators came up against competing priorities from below. Accounting for these dynamic perceptions was critical as they shaped agent behaviour and undoubtedly inform reintegration outcomes. This also implies acknowledging up front the likely tensions between pursuing a 'pragmatic peace' versus a 'justice-first' approach to DDR.[54] The Ugandan experience is a reminder that DDR is fundamentally wedded to politics and linked to broader aspects of the negotiation process and strategic outcomes more generally. In order to 'fast track' peace negotiations as parties work toward establishing security arrangements, DDR is frequently positioned as a technical 'stop-gap' intervention. Short-term gains in reducing the threat of spoilers and instability are privileged over longer-term investment in redressing real and perceived grievances. In the case of Uganda, DDR was designed explicitly to follow a political process rather than lead it. This was partly possible because the negotiations followed in the wake of several years of Ugandan experience with reintegration of ex-combatants, including with the LRA.[55]

A major lesson from the Ugandan experience was the elaboration of an upfront mediation strategy that linked DDR to wider security arrangements put in place during the negotiation process. The successful adoption of DDR protocol in 2008 – with clear provisions for reintegration – required explicit trade-offs that fell, in some instances, below international standards. In the Juba negotiations, for example, the drafters of the August 2006 Cessation of Hostilities Agreement made pragmatic decisions that were externally criticized for falling short of the ideal. In order to obtain agreement after two decades of war, priority issues such as the release of children and abductees was hidden deep in the text.[56] At the same time, the seeds of DDR were sown early in the negotiations even if conventional DDR was not explicitly on the table.[57]

In Uganda, the negotiations were from the outset facilitated with technical experts on DDR.[58] These experts could, on the basis of comparative experience, explain DDR and present a range of options relating to reintegration. They can also serve as advisers to the mediators and the parties. Even the presence of an adviser can potentially avoid the misrepresentation of DDR and overcome challenges such as those in Liberia, where the process lacked substantive up-front technical inputs.[59] Despite the apparent emergence of a multifaceted doctrine to guide DDR, there are in fact many (necessary) permutations and approaches to disarming, demobilizing and reintegrating ex-combatants. DDR is too often erroneously conceived as an end in itself, rather than a means. But form should always follow function and approaches to reintegration are no exception as the Ugandan case reveals.[60]

The strategy adopted during the Juba negotiations was to raise the issue of reintegration prior to disarmament as an incentive to encourage LRA participation. Ultimately, the art of negotiating DDR involved a careful balancing act: recognition of the way in which context and multiple framings informed strategic positioning. Negotiators cannot afford to ignore that DDR is neither linear nor uni-directional process as is often assumed. In most scenarios, the different phases of DDR transpire concurrently. Negotiating tactics may include discussing reintegration support packages up-front as an incentive with disarmament arrangements left for later. In some cases, DDR may not even be a recommended course of action.[61] The approach to DDR, and reintegration, should be empirically and analytically-based rather than a mechanical or knee-jerk response.[62]

Conclusions

It is too early to tell whether DDR will be effective in Uganda. Though the process will continue to face immense challenges, at the time of this writing there was an emerging separation between a *disarmament and demobilization* process with UN involvement (inside Sudan) and a *reintegration process* taking place in Uganda that built on conventional development programming. As is noted in other chapters of this volume, the functional division between the 'DD' and the 'R' was a response to the limitations of the existing aid architecture and the negotiating context on the ground. The 'de-linking' of DDR, then, was a pragmatic response to local conditions and realities. Another lesson emerging from the process is the importance of articulating attractive post-conflict 'futures' during negotiations, including options that account for reintegration as part and parcel of any agreement.

The Juba experience also raises a number of important insights related to timing and sequencing. Negotiators and DDR experts during the negotiations need to locate a common approach to determining the *appropriate timing* for raising reintegration concerns. Mediators may, for good reason, seek to delay or postpone the reintegration question while DDR experts may seek to force the issue too early and with too technical an orientation. The approach eventually adopted in Juba was to plant seeds for DDR in a range of discrete protocols. But this required the presence of DDR experts in the mediation team throughout negotiation process, and not reservedly when DDR was formally tabled.

Lessons from other countries offer some instructive insights into how successful approaches to negotiating DDR can be enhanced. Ultimately, reintegration involves the coordination between a wide variety of stakeholders – from multilateral and bilateral agencies, host governments, public and private security actors, commanders and combatants with competing interests and competencies. Identifying and mapping out interests and connections between reintegration and broader sector-specific capacities[63] is a sine qua non of effective reintegration planning. Developing unity of interest and common cognitive framings, together with formal implementation architecture, will shape the design, budgeting and execution of reintegration for the better.

Adjusting expectations and investing in evidence-generation is equally critical, and a central concern of this volume. While there are often temptations to over-promise during negotiations, a major long-term failure of reintegration relates to the incommensurability between anticipated outcomes and actual practice. Mediators should develop a reasonably sound grasp of the absorptive capacity in areas of 'return', the relative capacity of public and private service-providers and the ways legitimacy and authority are locally conferred. Ensuring that negotiations reflect to some extent what is possible is crucial for elaborating a realistic peace agreement. Before DDR – especially reintegration – is launched it is crucial that reliable and valid socio-economic profiling data is generated on commander and ex-combatant endowment sets and mobilization patterns. For obvious reasons lists of combatants (and their profiles) are regularly provided after negotiations, or even well into DDR implementation. But investment in a combination of quantitative and qualitative surveys of combatants and areas of return, together with focused studies on the spatial distribution of arms flows and stocks is critical for targeting and prioritizing budgets, short to medium-term employment and identifying linkages to national planning frameworks.

Even with the relative success of the Juba negotiations, the parties must anticipate the possibility of things going badly wrong in the course of DDR. It is therefore essential to establish legitimate and adequately resourced and empowered mechanisms to monitor and oversee reintegration as well as to adjudicate disputes among parties. For example, the Juba agreement on paper successfully embedded reintegration in Uganda's national recovery and poverty reduction framework by seizing on existing recovery plans for northern Uganda. However, such opportunities may be the exception and not the rule. Either way, due attention should be paid at the earliest stage of DDR planning to ways of ensuring reintegration is sustainable,[64] including by embedding strategies in international and national development frameworks.[65] Missed opportunity and last ditch efforts to do so in, for example, Rwanda and Burundi, reinforce the point that DDR mediators and practitioners need to establish early and effective interaction with development planners and agencies (DPRO 2007).

An approach to reintegration that addresses individuals but is also sufficiently broad to account for the interests of communities is key. A major challenge for DDR is linking individual returning officers and rank and file to broader community networks, markets and institutions. There is growing awareness of the importance of developing community-based approaches to reintegration, particularly in relation to supporting national and municipal capacities to promote recovery. Such strategies need to ensure that reintegration benefits include a combination of *private benefits* even as more conventional community development programmes emphasize *public goods*.[66] These two types of benefits generate fundamentally different incentives for ex-combatants.

Notes

1 Credit must be extended to many expert commentators on earlier versions of this draft. They include, *inter alia*, Laurie Nathan, Desmond Molloy, Macartan Humphreys, James Pugel, Gordon Peake, Sarah Nouwen, Antonio Donini and others.
2 Fisher (2001: 11) distinguishes between 'pure mediation' and 'power mediation'. The former refers to efforts by third-parties to facilitate a negotiated settlement on substantive issues through the use of reasoning, persuasion and effective control of information and the suggestion of alternatives. The latter refers to a process that while including pure mediation, applies leverage and coercion in the form of rewards or threatened punishments and may involve the third party as a monitor and guarantor of the agreement.
3 Previous HDC articles focused on 'disarmament' in relation to DDR and mediation. See, for example, HDC (2006).
4 There is an emerging consensus among senior UN practitioners that the IDDRS constitutes a major advance in enhancing and harvesting synergies between UN and international agencies. It cannot account for challenging 'personalities' but does offer a template for improved coordination. See, for example, DPKO (2007).
5 DPKO (2007) highlighted just a few, including:

 1 internal DDR section and partner coordination;
 2 appropriate staffing availability;
 3 complexity of implementation in volatile situations;
 4 contradictions of national ownership and international direction;
 5 difficulties of managing partnerships;
 6 vertical expectations management (between HQ and field);
 7 the need for strategic vision within country missions;
 8 the development of the next generation of DDR managers;
 9 the strengthening of the implementation of IDDRS;
 10 the clarification of the position of DDR in relation to peace-keeping, peace-building and transitional activities related to development;
 11 the relationship between DPKO and UN agencies at the country level in relation to the challenges to autonomy and the 'Resident' system; and
 12 the mobilization of resources for DDR from assessed budgets, voluntary and bilateral contributions and the rest.

6 The difficulties presented by a contrary government in relation to the UN Mission in Sudan (UNMIS) are noteworthy. Despite the establishment of national commissions for the north and south, the SRSG has been expelled on several occasions and there are few mechanisms to establish common understandings of DDR.
7 Molloy laments how 'reintegration' is seldom envisioned 'holistically': 'it should not be a reward for ex-combatants ... but an operation to strengthen community security' (correspondence in February 2008).
8 This can be achieved either through regular disarmament (including formal collection and destruction) or by 'putting arms beyond use' (ibid.).
9 Correspondence with Pugel, February 2008.
10 In Afghanistan, for example, the unprecedented variety of actors ensures a varied

interpretation of the purpose and outcomes of DDR. External observers, particularly the media and among human rights organizations, often conceive it as a total disarmament campaign rather than as the DDR of the AMF. Ex-combatants for their part often understand DDR as an entitlement that they are owed. Commanders frequently view DDR as a vehicle through which to exercise their right of rule. Meanwhile, NATO coalition representatives and many local private security companies (PSCs) continue to rely on these same commanders for counter-insurgency and security operations.

11 Humphreys notes how such divergence of views may in fact be crucial to getting parties on-board. Constructive ambiguity may be an important feature to generating consensus on problematic issues (correspondence with Humphreys, February 2008).

12 It should be recalled that while this definition is widely accepted by DDR practitioners, most donors and agencies likely conceive of reintegration in even more general terms – as a return to 'normality' or 'restoration' of development. It is only at the planning and implementation stages that a nuanced or more subtle definition emerges (credit to Pugel for these observations; correspondence in February 2008).

13 Reinsertion is the assistance offered to ex-combatants during demobilization but prior to the longer-term process of reintegration. Reinsertion is a form of transitional assistance to help cover the basic needs of ex-combatants and their families and can include transitional safety allowances, food, clothes, shelter, medical services, short-term education, training, employment and tools. While reintegration is a long-term, continuous social and economic process of development, reinsertion is a short-term material and/or financial assistance to meet immediate needs, and can last up to one year. Molloy describes reinsertion as a 'fiction' that 'permits assessed budget funding to get the [DDR] process through a bumpy start-up while waiting for voluntary contributions' (correspondence in February 2008).

14 The issuance of multiple agreements with competing timelines only adds to the complexity and margin for misunderstanding (DPKO 2007: 4).

15 Notwithstanding the potential use of reintegration as an 'incentive' or 'cover' in lieu of more tricky issues such as disarmament.

16 A recent workshop overseen by DPKO sought to unpack the 'red box'. They found that the pre-negotiation and pre-implementation phase of a peace agreement was a critical period for 'right tracking' DDR. They determined that more concerted focus on this period could avoid reserving DDR to after UN missions were deployed (DPKO 2007).

17 But as the recent experience of Haiti demonstrates, there may also be severe disagreements between donors (and the UN Special Representative) and national actors about the direction and modalities of DDR. Where governments are 'difficult' or 'fragile', donors may be less inclined to support them through direct budgetary support opting instead to channel resources through UN agencies such as UNDP (through National Execution functions, or NEX).

18 See, for example, HSBA publications at www.smallarmssurvey.org/sudan.

19 According to DPKO (2007: 6) there is no reintegration plan for the MDRP and disarmed elements are sent home with USD25 per month for a single year with no clear safety-nets or follow-on activities.

20 The CPA allows the SPLA/SPLM to retain an army and to 'integrate' all other armed groups into joint integrated units. Those groups that do not elect to join the army are thereafter to be forcibly disarmed as is occurring in Lakes, Jonglei and eastern Equatoria. See, for example, www.smallarmssurvey.org/sudan.

21 A similar situation arises during 'resistance wars' as in the case of Timor-Leste (see Chapter 6, this volume).

22 See, for example, Kiplagat (2002).

23 These aggressive campaigns continue and include a combination of forcible

disarmament, cordon and search operations and the regroupement of displaced populations into camps in order to isolate insurgents from their popular base (see HSBA
2007).

24 Not only was Sudan's role in supporting the LRA condemned, but the issue of child
abductions, sex slavery and the targeting of civilians in a messianic war of attrition
based on the Ten Commandments were documented. Between 2000 and 2001 the
donor discourse on the LRA focused primarily on these regional aspects even if they
excluded the Ugandan support to the SPLA.

25 UN OCHA – particularly the then UN Undersecretary-General for Humanitarian
Affairs Jan Egeland, identified northern Uganda as a humanitarian catastrophe in 2006.

26 The UPDF operation was labelled *Operation Iron Fist* (Rodriguez 2004).

27 A former NRM minister for Northern Uganda (Bigombe) was unable to broker agreement in 1994. Efforts more than a decade later – dubbed the 'Bigombe 2' talks –
hinged on her personal efforts and supported by a so-called 'core group' of Kampala-
based donors that included the Netherlands, US, UK and Norway. See also
www.usip.org/specialists/bios/archives/bigombe.html.

28 The ICC indicted give top commanders in October 2005. It unsealed the warrants for
crimes against humanity and war crimes. The warrants named Joseph Kony, Vincent
Otti, Okot Odhiambo, Dominic Ongwen and Raska Lukwiya.

29 The GOSS/SPLA threatened the LRA with a 'leave, die or talk' ultimatum. The LRA
and the government of Uganda accepted to talk.

30 Before the parties agreed to talk there were bilateral meetings between Riek Machar
(Vice-President of Southern Sudan) and the LRA leadership.

31 See, for example, IRIN (2005).

32 See, for example, US-issued security updates at: http://northernuganda.usvpp.gov/
securityupdate.html.

33 The agenda items established in July 2006 included:

1 cessation of hostilities (August 2006);
2 comprehensive solutions ('principles' May 2007, 'implementation protocol' February 2008);
3 accountability and reconciliation ('principles' June 2007, 'annexure' February
2008);
4 permanent ceasefire (February 2008); and
5 disarmament, demobilization and reintegration, DDR (February 2008). Other
agenda items finalized included;
6 implementation and monitoring mechanisms (February 2008); and
7 Final Peace Agreement (pending).

34 See, for example, the Final Peace Agreement Juba Sudan initiated version, 25 March
2008.

35 Chissano was appointed as a Special UN Envoy to facilitate a solution to the conflict
and worked successfully to bring the parties to the table. The final agreements
included:

1 The Agreement on Comprehensive Solutions Between the Government of the
Republic of Uganda and the Lord's Resistance Army/Movement of 2 May 2007;
and
2 The Agreement on Accountability and Reconciliation Between the Government of
the Republic of Uganda and the Lord's Resistance Army/Movement of 29 June
2007.

36 Some in the international community was extremely sceptical about the peace negoti-
ations in the early stages of 2006. In one case they described it as a 'rogue initiative'.
They wondered aloud how a nascent government of the semi-autonomous region of
Southern Sudan could succeed where so many others had failed. They were also

concerned themselves about how to engage in negotiations in light of the ICC indictments and classification as a terrorist group. Nevertheless, a significant number of donors eventually supported a UN-managed *Juba Initiative Fund* to financially support the negotiations. In late 2007 a common international approach was abandoned when the US lent de facto credence to the 'military' approach: a 31 January 2008 deadline was set for the negotiations to produce 'results'. By March 2008, a new international consensus was reached and expressed in the witnessing of the final FPA protocols by the UN, Kenya, Tanzania, DRC, Mozambique, South Africa, Canada, Norway, the EU and the US.

37 Correspondence with Reik Machir, Vice-President of southern Sudan, January 2008.

38 The improvement of trade linkages between northern Uganda and southern Sudan was considered indispensable to reducing reliance on 'Arab' northerners. The dissolution of the LRA was also important in order to pre-empt the use of the LRA as a proxy force by Khartoum in the advent of the 2011 referendum on independence.

39 Instead, diplomatic and financial support for the Juba process eventually focused on whether the agreed protocols and their implementation could be adequate to move from a possibility *in principle* to support for *local legal practice* to put the LRA to trial in Ugandan courts under conditions *acceptable* under the *Rome Statute*.

40 See, for example, Agreement on Disarmament, Demobilization and Reintegration, Juba, 29 February 2008.

41 See, for example, Clause 4 and Clause 5 (ibid.). The latter focuses on demobilization and explicitly alludes to the IDDRS and the World Bank.

42 Ibid. Clauses 2.2 and 7. DDR negotiators took note of that two basic sets of preconditions needed to be applied. In Sudan, where the DD process is set to take place, the UN has a natural role and that frame was applied to the relevant DDR clauses. In Uganda, the frame applied is one of 'national ownership' that is clause to the frame of the Government of Ugandan and its development partners.

43 During negotiations the wording of Clause 2.2 of the DDR protocol evolved from '*adopting*' a policy to '*adapting*' an existing reintegration policy. The latter gives even more weight to a national frame for the R of DDR. Section 7 of the DDR protocol focuses on *'Reintegration Programme'* and establishes reintegration support as an entitlement (7.2, 7.3) and stresses education: '*7.4 All former LRA members who wish to go to school, including vocational training, shall be assisted to do so*'. Operationally it is important that this clause does not exclude LRA who left before the Juba FPA. Such details are left to the adapted reintegration policy.

44 It is difficult to talk about 'combatant views'. LRA commanders purport to talk on behalf of the men, women, boys and girls still in the LRA, but DDR negotiators had no real access to active LRA rank and file. Most of what is available for reference is based on studies and research done on/with former LRA. See, for example, http://www.sway-uganda.org/.

45 See for example the debate between Tim Allen and Richard Dowdon (2007).

46 The mediators' aim was to let the COHA acknowledge and provide a mechanism for, vulnerable groups to leave the LRA. This was not successful. The alternative at the time was a status quo situation without a COHA whereby the Ugandan army would continue treating women and children as combatants. 'Assembly', even with full control exerted by a fighting force, is nevertheless an important intermediary condition on route to full demobilization.

47 The government of south Sudan reckoned that its strategy of patient engagement was warranted due to the emergence of comparatively 'peaceful' conditions. Moreover, it felt that military engagement with the LRA ran the risk of scattering the entity resulting in it constituting a menace for years to come.

48 See, for example, the Agreement on Comprehensive Solutions. Note, in particular, Section 8 (on security organs); Section 9 (on IDPs); Section 10 on a strategy for recovery; and Section 12 on vulnerable groups. The Agreement on Accountability

and Reconciliation also makes specific reference to the needs and dignity of women and children that were precursory to the more specific DDR clauses focused on women and children discussed earlier.

49 See, for example, Clause 2.14 (ibid.) that states: 'The parties shall ensure that the DDR process fully incorporates the special rights and needs of women. In particular, Security Council Resolution 1325 on Women, Peace and Security (2000)'. UNSC Resolution 1325 mandates UN member countries to a range of women-specific actions aimed at the protection of and participation by, women in DDR and peace-building.

50 The 'Paris Principles' are referred to in Clause 2.7 of the Juba DDR protocol. Like the IDDRS, the international call is for the *unconditional and early release of children*. The wording 'unconditional' was after much debate and effort to include it, left out of the Juba DDR text that instead commits the LRA/M 'To ensure the earliest release and repatriation to Uganda of pregnant and lactating women along with all children under 18 years of age'.

51 But even among negotiators DDR meant different things to different people. For example, some interpreted provisions for DDR in terms of aspirations rather than 'must achieve' standards. Others envisioned DDR as a purely technical exercise along the lines observed by Brickhill (2007) in the case of southern Sudan.

52 At the time of the writing of this chapter, the central contention between the LRA and the NRM related to what came first – the lifting or suspension of the ICC indictment or the signing of the FPA to give effect to the Juba protocols.

53 The fact that DDR may have achieved success when 'ex-combatants are as poor as the rest' and women associated with fighting forces are 'as oppressed as the rest' does not rest easily with the self-aggrandising discourse of security and development actors.

54 At a minimum DDR interventions should ensure that an effective public information strategy is pursued and coordinate activities with the timing and launch of related transitional justice mechanisms. It is vital that such activities do not inadvertently impede DDR activities – particularly among senior combatants. See Chapter 10, this volume.

55 Two contextual factors are especially important: on the up side, the 'Juba DDR case load' of former LRA rank and file coincides with the Ugandan Amnesty Commission that has administered reintegration programmes for at least eight years. On the down side, these reintegration programmes actually consisted of 'reinserting' former LRA into IDP camps with a modest financial package. These issues were deliberately downplayed in Juba to avoid the possibility that the LRA would raise the issue of retroactive benefits for former members.

56 Issues relating to women, children and (other) abductees were addressed by a clause that opened up the possibility that the LRA could 'handover non-essential' members to humanitarian agencies. In the draft of the Final Ceasefire, however, the 'space' for applying international standards had increased and reference to Security Council Resolutions 1325 and 1612 were acceptable to the parties.

57 Indeed, it is only in February 2008 that a formal overview or protocols of possible DDR strategies were supplied by facilitators to LRA commanders.

58 Throughout the Juba process, Denmark and Sweden seconded a DDR and gender expert. UNICEF provided a child release and DDR expert. The importance of DDR expertise for negotiating teams has been acknowledged independently by DPKO (2007: 3–4). They recommend that 'consideration be given to pre-deployment training to DDR staffs [sic], civilian, military and police' and that 'DDR stores [sic] should be strategically deployed early in the mission'. DPKO also notes that appropriate MoUs should be formalized early, that dialogue and planning should be developed as soon as possible and that the UN architecture must be developed on a case by case basis. DPKO recommends that 'partnership operational references' could be developed in this regard.

59 Molloy claims that this led to more than 106,000 'beneficiaries' rather than the 39,000 planned for in the agreement (correspondence, January 2008).
60 In Haiti, for example, the UN Mission in Haiti (MINUSTAH) developed a 'traditional' approach to DDR in 2004. But basic prerequisites did not exist: there was an absence of a peace accord, political will, identifiable caseload, unitary command, legal framework, credible deterrents and clarity in relation to integrated missions. The 'DDR' programme was eventually converted into a community violence reduction programme by 2006, long after the launch of MINUSTAH (see Chapter 8, this volume).
61 This is because weakly-administered disarmament has contributed to a rise in armed violence. Demobilization has in some instances fuelled militia activity and banditry.
62 In some cases, as in where there is no UN Mission or where armed groups are tantamount to 'gangs', DDR may not be the most appropriate approach. In such environments, certain agencies conventionally associated with DDR, including DPKO, may not be best equipped to play central role in the process at all (DPKO 2007: 3).
63 This also includes recognizing the role of 'foreign' ex-combatants and the juridical and logistical requirements of 'repatriation' – as the experiences of UNHCR and IOM demonstrate in DRC, Rwanda, Burundi and Uganda.
64 DPKO (2007: 3) advises that 'reintegration planning [be] fully coordinated with national recovery plans'.
65 Such frameworks can include, but are not limited to, Poverty Reduction Strategy Plans (PRSPs), UN Development Assistance Frameworks (UNDAFs) and national development plans. Ensuring that reintegration is adequately 'linked-up' with these mechanisms can be enhanced by accounting for related activities in Common Country Assessments (CCAs) and bilateral programming plans. See, for example, OECD (2008, forthcoming).
66 See, for example, World Bank Indonesia (2006).

Bibliography

Afako, B. (2003) 'Pursuing Peace in Northern Uganda: Lessons from Peace Initiatives', Commissioned by Civil Society Organizations for Peace in Northern Uganda. Kampala, May.

Allen, T. and Dowdon, R. (2007) *Project Magazine* (134), May.

Anderson, M. (1999) *Do No Harm: How Aid Can Support Peace – or War*, Boulder: Lynne Rienner.

Baaré, A. (2004) 'Development Aid as Third-party Intervention: A Case Study of the Uganda National Rescue Front II Peace Process', *Journal of Peacebuilding and Development* 2 (1): 21–36.

Baaré, A. (2006) 'An Analysis of Transitional Economic Reintegration', *Stockholm Initiative on Disarmament Demobilization and Reintegration Background Studies*, Ministry of Foreign Affairs, Sweden, 17–54.

Brahimi Report (1999) *Report of the Panel on United Nations Peace Operations* (A/54/1).

Brickhill, J. (2007) *Protecting Civilians through Peace Agreements. Challenges and Lessons of the Darfur Peace Agreement, ISS Paper 138.* Institute for Security Studies, South Africa.

Brown, S. (2007) 'Sustaining Positive Momentum in Northern Uganda', *US Government Public Statements*. Online, available at: northernuganda.usvpp.gov/momentum.html.

Buxton, J., Ginifer, J., Greene, O. and Muggah, R. (2006) *Options for Arms Management and DDR in Nepal: Lessons from Past Experience*, London: DfID and CICS.

Collier, P., Hoeffler, A., Elliot, L., Hegre, H., Reynal-Querol, M. and Sambanis, N. (2003) *Breaking the Conflict Trap: Civil War and Development Policy*, New York: Oxford University Press and the World Bank.

DPKO (2007) *Report on the First Workshop for Chiefs of DDR Sections in Missions*, Brindisi: UNLB, 25–29 July.

Duffield, M. (2001) *Global Governance and the New Wars: The Merging of Development and Security*, London: Zed Books.

Duffield, M. (2007) *Development, Security and Unending War Governing the World of Peoples*. London: Polity Press.

ECA (2006) *Analysis of Disarmament, Demobilization and Reintegration (DDR) Programs Existing in the World During 2005*, Barcelona: Escola de cultura de Pau.

Fisher, R. (2001) 'Methods of Third Party Intervention', *Berghof Handbook for Conflict Transformation*. Online, available at: www.berghof-handbook.net.

Goodhand, J. (2001) *Conflict Assessments – A Synthesis Report: Kyrgyzstan, Moldova, Nepal and Sri Lanka*, London: King's College.

Ghobarah, H., Huth, P. and Russett, B. (2003) 'Civil Wars Kill and Maim People – Long After the Shooting Stops', *American Political Science Review* 97 (2), May.

Harbom, B. and Wallensteen, P. (2007) 'Armed Conflict, 1989–2006', *Journal of Peace Research* 44 (5): 623–634.

HDC (Henri Dunant Centre) (2006) 'Negotiating Disarmament: Civilians, Guns and Peace Processes: Approaches and Possibilities', *Briefing Paper* 1. Geneva: HDC.

Hoeffler, A. and Reynal-Querol, M. (2003) *Measuring the Costs of Conflict*, Oxford: Center for the Studies of African Economies.

HSBA (Human Security Baseline Assessment) (2007) 'Responses to Pastoral Wars: A Review of Violence Reduction Efforts in Sudan, Uganda and Kenya', *Issue Brief* 8, Geneva: Small Arms Survey.

IRIN (2005) 'Sudan–Uganda: SPLM/A Leader Pledges to Help Ugandan Peace Effort', UNOCHA-IRIN report 31, January.

Keen, D. (1999) 'The Economic Functions of Violence in Civil Wars', *Adelphi Paper 320*, Oxford: Oxford University Press.

Kiplagat, B. (2002) Online, available at: www.c-r-org/our-work/accord/northern-uganda/-reaching-nairobi-agreement.php.

Moser, C. and McIlwaine, C. (2001) *Violence in a Post-Conflict Contexts*, Washington, DC: World Bank. Online, available at: wwwwds.worldbank.org/external/default/WDSContentServer/WDSP/IB/2001/12/11/000094946_01112104010285/Rendered/PDF/multi0page.pdf.

Muggah, R. (2004) 'The Anatomy of Disarmament, Demobilization and Reintegration in the Republic of Congo', *Journal of Conflict, Security and Development* 4 (1).

Muggah, R. (2005) 'No Magic Bullet: A Critical Perspective on Disarmament, Demobilization and Reintegration and Weapons Reduction during Post-Conflict', *The Commonwealth Journal of International Affairs* 94 (379).

Muggah, R. (2006) 'Emerging from the Shadow of War: DDR and Arms Reduction during Post-Conflict', *Journal of Contemporary Security Policy (Special Edition)* 25 (2).

Muggah, R. (2007) 'Great Expectations: (Dis)integrated DDR in Sudan and Haiti', *Humanitarian Practice Network* 40. London: ODI.

Muggah, R. (2008) 'Comparing DDR and Durable Solutions: Some Lessons from Ethiopia *Humanitarian Practice Network*, 39. London: ODI.

OECD (2005a) *Principles for Good International Engagement in Fragile States:*

Learning and Advisory Process on Difficult Partnerships (LAP), Paris. Online, available at: www.oecd.org/dataoecd/59/55/34700989.pdf.

OECD (2005b) *Security System Reform and Governance*, Paris. Online, available at: www.oecd.org/dataoecd/8/39/31785288.pdf.

OECD (2005c) *Preventing Conflict and Building Peace: A Manual of Issues and Entry Points*, Paris. Online, available at: www.oecd.org/dataoecd/26/3/35785584.pdf.

OECD (2006) *Evaluating Conflict Prevention and Peace-building Activities*, Norway. Online, available at: www.oecd.org/dataoecd/5/44/37500040.pdf.

OECD (2008, forthcoming) *Guidance on Preventing and Reducing Armed Violence*, Paris: OECD (by Small Arms Survey and SecDev Associates).

OECD-DAC (2001) *Guidelines on Helping Prevent Violent Conflict*, Paris. Online, available at: www.oecd.org/document/32/0,2340,en_2649_34567_33800800_1_1_1_1, 00.html DCD/DAC/CPDC(2007)2 31.

Patel, A. (ed.) (2008, forthcoming) *Transitional Justice and Disarmament, Demobilization and Reintegration (DDR)*, New York: International Centre for Transitional Justice.

Rodriguez, C. (2004) 'The Northern Uganda War: The "Small Conflict" that Became the World's Worst Humanitarian Crisis', *Health Policy and Development*, 2 (2) 81–84.

Small Arms Survey (2005) 'Post-Conflict: Considering DDR and Arms Reduction in the Aftermath of Conflict', *Small Arms Survey: Weapons at War*, Oxford: Oxford University Press.

Stockholm Initiative (2006) *Stockholm Initiative on Disarmament, Demobilization, Reintegration*. Online, available at: www.sweden.gov.se/sb/d/4890.

UNWG (2006) *Integrated Disarmament, Demobilization and Reintegration Standards (IDDRS)*. www.unddr.org/iddrs/.

Uganda Conflict Action Network (2005) 'Seizing the Ripe Moment for Peace in Northern Uganda', *Uganda-CAN Working Policy Paper no 1*. www.UGANDACAN.org.

World Bank Indonesia (2006) *GAM Reintegration Needs Assessment Enhancing Peace through Community-level Development Programming*. Manila: World Bank.

10 Transitional justice and DDR[1]

Ana Cutter Patel

Introduction

Since the mid-1980s, societies emerging from violent conflict or authoritarian rule have often chosen to confront the legacies of serious human rights abuses with transitional justice measures. Such interventions may include criminal prosecutions, truth commissions, reparations for victims and vetting or other forms of institutional reform. At the same time, programmes for DDR of combatants have become integral elements of peacemaking, peacekeeping and peacebuilding efforts. These two types of initiatives – one focused on justice and accountability for victims and the other on stability and former combatants – often coexist or overlap in the post-conflict period. Yet DDR programmes are seldom analysed, designed or implemented in relation to justice-oriented aims. Likewise, transitional justice mechanisms seldom articulate strategies for coordinating with DDR programmes.

While there is a growing body of research on DDR, there is little focused research that explores the specific connections between DDR and transitional justice. Rather, DDR programmes are often analysed in a vacuum, as if they had no implications for parallel efforts to achieve justice. An inability to better understand the relationships between DDR and transitional justice may frustrate the ability of traumatized societies to achieve both reintegration and justice (de Greiff and Duthie 2005). This chapter finds that DDR programmes potentially serve as an important first step in limiting violence by disarming large numbers of armed actors and disbanding illegal, dysfunctional or bloated military structures. The failure to remove the weapons from the hands of fighters and re-establish state control over the legitimate use of force may undermine security and the prospects for transitional justice. Conversely, DDR carried out in situations without recourse to, or coordination with, justice mechanisms can result in increased tensions and missed opportunities. These can include gross inequities between ex-combatants and victims that can foster resentment and impede long-term integration. But while there may be inherent tensions between these two types of initiatives, the long-term goals of both DDR and transitional justice measures are broadly analogous. With a moderate degree of cooperation and coordination, they may ultimately reinforce each other in positive ways.

Post-conflict countries in Africa witnessed some of the most renowned efforts in the emerging field of transitional justice. Examples include the South African Truth and Reconciliation Commission, the International Criminal Tribunal for Rwanda, the *gacaca* process in Rwanda, the Special Court for Sierra Leone, the Sierra Leone Truth and Reconciliation Commission and the first arrest warrants issued by the International Criminal Court (ICC) against political leaders and leaders of armed groups in Democratic Republic of the Congo (DRC), Sudan and Uganda.[2] Africa has also been the site of the greatest number of DDR operations (see Introduction, this volume). In considering recent experiences in Africa, this chapter seeks to simulate debate about the relationships between DDR and transitional justice. It draws primarily from a research project of the International Centre for Transitional Justice (ICTJ) entitled, 'Transitional Justice and Disarmament, Demobilization, and Reintegration'.[3]

The chapter is organized into three sections. The first provides an introduction to transitional justice and explores some of the shared aims and possible tensions with DDR. The second section presents an overview of the four primary approaches to transitional justice: prosecutions, truth-telling, reparations and institutional reform. It also provides a brief reference to the international law or norm that supports each mechanism and examines its relationship to DDR. The final section explores prospects for coordination between transitional justice efforts and DDR in specific areas or moments of the post-conflict or transitional period.

What is transitional justice?

Transitional justice focuses on the question of how societies transitioning from authoritarian rule to democracy, or from war to peace, address a history of massive human rights abuse. It is concerned primarily with gross violations understood as torture, summary executions, forced disappearances, slavery and prolonged arbitrary detention, as well as certain 'international crimes', including genocide, crimes against humanity and serious violations of the laws and customs applicable in armed conflicts, whether of a national or international character (Freeman 2003). Transitional justice refers to the range of approaches that societies use to contribute to a holistic sense of justice for all citizens, to establish or renew civic trust, to reconcile people and communities and to prevent future abuses.

What distinguishes transitional justice as a distinct discipline within the broader field of human rights? First, transitional justice focuses on legacies of past human rights violations and international crimes. While the main approaches to transitional justice – prosecutions, truth-seeking initiatives, reparations and institutional reform – feature forward-looking aims such as building trust between and among victims, citizens and institutions, these mechanisms are primarily concerned with accountability for mass atrocities committed during a specific period of time in the past. Second, transitional justice advocates do not 'argue for retroactive justice at any cost' (ibid.: 1). There is an understanding that in transitional societies the demand for justice must be balanced against the need for peace, democracy, equitable development and the rule of law. Third, transitional justice emphasizes the need for a comprehensive approach. The different measures of transitional justice are not meant to be implemented in isolation, but to complement each other. Fourth, transitional justice aims for a victim-sensitive approach. Mark Freeman (2003: 1–2) states that the 'legitimacy of transitional justice mechanisms is measured by the extent to which victims oppose or support them, and the degree to which they are able to participate in and benefit from them'.

Is it worth examining the relationships between transitional justice and DDR at all? In Africa, the answer appears to be yes. In the last 20 years, there were at least 11 UN peacekeeping operations in Africa in which the DDR of combatants was included in the mandate. In seven of these, there was also some form of an internationally assisted transitional justice process.[4] There are good reasons to anticipate a rise in post-conflict situations where DDR processes and transitional justice initiatives will coexist. At the outset, the likelihood of DDR operations to continue is comparatively high (see Introduction, this volume). In 2002, UN Secretary-General Kofi Annan stated in a report to the Security Council that DDR 'has repeatedly proved to be vital to stabilizing a post-conflict situation' (UN 2000b: 1). Likewise, there have been significant advances in international norms and standards relating to transitional justice, particularly regarding amnesties, accountability, the right to truth and the right to reparation. Transitioning states are increasingly using transitional justice mechanisms to address past human rights violations – a trend characterized as a 'revolution in accountability' (Sriram 2003). In many cases, international and domestic advocates for accountability are asserting their claims earlier in the peace process. In Liberia and Sierra Leone, for example, transitional justice initiatives were implemented during the final stages of DDR, leading to an overlap between DDR programmes and transitional justice mechanisms. The establishment of the ICC provides yet another accountability forum where DDR and transitional justice imperatives are likely to become ever more interconnected. The ICC warrants for armed actors and government representatives in the DRC, Sudan and Uganda, for example, were presented in the context of ongoing DDR efforts in all three countries (see Chapter 9, this volume).

The relationship between DDR and transitional justice is important to consider not just because they overlap in a practical sense, but because they share the same long-term aims for peace and reconciliation. According to the UN, the aims of transitional justice are to ensure accountability, serve justice and achieve reconciliation (UN 2005). The guarantee of the non-recurrence of mass atrocities and the prevention of human rights violations and international crimes is recognized as the 'first imperative' of justice efforts (UN 2006b). The establishment or renewal of civic trust is also an important complementary objective of transitional justice. By way of comparison, the UN (2006b) integrated standards for DDR (IDDRS) defines such processes as a means of increasing security, re-establishing state control over the use of force, preventing renewed violence, encouraging trust and confidence and reconciliation. Trust-building, the prevention of renewed violence and reconciliation therefore emerge as essential objectives for both types of processes.

Interactions between transitional justice and DDR, limited as they may be, tend to be more ad hoc and reactionary than proactive or collaborative. Few cases in Africa exhibit any clear institutional relationship between transitional justice initiatives and DDR programmes. There are likely multiple explanations for this lack of institutional linkage. For instance, it may arise from the tendency to approach DDR, particularly disarmament and demobilization, narrowly as a technical military exercise with fewer implications for economic, justice or social transformation (see Chapter 8, this volume). Likewise, DDR processes and transitional justice initiatives have very different constituencies: DDR programmes are overseen in large part by military entities and are directed primarily at ex-combatants while transitional justice initiatives are advanced by legal entities with a focus more on the victims and the human rights violations suffered by victims. Predictably, these constituencies exhibit different objectives, particularly with respect to accountability: victims seek it, while ex-combatants for the most part seek to minimize or reduce it. In some cases, the different timings of DDR and transitional justice delimit the forging of more formal institutional interconnections. Disarmament and demobilization components of DDR are frequently initiated during a ceasefire, or immediately after a peace agreement is signed; national transitional justice initiatives often require the forming of a new government and some kind of legislative approval, which can delay implementation by months or, not uncommonly, years.

This lack of coordination between the two processes yields unbalanced outcomes and missed opportunities. One potential outcome, for example, is that many victims receive markedly less attention and resources than ex-combatants. The inequity is most apparent when comparing benefits for ex-combatants with reparations for victims. The annual overview of DDR programmes undertaken by the Escola de Cultura de Pau, for example, found that of the 22 countries worldwide featuring DDR programmes in 2006, not one had implemented a reparations initiative for victims. In terms of missed opportunities, information is rarely shared between DDR and transitional justice processes. While sharing information about ex-combatants with a prosecutions process may be problematic, certain kinds of information could be shared with truth-seeking initiatives, for example, to contribute to the creation of a historical record of the conflict (de Greiff 2007a).

Approaches to transitional justice

It is useful to review the four main mechanisms of transitional justice and the prospects for institutional synergies with DDR. Prosecutions, truth commissions, reparations and institutional reform and related issues of local justice and reconciliation initiatives as well as justice for women are all considered in the following section. For each mechanism, a quick summary of the relevant international law, norms and standards is offered together with an exploration of their relationships to DDR.

Prosecutions and amnesties

The first broad category of transitional justice approaches consists of prosecutions – i.e. conducting of a criminal trial in a court against a person suspected of human rights violations or international crimes.[5] The form, function and mandate of a prosecutions process can vary widely. They can be wide in scope, aiming to try as many people as possible for their involvement in human rights crimes, or they can be narrow, focusing on leaders and those most responsible for crimes and violations. International human rights law creates an obligation for governments to investigate human rights crimes. The law establishes the duty to put an end to impunity[6] and states that governments:

> [s]hall undertake prompt, thorough, independent and impartial investigations of violations of human rights and international humanitarian law and take appropriate measures in respect of the perpetrators, particularly in the area of criminal justice, by ensuring that those responsible for serious crimes under international law are prosecuted, tried, and duly punished.[7]

Criminal punishment through prosecutions is considered by many to be the most effective insurance against future human rights violations. These proceedings aim to create a deterrent effect, to offer public denunciation of criminal behaviour and to provide a direct and individual form of accountability for perpetrators. They also seek to contribute to increased confidence of victims in the government's willingness to implement the law. The achievement of these aims can be hindered by a number of factors. In post-conflict contexts, prosecutions can face stiff obstacles such as inadequate human or financial resources, a corrupt or weak judicial sector, a perception of victor's justice and the logistical challenges of contending with a potential pool of victims and perpetrators numbering in the hundreds, thousands, or hundreds of thousands.

Amnesties, which effectively grant immunity to a designated group of people for a certain class of offences, also play a critical role in either eliminating prosecutions as an option or shaping a prosecutions strategy. There are many different kinds of amnesties, from those referred to as blanket amnesties, which grant a very broad scope of immunity for all criminal acts and human rights crimes to all combatants, to more narrow ones, which grant immunity for lower level crimes such as illegal possession of a weapon. For peace mediators amnesty is considered a critical tool in bringing the different parties of a conflict to the negotiating table and convincing combatants to disarm and demobilize (Freeman 2008).

Broad amnesties, however, are often undesirable from a transitional justice viewpoint because they can violate victims' right of redress, and can be inconsistent with a state's obligation under international law to punish perpetrators of human rights crimes. Broad amnesties can undermine the law's function as a deterrent against crime and create the impression that human rights crimes can be committed with impunity. Victims tend to view such amnesties with disillusionment and cynicism, and in response may be motivated to take the law into their own hands. In his 2004 report on transitional justice, UN Secretary-General Kofi Annan noted that there is a 'growing shift in the international community, away from a tolerance for impunity and amnesty and towards the creation of an international rule of law' (UN 2004: 14). The Secretary-General's Report rejects:

> any endorsement of amnesty for genocide, war crimes, or crimes against humanity, including those relating to ethnic, gender and sexually based international crimes, and ensures that no such amnesty previously granted is a bar to prosecution before any United Nations-created or assisted court.
>
> (UN 2004:14)

As nation states have the primary responsibility to pursue accountability, domestic court systems are the preferred venue for addressing human rights violations. Domestic prosecutions processes are more likely to strengthen local prosecutorial capacity and are generally more accountable and locally credible from a victim perspective. Yet in post-conflict situations, the domestic court system is often in ruins. Thus important options are international or 'internationalized' courts. The creation of international or hybrid tribunals in situations where national actors are unwilling or unable to prosecute alleged perpetrators is a revolutionary step in establishing accountability for human rights violations and international crimes.[8] Beyond the ICC there are two such tribunals operating in Africa: the International Criminal Tribunal for Rwanda (UN 1994) and the Special Court for Sierra Leone (UN 2000a).

The pursuit of accountability through trials is often seen as the transitional justice measure most in tension with DDR efforts. The concern is that the threat of prosecution will derail ceasefire or peace agreements, deter combatants from entering a DDR programme, and/or inhibit the effort to reintegrate former fighters into communities. Some tension between prosecutions processes and DDR may be inherent, as DDR requires the cooperation of ex-combatants, while prosecutors seek to hold the war criminals among them accountable for their actions during the conflict. Even so, bad or partial information about prosecutions efforts can further contribute to this tension. Ex-combatants are often uninformed of the mandate of a prosecutions process and oblivious to the basic tenets of international humanitarian law. They may assume that all war crimes will be prosecuted or that all ex-combatants will face arrest.

As a result, DDR administrators often seek to isolate the DDR process from ongoing prosecutions efforts. In Rwanda, for example, the Demobilization and Reintegration Commission refused to give investigators from the International Criminal Tribunal for Rwanda access to its demobilization camps. One of the Rwandan commissioners stated: 'for us, when they [ex-combatants] come, we assume everyone is innocent'.[9] A similar incident occurred in Sierra Leone, where, after receiving permission from the National Committee for Disarmament, Demobilization and Reintegration, the Special Court Working Group attempted to visit ex-combatants in cantonment to explain the mandate of the Special Court. Representatives of the working group were driven out of the camp by a Nigerian captain representing the Economic Community of West African States (ECOWAS) who feared that any discussion of the Special Court for Sierra Leone might influence ex-combatants to refuse to continue their participation in the DDR process.[10]

Prosecutions may exert a particularly negative effect on efforts to demobilize or release children associated with armed forces and groups (CAAFG). While international law does not prohibit children under the age of 18 accused of human rights crimes to be prosecuted in a court of law, it also calls on governments to look for alternatives. Children require special treatment because they are often forcibly recruited or volunteer under coercion or without a clear understanding of what their service will require. Depending on the context and the individual case, there may be more appropriate transitional justice measures than prosecutions for addressing child perpetrators.

Importantly, prosecutions may also make positive contributions to DDR. While the mandates of prosecutors and DDR administrators are probably most at odds during disarmament and demobilization, prosecutions may sometimes aid these phases of DDR by removing (real and potential) spoilers from the process. For instance, many people believe that the indictment of Liberian President Charles Taylor by the Special Court for Sierra Leone in 2003 allowed for the successful conclusion of the Accra peace process and the start of the DDR process in Liberia (see Chapter 3, this volume).

The experiences of several recent post-conflict countries reveal that there may in fact be greater potential for harmony between transitional justice and DDR during the reintegration phase. This is particularly the case where prosecution mandates are limited to top-level offenders, as was the case in Sierra Leone. Prosecutions can reduce the culture of impunity that often surrounds ex-combatants and therefore help contribute to the consolidation of the rule of law. They may also serve to individualize the guilt of specific perpetrators and therefore lessen the public perception that all ex-combatants are guilty of human rights crimes, thereby reducing stigmatization and potentially facilitating the reintegration process. Providing communities with some assurance that the worst perpetrators of human rights crimes are not benefiting from the DDR may enhance the prospects for trust between ex-combatants and other citizens.

Truth commissions

In an increasing number of transitional countries, local actors have begun to emphasize non-judicial truth-seeking measures as a means of accountability and a contribution to trust-building and reconciliation. These have often taken the form of truth commissions – official local or national inquiries into patterns of past abuse that seek to establish an accurate historical record of events. Truth commissions employ investigations and hearings to this end, often identifying the individuals and institutions responsible for abuse, the patterns of human rights violations, and the enabling conditions for abuse. Truth-seeking bodies frequently feature a relationship with other transitional justice measures such as prosecutions and reparations and are frequently empowered to make recommendations for national policy. It is the right of all people to know the truth, and the state has responsibility in giving effect to this right to know. According to the UN's *Updated Set of Principles for the Protection and Promotion of Human Rights through Action to Combat Impunity*:

> [e]very people has the inalienable right to know the truth about past events concerning the perpetration of heinous crimes and about the circumstances and reasons that led, through massive or systematic violations, to the perpetration of those crimes. Full and effective exercise of the right to the truth provides a vital safeguard against the recurrence of violations.[11]

Ex-combatants may also perceive truth-seeking initiatives as a threat. In Sierra Leone, for example, the concurrence of a tribunal and a truth commission generated considerable misunderstanding. Ex-combatants assumed that testimony taken by the Truth and Reconciliation Commission (TRC) would be handed over to the prosecutor of the Special Court. Civil society efforts to provide information to ex-combatants did help increase their understanding of the separate mandates of each institution. Alternatively truth-seeking initiatives may be regarded as an opportunity for ex-combatants to tell their side of the story and/or an opportunity to apologize. In some cases, truth-seeking efforts, with a sufficient public information and outreach capacity, could help break down rigid representations of victims and perpetrator by allowing perpetrators to tell their own stories of victimization and by exploring and identifying the structural roots of violent conflict.

In Sierra Leone, all parties to the Lomé peace agreement, including the national government and the rebel forces of the Revolutionary United Front (RUF), backed the establishment of a TRC, which began operations in 2002.[12] Ex-combatants there had a 'great deal of hope in the TRC to act as an effective and essential mechanism for promoting reconciliation' (PRIDE 2002: 16). Support for the TRC amongst ex-combatants rose from 53 to 85 per cent after ex-combatants understood its design and purpose, while those who believed it would bring reconciliation rose from 52 to 84 per cent. As one former combatant explained, the truth 'will help families and victims forgive us' (ibid.: 12). For those ex-combatants who were found guilty of committing a human rights crime, the TRC offered an opportunity to take responsibility for their actions. According to one report: 'They want to confess to the TRC because they think it will enable them to return to their communities (ibid.: 13).

Often, however, ex-combatants (who in some cases have experienced extreme victimization) are reluctant to identify themselves as victims. In South Africa, for example, ex-combatant participation in that country's TRC was limited primarily to the amnesty hearings – relatively few made statements as victims of abuse or were given a chance to testify at victim hearings. As a result, many of these victims (ex-combatants) were marginalized. Ex-combatants in South Africa, for instance, expressed a sense that 'they had been left out of the process' (Gear 2002). Such marginalization may hinder successful reintegration.

Reparations

Reparations refer to attempts to provide direct benefits to victims. These benefits can include a wide variety of goods such as direct cash payments to victims or to their families, access to medical treatment and access to education benefits. Reparations programmes aim to present either material or symbolic benefits to victims of certain types of crimes through individual or collective distribution. Such initiatives generally have two goals: first, to provide a measure of recognition for victims and their losses; and, second, to encourage trust among citizens and particularly between citizens and the state, by demonstrating that past abuses are regarded seriously by the new government. Reparations programmes are also the only transitional justice measure enacted primarily for the benefit of victims, rather than against perpetrators of human rights crimes (de Greiff 2006: 2).[13]

Reparations for victims of human rights crimes can contribute to the reintegration efforts of a DDR programme by reducing the resentment victims and communities may feel in the aftermath of violent conflict. The absence of reparations in the context of a DDR programme can add to the perception that ex-combatants are receiving special treatment (de Greiff 2007a). In Sierra Leone, for example, radio phone-ins received comments full of resentment, such as, 'those who ruined us are being given the chance to become better persons financially, academically, and skills-wise' (Ginifer 2003: 46).

Generally, programmes for ex-combatants and reparations programmes for victims are developed in isolation of each other. Reinsertion assistance is offered to demobilized combatants in order to assist with their resettlement – to get them home and provide them with a start toward establishing a livelihood – alongside longer-term support for reintegration.[14] Support to ex-combatants is motivated by a concern that without such assistance ex-combatants will become frustrated and threaten the peace process. The result is that ex-combatants participating in DDR often receive aid in the form of cash, counselling, skills training, education opportunities, access to micro-credit loans and/or land, while, in most cases victims of human rights violations receive nothing (de Greiff 2007a).

The 2002–2007 DDR programme in Rwanda financed by the World Bank, for example, had a budget of US$53.7 million. Ex-combatants received reinsertion and reintegration benefits including cash payments of between US$150 to US$2,000 each according to their rank and affiliation.[15] More than a decade after the genocide the government has yet to create a compensation fund for genocide survivors that it committed to in 1998. Representatives of survivors' organizations express bitterness about the lack of reparations, as do individual survivors. A representative of a genocide widows' association stated that 'the government says it is poor, but that doesn't satisfy us. [The absence of reparations] is killing us a second time' (Waldorf 2008: 13).

Institutional reform

Institutional reform to prevent serious abuses from recurring constitutes an important element of transitional justice. Such reforms aim to prevent violent conflict and human rights crimes by eliminating or transforming the structural conditions that gave rise to them in the first place. While institutional reform frequently includes skills training, supplying resources and increasing organizational efficiency; institutional reform that aims to prevent human rights abuse would also include efforts to increase the legitimacy of the institution through activities such as 'vetting, structural reform to provide accountability, build independence, ensure representation, and increase responsiveness, as well as verbal and symbolic measures that reaffirm a commitment to overcome the legacy of abuse and an endorsement of democratic values and norms' (Mayer-Rieckh 2007). Given that systematic human rights violations are primarily carried out by state security forces or (non-state) armed groups, the relationship between transitional justice, DDR and security sector reform (SSR) are especially critical areas.

The UN's *Updated Set of Principles on Combating Impunity*, provide a normative framework for institutional reform. They observe that: '[s]tates must take all necessary measures, including legislative and administrative reforms, to ensure that public institutions are organised in a manner that ensures respect for the rule of law and protection of human rights.'[16] Likewise, SSR offers a template for institutional reform. SSR entails the 'transformation of the security system – which includes all actors, their roles, responsibilities and actions – working together to manage and operate the system in a manner that is more consistent with democratic norms and sound principles of good governance'.

In theory, SSR seeks to provide efficient and effective state and human-centred security within a framework of democratic governance. It is concerned with re-establishing the state's legitimate control over the use force and addressing both physical and human capability deficits. From a justice perspective, SSR should also aim to build the integrity of the security system, promote its legitimacy and empower citizens in order to transform an overall abusive system into one that both respects and protects human rights (Mayer-Rieckh 2006). Vetting procedures, for example, can screen current and new members of the armed forces, some of whom may come from the armed groups that fought the war, for their possible implication in human rights violations or international crimes.

DDR is intrinsically connected to SSR. For example, decisions concerning the overall caseload of combatants to be demobilized, as well as those relating to who will be kept on or eligible for reconstituted security forces, sets important parameters for SSR. Furthermore, criteria for entry into a DDR programme, and the manner in which employment choices are presented to ex-combatants, may provide incentives or disincentives for reintegration in the armed forces. Such choices can potentially affect the representation of women or minorities in the security sector.

The fact remains, however, that in practice, DDR programmes often operate alongside, but without a connection to, SSR initiatives. This lack of coordination or cohesion can lead to the reappointment of human rights abusers into a fragile, albeit legitimate, security sector. For example, in Uganda, Taban Amin, the son of the former dictator, was named as an alleged perpetrator of human rights crimes. He was then provided with amnesty under the Ugandan Amnesty Act, which shields him from future prosecutions. He was consequently offered a position in the Ugandan security forces. Such cases undermine public faith in security sector institutions, and can also lead to distrust within the armed forces.

Local justice and reconciliation

Locally-occurring processes of justice and reconciliation ranging from informal courts to traditional ceremonies have taken place in countries such as Rwanda, Sierra Leone, Mozambique and Uganda. Such processes are often referred to colloquially as 'restorative justice'. According to Maiese (2003), restorative justice involves victims and communities directly in defining the responsibilities and obligations of offenders. Roger Duthie (2006 and 2008, forthcoming) argues that, 'while local justice and reconciliation processes do contain elements of restorative justice ... they also overlap with the functions of other transitional justice measures – prosecuting or punishing perpetrators, making reparations to victims, truth-telling, and institutional reform'. These local processes are regularly used to promote trust between ex-combatants and their communities. In Mozambique, for example, 'cleansing ceremonies' offered ex-combatants a way to reintegrate into communities by renouncing violence, acknowledging wrong-doing, and providing victims, or families of victims, with some kind of compensation (Lundin 2007).

Local processes can be more efficient in dealing with large numbers of perpetrators even though they also generate certain contradictions. The community-based nature of these processes renders them potentially more accessible and (locally) legitimate than other externally-imposed transitional justice measures. Locally planned and managed processes can be a particularly appropriate alternative to criminal prosecutions for certain groups, including child combatants. They can also be problematic. For example, local processes frequently operate outside of formal or 'modern' legal systems and thus do not always respect national or international legal and human rights standards, including standards of due process (Duthie 2008, forthcoming). Likewise as noted by Lars Waldorf (2008a), these local processes are often not equipped to handle more serious human rights violations such as war crimes, crimes against humanity, or genocide. For example, before the 1994 genocide, traditional *gacaca* courts in Rwanda involved mostly civil matters. Finally, local processes can often replicate gender or other biases that are present in community life and traditions (Amnesty International 2001: 39–45; Waldorf 2008).

The locally-based transitional justice mechanism underway in Rwanda offers up a paradigmatic case. Some 11,000 community courts (*gacaca*)[17] were launched in 2002 in order to try low-level suspects of genocidal acts. In contrast to the strategies of amnesty or selective prosecution selected by other countries in Africa faced with large perpetrator populations, the Rwandan government opted to pursue accountability through community courts. According to *Gacaca Law 2004*, government prosecutors will investigate the charges made in *gacaca* courts before transferring the files to national courts for trial (Waldorf 2008c, forthcoming).

The early outcomes of the *gacacas* are astonishing. Nearly 800,000 Rwandans have already been accused before these courts, including high-ranking officials. But the state's intent to prosecute these genocide suspects appears to contradict the objectives of a simultaneous DDR programme that reintegrated over 54,000 ex-combatants since 1995. Oddly, the risk of prosecution (by the *gacaca*) is not considered a threat by combatants and ex-combatants (Waldorf 2008b, forthcoming). There are two possible reasons for this. It is conceivable that those involved in *gacaca* differentiate between wartime killing and genocidal killing.[18] It is also possible that with the immense backlog of cases, ex-combatants are sceptical that the allegations made in *gacaca* courts will ever really come to trial. Even government officials admit that it will be impossible to arrest and try 800,000 people. More controversially, perhaps the tension between DDR and criminal accountability is less important than is commonly assumed (Waldorf 2008c, forthcoming).

Justice for women

The relationship between transitional justice and DDR has particular implications for women that transect the different approaches highlighted above. In the case of DDR, women are often not included in peace negotiations and their particular interests are usually marginalized from the political processes in which the parameters for DDR programmes are established. Narrow definitions of what constitutes a combatant and related identification criterion during the screening and registration of beneficiaries can restrict women's participation. In Sierra Leone and other countries, for example, the criteria for participation in DDR included possession of a gun (see Chapters 2 and 3, this volume). But female combatants either shared a gun with others, or were ordered by their commanders to give their guns to male combatants prior to the DDR process effectively disqualifying them from involvement. The imposition of (unintentionally) restrictive criteria may have long-term economic, political, social and legal repercussions, and often exclude or marginalize women (Specht 2006).

There are many subtle ways that women are excluded from DDR processes. In addition to negligent selection criteria for disarmament, cantonment sites during the demobilization phase often lack tailored facilities to meet the needs of women and girls. As a result, many females simply do not participate because of the absence of childcare services and issues relating to physical security or forced labour. Women combatants, supporters and dependents generally have not equally benefited from the entitlements – whether cash incentives, health-care, training, travel remittance, small business grants or housing support – that flow to their male counterparts. The result is that most women and girls particip-ate in DDR in much lower numbers than their actual forces (UNIFEM 2004). Women also face specific challenges with respect to reintegration. In some cases, women and men are encouraged to act out similar roles as part of an armed group, and then, post-conflict, women are expected to resume their tradi-tional roles in their community. Women frequently will not reveal their past experience as ex-combatants for fear of associated stigmatization and marginal-ization in their communities of 'return'. Likewise, women ex-combatants may receive less support from their families, suffer from a lack of education/ opportunity, and have to support children (Farr 2002; Mazurana *et al.* 2002; UNWG 2006: Module 5.10).

The failure of transitional justice measures to adequately incorporate a spe-cific focus on women may equally undermine the reintegration of ex-combatants and reinforce gender biases. Side-stepping gender-based violence committed by soldiers, while providing them with immediate DDR benefits, for example, can foster resentment among civilian victims. It can result in victims of gender-based violence going without assistance or redress that may be required to rein-tegrate into society. Furthermore, justice measures that are designed and implemented without concern for the implications for women may overlook such issues as the tension between acknowledging gender-based violence and the potential stigma and rejection that victims of such crimes may face in their communities (Mazurana *et al.* 2002: 119). Finally, transitional justice measures seldom consider the multiple roles of women in conflict. It is important, for example, that transitional justice measures acknowledge women not only as victims, but also in some cases as perpetrators, thereby challenging traditional gender biases (Farr 2002: 17).

Prospects for coordination

This chapter argues that concerted efforts to enhance coordination between tran-sitional justice and DDR can reinforce the aims and outcomes of both processes. A particular challenge is to understand how transitional justice and DDR can interact positively in the short-term in ways that, at a minimum, do not obstruct their respective objectives of accountability and stability. An emphasis on coordination and developing a shared language between transitional justice and DDR practitioners should, however, aim beyond that minimum. Practical efforts should be undertaken to constructively connect these two processes in ways that contribute to a stable, just peace in the long term. This section explores a few possible entry points for increased coordination. It focuses specifically on the prospects for coordinating legal frameworks, particularly during the design and implementation of DDR programmes and transitional justice measures. It also considers ways of enhancing their respective outreach strategies and prospects for integrating reintegration and reconciliation efforts.

Legal frameworks

The objectives and design of both DDR and transitional justice may be shaped during peace negotiations. It may also be guided by specific national legislation and during the preparation of analogous components of the legal framework regulating post-conflict situations, such as agreement about legal administration while a country is under some type of transitional authority.[19] When both types of initiatives are stipulated in a peace agreement, even if not explicitly connected by the parties to the conflict, a relationship between the two is necessarily created. Amnesties negotiated during a peace agreement, for example, can (unintentionally) limit the options for transitional justice, hindering the prospects for criminal prosecutions. They may also inadvertently increase the importance of non-judicial measures such as truth commissions and institutional reform.

While formal connections between transitional justice and DDR in peace agreements are limited in practice, a more opportunistic approach could harness synergies. Targeted amnesties for lower-level combatants, for example, can act as an incentive for their participation in demobilization while still allowing for prosecution of those (senior officers) most responsible for human rights crimes. For example, ex-combatants in Sierra Leone supported the work of the Special Court for Sierra Leone in part because of its promise to focus on those bearing the greatest responsibility for the violation of human rights and international crimes. Identifying an obligation to provide reparations for victims as part of a peace agreement could also comprise an important way to acknowledge the need to address the violations victims have suffered, and may reduce their resentment of the immediate benefits provided to ex-combatants through DDR. Conditionality is another way in which transitional justice measures and DDR programmes can be connected through the legal framework. For example, DDR benefits can be denied to ex-combatants accused of human rights crimes, or their access to those benefits could be conditional on their cooperation with transitional justice measures. Alternatively, combatants who have committed crimes can be offered a reduced penalty in exchange for demobilizing themselves and their unit as was being attempted in Colombia (see Chapter 1, this volume).

Design and implementation

The design and implementation of DDR and transitional justice measures in the early post-conflict period can also shape prospects for coordination. During the demobilization and reinsertion process, for example, DDR programmes can accommodate screening procedures for ex-combatants accused of human rights crimes. Screening, however, could also deter combatants from entering the DDR programme as they may fear it is a first step towards prosecution. Consideration may be given to how the design of the DDR process relates to the long-term goals of the SSR process, for example, by creating incentives or disincentives for ex-combatants, particularly women and minorities, to reintegrate into the security sector and vetting potential recruits on the basis of human rights criteria. DDR administrators and prosecutors could also collaborate more effectively in terms of sequencing their efforts. Prosecutors, for instance, can agree to delay the announcement of indictments of certain commanders until disarmament and demobilization operations have progressed beyond a pre-determined period.

The design and disbursements of reintegration benefits for ex-combatants through the DDR programme can also be sequenced with reparation initiatives. Assistance offered to ex-combatants is less likely to foster resentment if reparations for victims are provided at a comparative level and within the same relative time period. Similarly, truth commissions can include special outreach services to ex-combatants and extend efforts to recognize their varied experience as both perpetrators and victims. Particular attention could also be devoted to creating safe spaces for women and children associated with armed groups, who in some cases can be viewed as victims and perpetrators, to participate in the truth telling process.

Ultimately, both transitional justice and DDR measures can make a significant commitment to justice for women. DDR programmes can elaborate criteria for eligibility that allow women associated with armed groups and forces to take advantage of the benefits offered and increase efforts to protect them during disarmament and demobilization processes. Recruitment strategies that are explicitly inclusive of women and minorities (through, for example, quota systems) may yield a more representative security sector, while a lack of investment in this area may generate the opposite effect. On the side of transitional justice, prosecution strategies can select cases that reinforce the criminalization of rape and violence against women. Truth commissions can also potentially dedicate specific resources to create safe spaces for women to testify and provide information about the specific experience of women associated with armed groups and forces.

Information and outreach

Both DDR and transitional justice initiatives engage in gathering, sharing and disseminating information. Even so, information is seldom adequately shared in a systematic, transparent or coherent manner. Socio-economic and background data gathered through DDR programmes from ex-combatants could potentially be very useful for broader efforts to pursue transitional justice. In terms of sharing information with prosecutions processes, however, the risk of hindering the disarmament and demobilization of ex-combatants may be greater than the potential value of the information itself. There are arguably more possibilities for sharing certain kinds of data with truth commissions. Truth commissions often try to reliably describe broad patterns of past violence. Insights into the size, location and territory of armed groups, their command structures and recruitment processes, could assist in reconstructing an historical 'memory' of past patterns of collective violence. Such information generates fewer legal and ethical concerns than case-specific information provided by individual combatants.

The dissemination of information through outreach activities are crucial tasks of both DDR and transitional justice. Poor coordination in public outreach can lead to information asymmetries and generate conflicting and partial messages and rumour. In Liberia, for example, many ex-combatants expressed confusion about the mandate of the Special Court for Sierra Leone, which is limited to crimes committed in Sierra Leone, and decided not to participate in the DDR process because of fear of prosecution (see Chapter 3, this volume).[20] Increased consultation and coordination concerning what and how information is released to the public may, alternatively, reduce the spread of misinformation and reinforce the objectives of both transitional justice and DDR.

Reintegration and reconciliation

Reintegration and reconciliation are frequently the most neglected areas of both DDR and transitional justice (see Introduction, this volume). Paradoxically, they also offer amongst the best prospects for enhanced coordination between both sectors. During DDR programmes, far greater attention and resources are directed toward disarmament and demobilization. Considerably less emphasis is placed on preparing a coherent and long-term strategy and implementation of activities to support reintegration. In the rush to provide 'support', communities are not adequately consulted or prepared for the return of ex-combatants and the absorptive capacities of recipient communities are often unable to sustain integration.

Likewise, transitional justice initiatives too often focus on the short-term process of administering justice without sufficient investment in the impact of related processes on the ultimate goal of reconciliation. Despite claims to the contrary, transitional justice is often dispensed in a top-down fashion with limited information available or outreach to the public that explains about how justice and reconciliation will prevail at a local level.[21] For example, assessment of tribunals such as the ICTR, find that few nationals are actively involved in the trial process except for a handful who come as witnesses; and that the tribunal is invisible to most of the Rwandan population (ICG 2001).

Reconciliation can be defined as a function of the level of trust that exists between and among citizens and government. Trust involves more than relying on a person to do or refrain from doing certain things; it also involves the expectation of a commitment to shared norms and values (de Greiff 2004). DDR programmes seek to build civic trust between ex-combatants, society and the state. This is however, a 'thin' trust. As described by Pablo de Greiff:

> the sense of trust at issue here is not the thick form of trust characteristic of relationship between intimates, but rather, a thin disposition between

strangers that can be characterized initially as non-hostile disposition that contrasts not just with its direct opposite, but with one that puts a premium on surveillance and the threat of sanctions.

(2007a)

Transitional justice initiatives also aim to build trust between victims, society and the state. Unfortunately both DDR and transitional justice enterprises are hindered by poorer than expected implementation. Concepts of 'community-centred' reintegration may offer an alternative model to current focuses that tend to be individual- or ex-combatant-specific. Such approaches may also offer a bridge to link the claims and needs of ex-combatants with those of victims, together with those of the communities where they reside. At the very least, increased consultation with victims' groups, communities receiving demobilized combatants, municipal governments, faith-based organizations and the demobilized combatants and their families can inform and strengthen the legitimacy of DDR and transitional justice processes. The Stockholm Initiative for Disarmament, Demobilization, and Reintegration (SIDDR) proposes an approach to reintegration that includes a multi-donor trust fund with two targets: one committed to on the reintegration of ex-combatants and another dedicated to the needs of the recipient communities.[22]

This chapter offered a general treatment of the relationships between DDR and transitional justice. It proposes that while tensions may exist between the short-term goals of transitional justice processes and DDR in the immediate aftermath of conflict, both interventions share a common goal – the reestablishment of trust and the prevention of renewed violent conflict. Increasing awareness among practitioners about these shared aims, developing a shared language, working towards a minimum goal to do no intentional harm, and identifying possibilities for increased collaboration and communication, may successfully reinforce the goals of both.

Notes

1 This chapter builds on and draws from the research proposal for Transitional Justice and Disarmament, Demobilization, and Reintegration (DDR), written by Pablo de Greiff and Roger Duthie of the International Center for Transitional Justice (ICTJ).
2 The ICC is currently prosecuting political leaders and leaders of armed groups in the DRC, Sudan and Uganda: *The Prosecutor* v. *Thomas Lubanga Dyilo*, ICC-01/04–01/06; *The Prosecutor* v. *Ahmad Muhammad Harun ('Ahmad Harun') and Ali Muhammad Ali Abd-Al-Rahman ('Ali Kushayb')*, ICC-02/05–01/07 and; *The Prosecutor* v. *Joseph Kony, Vincent Otti, Okot Odhiambo and Dominic Ongwen*, ICC-02/04–01/05.
3 The ICTJ project explores the manifold ways in which DDR programmes and transitional justice measures may contribute to, or hinder, the achievement of the other's aims, including the prospects for a sustainable peace, through the elaboration of ten country case studies and eight thematic papers. The African examples referred to throughout the chapter are also included as country case studies developed for the ICTJ project. An edited volume of the research is forthcoming in 2008.
4 These seven UN missions include: United Nations Assistance Mission for Rwanda

(UNAMIR 1993), United Nations Assistance Mission in Sierra Leone (UNAMSIL 1999), The United Nations Organization Mission in the Democratic Republic of Congo (MONUC 1999), the United Nations Mission in Liberia (UNMIL 2003), the United Nations Operation in Burundi (UNOB 2004), and the United Nations Mission in the Sudan (UNMIS 2005). This information was gathered from the UN Department of Peacekeeping website at www.unddr.org/partners.php?id=5.

5 For the purposes of this paper, 'human rights crimes' is used to refer to 'gross human rights violations' and 'international crimes'.

6 See Commission on Human Rights Resolution on Impunity, UN Doc. E/CN.4/ RES/2005/81.

7 *Updated Set of Principles for the Protection and Promotion of Human Rights through Action to Combat Impunity*, UN Doc. E/CN.4/2005/102/Ad.1, Principle 32. [Hereinafter updated set of Principles on Combating Impunity.]

8 A hybrid tribunal usually includes both national and international judges and refers to both domestic and international law.

9 Cited from Lars Waldorf (2008c, forthcoming).

10 Interview with Osman Kamara, AFRC ex-combatant; this was confirmed later in an interview by Senesie Allieu a former CDF combatant. See, for example, Suma and Sesay (2008, forthcoming).

11 'Updated Set of Principles on Combating Impunity', Principle 2.

12 The Sierra Leone conflict ended with the signing of the Abuja Cease Agreement and Protocols in 2000; the Abuja Agreement reaffirmed a commitment to the Lomé Peace Agreement of 7 July 1999, including the establishment of the Truth and Reconciliation Commission.

13 The right to reparation is developed in the *Basic Principles and Guidelines on the Right to a Remedy and Reparation for Victims of Gross Violations of International Human Rights Law and Serious Violations of International Humanitarian Law*, which allows that reparation should be proportional to the violation and places the responsibility for reparations on the state (UN 2004: Principles 15 and 16).

14 The term reinsertion reflects the distinction between reinsertions (transitional) and reintegration (longer-term) drawn by the Integrated DDR Standards developed by the United Nations.

15 For example, ex-RDF and ex-FAR receive a 'recognition of service allowance'.

16 See 'Updated Set of Principles on Combating Impunity', Principle 36(a). See also Principle 36(c) and (e) according to which:

> Civilian control of military and security forces as well as of intelligence agencies must be ensured and, where necessary, established or restored. To this end, States should establish effective institutions of civilian oversight over military and security forces and intelligence agencies, including legislative oversight bodies … Public officials and employees, in particular those involved in military, security, police, intelligence and judicial sectors, should receive comprehensive and ongoing training in human rights and, where applicable, humanitarian law standards and in implementation of those standards.

17 In an effort to reduce the overwhelming number of genocide cases and prisoners, Rwandan officials turned for inspiration to *gacaca*, a local dispute resolution mechanism, where community elders make decisions on family and inter-family disputes over property, inheritance, personal injury, and marital relations. *Gacaca* means 'lawn' or 'small grass' and refers to the place where dispute resolution traditionally took place (Waldorf 2006).

18 Transitional justice in Rwanda has focused exclusively on accountability for the 1994 genocide, rather than the allegations of war crimes during the 1990–1994 civil war.

19 See for example the 1995 Abuja Accords that provided a temporary framework for

governance in Liberia, including DDR and the administration of justice, during the transitional period starting in 1995.
20 Conversation with researchers on the project entitled 'Successful Determinants of Reintegration', Columbia University (April 2007).
21 For example when information disseminated is communicated in complicated legal and technocratic language.
22 The Stockholm Report predicts that these two trust funds could increase social capital and local legitimacy if designed in ways that encourage inclusiveness (SIDDR 2006).

Bibliography

Amnesty International (2001) 'East Timor: Justice Past, Present and 'Future', *Index No. ASA 57/001/2001 Amnesty International, International Secretariat*. UK: AI.
de Greiff, P. (2006) 'Introduction Repairing the Past: Compensation for Victims of Human Rights Violations', in de Greiff, P. (ed.) *The Handbook for Reparations*. Oxford: Oxford University Press.
de Greiff, P. (2007a) 'Contributing to Justice and Peace – Finding a Balance Between DDR and Reparations', Paper prepared for the conference 'Building a Future on Peace and Justice's held from 25–27 June in Nuremberg, Germany. Online, available at: www.peace-justice-conference.info/.
de Greiff, P. (2007b) 'The Role of Apologies in National Reconciliation Processes: On Making Trustworthy Institutions Trusted', in Gibney, M. and Howard-Hassmann, R. (eds) *The Age of Apology*. Philadelphia: University of Pennsylvania Press.
de Greiff, P. and Duthie, R. (2005) *TJ and DDR Proposal* (unpublished).
Duthie, R. (2006) 'Transitional Justice and Social Reintegration', *Background Studies, Stockholm Initiative on Disarmament Demobilization and Reintegration*. Stockholm: Ministry for Foreign Affairs Sweden.
Duthie, R. (2008, forthcoming) 'Local Justice and Reintegration: Complementing Transitional Justice and DDR', Thematic paper for ICTJ's for ICTJ's research initiative on Transitional Justice and DDR. New York: ICTJ.
ECP (Escola de Cultura de Pau) (2007) *Analysis of the Disarmament, Demobilization, and Reintegration Program Existing in the World During 2006*, Barcelona: ECP.
Farr, V. (2002) *Gendering Demilitarization as a Peacebuilding Tool*. Bonn: International Center for Conversion.
Freeman, M. (2003) *What is Transitional Justice?* New York: International Center for Transitional Justice (unpublished).
Gear, S. (2002) 'Wishing Us Away: Challenges Facing Ex-combatants in the "New" South Africa', *Violence and Transition* series, Vol. 8.
Ginifer, J. (2003) 'Prioritizing Reintegration', in Malan, M. (ed) *Sierra Leone: Building the Road to Recovery*. Pretoria: Institute for Security Studies.
International Crisis Group (ICG) (2001) 'International Criminal Tribunal for Rwanda: Justice Delayed', *Africa Report No.* 30, June.
Lundin, I.B. (2007) 'Peace Process in Mozambique', Background paper for ICTJ's research initiative on Transitional Justice and DDR (unpublished).
Maiese, M. (2003) 'The Aims of Restorative Justice', *Beyond Intractability*, October. Online, available at: www.beyondintractability.org/essay/restorative_justice/.
Mayer-Rieckh, A. (2006) *A Justice Sensitive Approach to Security System Reform*. New York: International Center for Transitional Justice (unpublished).
Mayer-Rieckh, A. (2007) 'On Preventing Abuse: Vetting and Other Transitional

Reforms', in Mayer-Reickh, A. and de Greiff, P. (eds), *Justice as Prevention: Vetting Public Employees in Transitional Societies*. New York: Social Science Research Council.

Mazurana, D., McKay, S.A., Carlson, K.C. and Kasper, J.C. (2002) 'Girls in Fighting Forces and Groups: Their Recruitment, Participation, Demobilization, and Reintegration', *Peace and Conflict: Journal of Peace Psychology* 8 (2).

PRIDE (2002) *Ex-combatants Views of the Truth and Reconciliation Commission and the Special Court in Sierra Leone*, Freetown, September 12.

Rwanda's Demobilization and Reintegration Commission (RDRC) (nd) 'Demobilization and Reintegration brochure', *Multi-Country Demobilization and Reintegration Program Brief*. Online, available at: www.mdrp.org/PDFs/Media_Kit_eng.pdf.

SIDDR (Stockholm Initiative for Disarmament, Demobilization, and Reintegration) (2006) *Final Report*. Stockholm: Ministry of Foreign Affairs Sweden.

Specht, I. (2006) *Red Shoes: Experiences of Girl-combatants in Liberia*, Geneva, International Labour Office.

Sriram, C. (2003) 'Revolution in Accountability: New Approaches to Past Abuses', *American University International Law Review* 19 (2).

Suma, M. and Sesay, M. (2008, forthcoming) 'Transitional Justice in DDR in Sierra Leone', Case study for ICTJ's research initiative on Transitional Justice and DDR.

UN (1994) *Security Council Resolution 955: Statute of the International Criminal Tribunal for Rwanda* (S/RES/955). New York: UN.

UN (2000a) *Security Council Resolution 1315: Statute of the Special Court for Sierra Leone* (S/RES/1315). New York: UN.

UN (2000b) *The Role of United Nations Peacekeeping in Disarmament, Demobilization, and Reintegration: Report of the Secretary General*. New York: UN.

UN (2004) *The Rule of Law and Transitional Justice in Conflict and Post Conflict Societies: Report of the Secretary General*. New York: UN.

UN (2006a) *Basic Principles and Guidelines on the Right to a Remedy and Reparation for Victims of Gross Violations of International Human Rights Law and Serious Violations of International Humanitarian Law*. New York: UN.

UN (2006b) 'Rule of Law Tool for Post-Conflict States: Prosecutions Initiatives', *Report of the Office of the High Commissioner for Human Rights*. New York: UN.

UN Development Fund for Women (UNIFEM) (2004) *Getting It Right, Doing It Right: Gender and Disarmament, Demobilization and Reintegration*. New York: UN.

UNWG (2006) *Integrated Disarmament, Demobilization and Reintegration Standards (IDDRS)*. Online, available at: www.unddr.org/iddrs/.

Waldorf, L. (2006) 'Mass Justice for Mass Atrocity: Rethinking Local Justice as Transitional Justice', *Temple Law Review* 79 (1): 1–87.

Waldorf, L. (2008, forthcoming) 'Transitional Justice and DDR in Post-Genocide Rwanda', Case study for ICTJ's research initiative on Transitional Justice and DDR (unpublished).

Conclusions

Enter an evidence-based security promotion agenda

Robert Muggah, Mats Berdal and Stina Torjesen

Global anxiety over arms availability and armed groups and their role in ungoverned or liminal spaces shows no sign of abating any time soon. Counter-insurgency operations against insurgents, networked criminal entities and 'terrorists' persists and is growing in many parts of the world including in areas where state-building, peace-building and DDR are underway. Despite already being overburdened, multilateral peace support operations, under the auspices of the UN as well as a growing number of regional institutions, look set to continue expanding.[1] Likewise, the shift from narrowly conceived peace-keeping to more sustained investment in post-conflict peace-building, policekeeping and armed violence prevention and reduction is also set to continue. As the scope and scale of these large-scale interventions broadens, so too the expectations of DDR and SSR.

In spite of its growing appeal, the effectiveness of security promotion in low and medium-income countries remains largely untested. In laying out the evidence of what works and what does not, the authors of this volume aimed to close a number of gaps in relation to the (under) conceptualization of DDR and (in some cases falsely) attributed dividends of such activities. In drawing attention to the contradictions between policy prescriptions assigned from above and the outcomes from below, the volume seeks to assist policy-makers and practitioners do their jobs better. Taken together, the volume also fills a major research gap: each chapter highlights how comprehensive and comparative assessments of DDR are not only methodologically feasible, but they can also directly and positively inform policy and programming. Each chapter drew attention to a range of innovative research methods and instruments available to study DDR impacts.

The overall outcomes of DDR are mixed. This is arguably more novel a finding than it seems. The volume reveals the limitations of DDR as a broad spectrum treatment for contemporary armed violence, including that arising in the aftermath of war. But to expect that DDR could ever offer thorough and complete treatment is to place far too heavy a burden of expectations upon it. This is partly because there is no inherent or necessary relationship between DDR per se and the resolution of conflict much less a reduction in armed violence. DDR alone is unable to contend with the manifold and complex security challenges emerging in the wake of war, including quasi-political and criminal violence. Moreover, DDR is seldom able on its own to bring about positive and durable change in the lives of former soldiers as the cases of Sierra Leone, Liberia and Timor-Leste reveal. To believe that DDR could do otherwise is unrealistic in the extreme.

But the news is not all bad. In certain cases DDR appears to yield more immediate and positive effects. This was the case – and is likely to be the case elsewhere – when it formed part of, and was geared towards supporting, a wider political process aimed at addressing underlying sources of armed conflict. This suggests that a key concern animating this volume – how the framing and practice of DDR can be improved or modified to make it more effective in a narrow technical sense – is of fundamental importance. A more basic question, however, concerns the place of a given DDR process in the *wider* effort to stabilize armed conflict and concomitant efforts to lay the foundations for lasting peace.

The relationships between DDR as social engineering and as set of discrete technical practices has obvious implications for, among other things, assessing the metrics of 'success'. DDR seeks to effect change in attitudes and behaviours of a wide array of state and non-state actors and it also requires programmers and practitioners to constantly interrogate their own ontological framings and assumptions. In introducing new approaches to measuring DDR impact, the chapters generate much needed evidence-based reflections to help interventions along in this process. At the very least, DDR plans must be carefully attentive and tailored to the context in which they are crafted: the process is inevitably conditioned by a complex array of political interests and the broader imperatives of state consolidation. The bureaucratic architecture of DDR necessarily evolves over time. Other critical themes raised by authors in the volume relate to the persistent under-conceptualization of reintegration and the heterogeneity of stakeholders. This concluding chapter parses out these and other issues and considers their implications for security promotion more broadly.

Defining DDR?

Although a relatively new concept, DDR did not emerge in a *terra nullius*. From the early 1990s onward it was deeply connected to a parallel evolution in the doctrine of peace support operations and the changing discourse on security and development. Over a relatively short period of time peace-support interventions expanded from a relatively narrow focus on 'peacekeeping' intended to maintain stability between well-defined parties according to a negotiated ceasefire to include peace-enforcement and peace-maintenance in more indeterminate situations defined by multiple armed groups. Efforts soon expanded to address irregular forms of war and criminal violence, to include more robust peace enforcement operations and to engage in long-term post-conflict peace-building, some of them now under the auspices of the Peace-Building Commission, launched in 2006.[2] While the extent to which they are informed by an emerging doctrine of humanitarian intervention (much less a responsibility to protect) is open to question, peace support operations are increasingly adopting a multidimensional character and explicit military, policing and rule of law-oriented objectives.[3] Likewise, DDR interventions have clearly shifted from a narrow military focus to one that is more deeply invested in promoting sustainable development and progressive liberal transformations in the governance sector.

This volume highlighted the (varied) meanings different actors attribute to DDR. A number of authors noted the competing definitions and doctrines ascribed to DDR by donors, peace negotiators, affected governments, international agencies and former combatants. Terminological and ideological differences in turn generate divergent expectations of what DDR is supposed to accomplish, benchmarks of success and categories of beneficiaries. Many of these differences of course speak to differentiated assumptions of the meaning and purpose of security promotion. Such semantic variations are not esoteric or without consequence. They can have unambiguous consequences for planning, financing, implementing and monitoring the process. They directly inform more technical issues such as the selection criteria for prospective participants, the setting of incentives for disarmament and demobilization and the role of transitional justice and the security sector more generally. While a measure of constructive ambiguity may be desirable, in too large a dose it can undermine the viability and coherence of the process altogether.

Owing in part to the many layers of competing meanings attached to DDR, it is difficult to generate firm evidence as to whether the enterprise delivers on all of its promises. As noted in the case of Liberia, the multiplicity of objectives vested in DDR and the low priority awarded to data collection and monitoring and evaluation by donors delimited the setting and tracking of output and outcome indicators (see Chapter 3, this volume). In such cases, impact evaluators are required to string together an a priori theory of change in the absence of clearly articulated goals or benchmarks of success. This task is made all the more difficult in post-conflict contexts such as Afghanistan or Timor-Leste where surveillance data is limited, of poor quality and where levels of armed violence persist at alarmingly high rates (see Chapters 5 and 6, this volume).

The critical importance of establishing a coherent and consensus-based understanding of DDR throughout the duration of the process is clear. Achieving collectively determined conceptual and normative parameters for DDR – particularly vertically from affected communities to donor governments – is a laborious and time-consuming task. But the alternative risks undermining the legitimacy of the exercise from above and below. Equally, DDR planners must carefully think through what the exercise is designed (and not intended) to do and of how it can be measured: setting clear benchmarks is a critical first step to identifying pathways of success. Related, a dose of humility as to what is feasible in complex fragile state contexts should accompany the process. This is particularly so given the urgent political challenges accompanying DDR processes and the pressure to 'do something' during the negotiation of peace agreements and in the fast-paced investment in post-conflict recovery and reconstruction.

Politics and state-building

Not unlike other social engineering exercises associated with rapid development, population resettlement and governance promotion,[4] DDR is not immune to high and low politics. On the one hand, DDR is confronted with tensions amongst donors over the way it should be formulated, financed and executed. Issues relating to inclusive versus exclusive planning, bilateral versus multilateral funding and the involvement of specific agencies loom large. Likewise, DDR implementation is often profoundly influenced by competing strategic interests between and among international agencies, host governments and warring parties. The enterprise inevitably confronts pressures from a bewildering array of local power brokers and actors within civil society.[5] Although not a (technical) substitute for governance and broader democratic reform, DDR constitutes an inherently politicized sequence of activities (Pouligny 2004). Since DDR is, at one level, fundamentally about (re)establishing a state's monopoly of violence, politics necessarily lies at the heart of the enterprise.

It is useful to distil the many ways in which DDR is shaped by broader political processes. The chapter on reintegration and peace processes, for example, considers the ways in which competing visions of DDR – as livelihood promotion, the conferring of legitimacy from above, the acquisition of legitimacy from below and as a reward – required a capacity for compromise by all parties (see Chapter 9, this volume). Other authors observed that the inclusion of provisions for DDR in peace agreements is a necessary but insufficient means of ensuring commitment to the process, much less coherence or effective outcomes (see Chapter 8, this volume). At a minimum, mediators must ensure that central components of DDR are widely understood and supported by relevant actors before and during the preparation of ceasefires and accords. Central to the successful implementation of DDR is the establishment of real and perceived legitimacy, as was the case in Afghanistan (Chapter 5, this volume). These are all crucial areas for future policy development.[6]

The de facto practice of DDR can be an important factor in determining power, positions and influence of former military actors in the post-war period. Depending on how it is pursued, DDR can confer considerable degrees of legitimacy, from above and below, to groups that are included in DDR initiatives. Conversely DDR may deny legitimacy to groups that are otherwise excluded from the process (see Chapter 6, this volume). Likewise, DDR interventions can list off-course after they are launched because the political climate has yet to adequately 'ripen'. Despite the best intentions of external supporters, DDR may stall because the parties to the conflict (and their constituencies) may lack the confidence or will to engage the process transparently.[7] The need to surmount collective action dilemmas in relation to DDR against a backdrop of simmering (and likely unresolved) animosities between parties is not necessarily new. It is in some ways allied with classic game theoretic models deployed by political scientists: how is it possible to engender cooperation between otherwise competitive parties in repeat games when information asymmetries abound and the parties are not committed to peace?

A rationalist approach to DDR would likely focus on the fundamental security dilemmas associated with giving up arms and membership in armed groups in exchange for incentives. Realists would likely confer utility-maximizing motivations to commanders and rank and file and would focus on the relationships between the costs and the benefits accruing from DDR. In other words, to what extent does the surrendering of arms, demobilization and reintegration translate into tangible rewards and continued political influence? Do these rewards outweigh the fear of physical insecurity arising from the loss of one's arms? These concerns justified or not, inform future decisions to participate in the process. Drawing on this approach, they would be right to ask why such armed groups would engage in DDR if the process promised to strip away the very basis of their influence – a capacity to exert coercive force and seek rents. They would also be correct in asking how armed groups can be sure that other parties to a DDR process would surrender their weapons. Rationalists would therefore urge DDR planners to place a high priority on providing reliable information to all parties, getting the incentives 'right' and supplying proven security guarantees together with political and economic incentives in order to ripen the prospects for combatant participation.

By contrast, a constructivist approach would begin by interrogating the way DDR is cognitively understood and the values and norms underpinning the rules of the game. They might focus less on presumptions of a security dilemma, but rather the communicative processes associated with DDR and its prospects for triggering attitudinal and behavioural change. They would not necessarily be troubled by the apparent poor returns of DDR – whether in terms of arms returned or combatants demobilized – but rather its symbolic dividends and potential to influence the way combatants perceive each other and themselves. In fact, both rationalists and constructivists would anticipate a certain quantity of arms to be retained by armed groups as 'insurance' against failed promises. But rather than holding their surrender of arms as evidence of DDR effectiveness, constructivists would emphasize the role of communicative action and attitudinal shifts as more significant benchmarks.[8] Both rationalists and constructivists, then, might acknowledge that while holding back weapons may present a potential early challenge to DDR, in some cases it is precisely this insurance that enables armed groups commit to a peace process and subsequent demobilization and reintegration programmes (Torjesen and MacFarlane 2007).

Whatever the epistemological approach that informs DDR, it is important to recognize that such activities are fundamentally connected to state- and nation-building. This of course immediately begs the question of what *kind* of state is being built. International efforts over the past 15 years to build and strengthen the state in fragile states, including Somalia, Haiti and other countries have been disastrously misconceived, running against the grain of powerful local, historical and cultural forces and dynamics.[9] In Somalia for example, poorly planned interventions to resurrect the state provide one explanation for why the south of the country remains mired in endemic levels of violence and political instability. By contrast, relative peace and degree of order have come to the northern provinces of the former Somali Republic (the unrecognized Somaliland and Puntland) – where, not coincidentally, external intervention has been more limited. It is in Somaliland and Puntland where, paradoxically, the record of DDR since 1994 is more impressive; paradoxically because it occurred in the absence of central government, unaccompanied by national reconciliation or SSR, and without outside significant assistance from external actors.[10] That experience alone should give pause for thought regarding the role and place of donors, and of DDR, in facilitating stability and lasting peace, suggesting as it does that progress in DDR is consequential rather than causal of progress in other areas.

The Afghanistan and Timor-Leste experiences are also sober reminders of the relationship between state consolidation and the monopolization of force. In both cases, DDR could be conceived as an instrumental process of governmentality – in the Foucauldian sense – an explicit effort to reshape the rationalities, techniques and organizing practices of armed violence.[11] But in both countries, the DDR process neglected the complex critical interests and motivations of armed groups within the cycle – both before and after interventions were undertaken (see Chapters 5 and 6, this volume). As authors in this volume show, unless the variegated interests of different types of actors are taken into account and acknowledged, legitimized or deterred, some may seek to spoil the process. There are inevitably trade-offs in dealing with potential spoilers. On the one hand, bestowing legitimacy on certain actors in order to avoid future insecurity constitutes one widely applied strategy. The expectation is that they might calmly adopt more civic dispositions in the new post-war state structure – a hope that is not always borne out by experience.

In most DDR interventions, planners purposefully include problematic (and promising) commanders and combatants into new law enforcement and government structures. While these concessions may yield short-term dividends in terms of peace and stability, they can also problematize the creation of viable state institutions such as the armed forces, police, customs and tax authorities. As the case of Afghanistan amply shows, the inclusion of erstwhile warlords in the state-building project, while to some extent unavoidable, jeopardizes the perceived legitimacy of state institutions and even post-war economic development (see Chapter 5, this volume). Ultimately, the ability of states to regulate, tax and engage in a functional market economy and deliver basic social welfare goods is potentially compromised by those whose interest may be shaped by short-term acquisition of rents and profit (Torjesen and MacFarlane 2007; Keen 1999).[12]

Context matters

No post-conflict society offers up a blank slate on which discrete technocratic interventions can be readily grafted. Rather, the dynamics of the war, the complex factors shaping the mobilization of fighters, and the manner in which peace is negotiated (if at all) are all of critical importance in shaping the tenor and direction of DDR and related security sector strategies. The political, social, economic and cultural circumstances in which DDR is undertaken matter fundamentally. The recent war between Ethiopia and Eritrea is fundamentally distinct from the civil conflict engulfing Colombia or the two-decade long resistance against Indonesia in (now independent) Timor-Leste. The political economy of contemporary armed conflict – a subject that has received increasingly sensitive analysis over the past decade – is one key contextual factor that powerfully affects the incentive/disincentive structure for ex-combatants in aftermath of war (Ballentine and Sherman 2003). But while there may be a convergence of understanding of the ways in which certain intrinsic or structural factors shape war onset or closure, the preferences of armed groups and their respective members vary widely across time and space and tend to be highly dynamic.

Context is therefore a critical factor in shaping the design, implementation and outcomes of DDR. While DDR may be strategically inserted into UN Security Council Resolutions as was the case in Haiti (in spite of the absence of necessary preconditions) or Sudan, it is critical that the parameters of any programme reflect idiosyncratic realities on the ground. As is well known to practitioners, the failure to adequately account for regional and local dynamics can undermine the effectiveness of interventions. Comparatively simple measures from learning local histories, languages and dialects to building genuine dialogue with partners and finding ways to build on existing capacities can go a long way to fostering a foundation for serious engagement. As noted in Pouligny (2004: 12): 'one of the most worrisome consequences (of weak analysis is) that they neglect local anthropological but also historical variables' thus reinforcing technocratic approaches over ones grounded in local specificity. Fortunately, the authors in this volume point to a rash of interdisciplinary approaches to better apprehend local context while remaining faithful to methodological rigour. While certainly no panacea, better harnessing social sciences more effectively and using knowledge in real time could enhance DDR outcomes.

Whether a country is emerging from an internal war, a war of independence, a cross-border war or a state of generalized collective violence matters fundamentally in shaping the parameters of DDR. As was amply demonstrated in the case of Ethiopia's demobilization and reintegration initiative, veterans came home to communities that were comparatively unscathed by the war. Heralding from disciplined army units, these returnees were considered 'heroes' by their communities. This shaped their entitlements and the ways in which they were provided – generally for the better. But over time, conditions changed. The DDR programme struggled to build on latent good will and social capital over the long-term, even if the overall reintegration outcomes were tentatively successful (see Chapter 7, this volume). By way of contrast, returning fighters from Sierra Leone and Liberia's devastating internal conflicts returned to areas where absorptive capacities were frayed and often depleted. As former rebels with loose affiliations, they faced a drastically less favourable reception, including acute stigmas for women and children. Most displayed few marketable skills which undoubtedly shaped the nature of reintegration outcomes (see Chapters 2 and 3, this volume).

From the first to the second generation

The Introduction highlighted the many ways in which DDR programmes are adjusting to the changing landscape of armed violence, particularly from the late 1990s onward. Interventions are transforming and expanding as practitioners begin to acknowledge the ways in which DDR processes are politicized and conditioned by local context, but also in a bid to maximize coherence, coordination and reduce competitive friction between and among various actors. In certain cases what is described in this volume as 'conventional' DDR focused on structural stability and narrow military objectives is giving way to new wave of second generation activities focusing on, among other things, preventing and reducing armed violence. In some cases as in Haiti and Sudan, these second generation activities are undertaken in parallel with DDR[13], while in others they are administered independently. The fact that a number of DDR interventions are undergoing subtle transformations and adapting to their environment potentially reflects a level of dynamism in the (literal) field. This capacity of key actors to evolve, register and respond to changes on the ground is a positive sign.[14]

Taken together, first generation or conventional DDR consists of an interlocking cluster of activities often administered with external support and designed to promote stability. It can occur in the context of UN peace-support operations or outside of them with regional entities such as NATO, the EU or the AU. They may even take place unilaterally outside of a peace agreement altogether as was the case in Nigeria in the 1990s.[15] For example, DDR may occur as part of a general military reform process, including the integration of regular soldiers and militia into formal security structures and shedding of excess personnel. While traditionally the preserve of governments and their security sectors, an increasingly wide range of multilateral and bilateral aid agencies waded into the DDR sector in the past decade. This is due in part to their growing expertise in post-conflict environments, but also as a result of persistent pressures on them from multilateral and bilateral donors to engage more proactively in societies emerging from war (see Introduction, this volume). Conventional approaches to DDR increasingly feature a number of shared characteristics. In addition to their focus on rapid stabilization, supporters are adamant that DDR be 'nationally owned', conform to the pro-poor rhetoric of Western donors and inclusive and equitable in its treatment of all participants. In the vernacular, they are supposed to adopt a people-centred and rights-based approach all of which is in line with international law and the promotion of human rights more generally.[16]

Second generation approaches to containing arms and spoilers in post-conflict and seriously violence-affected societies are fast emerging, particularly in Latin America and the Caribbean. In contrast to DDR, these second generation approaches tend to endorse evidence-led activities focusing at the outset on identifying and responding to demonstrated risk factors, enhancing resilience at the municipal level and constructing interventions based on the basis of identified needs. Armed violence prevention and reduction programmes launched in municipal centres in Colombia, El Salvador, Nicaragua, Haiti and Brazil during the 1990s and early 2000s combined a rash of activities ranging from voluntary weapons collection, temporary weapons-carrying and alcohol restrictions and targeted environmental design (Muggah and Jutersonke 2008). In Colombia, and on the basis of robust longitudinal evidence, focused interventions targeting 'at-risk' youth and paramilitaries led to the fastest drop in homicidal violence ever recorded in the Western hemisphere (see Chapter 1, this volume). These and other interventions explicitly targeted the diverse dimensions of arms availability, including the preferences of actors using them together with the real and perceived factors contributing to armed violence.

Second generation activities tend to adopt a more holistic approach to armed violence prevention and reduction than does either conventional DDR or disarmament. Because action plans tend to be formulated by municipal authorities in concert with public and private security entities, academic institutions and civil society, they unconsciously adopt an 'all of government' approach. These interventions also purposefully seek to build-up confidence and legitimacy through the deliberate engagement of local actors. They rely, however, on comparatively robust and decentralized local authorities and civil society – institutions that may be weakened by prolonged periods of warfare and comparatively underdeveloped.

Second generation initiatives explicitly privilege a bottom-up approach by focusing on community and people-centred security promotion rather than the formation of national institutions. The introduction of 'weapons for development' programmes in the Republic of Congo, Mali and Liberia, 'weapons lotteries' in Mozambique and 'gun free zones' in South Africa all reflect the emergence of a more sophisticated approach to reducing arms availability and armed violence than before (Muggah 2006). More recently, second generation interventions emerging in the wake of DDR in Sudan and Haiti highlight how they can reinforce conventional DDR. Such activities can complement the current preoccupation of security and development actors with strengthening the national regulatory framework associated with civilian arms ownership, enhancing accountability over the stockpiles of public security providers and reinforcing civilian oversight over the security sector.[17]

While still early days, there are potentially important lessons from second generation activities for DDR practitioners and policy-makers. For example, an underlying principle of second generation activities is the insistence on international agencies playing a more scaled-back and facilitative role rather than being heavily invested in project implementation. Instead of recreating new national-level institutions such as commissions or focal points, second generation activities are forged on the basis of cooperation with existing formal and customary institutions at the sub-national level. Likewise, in explicitly adopting a holistic approach, second generation activities also encourage public and private actors to themselves define and design a cluster of related and targeted activities. Mirroring to some extent the orthodoxies of participatory development,[18] the initiative, control and responsibility of overseeing second generation activities rests as much (if not much more) with local partners as with expatriates. Although many second generation interventions are nascent and empirically demonstrated evidence of their effectiveness is only gradually being assembled, they offer a promising approach to dealing with the tools of war through demonstrated reductions in real and perceived armed violence.[19]

Rethinking the bureaucratic architecture

The bulk of the existing literature on DDR and SSR tends to focus on the normative and bureaucratic mechanics of intervention. Whereas interventions were at one time overseen by a small coterie of multilateral and bilateral donors with short time horizons, there is currently a bewildering array of external agencies preoccupied with the issue. While in many ways a positive sign of the importance attached to DDR, the resulting complexity has generated new forms of information asymmetries, collection action dilemmas, mandate battles and semantic challenges. As noted by Muggah *et al.* (Chapter 8, this volume), the comparatively recent drive within the UN to promote integrated, unified and joined-up missions – while to some extent misunderstood – is an attempt to promote more coordinated, predictable and effective approaches to DDR in what is an otherwise crowded field.

Advocates for so-called integrated missions in transitional or post-conflict contexts anticipate the creation of system-wide approaches to planning and programming. They contend that an integrated approach to DDR requires, among other things, the deliberate (re)positioning of core activities into the overall post-conflict stabilization and recovery process. Put another way, DDR can not be implemented in isolation from broader peace-building and recovery activities and must be integrated into development frameworks.[20] They also champion the value of forming more coherent partnerships between agencies and implementing entities. But the case of Sudan and Haiti where integrated DDR was first piloted is a reminder that while integrated approaches are desirable in principle, they are much more difficult to achieve in practice. The integration zeal emanating from within the UN system (by a host of donors) encountered a degree of friction. Integration inertia was provoked by challenges from above (e.g. normative disagreements and lack of higher-order political support) and from below (e.g. inter and intra-agency tensions). An outcome of these intervening factors was that integration emerged more slowly than expected (or not at all in the case of Haiti) and that conventional DDR was restructured according to demonstrated competencies and expressed needs on the ground. The IDDRS provide a set of rules to guide institutional behaviour, but they were only as strong as the people backing them.

Promoting ownership from below

In spite of the contemporary fashion for encouraging local ownership of development processes, managing the relationships and practices of DDR proponents and fragile host governments is a tricky one. In some cases, DDR supporters – bilateral and multilateral agencies, non-governmental agencies and civil society actors – may express concerns over government legitimacy and capacity to oversee and execute related interventions. These same donors and agencies may see a range of strategic and economic advantages of overseeing DDR on their own. Alternatively, host governments and demobilized commanders may justifiably and legitimately seek to coordinate the activities through their own representatives. Although national ownership has assumed a kind of orthodoxy in development circles with direct budgetary support assuming greater importance as a strategic approach, there are enormous practical constraints to realizing genuine ownership in relation to security promotion.

Typically, supporters of conventional DDR interventions pay lip service to the importance of enhancing national state capacities. Even where DDR is entirely funded and administered by development agencies, benefactors may claim that they are promoting in the vernacular, 'local ownership'. Experts contend that the development of institutional capacity of both public and civil society entities is critical to enhance their potential to bargain for service provision – a central feature of good (enough) governance (Welsh and Wood 2007). This volume highlights a number of tricky cases where states are either unable or unwilling to manage the DDR process. In certain instances, this is a function of state capacity: post-conflict governments are frequently severely institutionally weakened and lack the means and legitimacy to provide basic services. In most cases they do not exercise the full control over their territory or bureaucratic machinery. In such challenging circumstances, with host governments being either internally divided, hostile to the DDR process or lacking capacity, it is critical that international agencies operate with both the greatest possible degrees of flexibility and sensitivity.

In theory, UN agencies and the World Bank are expected to support national actors in undertaking DDR. Specifically, they are mandated to strengthen and reinforce national institutions within the public sector to undertake the process and related follow-on activities in an accountable and expedient manner. In situations described above, there will likely be comparatively modest DDR expertise in programme development and management (among both international and local staff).[21] In practice, DDR is frequently overseen by a newly-created national enabling mechanism – a department, commission or committee with clear authority and discretion and with civil society representation – so that the process is seen to be transparent and credible. Though often overlooked in the rush to do something, the credibility of the participants, composition and structure of these mechanisms are as critical as their mandate. Moreover, the imperative of ensuring a genuinely locally-owned rather than outside-led process is paramount, particularly since outsiders are less likely than insiders to understand the insidious challenges of re-building state institutions. Ensuring fulfilment of these criteria is no simple task. What is certain, however, is that a UN intervention that is not 'at peace with itself' is unlikely to constitute a constructive and coherent partner for the host government.

Rethinking reintegration

Reintegration has long been singled out as the 'Achilles heel' of DDR. While not a novel finding in itself, each of the chapters highlighted the under-conceptualization of reintegration as a set of outcomes and the many profound challenges confronting efforts to achieve sustained improvements in ex-combatant livelihoods. They reveal how reintegration is not only poorly developed in the academic and policy literature but how it is also rarely adequately defined in peace agreements, in DDR programme documents and in routine interventions (see Chapter 9, this volume). Where it is considered at all, donors and practitioners tend to adopt an economic-bias focusing on expanding labour opportunities or income earned following demobilization. Chapters on Sierra Leone, Liberia, Ethiopia, Timor-Leste and Uganda all introduced novel conceptual frameworks and new methodological tools to begin reframing the concept. These approaches offer important insights into understanding how programme effects can affect the attitudes towards democratic governance (Sierra Leone), participation in local level political structures (Ethiopia) and the dismantling of command and control of armed groups (Timor-Leste).

The chapters also make clear that reintegration remains a frustrating element of DDR programmes both in terms of financing and implementation. Certain authors argued for a serious rethinking of whether reintegration should be included as a component of DDR and not in fact detached or undertaken separately as part of mainstream development process (see Chapter 3, this volume).[22] Current best practice determines that at a minimum, UN and non-governmental agencies that are mandated to address reintegration must be integrated into the planning and design of DDR programmes at the earliest stage so as to ensure that the requisite resources are in place in a timely fashion (UNWG 2006). This is especially important given that key aspects of the reintegration enterprise must be established well before demobilization takes place.

Related, while there is a temptation to envision DDR as a linear process, the authors observe that this seldom occurs in practice. Indeed, the very way in which disarmament, demobilization and reintegration as activities are conflated in the DDR concept appears to imply a *sequential* approach to the activities themselves. But experiences noted in this volume demonstrate that not only do DDR activities overlap and occur in parallel, but the ordering of individual components will likely stray from the formulation implied by the now ubiquities acronym. As Torjesen and MacFarlane (2007) have noted elsewhere in context of Tajikistan, it may in some cases be necessary to start with 'reintegration' before thinking of demobilization, let alone disarmament. Ultimately, the scale and complexity of reintegration in terms of both mobilizing resources but also investing in capacities to ensure that ex-combatants are successfully absorbed in communities of return, require a forward-looking strategy with reintegration adequately aligned to market and societal absorptive capacity well in advance.

Closing reflections

DDR is part of a wider effort aimed at encouraging fundamental changes in how former fighters see and act in the world. By targeting potential spoilers, creating the enabling conditions for productive livelihoods to proceed and reducing the prospect for a return to war, DDR is expected to dismantle systems of (illicit) profit and power (Keen 1999). In its conventional formulation, DDR is comprised of a straightforward combination of sticks and carrots. In assuming a level of rational choice among 'beneficiaries' – though acutely conscious of the limits of simplistic rational choice thinking – DDR is expected to steer a complex assortment of actors from the paths of war to the road of peace.

But the realities on the ground frequently confound expectations. Peace processes themselves bring the divergence of interests between leaders and their followers into stark relief. As chapters on Afghanistan and Timor-Leste show, armed groups constitute highly heterogeneous subsets of the population and require differentiated solutions (see Chapters 5 and 6, this volume).[23] But these and other chapters also demonstrate the importance of accounting not just for the motivations of different categories of former combatants, but also the competing interests of donors, governments, international and national agencies and host communities.

Given these complexities both among actors in the host country and among international actors, a pertinent and legitimate question seems to be whether the kind of ambitious social engineering embodied within DDR initiatives is at all appropriate and realistic. Is DDR merely a harmful and unreflexive set of practices imposed by the international aid community? Does it constitute a useful policy tool that can be continuously improved upon? As noted at the outset, the authors of this volume contend that there can be, despite a range of challenges and pitfalls, real and large-scale benefits associated with DDR. But social change promised by DDR initiatives can also be sub-optimal, even potentially destructive. A useful starting point for moving DDR forward might be to begin with the calls stemming from many of the contributing authors: to take evaluation and assessment of DDR more seriously, while also humbly acknowledging the limits to what can realistically be achieved through social interventions to secure protection at war's end.

Notes

1 The UN alone fielded more than 83,000 uniformed peace-keepers and another 20,000 civilian staff as part of peace support operations in 2007 alone. Non-UN organizations such as the EU, AU and NATO maintained over 78,000 military and police personnel in the field – the bulk of which were in Afghanistan and Kosovo. See, for example, CIC (2008).

2 See, for example, Cockayne and Pfister (2008); Bellamy and Williams (2007); Bellamy (2004); and Paris (2004).

3 CIC (2008: 9) notes how despite the strains of over-stretching mandates and limited reserves, UN police deployments rose from 6,167 (2005) to 9,414. Another 3,700 are to be deployed to Darfur and 300 more to Chad and CAR.

4 See, for example, Scott (1998) for a review of the way in which social engineering and aspirations of high modernism infused development policy and practice in the twentieth century.

5 White (1994) describes civil society as:

> an intermediate associational realm between state and family populated by organisations which are separate from the state, enjoy autonomy in relation to the state and are formed voluntarily by members of society to protect or extend their interests or values.

It should be noted that there is nothing inherently positive in civil society per se.

6 See also HDC (2008) for a review of 'negotiating disarmament' during peace agreements.

7 This was recently the case with the failed efforts to restart negotiations for the Darfur Peace Agreement (DPA) in late 2007 and early 2008. See, for example, Nathan and Muggah (2007).

8 Each of the chapters identifies concrete ways to contend with the political challenges associated with DDR. In certain cases where a peace process is especially fragile, confidence building arrangements will likely be required. Operationally, this may amount to at first emphasizing the disarmament, demobilization and reintegration of children, women fighters and physically disabled ex-combatants before larger-scale activities are launched as was the case in Sudan.

9 Indeed, according to Mayall and Lewis (2007: 138), 'in Somalia there was an ancient and powerful national culture but no recoverable state'.

10 On the success of self-generated DDR in parts of Somalia, see Menkhaus (2004).

11 Hunt and Wickham (1994: 76) define governmentality as 'the dramatic expansion in the scope of government, featuring an increase in the number and size of the governmental calculation mechanisms'.

12 The Colombian and Ugandan cases are also important reminders of how the administration of 'local' justice is often balanced against the trade-offs of reduced violence and stability. See, for example, Chapters 1 and 9, this volume.

13 In Haiti and Sudan, for example, community security promotion activities are being undertaken in tandem with more conventional DDR activities. See, for example, Chapter 8, this volume.

14 A related question, however, is whether these transformations are occurring as a consequence, or independently of, broader influence of the expanding peace-support and peace-building architecture.

15 The Nigerian government has attempted a number of disarmament exercises in the country over the past several decades. Many of these have taken place in the Delta region, but none have proven successful. Between 1997 and 1999 the Delta state government initiated a disarmament programme for the warring ethnic factions from the Ijaw, Urhobo and Itsekiri ethnic groups, while the governor of Warri offered cash, short-term training and employment to militant youths to give up their weapons. These initiatives failed to significantly reduce the number of arms in circulation. In July 2004 the governor of Rivers state initiated a disarmament programme to address the escalating violence in the Niger Delta. This programme never took hold and renewed fighting between heavily armed militant groups led to the intervention of the federal government. In October 2004 (former) President Olusegun Obasanjo negotiated a temporary end to the violence, which led to the establishment of a new DDR programme. The key element preventing real progress on this initiative was the lack of attention to reintegration efforts and opportunities for former militants to earn gainful employment. See, for example, Hazen with Horner (2007).

16 Including the Rome Conventions on the International Criminal Court and the Operational Protocol on the Convention of the Rights of the Child. Conventional DDR programmes therefore tend to focus on a variety of different people:

1   male and female adult combatants;
2   children associated with armed forces and groups;
3   those working in non-combat roles;
4   ex-combatants with disabilities and chronic illnesses; and
5   dependents and family members.

A particular focus on women and girls – and specialized care and support for victims of sexual and gender-based violence – during the cantonment period is widely coun-selled. Regular consultation with ex-combatants, but also support for communities of return is crucial so that sustainable rehabilitation and reintegration can proceed. See, for example, UNWG (2006) and UNDP (2006).

17 Second generation approaches should in practice complement conventional DDR. But the remarkable results generated by a rash of new low-cost second generation initi-atives also sends a powerful message about the different kinds of ideologies and cog-nitive assumptions that may underpin peace-building efforts and renew interest in investing in innovation and flexibility.

18 See, for example, Pearce (2007) and Chambers (1994).

19 See, for example, Muggah (2008) for a review of such interventions in Africa.

20 Integration of DDR with parallel humanitarian, development, peacekeeping and fiscal priorities is gradually being encouraged in Common Country Assessments (CCA) and UN Development Assistance Frameworks (UNDAF).

21 In such situations, technical assistance, training and financial support, as well as the involvement of local authorities, affected communities, ex-combatants and their dependents, becomes a priority.

22 Some critics have called for restricting reintegration arguing that 'it might make more sense to redefine and limit the "R" portion of DDR as "reinsertion" and view reinser-tion as the bridge between demobilization and longer-term reintegration' which should be provided by mainstream development programmes (Ball and van de Goor 2006: 3).

23 Pouligny (2004: 9) observes how in Mozambique, the economic packages offered to commanders bore little similarity to what was offered ordinary soldiers. By 1994, revolts occurred involving the taking of hostages, and pressure was applied on the UN to fill the gap. By October of that year on the eve of elections, former soldiers threat-ened the democratic process.

Bibliography

Ball, N. and van de Goor, L. (2006) *DDR: Mapping Issues, Dilemmas and Guiding Prin-ciples*, Clingendael, August.

Ballentine, K. and Sherman, J. (eds) (2003) *The Political Economy of Armed Conflict: Beyond Greed and Grievance,* Boulder: Lynne Rienner.

Bellamy, A. (2004). *Understanding Peacekeeping*, London: Polity.

Bellamy, A. and Williams, P. (eds) (2007) *Peace Operations and Global Order*, London: Routledge.

Berdal, M. (1996) 'Disarmament and Demobilization after Civil Wars', *Adelphi Paper* 303, Oxford: Oxford University Press.

Chambers, R. (1994) *Poverty and Livelihoods: Whose Reality Counts?* Policy Paper No. 1, New York: UNDP.

CIC (Center on International Cooperation) (2008) *Annual Review of Global Peace Opera-tions: 2008*, New York: Center on International Cooperation at New York University.

Cockayne, J. and Pfister, D. (2008) *Peace Operations and Organised Crime.* Report of the International Peace Institute and Geneva Centre for Security Policy, New York.

Colletta, N., Koster, M. and Wiederhofer, I. (1996) *The Transition from War to Peace in Sub-Saharan Africa*, Washington, DC: World Bank.

Collier, P. (1994) 'Demobilization and Insecurity: A Study in the Economics of the Transition from War to Peace', *Journal of International Development* 6: 343–351.

Collier, P. (2004) *Reducing the Global Incidence of Civil War: A Discussion of the Available Policy Instruments.* Online, available at: www.inwent.org/ef-texte/military/collier.htm.

Collier, P., Hoeffler, A., Elliot, L., Hegre, H., Reynal-Querol, M. and Sambanis, N. (2003) *Breaking the Conflict Trap: Civil War and Development Policy*, New York: Oxford University Press and the World Bank.

Duffield, M. (2007) *Security, Development and Unending War*, London: Polity Press.

Ghobarah, H., Huth, P. and Russett, B. (2003) 'Civil Wars Kill and Maim People – Long After the Shooting Stops', *American Political Science Review*, 97 (2), May.

Harbom, L. and Wallensteen, P. (2007) 'Armed Conflict, 1989–2006', *Journal of Peace Research* 44 (5): 623–634.

Hazen, J. with Horner, J. (2007) 'Small Arms, Armed Violence, and Insecurity in Nigeria: The Niger Delta in Perspective', *Occasional Paper 20*. Geneva: Small Arms Survey.

HDC (Henri Dunant Center) (2006) 'Negotiating Disarmament: Civilians, Guns and Peace Processes: Approaches and Possibilities', *Briefing Paper*, 1.

HDC (2008) 'Negotiating Disarmament: Reflections on Guns, Fighters and Armed Violence in Peace Processes', Geneva: Centre for Humanitarian Dialogue.

Hunt, H. and Wickham, G. (1994) *Foucault and Law*, London: Pluto Press.

Jutersonke, O., Krause, K. and Muggah, R. (2007) 'Guns and the City: Analysing Urbanisation and Armed Violence', *Small Arms Survey 2007*, Cambridge: Cambridge University Press.

Keen, D. (1999) 'The Economic Functions of Violence in Civil Wars', *Adelphi Paper 320*, Oxford: Oxford University Press.

Ljungman, C. (2004) 'Applying a Rights-based Approach to Development: Concepts and Principles', *Conference Paper, Winners and Losers from Rights-based Approaches to Development*, Manchester.

Mayall, J. and Lewis, I. (2007) 'Somalia', in Berdal, M. and Economides, S. (eds) *United Nations Interventionism, 1991–2004*, Cambridge: Cambridge University Press.

Menkhaus, K. (2004) 'Somalia: State Collapse and the Threat of Terrorism', *Adelphi Paper 364*, Oxford: Oxford University Press.

Moser, C. and McIlwaine, C. (2001) *Violence in a Post-Conflict Context*, Washington, DC: World Bank.

Muggah, R. (2006) 'Emerging from the Shadow of War: DDR and Arms Reduction during Post-Conflict', *Journal of Contemporary Security Policy Special Edition* 25 (2).

Muggah, R. (2008) 'Post-Conflict Transition: Reviewing DDR and Arms Control in Africa', *Africa Development Report 2008*, Tunis/Washington, DC: African Development Bank.

Muggah and Jutersonke (2008) 'Dealing with Endemic Urban Violence', background paper for the Human Security and Cities Programme, Ottawa: DFAIT.

Muggah, R. and Krause, K. (2006) 'The True Measure of Success? Considering the Emergence of Human Security in Haiti', in Shaw, T., Maclean, S. and Black, D. (eds) *Human Security: A Decade On,* New York: Lynne Rienner.

Nathan, L. and Muggah, R. (2007) 'The Time for Mediation Is Over in Darfur', *Globe and Mail*, 24 November.

Paris, R. (2004) *At War's End*, Cambridge: Cambridge University Press.

Pearce, J. (2007) 'Violence, Power and Participation: Building Citizenship in the Contexts of Chronic Violence', *IDS Working Paper 274*, Brighton: IDS, March.

Pouligny, B. (2004) 'The Politics and Anti-Politics of Disarmament, Demobilization and Reintegration Programs', Science-Po Report, Paris: Science-Po.

Scott, J. (1998) *Seeing like a State: How Certain Schemes to Improve the Human Condition have Failed*, New Haven: Yale University Press.

Suhrke, A. and Samset, I. (2007) 'What's In a Figure? Estimating Recurrence of Civil War', *International Peacekeeping* 14 (2).

Torjesen, S. (2006) *The Political Economy of Disarmament, Demobilization and Reintegration (DDR)* (mimeo). Online, available at: www.nupi.no/publikasjoner/notater/2006/the_political_economy_of_disarmament_demobilization_and_reintegration_ddr.

Torjesen, S. and MacFarlane, N. (2007) 'R Before D: The Case of Post Conflict Reintegration in Tajikistan', *Journal of Conflict, Security and Development*, 7 (2).

UNDP (2006) *Practice Note: Disarmament, Demobilization and Reintegration of Ex-combatants*, April. Online, available at: www.undp.org/bcpr/whats_new/ddr_practice_note.pdf.

UNDPKO (1999) *Disarmament, Demobilization and Reintegration of Ex-combatants in a Peacekeeping Environment*, New York: UNDPKO, December.

UNWG (2006) *Integrated Disarmament, Demobilization and Reintegration Standards (IDDRS)*. Online, available at: www.unddr.org/iddrs/.

Welsh, J. and Wood, N. (2007) *Exporting Good Governance*, Waterloo: Wilfred Laurier University Press.

White, G. (1994) 'Civil Society, Democratization and Development (I): Clearing the Analytical Ground', *Democratization* 1 (3), Autumn.

Index

Figures are indicated by **bold** page numbers, tables by *italic* numbers

11671380R00173

Printed in Great Britain
by Amazon.co.uk, Ltd.,
Marston Gate.